SEXUAL DIMORPHISM
IN *HOMO SAPIENS*

SEXUAL DIMORPHISM IN *HOMO SAPIENS*

A Question of Size

EDITED BY
Roberta L. Hall

PRAEGER

PRAEGER SPECIAL STUDIES • PRAEGER SCIENTIFIC

Library of Congress Cataloging in Publication Data

Main entry under title:

Sexual dimorphism in homo sapiens.

Includes bibliographies and index.
1. Proportion (Anthropometry)—Addresses,
essays, lectures.   2. Body size—Addresses,
essays, lectures.   3. Sex differences—Addresses, essays, lectures.   I. Hall, Roberta L.
GN66.S42   573'.6   81-5907
ISBN 0-03-056963-X   AACR2

Published in 1982 by Praeger Publishers
CBS Educational and Professional Publishing
a Division of CBS Inc.
521 Fifth Avenue, New York, New York 10175 U.S.A.

© 1982 by Praeger Publishers

23456789   145   987654321

Printed in the United States of America

Contributors

Stephen M. Bailey

Department of Sociology and Anthropology, Tufts University, Medford, Massachusetts. Dr. Bailey received his Ph.D. in physical anthropology from the University of Michigan. His research is in the areas of human growth and environmental influences on body composition.

Gerhard W. Brauer

Research Coordinator, Epidemiology Division of the Cancer Control Agency of British Columbia, Vancouver, British Columbia, Canada. From 1975 to 1978 Mr. Brauer was a research fellow in epidemiology and physical anthropology, working with the Wellington Hospital Epidemiology Unit in Wellington, New Zealand. He is a doctoral candidate in medical anthropology at the University of British Columbia.

David J. Finkel

Pleasantville, New York. Dr. Finkel's Ph.D. in physical anthropology was completed at the University of Oregon in 1974. Research interests include fossil man, especially in the Middle East and Europe, medical anthropology and social epidemiology, and demography. Dr. Finkel has taught at Fordham University and has been a research associate at the New York City Health Department, Bureau of Biostatistics, and at the New York University Graduate School of Public Administration.

J. Patrick Gray

Department of Sociology and Anthropology, North Texas State University, Denton, Texas. Dr. Gray is a cultural anthropologist who received his Ph.D. from the University of Colorado in 1976. His research concerns symbolic systems in both nonliterate and literate societies, witchcraft, and human sexual behavior.

Roberta L. Hall

Department of Anthropology, Oregon State University, Corvallis, Oregon. Dr. Hall earned a Ph.D. at the University of Oregon in 1970. She taught at the

University of Victoria from 1970 to 1974 and has published research in all areas of anthropology. With Henry Sharp she is co-editor of the book *Wolf and Man: Evolution in Parallel.*

Margaret E. Hamilton

Department of Anthropology, University of Delaware, Newark, Delaware. Dr. Hamilton holds a Ph.D. from the University of Michigan. She has written papers on human sexual dimorphism and the evolution of human female sexuality and is currently beginning research on the etiology of difficult childbirth.

Grover S. Krantz

Department of Anthropology, Washington State University, Pullman, Washington. Dr. Krantz earned a Ph.D. at the University of Minnesota. He is the author of several books on human origins and variation and is well known for his provocative models in human paleontology.

Walter Leutenegger

Department of Anthropology, University of Wisconsin, Madison, Wisconsin. Born in Switzerland, Dr. Leutenegger earned his doctorate in biological anthropology and zoology at the University of Zurich. His research interests range from functional anatomy and reproductive biology in primates to the reconstruction of social organization and behavior in early hominids.

Leslie Sue Lieberman

Departments of Anthropology and Pediatrics, University of Florida, Gainesville, Florida. Dr. Lieberman earned a Ph.D. at the University of Connecticut. Her chief interests are in nutritional anthropology, medical anthropology, and the study of growth and development. A text on nutritional anthropology is forthcoming.

Elizabeth R. McCown

Carmel, California. Dr. McCown's Ph.D. was earned at the University of California at Berkeley. She has served as managing editor for the last three volumes of the series *Perspectives on Human Evolution.* Currently she is studying and photographing subtidal invertebrates on the Monterey Peninsula.

William D. Ross

Department of Kinesiology, Simon Fraser University, Burnaby, British Columbia, Canada. Dr. Ross did undergraduate, graduate, and postdoctoral studies at the University of British Columbia, the University of Oregon, and the Institute of Child Health of the University of London. He is identified with the newly emerging scientific specialization known as kinanthropometry, the practical interface between anatomy and physiology, and currently serves as the secretary general of the International Working Group on Kinanthropometry.

William A. Stini

Departments of Anthropology and Family and Community Medicine, University of Arizona, Tucson, Arizona. Dr. Stini's primary interests lie in the interaction of human growth, development, and aging with environmental factors such as disease, nutrition, and climatic stressors. He has done field work in Colombia where he studied the effect of low protein diet on human growth and disease. Recently he has done research in the area of comparative growth performance of breast-fed versus bottle-fed infants and their disease experience.

Richard Ward

Department of Kinesiology, Simon Fraser University, Burnaby, British Columbia, Canada. Mr. Ward graduated with a B.Sc. from Loughborough University of Technology, England, in human biology, and has completed a master's degree in kinesiology at Simon Fraser. Research for his doctoral thesis concerns examination of the proportional growth of children and its implications.

Linda D. Wolfe

Department of Anthropology, University of Florida, Gainesville, Florida. Dr. Wolfe earned her Ph.D. in physical anthropology from the University of Oregon. Her interests include the analysis of models utilized to explain the evolution of primate behavior, the sociosexual behavior of primates, and the incorporation of biological models into popular culture.

Contents

Preface

That men in all populations tend to be physically larger than women is a truism that holds for many, but not all, parts of the anatomy. Going beyond this truism, human biologists are investigating the topic of sex differences in size because of the many provocative questions it raises. Among them are: What evolutionary forces are related to the level of size dimorphism that we now see in *Homo sapiens*? Has it changed during hominid history? In what way or ways do size differences relate to behavioral differences? How does sexual dimorphism in humans compare with that in other primates? Is sexual dimorphism constant throughout all segments of the species or is it greater in some populations than in others? If it is not uniform, are the differences due to natural selection or to variation in nutrition, work patterns, or other environmental and behavioral features? Do the sexes differ in their response to environmental pressures?

The inquiries summarized above prompted the research that grew into this book. By the mid-1970s it had occurred to most human biologists that the old adage "Men are larger than women" was neither explanatory nor descriptive. It became generally realized that it was not meaningful to say, as many of us did, that *Homo sapiens* has "more size sexual dimorphism than gibbons but less than gorillas and baboons." The time had come for more detail in description and for research strategies that would permit at least tentative explanations.

During the 1970s when more explicit work was being done on sexual dimorphism in primates, sociobiological theory was crystallizing. Sociobiological theory offers a means of interpreting selection for size as a response to the different reproductive strategies practiced by each sex. Translation of these strategies into selection for size is dependent on the unique ecobehavioral niche that each species (or in the case of humans, each culture) occupies. Though sociobiological theory offers a plan for analyzing heterogeneous data, it does not offer a formula that can predict appropriate size norms for all mammals. But if applied properly, sociobiological theory can reintroduce dynamic, interactionist concepts imbedded in evolutionary theory; it can remind researchers that morphology and behavior are two sides of one coin, and that in life forms, change is the only constant.

Sex differences in size cannot be divorced from morphology, since the two factors intersect at the level of function. Size exerts physical constraints on form, and form places limits on size. To explore size sexual dimorphism adequately, morphology, function, and behavior must, necessarily, be addressed as well. The emphasis in this volume is on size, which can be viewed as a dependent variable. Behavior, morphology, and environmental attributes can be considered the independent variables, treated variously by contributing authors.

The study of sexual dimorphism reaches across all aspects of human biology. I have tried to include representatives of most of them in this volume. Topically they can be subdivided as: mammalian sexual dimorphism; early hominid sexual dimorphism; interpopulational comparisons of sexual dimorphism in prehistoric and modern populations; sexual dimorphism in growth, in health, and in disease; and sexual dimorphism of body composition.

This volume was launched in an attempt to chart the dimensions of human sexual dimorphism. The goal is to set standards for the continuing study of the topic. In the end, the greatest use for inquiries into size sexual dimorphism may be that they enrich the study of effects of behavior, climate, nutrition, activity patterns, disease, and genetic background on human growth. Or, we may discover a new perspective from which to view the male-female dichotomy. In any case, the endeavor has provided a challenge that all of the authors who contributed to this volume have enjoyed.

One

Mammals, Primates, and Prehistoric Hominids

One

Introduction: Consequences of Sexuality

Roberta L. Hall

The concept of sexuality is so pervasive and is learned by most of us at such an early age that we seldom inquire as to its biological function. Yet not all plants and animals possess sexuality. The history of life forms on planet Earth may extend more than three billion years into the past (Volpe 1977), yet for most of that time life forms were single-celled and probably asexual in their reproductive behavior. One of the most striking features in a survey of life history is that the relatively recent biological periods have been characterized by a growing richness of life forms, that is, an increase in diversity. Novelties have emerged among both the complex and the simply structured forms. Clearly, the increase in kinds of life forms has, in itself, been responsible in part for an increase in the momentum of evolutionary experiments, in that life forms create new niches and new opportunities—simply by their presence as well as by the effects they have on the environment. But sexual reproduction also is an important factor promoting variability (Mayr 1966).

An asexual organism that is haploid (meaning that it has only one set of chromosomes) reproduces by replication of itself. Therefore, it has only one way to evolve: by mutation. A mutation is essentially an imperfection that occurs in the genetic copying process. It is random in respect to the external environment and is not related to the organism's own requirements. Indeed, mutations disrupt the delicate chemical balance that natural selection has put together through many generations; hence, most mutations doom the individual organisms that inherit them. Only occasionally does a mutant individual survive, flourish, and outdo its own forbears in fitness.

By contrast, sexual reproduction results in every offspring's being genetically unique and, because there are two sets of chromosomes, individuals are, to some extent, protected from the deleterious effects of mutations when they do occur. Each of two parents contributes only one-half of its own genetic material to every sex cell that it produces. Individuals are always diploid (meaning that they contain a double set of chromosomes); but prior to reproducing, "meiosis"—a process in which haploid reproductive cells are formed—occurs. During meiosis, the paternal and maternal chromosomes pair with each other, break in several places, and exchange segments. This event, called "crossing over," results in the production of novel chromosomes, slightly different from those that the reproducing individual itself inherited. In meiosis the chromosomes double only once, but there are two cell divisions: four sex cells, each with only one set of chromosomes, are formed.

These four individual cells are now free to unite with haploid cells from another individual and the resulting offspring—even without mutations—will vary slightly one from another and from their parents. In an animal like the human with 23 pairs of chromosomes, the number of different genetic combinations that can be produced from one set of parents is in the trillions.

Along with the potential for variation that is the consequence of sexual reproduction comes the lack of perfect stability that, at times, in stable environments, can also benefit a species. Some insects and some microorganisms have found the ideal solution in the ability to shift between asexual and sexual reproduction. Though asexual parthenogenetic reproduction is not impossible in mammals, it is not probable and cannot be relied on to benefit the species in a natural situation, leaving aside the possibility of laboratory managed cloning. For complex animals, variation is an obligatory part of the adaptive pattern, and it is rooted in sexual reproduction.

From an evolutionary perspective, we have to postulate that some major benefit *must* flow from sexual reproduction in order to compensate for the major physiological and behavioral investments that animals make in it. And this benefit is variation.

It must be granted that the division of the reproductive unit into two parts has selective importance, particularly for large and complex organisms whose generations are long and that reproduce so few offspring that they cannot afford the risk of producing variation only by mutation. *How* are the two reproductive units different? How are they distinguishable; what defines male and female at the basic, cellular level?

THE MALE-FEMALE DICHOTOMY

Dawkins (1976) notes that in some relatively simple organisms—for instance, in some fungi—a kind of sexual reproduction that does not include the male-female dichotomy occurs. Though new individuals are formed by the fusion of two haploid cells, all sex cells are the same. Both of the haploid cells that unite to form a new individual contribute not only half of the required genetic material but an equal amount of food reserves as well. This last point distinguishes the more common male-female form of sexual reproduction from the primitive type. For in sexual reproduction in which males and females are differentiated, the female sex cell (the egg) contributes not only half the genetic material but also a certain amount of food reserves; the male sex cell (the sperm) contributes half of the genetic material but no food reserves.

Dawkins (1976, p. 153) remarks—facetiously, one hopes—that "female exploitation begins here!"

One effect of this dichotomy is that females tend to produce relatively fewer sex cells but these cells are larger and a greater percentage of them become fertilized. By contrast sperm cells are produced in great quantities but far fewer of them survive to contribute to a living organism. In human females, the outcome of meiosis is that one well-endowed, viable egg is produced; the other three cells produced by the double split are inviable and are called "polar bodies." The outcome of a meiotic act in the human male is four viable sperm cells.

One of the further consequences of sexual dimorphism is that there exists the potential for greater variability, among males, in reproductive output (Mayr 1976). Since sperm cells are produced in greater quantities and all are competing to join with the relatively fewer but better endowed female cells, greater variability in successful reproduction can be expected in males than females. That is, the chance of an individual leaving no descendants or leaving many descendants is greater, in general, for males than for females, whose reproductive records tend to vary much less.

The extent to which there is a real difference in variability between male and female reproductive output, however, varies according to the ecobehavioral adaptation of the species. In general, the potential for sexual dimorphism in reproduction is exaggerated in mammals.

What is there about mammals that exaggerates the male-female dimorphism? The basic factor is that mammals are distinguished by the female's providing nourishment to the young not only before birth but also in the immediate postnatal period. This simple biological fact entails several consequences directly relevant to the topic of sexual asymmetry. This means, for one thing, that the female can only fertilize one or at best a small number of eggs each season, since only a limited amount of energy is available for the feeding of the young. This requirement stands in marked contrast to female fishes, for example, whose upper reproductive limit is imposed by their physiological ability to carry eggs. At the point of release of the eggs, in most fishes, the mother's responsibility ends. Clearly this is not so for mammals!

In contrast to its female partner, the male mammal is not constrained physiologically in the number of sex cells that he can produce or in the number of female cells that can be fertilized. Hence, in mammals the *potential* for differences in male-female variability in reproductive output is inherently greater than in other groups of animals.

NURTURING IN NONMAMMALIAN VERTEBRATES

As in many other biological areas, birds represent a unique combination of mammalian and nonmammalian adaptations. Though females are, by definition, the individuals who lay the eggs, both parents are equally capable, anatomically, of rearing offspring. In many species of birds, both parents provide nurturing of the young, and frequently the sexes share incubation duties as well. Male-female differences in the variability of offspring production among birds that mate monogamously and rear their offspring jointly are probably quite low. Though courtship behavior of the two sexes of birds clearly differs, and though most birds are clearly distinguishable by sex, these dimorphic factors do not affect their joint commitment to their offspring.

Among fish and amphibians, however, there exists an immense potential for variety in the ways in which male and female behavior can be structured, all equally suitable for the prime goal of successful reproduction. Courtship and mating behavior of the stickleback has been studied thoroughly and presents some interesting features (Kass-Simon 1976). In this species of fish, the male is the family nest builder and he also tends the young fry after they hatch. The dutiful father rides herd on the young and when one strays from the school he catches it in his mouth and brings it back. By contrast, female sticklebacks are likely to devour their young if they chance to encounter them. Therefore, after mating a male must see to it that his mate, as well as other sticklebacks, stays away from his nest.

To us as mammals this example appears to indicate an "abnormal" reversal of sex roles. But it should not be considered so since among fishes—in this case, sticklebacks—females are no more suited for the role of nurturing than are males. Among fishes, a wide variety of courtship and mating techniques are found, each meeting particular requirements of particular environmental niches. The anatomy of the sexual dimorphism of fishes, in general, is not rigidly restrictive.

We are accustomed to thinking of our own class of animals— mammals—as the one that offers its species the greatest potential for freedom of action. But in many respects this is not true. For example, though warm-bloodedness permits mammals to be active even in cold weather, it carries the prescription to eat well in all seasons; the alternative is starvation. The superior nurturing system that acts before birth as well as postnatally permits a much larger percentage of young to survive but it also makes it impossible for mammals to rear a large number of young. In nature there is no such thing as a free lunch! And with mammalian dimorphism, males and females have a somewhat more restricted set of alternatives open to them. Following the birth of offspring, females must spend at least a minimal amount of time and energy on nurturing.

NURTURING AND SEXUAL DIMORPHISM IN MAMMALS

Still, behavioral options exist, and mammals vary greatly in the degree to which male and female roles differ. For example, among the carnivores, members of the family *Canidae* tend generally to equalization or symmetry of male-female roles. Using the North American wolf as an example, we note that wolves live in stable social groups in which usually only one adult female produces a litter of young each year (Hall and Sharp 1974). Other members of the pack, both male and female, participate in the rearing. This includes bringing food to the young, baby-sitting (keeping predators away while pups play near the den), and teaching the pups to hunt. Though the female who gives birth to the young provides them with nourishment in the first few weeks of life, other pack members provide sustenance for the mother and very soon provide meat for the pups as well. For her part, the female appears eager to resume her place in the pack's hunting forays (Mech 1970). It also is interesting that one of the chief behavioral consequences of domestication of the dog is that males lack the ability, interest, or training to participate in pair bonding and the rearing of offspring. As a consequence, the offspring of male dogs and female wolves receive insufficient care and have a low probability of survival. This example emphasizes the adaptive value of the wolf's social structure within its own niche.

Among the great cats who also are considered social carnivores, males play a much less active role in the nurturing of young. Though male lions merely by their presence provide defense for the young in their prides (Schaller 1972), the male-female nurturing role differs to a much larger extent than among the wild dogs; among lions and other great cats the female assumes the parent role almost exclusively. Female lions are great hunters, however, and also provide food for the males of their own pride; males specialize in defense.

Canids and Felids differ as well in the morphology of sexual dimorphism. Male wolves tend to measure, on the average, only about 4 percent larger than females in linear measurements (Jolicoeur 1959), with much overlap between sexes, and a wolf's sex is hard to distinguish at a distance. Sex of adult lions, however, is immediately apparent.

Within the order Primates, sexual dimorphism in size, shape, and behavior varies greatly. Even among the apes, our closest phylogenetic relatives, there is great variation. (The following two chapters offer detailed analyses of primate sexual dimorphism.) The mammalian physiology, though it provides a basis for role and morphological dimorphism, is not a straitjacket either. Rather, evolution appears to reward those major groups of animals that are able to diversify maximally. That is, those groups that evolve diversified niches (a large number of morphological patterns and survival strategies) are most widespread. Human cultures, which exploit different habitats by varied technologies and social structures, are analogous to biological species in that they foster the success of the total group by providing diverse exploitative mechanisms. Is the cultural unit, then, the appropriate one for study of sexual dimorphism in human behavior, size, and morphology? If so, we must ask what controls human plasticity in adapting to diverse habitats. How is the mammalian pattern of sexual dimorphism variously expressed in groups of *Homo sapiens*?

SUMMARY

Sexual reproduction is a means of ensuring variation in plants and animals. The general biological difference between females and males is that female sex cells provide nourishment as well as genetic material for offspring; male cells provide genetic material only. In mammals, females also provide nourishment for the infant. In nonmammalian vertebrates there are abundant examples of animals in which nurturing of the young is performed by male or female parent alone, by both parents, and by neither. Among mammals, nurturing is sometimes done by the female parent, by both parents, and by the female parent and a wider group of kin. Though there exists a mammalian potential, there is no universal mammalian pattern that all species follow. Similarly, but at a lower level in biological taxonomy, no universal pattern of rearing of human children exists, but rather a variety of patterns are observed in various human cultures. Morphology and behavior interact at many points in individual development. Our job as human biologists is to clarify these points; the succeeding chapters will strive to do so.

BIBLIOGRAPHY

Dawkins, Richard. 1976. *The Selfish Gene.* New York: Oxford University Press.

Hall, Roberta L., and Henry Sharp, eds. 1974. *Wolf and Man: Evolution in Parallel.* New York: Academic Press.

Jolicoeur, Pierre. 1959. "Multivariate Geographical Variation in the Wolf *Canis lupis* L." *Evolution,* 13:283-299.

Kass-Simon, G. 1976. "Female Strategies: Animal Adaptations and Adaptive Significance." In *Beyond Intellectual Sexism,* edited by J. I. Roberts, pp. 74-84. New York: David McKay Co.

Mayr, Ernst. 1966. *Animal Species and Evolution.* Cambridge: Harvard University Press.

———. 1976. *Evolution and the University of Life.* Cambridge: Harvard University Press.

Mech, L. David. 1970. *The Wolf: The Ecology and Behavior of an Endangered Species.* Garden City, N.Y.: Natural History Press.

Schaller, George B. 1972. *The Serengeti Lion.* Chicago: University of Chicago Press.

Volpe, E. Peter. 1977. *Understanding Evolution,* 3rd ed. Dubuque: Wm. C. Brown.

Two

Sexual Dimorphism in Nonhuman Primates*

Walter Leutenegger

Secondary sexual differentiation in humans leads to more or less pronounced sexual dimorphism in an array of interrelated morphological, physiological, and behavioral features. Such sexual dimorphism is not unique to humans but also occurs in other sexually reproducing vertebrates, invertebrates, and plants (Wilson 1975; Brown 1975; Ralls 1977; Onyekwelu and Harper 1979; Willson 1979). In this chapter I examine sexual dimorphism in the closest relatives of humans, the nonhuman primates.

The question of the nature and evolution of sexual dimorphism in nonhuman primates has received increasing attention recently and interest in it has developed along several lines. First, paleoanthropologists started to realize that in order to meaningfully assess taxonomy and phylogeny and to reconstruct ecology and behavior of early hominids, estimates of the expected degree of sexual dimorphism within fossil populations are essential (Brace 1972; Pilbeam and Gould 1974; Wolpoff 1976; Zihlman 1976; Leutenegger 1977). These estimates, in turn, are arrived at by analogy from studies of variability and sexual dimorphism in other primates. Second, it became clear that when sexual differences in humans are examined from a comparative nonhuman primate and mammalian point of view, new insights may be gained (Alexander et al. 1979). Third, the nature of sexual dimorphism in nonhuman primates is of course of interest per

*Much of this research is based on studies that were supported, in part, by Faculty Research Grants from the Graduate School, University of Wisconsin-Madison. I wish to thank Susan Larson for constructive criticism of the manuscript, and Jan Noda and Steve Rokicki for technical assistance.

11

se, as it reflects a major aspect of the socioecology of each species (Crook 1972; Clutton-Brock and Harvey 1977; Leutenegger and Kelly 1977; Post, Goldstein, and Melnick 1978). I focus here on these more general aspects of sexual dimorphism in nonhuman primates. More specifically, I will examine species-specific differences in sexual dimorphism in terms of their evolutionary and adaptive significance. A recent study has reviewed in great detail physiological and behavioral sex differences in nonhuman primates (Mitchell 1979). To avoid unnecessary duplication, this chapter is restricted largely to a consideration of sexual dimorphism in morphological features. Because of extensive documentation, particular attention will be given to an analysis of sexual dimorphism in body weight and canine size. Also included is a discussion of other sexually dimorphic internal and external features that have been of particular interest not only to mammalogists and primatologists but may also be important to anthropologists.

VARIATION IN SEXUAL DIMORPHISM AND ITS CAUSES

Among nonhuman primates morphological sexual dimorphism occurs in a wide range of features, including (1) size (weight and linear body dimensions, such as body, head, and tail length); (2) dentition, such as canine size; (3) skull characteristics, such as prognathism, sagittal and nuchal crests; (4) locomotor apparatus (size and shape of axial and appendicular skeleton, muscular development); (5) internal organs, such as brain and heart size; (6) external features, such as pelage color and markings, shoulder capes and manes, permanent skin ridges and coloration, particularly on the face; and (7) maturational, seasonal, or periodic morphological changes associated with reproductive cycles.

Sexual dimorphism not only occurs in a wide range of features but also shows considerable variation between species. The degree of body weight dimorphism, for example, ranges from species in which males on the average are slightly more than twice as heavy as females to those in which females are slightly heavier than males (Clutton-Brock and Harvey 1977; Leutenegger and Kelly 1977). Similarly, canine size dimorphism ranges from species in which males have markedly larger canines than females to those in which canine size is virtually the same in the two sexes (e.g., Swindler 1976; Leutenegger and Kelly 1977; Harvey, Kavanagh, and Clutton-Brock 1978a,b).

Two principal theories offer causal explanations of such variation in sexual dimorphism. The more traditional one explains sexual dimorphism in terms of sexual selection (Darwin 1871). The argument is based on the competition among members of one sex for those of the other and the different selective pressures affecting the competitor and the object of competition. There is both empirical and theoretical evidence that in populations the ratio of adult males to females approximates 1:1. Consequently, if either individual males are able to father the offspring of several females or individual females are able to monopolize the reproductive effort of several males, then sexual competition will be relatively stronger in the sex that includes the disproportionately successful individuals. In other words, it will be more difficult for any individual to reproduce successfully in the sex in which some individuals are unusually successful. Thus, in a polygynous species (one in which some males mate with two or more females and in which the adult sex ratio approximates 1:1), reproductive success will vary more among males than females, and fewer males than females will contribute genetically to subsequent generations. In a polyandrous species (one in which some females mate with more than one male) the reverse will be true. Finally, in a monogamous species (one in which one male and one female form an exclusive mateship), variance in reproductive success is predicted to be equal in the two sexes. All this means that the greater the sexual competition is, the stronger selection will be for attributes leading to success in that context. Since in all but monogamous species there will be asymmetry between the sexes in this regard, selective pressures on males and females will be divergent and thus result in the development of sexual dimorphism.

Trivers (1972) extended these ideas and proposed a more inclusive model in which parental investment is the key factor influencing sexual selection. In short, he argues that the sex contributing most to parental care will be short in supply and hence will be the object of competition. In most mammalian species, primates included, females generally invest more in each offspring than do males because they have a lower reproductive potential. For a female the number of offspring produced during her reproductive period is limited by the time taken up by gestation and lactation. Female primates spend most of their adult life either pregnant or nursing, but even so the maximum number of offspring a single female can produce is about 15 to 20. As a rule, a female gains no advantage in mating with many males or competing with other females for mates; there are always plenty of males willing to mate, thus ensuring conception. It is advantageous, however, for the female to be mated only by the strongest and most vigorous male, for he will pass on these qualities to their offspring, thus maximizing not only his reproductive success but also hers. Furthermore, in species that live in permanent troops, as most higher primates do, the female consorts of the most dominant males and her offspring profit by sharing aspects of his privileged position. These may include preferential access to rare or scarce food resources and better protection against predators.

Among the most important aspects influencing a female's reproductive success is the quality of her behavior as a mother. Since she can produce only a limited number of offspring, her most effective strategy is to take the best possible care of each of them and to ensure that every one of them reaches sexual maturity.

In contrast, the reproductive strategy of males is not limited by such physiological constraints as gestation and lactation. Whereas the female's basic strategy is one of intensive nurture, the male's strategy is one of maximization of copulations. A male can sire a virtually unlimited number of offspring, provided he can successfully compete with other males in attracting and holding females. Since males spend more time and energy in competing with each other and courting the other sex, they have less time and energy available for parental care. Ultimately, it is this disparity in parental care that explains why males enhance their reproductive success by trying to maintain exclusive mating access to several mates, whereas females cannot enhance theirs by doing the same.

Therefore, it is because of this asymmetry between the sexes that among mammals polygyny is very widespread and its converse, polyandry, exceedingly rare. The third kind of mating strategy, monogamy, is also relatively infrequent, although not as uncommon as polyandry. For example, among 53 primate species I have investigated, 42 are polygynous, 11 are monogamous, and none are polyandrous. Monogamy occurs when the male's parental role (because of specific ecological circumstances that will be elucidated later) increases to match that of the female. Males of monogamous species typically spend much of their time and energy to help protect and raise their offspring. In a monogamous system a male must be certain that the offspring are his own, otherwise he risks expending energy raising offspring of another male. Thus, while monogamous males do not as much try to enhance their reproductive success by mating with as many females as possible, they jealously guard their female against stolen copulations.

Based on what has been discussed so far, the following prediction on the relationship between parental investment mating system and sexual dimorphism can be made: the more strongly asymmetrical parental investment is in a species, the more highly polygynous it should be. Furthermore, it is expected that the more highly polygynous a species is, the more sexually dimorphic it should be.

The second principal explanation of sexual dimorphism is that differences between males and females are a means of reducing intraspecific competition for resources, especially food (Amadon 1959; Selander 1972; Myers 1978). While such an explanation holds for a number of bird species, it has yet to be adequately tested for primates.

While much of the variance in sexual dimorphism among primates can be accounted for by sexual selection and parental investment theories, it is clear that there are other factors which influence the degree of sexual dimorphism, especially body-weight dimorphism. Ecological factors that have been suggested to affect sexual dimorphism in body weight include habitat, abundance and distribution of food, predator defense or avoidance, and positional behavior (e.g., Crook and Gartlan 1966; Crook 1972; Eisenberg, Muckenhirn, and Rudran 1972; Clutton-Brock and Harvey 1977, 1978; Leutenegger and Kelly 1977; Ralls 1977; Clutton-Brock, Harvey and Rudder 1977; Leutenegger 1978; Alexander et al. 1979). Evolutionary factors, in the sense of "phylogenetic legacy" (Raup 1972) or "phylogenetic inertia" (Wilson 1975), may also affect sexual dimorphism.

A factor that has received only sporadic attention, but clearly should be considered in any analysis of sexual dimorphism, is body size. Rensch (1950, 1954) showed, more than 25 years ago, that sexual dimorphism in appendicular structures tends to increase with increasing body size in various arthropoid and avian taxa. More recently, Ralls (1977) observed that extreme body size dimorphism evolves much more frequently in large species of mammals than in small ones. In preliminary reports both Clutton-Brock, Harvey and Rudder (1977) and Leutenegger (1978) demonstrated positive allometry for body-weight dimorphism in primates. While evidence for a positive relationship between body-weight dimorphism and body weight is accumulating for various mammalian taxa (including primates, pinnipeds, ungulates, rodents, and carnivores), its adaptive significance is not well understood at the present and different interpretations have been offered (Clutton-Brock, Harvey, and Rudder 1977; Leutenegger 1978; Alexander et al. 1979). Thus in the following section special attention will be focused on the scaling of sexual dimorphism in body weight in terms of its functional significance and its relationship with other forces postulated to affect body weight dimorphism.

The question of sexual dimorphism in canine size in primates, particularly as it relates to the problem of canine reduction in hominid evolution, has been discussed for more than a century (e.g., Darwin 1871; Washburn and Ciochon 1974). Although there seems to be general agreement on the kind and direction of selective forces affecting the degree of canine size dimorphism in nonhuman primates, much disagreement characterizes the various adaptive scenarios that have been advanced as explanations of hominid canine reduction (Jungers 1978). In neither case, however, has there been much attention paid to the influence of body size on canine size, as vehemently pointed out by Clutton-Brock and Harvey (1978). It is only very recently that systematic studies on the influence of body size on canine size dimorphism in nonhuman primates have begun (Harvey, Kavanagh, and Clutton-Brock 1978a,b; Leutenegger 1981), and a further analysis of this problem is presented in the section on canine size dimorphism.

It is important to distinguish between sexual dimorphism in body weight and other sexually dimorphic characteristics (Ralls 1977). While the degree of body weight dimorphism appears to be affected by a multitude of selective pressures, the degree of sexual dimorphism in structures such as canines (or horns as in ungulates) used in displays or as weapons seems to be most strongly influenced by the intensity of sexual selection and antipredator strategy (Leutenegger and Kelly 1977; Harvey, Kavanagh, and Clutton-Brock 1978a). Because of these differences in selective action on sexual dimorphism in body weight and canine size, the strength of their correlation appears to vary somewhat. Leutenegger and Kelly (1977) found a positive, but only moderate, correlation between canine-size dimorphism and body-weight dimorphism in a sample of 18 anthropoid species. Gautier-Hion (1975) found a stronger correlation between sexual dimorphism in body weight and canine size in several African cercopithecids, as did Orlosky (1973) in cebids. A brief reexamination of the relationship between canine-size dimorphism and body-weight dimorphism based on comparison of their distribution patterns among primates represents another focus of this chapter.

BODY-WEIGHT DIMORPHISM

Variation in the degree of sexual dimorphism in body weight is considerable among nonhuman primates (Table 2.1). The largest degree of body weight dimorphism amounts to males being about twice as heavy as females in some cercopithecid monkeys and great apes such as savanna baboons (*Papio cynocephalus, P. anubis*), mandrills (*Mandrillus sphinx*), proboscis monkeys (*Nasalis larvatus*), orangutans (*Pongo pygmaeus*) and gorillas (*Pan gorilla*). The majority of species exhibit a moderate degree of body-weight dimorphism (males heavier than females by about 15 to 85 percent) and includes one strepsirhine, the ruffed lemur (*Lemur variegatus*), and many cebid and cercopithecid monkeys. The least amount of body-weight dimorphism is found in strepsirhines (except the ruffed lemur), marmosets and tamarins (Callitrichidae), titi monkeys (*Aotus trivirgatus*), spider monkeys (*Ateles geoffroyi*), many colobine monkeys (*Colobus verus, Presbytis aygula, P. melalophos, P. frontata, P. rubicunda, P. cristatus*), and the gibbons and siamangs (Hylobatidae). In this latter group, males and females are virtually equal in weight, so they may be considered monomorphic.

Sexual selection theory predicts that this variation in body-weight dimorphism is the result of species differences in the degree of polygyny. The data in Table 2.1 bear out this prediction. The average degree of body-weight dimorphism in polygynous species amounts to males being 40 percent heavier than females, whereas in monogamous species males are heavier than females by only 4 percent. Using a slightly different sample of primate species than presented here, Clutton-Brock and Harvey (1977) and Clutton-Brock, Harvey, and Rudder (1977) have also tested this prediction and found a positive correlation between body weight dimorphism and socionomic sex ratios (mean number of adult females per adult male in breeding groups). They also found that this relationship is largely due to the fact that monogamous species show considerably less dimorphism than polygynous ones, and when only polygynous species are considered, no relationship exists. Their explanation for the lack of a correlation among polygynous species is that the socionomic sex ratio may be a poor indicator of intensity of competition among males. They argue that it would, for example, be likely to underestimate the degree of intermale competition in multimale troups (as in *Papio* or *Macaca* species) where a marked dominance hierarchy exists and mating access is not equally shared among males. Indeed, if only single-male troups are considered, there is a significant relationship between body-weight dimorphism and harem size (Alexander et al. 1979). Thus, the successful confirmation of the prediction of a correlation between degrees of body-weight dimorphism and degrees of polygyny seems to depend primarily upon finding an adequate measure of the degree of polygyny.

Another factor which has to be taken into consideration in an analysis of body weight dimorphism is body weight per se. Based on the figures presented in Table 2.1, regressions of $\log_{10}$ (male weight) on $\log_{10}$ (female weight) were fitted by least squares techniques. For the total sample of 53 species, male weight scales strongly at a power of female weight of 1.081 (Table 2.2). The slope is significantly different from the isometric slope of 1.0 at $P < 0.01$. This suggests that sexual dimorphism in body weight tends to increase exponentially with increasing body weight. It is crucial to note, however, that positive allometry in body-weight dimorphism is solely due to the fact that the sample contains a much larger number of polygynous than

TABLE 2.1
Sexual Dimorphism in Body Weight and Canine Size Among Nonhuman Primates.

Species	Weight			Canine Size			Mating System
	Male (g)	Female (g)	Sex Dim.	Male (mm)	Female (mm)	Sex Dim.	
Strepsirhini							
Lemur variegatus	3,004	2,380	126	—	—	—	P
Lepilemur mustelinus	913	846	108	—	—	—	P
Microcebus murinus	50	45	111	—	—	—	P
Propithecus verreauxi	3,585	3,183	113	—	—	—	P
Perodicticus potto	1,125	1,165	105	4.3	4.1	105	P
Nycticebus coucang	—	—	—	3.6	3.3	109	P
Galago crassicaudatus	—	—	—	4.6	4.1	112	P
Galago senegalensis	—	—	—	2.3	2.2	105	P
Galago demidovii	64	61	105	—	—	—	P
Haplorhini							
Callitrichidae							
Callithrix jacchus	362	381	95	2.06	2.11	98	M
Saguinus mystax	595	529	112	—	—	—	M
Saguinus oedipus	558	537	104	—	—	—	M
Saguinus geoffroyi	—	—	—	2.8	2.9	97	M
Cebidae							
Aotus trivirgatus	922	900	102	3.1	3.0	103	M
Pithecia pithecia	1,295	1,059	122	—	—	—	P

Species							
Alouatta villosa	8,960	7,600	118	7.6	6.2	123	P
Alouatta palliata	7,400	5,970	124	—	—	—	P
Alouatta seniculus	8,060	6,440	125	8.09	6.30	128	P
Alouatta caraya	7,616	4,893	153	—	—	—	P
Cebus capucinus	3,812	2,666	143	—	—	—	P
Cebus apella	2,646	2,192	121	7.36	6.21	119	P
Saimiri sciureus	785	620	127	3.5	2.7	130	P
Saimiri oerstedii	893	737	121	3.9	2.7	144	P
Ateles geoffroyi	7,390	7,888	94	6.1	5.5	111	P
Cercopithecidae							
Cercopithecus aethiops	5,080	3,560	143	7.42	5.16	144	P
Cercopithecus neglectus	6,570	4,700	140	8.3	5.6	148	P
Cercopithecus nictitans	6,460	4,000	162	7.5	4.9	153	P
Cercopithecus ascanius	4,080	3,080	132	6.13	4.40	139	P
Cercopithecus mitis	—	—	—	7.9	5.5	144	P
Cercopithecus mona	—	—	—	7.2	4.9	147	P
Erythrocebus patas	11,500	6,500	177	—	—	—	P
Cercocebus galeritus	—	—	—	9.7	6.0	162	P
Cercocebus torquatus	—	—	—	8.5	6.5	131	P
Cercocebus albigena	—	—	—	7.71	6.08	127	P
Macaca nemestrina	9,400	5,980	157	11.7	7.3	160	P
Macaca fascicularis	4,740	3,000	158	9.2	5.8	159	P
Macaca mulatta	9,720	6,020	161	8.9	6.0	148	P

(continued)

19

TABLE 2.1

Sexual Dimorphism in Body Weight and Canine Size Among Nonhuman Primates.

Species	Weight			Canine Size			Mating System
	Male (g)	Female (g)	Sex Dim.	Male (mm)	Female (mm)	Sex Dim.	
Macaca cyclopsis	6,000	4,945	121	—	—	—	P
Macaca fuscata	13,720	9,180	149	—	—	—	P
Macaca niger	—	—	—	7.6	6.3	121	P
Macaca speciosa	—	—	—	10.3	7.1	145	P
Papio cynocephalus	23,100	11,200	206	14.0	8.3	169	P
Papio anubis	24,400	12,440	196	—	—	—	P
Papio ursinus	24,330	14,530	167	—	—	—	P
Papio hamadryas	28,000	16,500	170	—	—	—	P
Mandrillus sphinx	26,000	11,000	236	—	—	—	P
Theropithecus gelada	—	—	—	14.8	7.4	200	P
Colobus verus	3,800	3,600	106	—	—	—	P
Colobus badius	—	—	—	9.8	6.9	142	P
Colobus polykomos	—	—	—	9.8	7.0	140	P
Presbytis aygula	6,680	6,710	100	6.1	5.5	111	P
Presbytis melalophos	6,590	6,660	99	—	—	—	P
Presbytis frontata	5,600	5,660	99	—	—	—	P
Presbytis rubicunda	6,250	5,900	106	—	—	—	P
Presbytis cristatus	6,450	5,850	110	6.23	5.35	116	P
Presbytis obscurus	7,320	5,620	130	—	—	—	P
Presbytis johnii	—	—	—	8.3	6.4	130	P
Pygathrix nemaeus	—	—	—	6.8	5.4	126	P
Nasalis larvatus	20,370	9,820	207	8.2	6.1	134	P

Hylobatidae							
Hylobates lar	6,420	5,310	121	—	—	—	M
Hylobates moloch	5,890	6,300	93	7.4	7.6	97	M
Hylobates agilis	5,822	5,500	106	7.2	6.9	104	M
Hylobates hoolock	6,900	6,100	113	—	—	—	M
Hylobates concolor	5,600	5,800	97	—	—	—	M
Hylobates klossi	5,700	5,900	97	—	—	—	M
Hylobates syndactylus	10,940	10,600	103	—	—	—	M
Pongidae							
Pongo pygmaeus	72,750	36,630	199	16.4	12.5	131	P
Pan troglodytes	44,500	36,900	121	15.0	11.7	128	P
Pan paniscus	—	—	—	11.1	9.0	123	P
Pan gorilla	158,600	72,320	219	21.4	15.0	143	P

Note: The body-weight data presented in the table are those of adult males and females. Each of the 53 species is represented by male and female means of a total of at least 16 individuals, with approximately equal numbers of each sex. Although the data are taken from various sources and are, therefore, not perfectly comparable, a major source of error usually found in body-weight studies has been eliminated by disregarding that from captive animals and using data only from wild-trapped and wild-shot animals. All the body-weight data were extracted from Leutenegger (1973a, 1978), Rothenfluh (1976), and Leutenegger and Kelly (1977).

Canine size is represented by male and female means of the mesiodistal diameter of the maxillary permanent canine of 42 species. The maxillary canine rather than the mandibular canine was selected because of its larger size and greater importance in behavioral displays. The decision to use the mesiodistal diameter of the maxillary canine was based upon two criteria: (1) wear has less influence on the mesiodistal diameter than on height; and (2) more data are available on the mesiodestal diameter than on height. All the canine dimensions were extracted from Leutenegger (1976), Swindler (1976), and Leutenegger and Kelly (1977).

Sexual dimorphism in both body weight and canine size is expressed as male mean in percentage of female mean. Mating system is denoted by P = polygynous and M = monogamous.

TABLE 2.2

Regressions of Log_{10} (Male Weight) on Log_{10} (Female Weight) for Primates on the Basis of the Breeding System.

Breeding System	N	a	b	S_b	r^2	t	P
Combined polygynous and monogamous species	53	−0.182	1.081	0.022	0.979	3.66	< 0.01
Polygynous species	42	−0.172	1.085	0.024	0.981	3.54	< 0.01
Monogamous species	11	0.008	1.002	0.022	0.996	0.10	n.s.

Note: N, sample size (number of species); a, y-intercept; b, least squares slope; S_b, standard error of b; r^2, squared correlation coefficient; t, t-value of difference of slope from isometric slope at 1.0; P, probability; n.s., not significant.

monogamous species. In other words, the contribution of polygynous species to the slope tends to obscure that of monogamous species. An analysis with the species separated on the basis of the breeding system makes this clear (Table 2.2 and Figure 2.1).

While for 42 polygynous species male weight is positively related to female weight, with a slope of 1.085 being significantly different from 1.0 at $P < 0.01$, for 11 monogamous species the slope of 1.002 shows equality with the isometric slope of 1.0. Furthermore, the y-intercept is practically zero. As a numerical example, a polygynous species in which adult females weigh 1000 gm would have adult males that weigh 1211 gm, while a monogamous species with the same female weight would have males that weigh 1033 gm. For females averaging 10,000 gm, the predicted weight for males of a polygynous species would be 14,730 gm, whereas male weight of a monogamous species would be 10,380 gm. This suggests that whereas in polygynous species body-weight dimorphism increases exponentially with increasing body weight, in monogamous species body-weight dimorphism not only remains constant throughout the size range, but actually is minimal or lacking at any given body weight.

A multifactorial model can be used to explain why in polygynous species sexual dimorphism in body weight tends to increase exponentially with increasing body weight (Leutenegger 1978). I suggested that the more highly polygynous a species is, the more intense is sexual selection and thus selection for larger male size, which, in turn, is interrelated with an increase in sexual dimorphism. In an intricate feedback system, increased sexual dimorphism and larger male size promote polygyny. This model is in accordance with similar ones developed on the basis of observation of grouse (Wiley 1974), grassland herding ungulates, and primates (Alexander et al. 1979).

All models entail that the evolution of polygyny is inseparable from the evolution of large size.

While many primate species fit the predicted degree of sexual dimorphism based on polygyny and body weight, several species are more or less deviant (Figure 2.1). In general, deviations from the predicted degree of sexual dimorphism can be related to known ecological and evolutionary pressures. For example, the majority of terrestrial species show substantially greater body-weight dimorphism than predicted on the basis of polygyny and body weight. There are two explanations that may account for this observation. First, in terrestrial species increased body weight does not restrict the male's access to food supplies (which are often located on fine branches or terminal twigs) to the same extent as it would in arboreal species (Clutton-Brock, Harvey, and Rudder 1977). Actually, increased sexual dimorphism may act to reduce male-female competition for food resources (Selander 1972; Clutton-Brock 1977). Second, as observed in yellow baboons (*Papio cynocephalus*), increased size and weight may be important in regard to the male's role of intimidation or displacement of predators (DeVore and Washburn 1963; Altmann and Altmann 1970).

Not all terrestrial species are excessively dimorphic, however. Gelada baboons (*Theropithecus gelada*), for example, show a moderate degree of body-weight dimorphism that virtually coincides with a degree to be expected if they were not terrestrial. In other words, if in gelada baboons there is selection pressure for large male size due to terrestrialism, it is counteracted by selection against large weight due to other factors. As detailed elsewhere, these constraining factors most probably relate to the arid habitat and seasonally limited food resources (Leutenegger and Kelly 1977).

While in many arboreal species observed and predicted degrees of body-weight dimorphism coincide or at least come very close, several species show strong negative deviation from the predicted degree. For example, in the blackhanded spider monkey (*Ateles geoffroyi*), and in some colobines, such as the olive colobus monkey (*Colobus verus*), the Sunda Island leaf monkey (*Presbytis aygula*), the banded leaf monkey (*P. melalophos*) and the white-fronted leaf monkey (*P. frontata*), body-weight dimorphism is as minimal or lacking as in monogamous species. Because of lack of quantitative behavioral and ecological data in many cases, it is difficult to assess the species-specific pressures that tend to reduce male weight and thus constrain sexual dimorphism. Thus, explanation of their position depends on further information.

The observation that for monogamous species, sexual dimorphism in body weight is minimal or lacking and independent of body

FEMALE   WEIGHT (g)

weight may be explained by the finding that for all species for which data are available, the intensity of sexual selection and the degree of behavioral dimorphism are consistently low, while male parental investment is generally high. For example, as Kleiman (1977) demonstrated, the summarized intensity of paternal investment reflected by particular types of behavior such as defending a territory, and defending, grooming, feeding, carrying, and teaching the young is almost identical for small-sized species, such as marmosets and tamarins, to that for the largest-sized monogamous species, the siamang (*Hylobates syndactylus*). It is also notable that monogamy, not only in primates, but also in other mammals such as ungulates (Alexander et al. 1979) and carnivores (Kleiman 1977) is almost entirely limited to small- and medium-sized species. This may be explained by the lowered intensity of sexual selection, thus reducing

Figure 2.1. Double-logarithmic representation of the relationship between adult male and female weights for 53 primate species (based on Table 2.2). The upper line (P) represents the regression for 42 polygynous species (designated by solid dots); The lower line (M) represents the regression for 11 monogamous species (designated by circumscribed dots). Numerical designation of species: 1, *Alouatta villosa*; 2, *Alouatta seniculus*; 3, *Alouatta caraya*; 4, *Ateles geoffroyi*; 5, *Cebus capucinus*; 6, *Cebus apella*; 7, *Cercopithecus aethiops*; 8, *Cercopithecus neglectus*; 9, *Cercopithecus nictitans*; 10, *Cercopithecus ascanius*; 11, *Colobus verus*; 12, *Erythrocebus patas*; 13, *Galago demidovii*; 14, *Lemur variegatus*; 15, *Lepilemur mustelinus*; 16, *Macaca nemestrina*; 17, *Macaca fascicularis*; 18, *Macaca mulatta*; 19, *Macaca cyclopsis*; 20, *Macaca fuscata*; 21, *Mandrillus sphinx*; 22, *Microcebus murinus*; 23, *Nasalis larvatus*; 24, *Pan gorilla*; 25, *Pan troglodytes*; 26, *Papio anubis*; 27, *Papio cynocephalus*; 28, *Papio ursinus*; 29, *Papio hamadryas*; 30, *Perodicticus potto*; 31, *Pithecia pithecia*; 32, *Pongo pygmaeus*; 33, *Presbytis aygula*; 34, *Presbytis melalophos*; 35, *Presbytis frontata*; 36, *Presbytis rubicunda*; 37, *Presbytis cristatus*; 38, *Presbytis obscurus*; 39, *Propithecus verreauxi*; 40, *Saimiri sciureus*; 41, *Saimiri oerstedii*; 42, *Theropithecus gelada*; 43, *Callithrix jacchus*; 44, *Saguinus oedipus*; 45, *Saguinus mystax*; 46, *Aotus trivirgatus*; 47, *Hylobates lar*; 48, *Hylobates moloch*; 49, *Hylobates agilis*; 50, *Hylobates hoolock*; 51, *Hylobates concolor*; 52, *Hylobates klossi*; 53, *Hylobates syndactylus*.

selection for large male weight, one consequence of which is a slowing in phyletic size increase. It may even be argued that phyletic dwarfism as suggested for marmosets and tamarins (Leutenegger 1973a, 1979; Peters 1978) is at least partially associated with monogamy in these primates (Leutenegger 1980). Because of lack of selection for larger male size, selection for a size decrease as an adaptive response to a secondary shift to a higher energy diet (Kay 1973; Rosenberger 1977) may have acted more strongly and resulted in a phyletic size decrease.

As to the aforementioned observation that monogamous primates are generally smaller than their polygynous relatives, Alexander et al. (1979) offer an alternative explanation. Their argument is based on different methods of escaping predation in polygynous and monogamous species. Monogamous species, they argue, have a sedentary nature, are territorial, and tend to live in forests, or habitats with considerable cover. They avoid predators primarily by concealment and escape into trees. Such an antipredator strategy most likely results not only in selection for maintenance of a smaller size, but also in selection for equality in size of adults of the two sexes. While I agree with Alexander et al. (1979) that there seems to be a positive relationship between antipredator strategy, body size, and body-size dimorphism, I do not believe that there is a strong association between antipredator strategy and breeding system. Avoidance of predators by means of escape and concealment and consequent selection for small size and tendency toward monomorphism is not limited to monogamous species but may also occur in arboreal, polygynous species such as the blackhanded spider monkey and some colobine species (as discussed earlier), as well as in nocturnal strepsirhines such as mouse lemurs (*Microcebus murinus*), slow lorises (*Nycticebus coucang*), pottos (*Perodicticus potto*), and lesser and greater bushbabies (*Galago senegalensis, G. crassicaudatus*).

CANINE-SIZE DIMORPHISM

The extent of variation in canine-size dimorphism is somewhat smaller than that of body-weight dimorphism. It ranges from a species (gelada baboons) in which males have canines twice the size of those of females to species (marmosets, tamarins, night monkeys, gibbons) in which canine size is virtually the same in the two sexes (Table 2.1). As with the variation in body-weight dimorphism, much of the variation in canine-size dimorphism can be accounted for on the basis of differences in the degree of polygyny. Using the figures presented in Table 2.1, the average canine-size dimorphism amounts to 35 percent for polygynous species, while for monogamous species canine-size dimorphism is nonexistent (zero percent). Using a somewhat different sample of primate species, Harvey, Kavanagh, and Clutton-Brock (1978a) also found a significant difference in the degree of canine-size dimorphism between polygynous and monogamous species. Among polygynous species, however, they found no significant difference between uni-male and multi-male species.

Since body size has been demonstrated to affect body-weight dimorphism, I also tested its influence on canine-size dimorphism. Table 2.3 shows that for the total sample of 42 species male canine size scales at a power of female canine size of 1.156. The slope is significantly different from the isometric slope of 1.0 at $P < 0.05$. This indicates that canine-size dimorphism tends to increase exponentially with increasing female canine size. Since female canine size is very strongly correlated with female body weight, as shown by Harvey, Kavanagh, and Clutton-Brock (1978a,b), this further suggests that canine-size dimorphism also increases exponentially with increasing weight. As with the variation in body-weight dimorphism, it is important to note that positive allometry in canine-size dimorphism is solely due to the fact that the sample contains a much larger number of polygynous than monogamous species. An analysis with

TABLE 2.3

Regressions of Log_{10} (Male Canine Size) on Log_{10} (Female Canine Size) for Primates on the Basis of the Breeding System.

Breeding System	N	a	b	S_b	r^2	t	P
Combined polygynous and monogamous species	42	−0.007	1.156	0.066	0.960	2.37	< 0.05
Polygynous species	37	0.026	1.131	0.059	0.963	2.21	< 0.05
Monogamous species	5	−0.015	1.029	0.016	0.997	1.77	n.s.

Note: N, sample size (number of species); a, y-intercept; b, least squares slope; S_b, standard error of b; r^2, squared correlation coefficient; t, t-value of difference of slope from isometric slope at 1.0; P, probability; n.s., not significant.

the species separated according to the breeding system confirms this (Table 2.3 and Figure 2.2).

Whereas for 37 polygynous species, male canine size is positively related to female canine size, with a slope of 1.131 being significantly different from 1.0 at $P < 0.05$, for 5 monogamous species the slope of 1.029 is not significantly different from the isometric slope of 1.0. This parallels the variation in body-weight dimorphism observed earlier. It suggests that while in polygynous species canine-size dimorphism increases exponentially with increasing canine size (and body weight), in monogamous species canine-size dimorphism not only remains constant throughout the size range, but is minimal or lacking at any given size and weight.

While the gross distribution of canine-size dimorphism is consistent with the pattern predicted by breeding system and size, several species are more or less deviant (Figure 2.2). As with the variation in body-weight dimorphism, this indicates that the degree of canine-size dimorphism is affected by additional selective pressures. The strongest positive deviation in canine-size dimor-phism from the predicted degree is found in yellow baboons. This suggests that not only excessive male weight but also excessive male canine size may have been selected for as predator deterrents. The only other terrestrial Old World monkey for which data on canine size are available, the gelada baboon, also shows much greater male canine size than predicted, thus supporting the argument of a relationship between active predator defense and marked canine-size dimorphism (e.g., Lauer 1975; Leutenegger and Kelly 1977; Harvey, Kavanagh, and Clutton-Brock 1978a,b). Those species displaying the strongest negative deviation in body-weight dimorphism, such as the blackhanded spider monkey and the Sunda Island leaf monkey, also

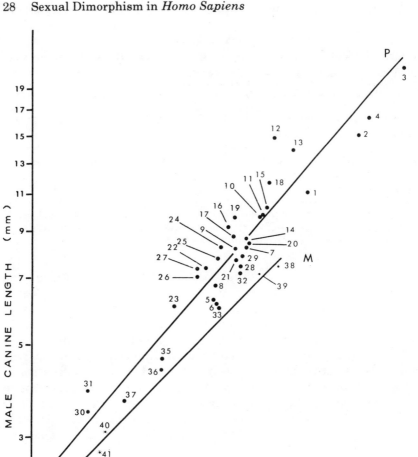

are characterized by a marked reduction in canine-size dimorphism. It is interesting to note, however, that while the Sunda Island leaf monkey is virtually monomorphic in weight and spider monkey females tend to be slightly heavier than males, in both species males have slightly larger canines than females. This suggests that whatever selective pressures tend to keep sexual dimorphism minimal in these two species, they apparently act more strongly on body weight than on canine size.

As predicted by sexual selection and parental investment theories, monogamous primates are virtually monomorphic in canine

Figure 2.2. Double-logarithmic representation of the relationship between male and female maxillary canine length for 42 primate species (based on Table 2.3). The upper line (P) represents the regression for 37 polygynous species (designated by solid dots); the lower line (M) represents the regression for 5 monogamous species (designated by circumscribed dots). Numerical designation of species: 1, *Pan paniscus*; 2, *Pan troglodytes*; 3, *Pan gorilla*; 4, *Pongo pygmaeus*; 5, *Presbytis cristatus*; 6, *Presbytis aygula*; 7, *Presbytis johnii*; 8, *Pygathrix nemaeus*; 9, *Nasalis larvatus*; 10, *Colobus badius*; 11, *Colobus polykomos*; 12, *Theropithecus gelada*; 13, *Papio cynocephalus*; 14, *Macaca niger*; 15, *Macaca speciosa*; 16, *Macaca fascicularis*; 17, *Macaca mulatta*; 18, *Macaca nemestrina*; 19, *Cercocebus galeritus*; 20, *Cercocebus torquatus*; 21, *Cercocebus albigena*; 22, *Cercopithecus aethiops*; 23, *Cercopithecus ascanius*; 24, *Cercopithecus neglectus*; 25, *Cercopithecus mitis*; 26, *Cercopithecus mona*; 27, *Cercopithecus nictitans*; 28, *Alouatta villosa*; 29, *Alouatta seniculus*; 30, *Saimiri sciureus*; 31, *Saimiri oerstedii*; 32, *Cebus apella*; 33, *Ateles geoffroyi*; 34, *Galago senegalensis*; 35, *Galago crassicaudatus*; 36, *Perodicticus potto*; 37, *Nycticebus coucang*; 38, *Hylobates moloch*; 39, *Hylobates agilis*; 40, *Aotus trivirgatus*; 41, *Saguinus geoffroyi*; 42, *Callithrix jacchus*.

size. The very strong fit of all monogamous species to the predicted pattern suggests that other ecological and evolutionary pressures are of only minor importance in their influence on canine-size dimorphism.

A comparison of the gross distribution patterns of canine-size dimorphism and body-weight dimorphism shows that while rarely coinciding in degree, they depart in most species, if deviant, in the same direction from the predicted pattern. This similarity implies a positive relationship between canine-size dimorphism and body-weight dimorphism, thus confirming findings of earlier studies (Orlosky 1973; Gautier-Hion 1975; Leutenegger and Kelly 1977). This leads to the suggestion that, for primates in general, most of the variance in both canine-size dimorphism and body-weight dimorphism can be accounted for by the same three principal factors: sexual selection, antipredator strategy, and size. On the other hand, the finding that for several polygynous species canine-size dimorphism and/or body-weight dimorphism do not coincide with the degree predicted by sexual selection, antipredator strategy, and size supports the suggestion that additional ecological and evolutionary pressures may influence sexual dimorphism in canine size and body weight.

SEXUAL DIMORPHISM IN OTHER FEATURES

Secondary sexual dimorphism develops not only in regard to size and weight of the entire body but also in the proportions of component parts of the body, such as the dentition and the skeleton. As demonstrated in the preceding section, canine-size dimorphism varies among primates according to the degree of polygyny, antipredator strategy, and body size. Similarly, sexual dimorphism of the cranium varies directly with the degree of polygyny and also shows a strong allometric component, as exemplified by the development of prognathism, sagittal and nuchal crests.

One of the best studied parts of the skeleton from the point of view of sexual dimorphism is the pelvis (cf. Van den Broek 1911; Washburn 1942; Schultz 1949; Wettstein 1963; Leutenegger 1970a, b, 1973b, 1974; Black 1970; Gingerich 1972). While part of the variance in pelvic sexual dimorphism can be attributed to the effect of general body size differences (Mobb and Wood 1977), some of the variance is the result of interspecific differences in the neonatal-maternal size relationship (Leutenegger 1970a,b, 1973b, 1974), i.e., the dimensional relationship between the cranium of the fetus at term and the female true pelvis. Among the best measures of pelvic sexual dimorphism is the ischiopubic index. Since the pubis constitutes part of the birth canal, whereas the ischium does not, and since the ischium is highly correlated with body size (Leutenegger 1970a), sexual dimorphism in the ischiopubic index primarily reflects the relative enlargement of the female true pelvis, while at the same time the index is independent of general secondary sexual differentiation. In all primates studied so far, the mean for the ischiopubic index is higher in females than in males (Table 2.4). The most marked sexual dimorphism in the ischiopubic index is found in the squirrel monkey (*Saimiri sciureus*) and the capuchin monkey (*Cebus capucinus*), in both of which neonate cranial dimensions are largest compared to female true pelvic dimensions. In contrast, only slightly developed sexual dimorphism in the ischiopubic index exists in the African lorises (*Perodicticus potto* and *Arctocebus calabarensis*), the mantled howler monkey (*Alouatta villosa*), and the pongids, in all of which neonate cranial dimensions are strikingly smaller than corresponding female pelvic dimensions.

Sexual dimorphism also occurs in a variety of external features. Relatively rare among primates is the development of sexual dimorphism in pelage color. Among strepsirhines, striking sexual dichromatism is only known for the black lemur (*Lemur macaco*) in which males are almost entirely black and females reddish-brown to olive-brown, according to subspecies. Among haplorhines, sexual dichromatism has been observed for various species and subspecies of sakis (*Pithecia*), the black howler monkey (*Alouatta caraya*), and some gibbon species (*Hylobates*). In general, adult males are dominantly or entirely blackish, and the individual hairs unbanded.

TABLE 2.4

Sexual Dimorphism in Ischiopubic Index Among Nonhuman Primates.

Species	Male Mean	Female Mean	Sex Dimorphism*
Perodicticus potto	183.3	188.7	102.9
Arctocebus calabarensis	146.6	156.8	107.0
Callithrix jacchus	84.7	93.9	110.9
Saguinus tamarin	76.7	84.9	110.7
Aotus trivirgatus	71.8	83.3	116.0
Saimiri sciureus	73.0	92.9	127.3
Cebus capucinus	75.8	90.8	119.8
Alouatta villosa	111.3	115.3	103.6
Lagothrix lagothricha	98.7	112.9	114.5
Ateles geoffroyi	89.9	100.8	112.3
Macaca mulatta	82.9	95.7	115.4
Nasalis larvatus	86.4	96.9	112.1
Hylobates lar	92.7	101.6	109.6
Hylobates moloch	95.0	108.1	113.7
Pongo pygmaeus	97.8	107.0	109.4
Pan troglodytes	82.6	87.0	105.3
Pan gorilla	93.6	98.3	105.0

*Sexual dimorphism is expressed as female mean in percentage of male mean.

The females, in contrast, are partially, dominantly, or entirely reddish, the hair with or without bands (Hershkovitz 1977). As to the adaptive significance of sexual dichromatism, Hershkovitz (1979) suggests that it appears to have evolved among social species that are relatively predator-free and whose coloration serves mainly for recognition or display within the group.

Various species show sexual dichromatism in localized areas, such as the face and the perianal and genital areas. Among New World monkeys, for example, the male of the pale-headed saki (*Pithecia pithecia*) has a whitish to reddish crown, face, and throat, while the female has a dark face with paranasal stripes. Among Old World monkeys, the most remarkable development of localized sexual dichromatism is seen in the mandrill (*Mandrillus sphinx*). The males have a bicolored face with a red nose and nostrils and blue paranasal swellings. This color pattern is repeated in the perianal and genital regions. In females neither facial nor perianal nor genital coloration is developed. In vervet monkeys (*Cercopithecus aethiops*), sexual dichromatism is only slightly less striking with males exhibiting a bright red penis, bright blue scrotum, and white belly known as "the red, white, and blue display" (Mitchell 1979). This coloration, however, occurs only periodically, during the breeding season.

Sexual dimorphism may develop not only in coloration of hair but also in its pattern of distribution. Adult males of gelada baboons (*Theropithecus gelada*), hamadryas baboons (*Papio hamadryas*), and some macaque species grow thick manes of long hair on head and neck, and often on the shoulder and down the back. The manes and shoulder capes are poorly developed in females. In an attempt to explain the adaptive significance of sexual differences in hair distribution, Leutenegger and Kelly (1977) have found that in the large African monkeys, the development of manes and shoulder capes is inversely related to the degree of body-weight dimorphism, both of which vary with habitat quality and food supply. In a good quality habitat with abundant food supply, body-size dimorphism is accomplished exclusively by weight dimorphism and not by the presence of manes. On the other hand, in a poor quality habitat with restricted food supply, the development of manes and capes results in an apparent increase in size without a concomitant increase in the individual's biomass proportional to its appearance. This suggests that under energetic restrictions it is more economical for males to maintain a long coat of hair than a high body weight.

Sex differences in hair distribution and length are known for other localized areas as well (Schultz 1969). In mature male gorillas, for example, the entire chest becomes almost bare with advancing age. As another example, beards and moustaches develop in many male orangutans, but in only a few females.

The most extraordinary sexually dimorphic features develop in the faces of two South East Asiatic primates. The proboscis monkey (*Nasalis larvatus*), as implied by its name, has a highly unusual nose. In adult males it is very large, bulbous and drooping while in females it is less developed and slightly upturned. In orangutans marked facial dimorphism is the result of a hypertrophic development of cheek pads and gular pouches in adult males. While the proximate function of such peculiar anatomical structures is still obscure, there is little question that they are the result of intense intrasexual or epigamic selection.

SUMMARY

Among nonhuman primates, morphological sexual dimorphism not only occurs in a wide range of external and internal features, but shows considerable variation between species. While much of the variance in sexual dimorphism can be accounted for by sexual selection and parental investment theories, there is evidence of additional factors that may have an influence. Among these are ecological and behavioral factors—such as quality of habitat, abundance and distribution of food, predator defense or avoidance, and positional behavior. In their combination they produce what may be called "bioenergetic constraints" to sexual dimorphism. Evolutionary factors, in the sense of "phylogenetic legacy" or "phylogenetic inertia" may also have an effect. In addition, and as particularly emphasized in this chapter, an adequate explanation of sexual dimorphism should also consider the influence of body size, i.e., of allometric effects. Finally, it is crucial to realize that while general models on sexual dimorphism can be arrived at based on the interaction of the factors given above, extreme caution should prevail in attempts to explain the degree of sexual dimorphism in a specific feature of a given species.

BIBLIOGRAPHY

Alexander, R. D., J. L. Hoogland, R. D. Howard, K. M. Noonan, and P. W. Sherman. 1979. "Sexual Dimorphism and Breeding Systems in Pinnipeds, Ungulates, Primates and Humans." In *Evolutionary Biology and Human Social Behavior: An Anthropological Perspective,* edited by N. A. Chagnon and W. Irons, pp. 402-435. North Scituate, Mass.: Duxbury Press.

Altmann, S. A., and J. Altmann. 1970. "Baboon Ecology." *Bibliotheca Primatologica,* 12:1-220.

Amadon, D. 1959. "The Significance of Sexual Differences in Size Among Birds." *Proceedings of the American Philosophical Society,* 103:531-536.

Black, E. S. 1970. "Sexual Dimorphism in the Ischium and Pubis of Three Species of South American Monkeys." *Journal of Mammalogy,* 51:794-796.

Brace, C. L. 1972. "Sexual Dimorphism in Human Evolution." *Yearbook of Physical Anthropology,* 16:31-49.

Brown, J. L. 1975. *The Evolution of Behavior.* New York: Norton.

Clutton-Brock, T. H. 1977. "Some Aspects of Intraspecific Variation in Feeding and Ranging Behavior in Primates." In *Primate Ecology,* edited by T. H. Clutton-Brock, pp. 539-556. London: Academic Press.

Clutton-Brock, T. H., and P. H. Harvey. 1977. "Primate Ecology and Social Organization." *Journal of Zoology,* 183:1-39.

———. 1978. "Mammals, Resources and Reproductive Strategies." *Nature,* 273:191-195.

Clutton-Brock, T. H., P. H. Harvey, and B. Rudder. 1977. "Sexual Dimorphism, Socionomic Sex Ratio and Body Weight in Primates." *Nature,* 269:797-800.

Crook, J. H. 1972. "Sexual Selection, Dimorphism, and Social Organization in the Primates." In *Sexual Selection and the Descent of Man, 1871-1971,* edited by B. G. Campbell, pp. 231-281. Chicago: Aldine.

Crook, J. H., and J. S. Gartlan. 1966. "On the Evolution of Primate Societies." *Nature*, 210:1200-1203.

Darwin, C. 1871. *The Descent of Man and Selection in Relation to Sex.* London: John Murray.

DeVore, I., and S. L. Washburn. 1963. "Baboon Ecology and Human Evolution." In *African Ecology and Human Evolution*, edited by F. C. Howell and F. Bourlière, pp. 335-367. Chicago: Aldine.

Eisenberg, J. F., N. A. Muckenhirn, and R. Rudran. 1972. "The Relation Between Ecology and Social Structure in Primates." *Science*, 176:863-874.

Gautier-Hion, A. 1975. "Dimorphisme sexuel et organisation sociale chez les cercopithécinés forestiers Africains." *Mammalia*, 39:365-374.

Gingerich, P. D. 1972. "The Development of Sexual Dimorphism in the Bony Pelvis of the Squirrel Monkey." *Anatomical Record*, 172:589-595.

Harvey, P. H., M. Kavanagh, and T. H. Clutton-Brock. 1978a. "Sexual Dimorphism in Primate Teeth." *Journal of Zoology*, 186:475-485.

_____. 1978b. "Canine Tooth Size in Female Primates." *Nature*, 276: 817-818.

Hershkovitz, P. 1977. *Living New World Monkeys (Platyrrhini) with an Introduction to Primates*, Vol. 1. Chicago: University of Chicago Press.

_____. 1979. "The Species of Sakis, Genus *Pithecia* (Cebidae, Primates), with Notes on Sexual Dichromatism." *Folia Primatologica*, 31:1-22.

Jungers, W. L. 1978. "On Canine Reduction in Early Hominids." *Current Anthropology*, 19:155-156.

Kay, R. F. 1973. *Mastication, Molar Tooth Structure and Diet in Primates.* Ph.D. dissertation, Yale University.

Kleiman, D. G. 1977. "Monogamy in Mammals." *Quarterly Review of Biology*, 52:39-69.

Lauer, C. 1975. "A Comparison of Sexual Dimorphism and Range of Variation in *Papio cynocephalus* and *Gorilla gorilla* Dentition." *Primates*, 16:1-7.

Leutenegger, W. 1970a. "Das Becken der rezenten Primaten." *Morphologisches Jahrbuch*, 115:1-101.

_____. 1970b. "Beziehungen zwischen der Neugeborenengrösse und dem Sexual dimorphismus am Becken bei simischen Primaten." *Folia Primatologica*, 12:224-235.

_____. 1973a. "Maternal-Fetal Weight Relationships in Primates." *Folia Primatologica*, 20:280-293.

_____. 1973b. "Sexual Dimorphism in the Pelves of African Lorises." *American Journal of Physical Anthropology*, 38:251-254.

_____. 1974. "Functional Aspects of Pelvic Morphology in Simian Primates." *Journal of Human Evolution*, 3:207-222.

_____. 1976. "Metric Variability in the Anterior Dentition of African Colobines." *American Journal of Physical Anthropology*, 45:45-52.

_____. 1977. "Sociobiological Correlates of Sexual Dimorphism in Body Weight in South African Australopiths." *South African Journal of Science*, 73:143-144.

_____. 1978. "Scaling of Sexual Dimorphism in Body Size and Breeding System in Primates." *Nature*, 272:610-611.

————. 1979. "Evolution of Litter Size in Primates." *American Naturalist*, 113:525-531.

————. 1980. "Monogamy in Callitrichids: A Consequence of Phyletic Dwarfism?" *International Journal of Primatology*, 1:95-99.

————. 1981. "Scaling of Sexual Dimorphismus in Canine Size and Body Size in Primates." In *Folia Primatologica* (in press).

Leutenegger, W., and J. T. Kelly. 1977. "Relationship of Sexual Dimorphism in Canine Size and Body Size to Social, Behavioral, and Ecological Correlates in Anthropoid Primates." *Primates*, 18:117-136.

Mitchell, G. 1979. *Behavioral Sex Differences in Nonhuman Primates*. New York: Van Nostrand Reinhold.

Mobb, G. E., and B. A. Wood. 1977. "Allometry and Sexual Dimorphism in the Primate Innominate Bone." *American Journal of Anatomy*, 150: 531-538.

Myers, P. 1978. "Sexual Dimorphism in the Size of Vespertilionid Bats." *American Naturalist*, 112:701-711.

Onyekwelu, S. S., and J. L. Harper. 1979. "Sex Ratio and Niche Differentiation in Spinach (*Spinacia oleracea* L.)." *Nature*, 282:609-611.

Orlosky, F. 1973. *Comparative Dental Morphology of Extant and Extinct Cebidae*. Ph.D. dissertation, University of Washington.

Peters, S. M. F. 1978. "Dwarfism and Callitrichidae." *American Journal of Physical Anthropology*, 48:426.

Pilbeam, D., and S. J. Gould. 1974. "Size and Scaling in Human Evolution." *Science*, 186:892-901.

Post, D., S. Goldstein, and D. Melnick. 1978. "An Analysis of Cercopithecoid Odontometrics. II. Relations Between Dental Dimorphism, Body Size Dimorphism and Diet." *American Journal of Physical Anthropology*, 49:533-544.

Ralls, K. 1977. "Sexual Dimorphism in Mammals: Avian Models and Unanswered Questions." *American Naturalist*, 111:917-938.

Raup, D. M. 1972. "Approaches to Morphologic Analysis." In *Models in Paleobiology*, edited by T. J. M. Schopf, pp. 28-44. San Francisco: Freeman.

Rensch, B. 1950. "Die Abhängigkeit der relativen Sexualdifferenz von der Körpergrösse." *Bonner Zoologische Beiträge*, 1:58-69.

————. 1954. *Neuere Probleme der Abstammungslehre*. Stuttgart: Enke.

Rosenberger, A. L. 1977. "*Xenothrix* and Ceboid Phylogeny." *Journal of Human Evolution*, 6:461-481.

Rothenfluh, E. 1976. *Überprüfung der Gewichtsangaben adulter Primaten im Vergleich zwischen Gefangenschafts- und Wildfangtieren*. Universität Zürich: Semesterarbeit.

Schultz, A. H. 1949. "Sex Differences in the Pelves of Primates." *American Journal of Physical Anthropology*, 7:401-423.

————. 1969. *The Life of Primates*. London: Weidenfeld and Nicholson.

Selander, R. K. 1972. "Sexual Selection and Dimorphism in Birds." In *Sexual Selection and the Descent of Man, 1871-1971*, edited by B. G. Campbell, pp. 180-230. Chicago: Aldine.

Swindler, D. R. 1976. *Dentition of Living Primates*. London: Academic Press.

Trivers, R. L. 1972. "Parental Investment and Sexual Selection." In *Sexual Selection and the Descent of Man, 1871-1971*, edited by B. G. Campbell, pp. 136-179. Chicago: Aldine.

Van den Broek, A. J. P. 1911. "Über Geschlechtsunterschiede im Becken bei Primaten." *Archiv für Anatomie und Physiologie*, 35:163-184.

Washburn, S. L. 1942. "Skeletal Proportions of Adult Langurs and Macaques." *Human Biology*, 14:444-472.

Washburn, S. L., and R. L. Ciochon. 1974. "Canine Teeth: Notes on Controversies in the Study of Human Evolution." *American Anthropologist*, 76:765-784.

Wettstein, E. B. 1963. "Variabilität, Geschlechtsunterschiede und Altersveränderungen bei *Callithrix jacchus* L." *Morphologisches Jahrbuch*, 104:185-271.

Wiley, R. 1974. "Evolution of Social Organization and Life History Patterns Among Grouse." *Quarterly Review of Biology*, 49:201-227.

Wilson, E. O. 1975. *Sociobiology: The New Synthesis*. Cambridge, Mass.: Harvard University Press.

Willson, M. F. 1979. "Sexual Selection in Plants." *American Naturalist*, 113:777-790.

Wolpoff, M. H. 1976. "Primate Models for Australopithecine Sexual Dimorphism." *American Journal of Physical Anthropology*, 45:497-510.

Zihlman, A. L. 1976. "Sexual Dimorphism and Its Behavioral Implication in Early Hominids." Paper presented at Colloque IV, IX Congrès International des Sciences Préhistoriques et Protohistoriques.

Three

Sex Differences:
The Female as Baseline
for Species Description*

Elizabeth R. McCown

The nature and meaning of secondary sexual differences are old problems. In addition to primary sexual differentiation, males and females differ in body size and in a very wide variety of secondary characteristics. Recently sociobiologists have called attention to the behavioral, genetic, and evolutionary importance of sex differences (Wilson 1975, Barash 1977), but there is no guiding theory as to how such features are to be analyzed or described. The purpose of this chapter is to suggest a way of looking at sexual differentiation in primates that may help in the study of evolution, that is useful in analysis, and that can be correlated with behaviors.

In our scientific culture it has been customary to regard the male as best exemplifying the species. For example, in Elliot's review of 477 species of monkeys and apes (1913), the type specimens of all but four are adult males.

A tabulation of anthropoid collections in the United States by Krogman and Schultz (1938) also points to this bias—63 percent of the gorilla skulls in the collections of American museums at that time were males. Of a total of 503 gorilla specimens, 321 are males and 182 are females.

An exception to the general trend of making comparisons on the basis of male anatomy is Weidenreich's use of a female gorilla skull for comparison with Peking Man (1943).

*This study was supported, in part, by a grant from the Leakey Foundation.

When comparing males and females, females are generally referred to as being a percent of the male (Crook 1972; Napier and Napier 1967). For example, the size of the female is considered to be 90 percent of the male in humans and chimpanzees, 50 percent in orangs and gorilla, and 93 percent in gibbons (Napier and Napier 1967). Schultz (1962), on the other hand, reversed this procedure and used the females to represent the basic size of the species and described the males as a percent of the female.

At the present time both methods (male/female x 100 and female/male x 100) are used without any particular justification for either.

This conventional method of describing the female as a percent of the male is awkward for the purpose of analysis and may be misleading. In the case of *Cercopithecus aethiops* the weight of the female is 62 percent of the male; but the trunk height is 88 percent; temporal muscle weight, 36 percent; and canine tooth length, 78 percent. The degree of difference is dependent on the anatomical area being compared, and no theory guides the comparisons.

The anatomy of the female appears to be a more useful guide to the anatomy of the species. Aside from primary sexual anatomy and functions, females incorporate all the basic behaviors of the species in their repertoire: They travel, eat, sleep, and socialize in the characteristic manner of the species. To the basic species-specific anatomy, the male behavior of fighting and the anatomy upon which it is dependent have been added—not just agonistic behavior, but also the behavior of bluff (Guthrie 1970).

SEXUALLY DIMORPHIC AGGRESSION

Both male and female monkeys and apes may act aggressively. Their social systems cannot function without aggressive behaviors, but there is a great difference between male and female fighting. On Cayo Santiago rhesus males fight, primarily in the mating season (Wilson and Boelkins 1970), and during that season deaths and wounds are significantly more common among the males than the females. During the 2-year study period, 13 of the 15 male deaths occurred in the mating season. There is no doubt that fighting by the male with large canine teeth is lethal as compared to female biting.

Male aggressive behavior results in the development of structures needed for both bluff and serious fighting. Males may have long hair on the shoulders, manes, and neck ruffs—features needed for piloerection which results in the appearance of greater size, an important part of bluffing strategy. Males also have large, sharpened canine teeth and powerful mandibular muscles. Such secondary sex differences very likely are the result, through selection, of success in male-male fighting and bluffing within the same species.

Several conclusions that follow will briefly be mentioned here and will be fully treated in the discussion. First the traditional method of comparing the sexes can greatly underestimate sex differences. Second, looking at sex differences in relation to basic species anatomy reveals patterns of structure and behavior. Cranial dimorphism will then fall into measurable functional patterns; the male canine complex, for example, would be seen as a pattern reflecting the male aggressive anatomy (McCown 1978). Third, such different characteristics as male techniques of play, timing of maturity, learning various social behaviors, and longevity can be seen as having evolved in a feedback relation with fighting and aggression. Sex differences in play, learning, psychology, and fighting behaviors form a complex dependent on anatomy.

The reduction of aggressive anatomy in human beings (the specialized anatomy of bluff and the fighting teeth), may be the result of selection that no longer favors these structures because fighting has shifted from teeth to tools (Washburn 1968a, 1971; Washburn and Ciochon 1974). Sexual dimorphism in terms of strength still remains, however, and is much greater than is usually realized (Damon, Stoudt, and MacFarland 1966). The human female is 90 percent of the male in size, but in anatomy concerned with strength of grip and powerful throwing, the female is only 50 percent of the male (Tanner 1962). In primates the degree of male-female differences varies according to the anatomical area used for comparison. Sex differences due to the fundamentally diverse behavior patterns (D'Andrade 1966; B. A. Hamburg 1978), have been produced through natural selection working over a long interval of time and are of great importance for the success of the species.

RESEARCH STRATEGY AND MATERIALS

To illustrate these points, males, females, and subadult males of four series of crania of Old World monkeys and a small series of gorillas were measured, compared, and photographed.

The series of crania are from field collections. The *Macaca fascicularis* and *Presbytis cristatus*, collected in Borneo in 1937 by S. L. Washburn and A. L. Schultz for the Asiatic Primate Expedition, was a cooperative undertaking of Columbia, Harvard, and Johns Hopkins universities. The third series, *Cercopithecus aethiops*, was collected in Uganda in 1947 by S. L. Washburn. All three series were shot in the wild, and are of known provenience and sex. Morphological measurements of *C. aethiops* were taken in the field. Body weight, trunk length, and some muscle weights were recorded before the skeletons were prepared; these data have proven to be very useful in giving added information as to the relative sexual dimorphism found in specific parts of the skull.

The fourth series, *Gorilla gorilla beringei*, is from the Virunga Mountains, Rwanda, collected in the field by Dian Fossey in the late 1960s during her work at the Karisoke Research Centre, Ruhengeri, Rwanda. A small series of *Nasalis larvatus* from the Museum of Comparative Zoology, Harvard, also is included for comparative and illustrative purposes.

The crania in each species were sorted into males and females, the sex of the specimens having been established in the field. The skulls were then divided into age categories, based on the permanent teeth. Only the adult males, adult females, and the subadult males were used in this study. A cranium with a fully erupted M3 was considered adult. A cranium was considered subadult if the M2 was fully erupted and the canine was in the process of erupting. The female is treated as the norm for each species in this study and is considered as a baseline of 100 percent for each dimension.

The series consisted of the following number of crania:

Cercopithecus aethiops (from the University of California, Berkeley)
  19 females
  23 males
  3 subadult males

Macaca fascicularis (from the Museum of Comparative Zoology, Harvard University)
  24 females
  22 males
  13 subadult males

Presbytis cristatus (from the Museum of Comparative Zoology, Harvard University)
  30 females
  17 males
  5 subadult males

Gorilla gorilla beringei (from the Smithsonian Institution, Washington, D.C.)
  5 females
  5 males

(from the collection of Jay Matternes, Washington, D.C.)
  6 females
  8 males
  1 subadult male

Nasalis larvatus (from the Museum of Comparative Zoology, Harvard University)
  5 females
  4 males
  1 subadult male

MEASUREMENTS AND RESULTS

Between 22 and 24 measurements were taken on each skull (see Appendix for definition of the 24 measurements). Some are standard craniometric measurements (Montagu 1960), while others were specifically designed to measure those areas where the most marked sexual dimorphism is found. These areas are the nuchal and mastoid crests on the occipital bone and the glabella area on the frontal bone. Measurements were taken either on the left side of the skull or where appropriate, in the mid-sagittal plane, using dial calipers for the majority of the measurements.

In order to measure the thickness of cranial bone it was necessary to devise a new instrument, a modification of the Helios Dial Caliper in which longer rods were used in place of the conventional needle points. Two sets of rods with different angles were divised that could be used interchangeably. The calipers were designed to enable one end to be inserted into the foramen magnum to reach the desired endocranial landmark. This instrument was used to measure glabella thickness, mastoid crest thickness, and nuchal crest thickness.

The mean, standard deviation, and range were determined for all measurements and the significance of the differences was computed by means of a "student's" *t*-test, using a two-tailed hypothesis to assess the significance of the *t*-value. Percentages of the degree of sexual dimorphism between the males, females, and subadult males were calculated for all measurements using the following formula: female mean/male mean x 100.

The measurements taken on the skulls in the series studied show sexual dimorphism in all dimensions. The degree of dimorphism varies widely: the difference is small in some dimensions, and in others the male is 195 percent of the female. The female was not larger than the male in any dimension.

The more visible anatomical differences between the skulls of females and males—additions of buttresses of bone in the male, larger areas or crests for muscle attachments, and increased size of specific teeth—can be located and measured easily. The majority of these increments form a functional pattern that is related to fighting and aggression, a function not usually shared with the female. The male anatomical differences that make up this pattern can be usefully referred to as the "anatomy of aggression." Some of the most obvious expressions of the aggressive anatomy in the area of the head are the large brow ridges, heavy crests, large sharp canines, and heavy neck and mandibular muscles of the male, usually in great contrast to the smaller female. All of these features form a functional pattern—an adaptation for the purpose of fighting that can be measured and interpreted from this point of view. Using the female as the norm for the species makes it possible to determine where and when these sexual dimorphic expressions of the anatomy of aggression occur. The greatest amount of dimorphism found in the cranium was in the structures reflecting this anatomy. The degree of dimorphism found in each dimension varies with the species, so that each species has a characteristic and distinctive functional pattern associated with aggression.

Parts of the skull that are closely related to the size of the brain show the least dimorphism. Cranial breadth and minimum frontal breadth show very little dimorphism in any of the species and the slight differences that are found probably are a function of general body size. Cranial capacity shows a female-male difference of less than 10 percent where there is moderate body-size dimorphism, but as much as 19 percent where there is greater body-size dimorphism.

Canine length was one of the most strongly dimorphic measurements in all species, and canine size is one of the most important attributes in aggressive behavior. This is in complete contrast to the length measurement of M 1-3 where there is little dimorphism in any of the series. This result is expected as molars are not used for fighting or aggression.

The thickness of the nuchal and mastoid crests is consistently greater in the male than in the female which implies that the muscles attaching there (trapezius, splenius capitis, semispinalis capitis, longissimus capitis, sterno-mastoideus, cleido-mastoideus and cleido-occipitalis) are larger. All of these muscles must be strong and large for aggressive encounters and successful fighting with the head.

The measurements of the fossa length and breadth indicate the larger size of the infratemporal fossa in the male. This increased size accommodates the much larger temporalis and longer origin of masseter in the male. These muscles are used for fighting with the mouth and jaws, using the canines as weapons as well as for bluffing. Many other dimensions taken on the face reflect the presence of these same massive muscles, such as bizygomatic, bimalar, and bicanine. The larger facial dimensions of the male all demonstrate greater facial strength.

In order to show that the sex differences in the adult male skull can be viewed as additions to the basic species anatomy, the subadult male was compared to the adult female. This allows a comparison between a female skull and a male skull of the same size. It is possible to match an adult female cranium almost exactly with a subadult male cranium as shown in Tables 3.1 to 3.3, and in Figures 3.1-13, 15. The differences between the subadult male and the adult male are the same as those between the adult male and the adult female, implying that it is late growth—from the subadult to the adult—that results in

TABLE 3.1

Macaca fascicularis: Measurements Expressed in Percentages (Male / Female) Listed in Order of Greatest Sexual Dimorphism.

Measurement	Male Percentage of Female	Subadult Male Percentage of Female
Mastoid crest*	170.0	87.4
Canine length**	162.0	—
Interorbital breadth*	124.0	99.2
Petrotemporal width*	121.4	91.1
Fossa breadth*	119.6	86.3
Fossa length*	119.3	95.9
Palate length*	118.9	91.7
Glabella-prosthion*	118.7	92.5
Glabella thickness*	118.6	81.3
Bizygomatic breadth*	118.2	93.3
Maximum biorbital breadth*	115.4	95.6
Malar depth*	115.1	89.3
Base width*	112.5	99.1
Glabella-basion*	110.7	95.9
Nuchal crest	110.5	76.3
Cranial capacity*	109.3	100.4
Inner biorbital breadth*	108.7	96.4
Palate breadth*	106.5	96.0
Length*	106.5	99.1
Breadth	103.4	99.3
Minimum frontal breadth	103.4	99.9
M 1-3*	103.4	—

*Statistically significant differences between female and male means at $P < 0.01$.

**Statistically significant differences between female and male means and no overlap between female and male ranges.

TABLE 3.2

Cercopithecus aethiops: Measurements Expressed in Percentages (Male/Female) Listed in Order of Greatest Sexual Dimorphism.

Measurement	Male Percentage of Female	Subadult Male Percentage of Female
Mastoid crest**	182.3	138.5
Nuchal crest*	160.1	97.4
Interorbital breadth*	133.8	100.8
Fossa breadth*	133.5	92.4
Canine length*	128.7	—
Petrotemporal width*	123.6	98.6
Glabella thickness*	122.0	90.7
Glabella-prosthion*	121.6	99.2
Fossa length*	121.1	91.8
Bicanine breadth*	120.1	101.4
Bizygomatic breadth*	118.8	98.9
Palate length*	117.8	93.9
Bimalar breadth*	117.7	100.4
Maximum biorbital breadth**	116.6	101.5
Malar depth	114.0	101.4
Cranial capacity*	113.7	113.6
Glabella-basion*	112.9	97.7
Base width**	112.7	105.7
Inner biorbital breadth*	112.2	103.3
Palate breadth*	111.8	99.6
Breadth*	110.8	105.6
Length*	109.6	103.1
M 1-3*	107.5	—
Minimum frontal breadth*	105.9	107.4

*Statistically significant differences between female and male means at $P < 0.01$.
**Statistically significant differences between female and male means and no overlap between female and male ranges.

observed cranial differences between the sexes. The large canine in the subadult male is still in the process of erupting; presumably the hormonal stimulus has not yet resulted in changes in the cranium that result in an adult configuration.

Since the majority of the dimensions of the subadult male are comparable to those of the female, it can be inferred that the distinctive male cranial anatomy appears late. This also is true for serious fighting behavior. Other male-female differences in behavior that appear much earlier (Symons 1978) are not reflected anatomically in the skull.

TABLE 3.3

Presbytis cristatus: Measurements Expressed in Percentages (Male/Female) Listed in Order of Greatest Sexual Dimorphism.

Measurement	Male Percentage of Female	Subadult Male Percentage of Female
Nuchal crest*	130.3	95.9
Canine length*	130.0	—
Bicanine breadth**	122.4	104.3
Mastoid crest*	118.0	85.5
Fossa breadth*	112.6	89.9
Malar depth*	111.4	106.0
Glabella-prosthion*	110.7	100.1
Interorbital breadth	109.8	86.0
Palate length*	109.8	97.6
Bizygomatic breadth*	108.8	93.0
Cranial capacity*	108.8	99.1
Glabella-basion*	107.5	95.9
Bimalar breadth*	107.5	91.1
Fossa length*	107.2	94.0
Petrotemporal width*	107.0	86.7
Maximum biorbital breadth*	106.3	92.9
Base width*	106.2	97.4
Length*	106.0	96.5
Inner biorbital*	103.5	94.3
Palate breadth	102.5	94.0
Glabella thickness	102.5	65.0
Breadth	100.4	98.8
Minimum frontal breadth	100.2	99.5
M 1-3	100.1	—

*Statistically significant differences between female and male means at $P < 0.01$.

**Statistically significant differences between female and male means and no overlap between female and male ranges.

Macaca fascicularis

In the sample of *Macaca fascicularis*, mean values for all measurements showed sexual dimorphism, and, except for cranial breadth, minimum frontal breadth, and nuchal crest thickness, sample means were statistically significant by sex at $P < 0.01$. All male measurements were greater than 100 percent of the female measurements whereas the subadult male measurements were approximately 95 percent of the female measurements. The mean male supramastoid crest was 170 percent of that of the female mean, but the subadult male average was only 87 percent that of the female. The greatest sexual dimorphism in this species was shown in the supra-mastoid crest. Canine length was the second most dimorphic measurement, the male average value being 162 percent of the female. These two measurements were by far the most diagnostic for sex determination.

A group of eight measurements on the face was the next most diagnostic, being approximately 15 to 20 percent greater in the male than in the female. The measurements showing the least amount of sexual dimorphism are the length of M1-3, minimum frontal breadth, and cranial breadth. The percentage of male-female dimorphism in all measurements of *Macaca fascicularis* is listed in Table 3.1.

The superior view of the three skulls of *M. fascicularis* in Figure 3.1, male, female, and subadult male, demonstrates the similar braincase size in all three in contrast to the great difference in the size of the facial skeleton of the adult male as opposed to the subadult male and female. The adult male has only a slightly larger braincase than the female or the subadult male. The mean measurements and standard deviations are:

	Cranial Length		Cranial Breadth	
	$\overline{X}$	*S.D.*	$\overline{X}$	*S.D.*
Female	72.2	2.3	53.4	2.0
Male	76.9	2.3	55.3	2.0
Subadult male	71.6	1.8	53.1	1.6

The breadth measurement is very similar in all three. The greater length of the adult male skull is in the larger supraorbital crest as reflected in the glabella thickness dimension, whereas the subadult male does not yet show this trait. The means and standard deviations are:

	Glabella Thickness	
	$\overline{X}$	*S.D.*
Female	8.3	1.3
Male	9.9	1.0
Subadult male	6.8	1.0

The lateral view of *M. fascicularis* (Figure 3.2) illustrates the great size of the canine (canine length measurement) of the male in relation to that of the subadult male and adult female. This dimension is the second most diagnostic trait differentiating the male from the female, in direct contrast to the length of M1-3, the least diagnostic measurements in the species.

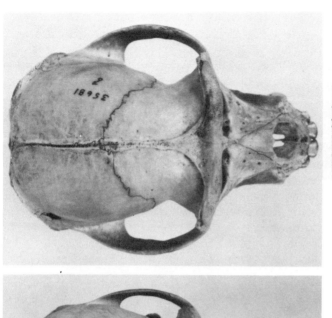

Adult Male

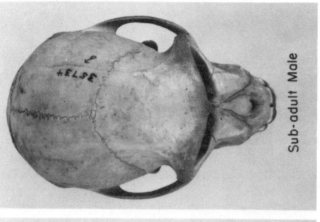

Sub-adult Male

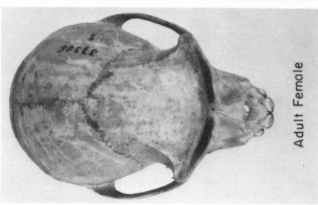

Adult Female

Figure 3.1. *Macaca fascicularis*, superior view.

47

	Canine Length		M 1-3 Length	
	X̄	S.D.	X̄	S.D.
Female	5.6	0.5	19.7	1.0
Male	9.1	0.8	20.4	0.8

The x-rays of the three skulls of *M. fascicularis* (Figure 3.3) again demonstrate the similar size of the braincase in female, male, and subadult male. The cranial capacity of the male is approximately 10 percent greater than in the female and the subadult male. The length of the palate and the size of the canine tooth complex are also greater in the adult male. The infratemporal fossa that accommodates the larger temporalis and masseter muscles for fighting is also much larger in the adult male.

	Fossa Length		Fossa Breadth	
	X̄	S.D.	X̄	S.D.
Female	25.3	1.4	17.3	2.1
Male	30.2	2.2	20.9	2.5
Subadult male	24.3	1.8	15.1	1.5

	Palate Length		Palate Breadth	
	X̄	S.D.	X̄	S.D.
Female	41.5	2.7	33.2	1.6
Male	49.4	2.9	35.4	1.3
Subadult male	38.1	2.3	31.9	1.7

Cercopithecus aethiops

In the *Cercopithecus aethiops* sample all measurements showed sexual dimorphism (Table 3.2). The *t*-test indicated that mean differences were significant at $P < 0.01$ for all traits except malar depth. The two dimensions showing the greatest dimorphism were those of the nuchal crest and the mastoid crest. The average value for the mastoid crest in the male is 182.3 percent of the female average, and the nuchal crest is 160.1 percent. The two least dimorphic dimensions are: length of M 1-3 (107.9 percent of the female) and the minimum frontal breadth (105.9 percent of the female). Cranial length and breadth differences are also minimal, the male being only 109.6 and 110.8 percent of the female average values.

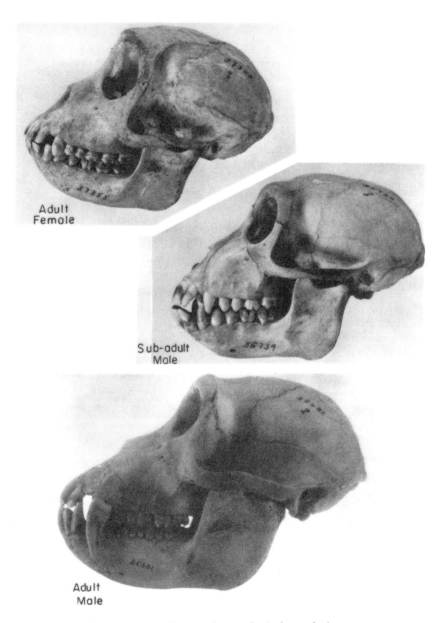

Figure 3.2. *Macaca fascicularis*, lateral view.

The superior view of the female, subadult male, and male skulls of *C. aethiops* shows only a slight variation in the size of the braincase in contrast to the large difference to be seen in bizygomatic breadth and bicanine breadth (Figure 3.4). Mean measurements and standard deviations are:

	Bizygomatic Breadth		Bicanine Breadth	
	X̄	S.D.	X̄	S.D.
Female	62.2	3.6	25.4	1.1
Male	73.9	3.4	30.6	1.6
Subadult male	61.5	4.8	25.8	2.8

These dimensions, almost identical in the female and subadult male, are in contrast to those in the adult male, and indicate the tremendous change that results at the time the male canine tooth erupts and the related muscles enlarge.

The great difference in size of the infratemporal fossa in the male and female is evident. Measurements for the series are:

	Fossa Length		Fossa Breadth	
	X̄	S.D.	X̄	S.D.
Female	25.3	1.3	15.1	1.3
Male	30.6	2.4	20.1	2.2
Subadult male	23.2	2.0	13.9	1.9

The minimal difference in braincase size between the adult female, subadult male, and adult male of *C. aethiops* is clearly visible in the x-ray of the three skulls (Figure 3.5). The means and standard deviations for the widths of the braincase are:

	Minimum Frontal		Cranial Breadth	
	X̄	S.D.	X̄	S.D.
Female	40.8	1.3	53.7	1.7
Male	43.2	1.6	59.9	2.1
Subadult male	43.8	1.6	56.7	2.5

Cranial length, because it incorporates the glabella thickness and the thickness of the nuchal crest, shows a greater difference.

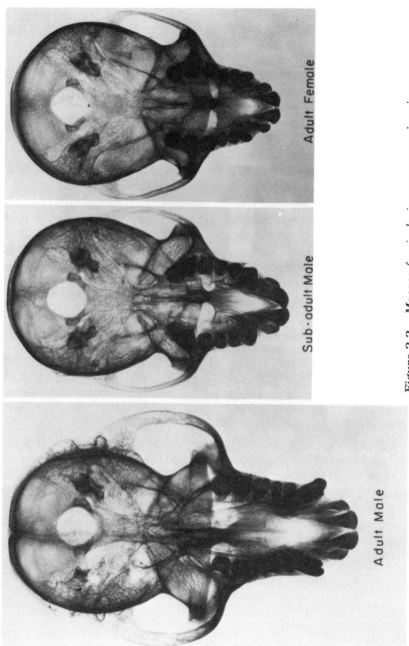

Figure 3.3. *Macaca fascicularis*, x-ray, superior view.

51

	Cranial Length		Glabella Thickness	
	X̄	S.D.	X̄	S.D.
Female	72.1	2.1	7.2	1.1
Male	79.1	2.9	8.8	1.1
Subadult male	74.3	1.5	6.6	0.5

	Nuchal Crest Thickness	
	X̄	S.D.
Female	3.1	1.0
Male	5.0	1.1
Subadult male	3.0	0.3

The overall cranial size is larger in the male because it incorporates the mastoid crests, nuchal crests, and the thickness of the glabella.

The differences in palate size are evident from these x-rays (Figure 3.5). Length of the palate reflects the larger male canines as does bicanine breadth. Breadth of the palate taken approximately at M 2 does not reflect the complex related to the canines.

	Palate Length		Palate Breadth	
	X̄	S.D.	X̄	S.D.
Female	39.1	1.9	32.5	2.0
Male	46.0	1.9	36.3	1.9
Subadult male	36.7	2.9	32.3	1.5

The lateral views of *C. aethiops* crania of a female, subadult male, and adult male illustrate the marked difference in canine length (Figure 3.6). The mean length for the female is 5.7 mm and for the male is 7.3 mm. In contrast only a slight difference in the length of M 1-3 can be seen; the female mean is 17.7 mm and the male mean 19.0 mm. Face length from glabella to prosthion (gl-pr), which measures the size of the facial projection, is a reflection of the large male canine complex.

	Glabella to Prosthion	
	X̄	S.D.
Female	43.0	3.6
Male	52.3	3.2
Subadult male	42.7	4.7

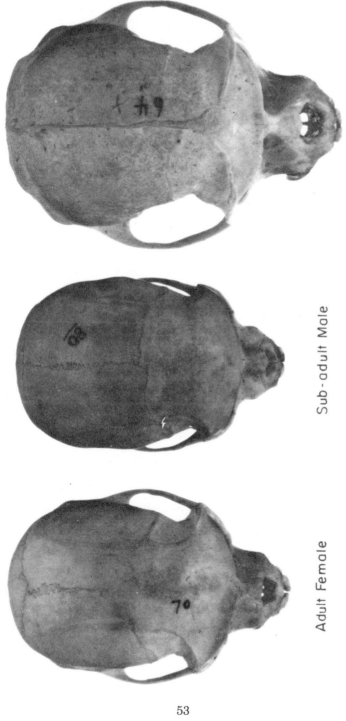

Adult Female

Sub-adult Male

Adult Male

Figure 3.4. *Cercopithecus aethiops*, superior view.

Presbytis cristatus

In the skull of *Presbytis cristatus* sexual dimorphism was less pronounced than in *Macaca fascicularis* or *Cercopithecus aethiops*. The degree of difference between the male and female measurements averaged less than 10 percent. The *t*-tests showed that sexual differences in six measurements were not significant; these included skull measurements such as cranial breadth, minimum frontal breadth, interorbital breadth, palate breadth, glabella thickness, and the M 1-3 length. These dimensions do not reflect male aggression. In only a few measurements were the male dimensions more than 10 percent greater than in the female, but in the nuchal crest, canine length, and bicanine breadth the male measurements were 122 to 130 percent greater than those of the female (Table 3.3).

Only in the anatomy directly related to aggression—the canine complex—is the male significantly larger than the female.

The most dimorphic measurements are those of the nuchal crest and canine length. But in both of these dimensions the male exceeds the female by only 30 percent. The least dimorphic dimensions, M 1-3, minimum frontal and cranial breadth, are identical in size in all three groups, female, male, and subadult male (Figures 3.7-3.9)

Gorilla gorilla beringei

The collection of *Gorilla gorilla beringei* is small but striking in the dimorphism seen between the males and females. There are 13 adult males, 11 adult females, and 1 subadult male available for comparison. The average male cranium value is 25 percent greater than the female in the measurement "greatest length" due to the much heavier, thicker browridges and the heavier nuchal crests. The strikingly large canine of the male is over 60 percent larger than that of the female, whereas the measurements of the molars (M 1-3) show only a 6 percent difference. The breadth measurement of the brain portion of the skull shows little difference (male 105 percent of the female). In contrast, the measurement incorporating the mastoid crests and reflecting the neck muscles is much larger in the male; the mean mastoid crest measurement of the male is 143 percent that of the female average (Table 3.4, Figures 3.10, 3.11).

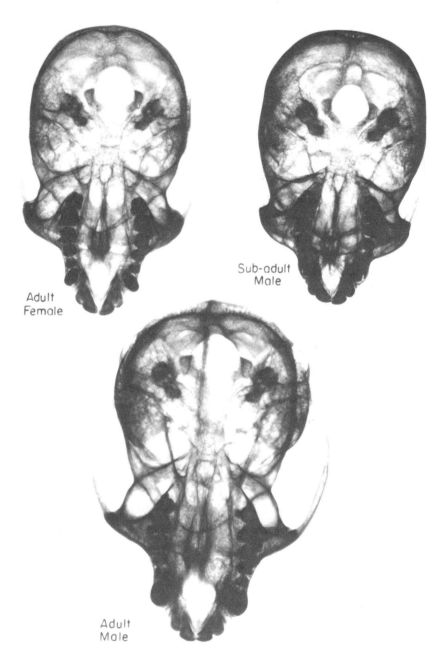

Adult
Female

Sub-adult
Male

Adult
Male

Figure 3.5. *Cercopithecus aethiops*, x-ray, superior view.

TABLE 3.4
Gorilla gorilla beringei: Measurements Expressed in Percentages (Male/Female) Listed in Order of Greatest Sexual Dimorphism.

Measurement	Male Percentage of Female
Nuchal crest	195
Canine length*	161
Mastoid crest	143
Interorbital breadth	134
Fossa breadth*	132
Fossa length*	129
Bicanine width*	126
Glabella-prosthion	126
Greatest length*	125
Palate length*	124
Bizygomatic breadth*	119
Outer biorbital breadth*	119
Brow ridge breadth*	118
Base width*	118
Face breadth*	116
Length	115
Inner biorbital breadth*	114
Cranial capacity	114
Glabella-basion*	113
Palate breadth*	108
M 1-3	106
Breadth	105
Minimum frontal breadth	99

*No overlap between male and female sample distributions. Except for minimum frontal breadth, mean values of female and male samples are significantly different at P < 0.01.

| | *Gorilla gorilla beringei* | | | |
| | Female | | Male | |
	$\overline{X}$	S.D.	$\overline{X}$	S.D.
Most dimorphic measurements				
Nuchal crest	20.5	6.1	40.1	7.7
Canine length	14.0	2.0	22.5	1.6
Mastoid crest	24.1	3.6	34.6	4.0
Least dimorphic measurements				
Minimum frontal breadth	68.7	2.5	68.1	4.2
Breadth	101.9	4.0	106.7	5.3
Molars 1-3	46.4	1.2	49.3	1.4

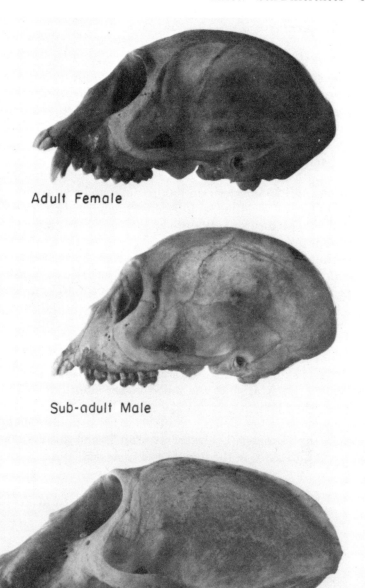

Adult Female

Sub-adult Male

Adult Male

Figure 3.6. *Cercopithecus aethiops*, lateral view.

Nasalis larvatus

Although the series of *Nasalis larvatus* is very small (consisting of only five females, four males, and one subadult male), it has been included because the sex differences are marked and are useful in demonstrating the theory. The functional pattern, the anatomy of aggression, is evident here as in the other series. The amount of sexual dimorphism is great, the males being an average of 122 percent of the female in all measurements (Table 3.5). The dimorphism shown in the length of the canine tooth was greater than in any of the other series measured. A pattern similar to that found in the other species is repeated here, the canine length being the most sexually diagnostic trait. Least dimorphic traits are M 1-3 length, cranial breadth, and minimum frontal breadth.

Schultz (1962), in his study of a series of 51 proboscis monkeys (*Nasalis*) and 41 of the resulting skeletons, reported the sex difference in size as 2:1. The weight of the females averaged 9.87 kg and the males 20.3 kg. This great dimorphism in body size is reflected in more dimorphic dimensions of the cranium, especially in the extreme differences seen in the canine tooth.

The superior and lateral views (Figures 3.12, 3.13, and 3.14) of the *N. larvatus* skulls illustrate the small size of the adult female and the subadult male relative to the much larger adult male. The x-rays (Figure 3.15) show the similar size of the braincase in female, male, and subadult male, which is in contrast to the variations in the canine size. Cranial capacity is larger in the male, and this correlates with the great difference in the female and male body size.

	Cranial Length		Cranial Breadth	
	$\overline{X}$	*S.D.*	$\overline{X}$	*S.D.*
Female	83.2	3.0	61.8	1.0
Male	91.8	1.7	63.8	2.2
Subadult male (1)	84.0	—	60.0	—

	Cranial Capacity	
	$\overline{X}$	*S.D.*
Female	85.3	7.3
Male	101.3	8.1
Subadult male (1)	87.0	—

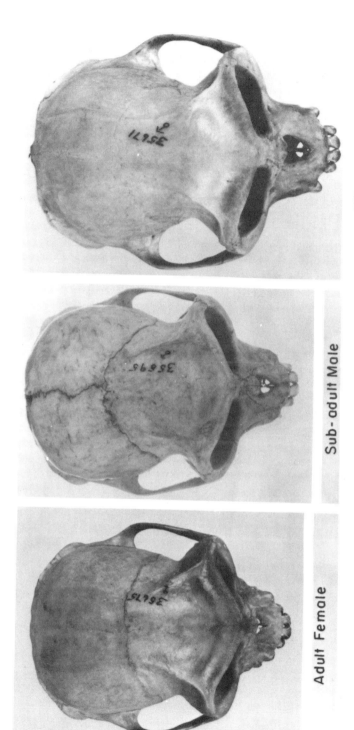

Figure 3.7. *Presbytis cristatus*, superior view.

TABLE 3.5

Nasalis larvatus: Measurements Expressed in Percentages (Male/Female) Listed in Order of Greatest Sexual Dimorphism.

Measurement	Male Percentage of Female
Canine length**	193.9
Mastoid crest**	140.4
Interorbital breadth**	133.3
Bicanine breadth**	129.8
Glabella-prosthion*	128.9
Palate length**	125.3
Fossa breadth**	124.3
Nuchal crest*	124.0
Malar depth**	123.0
Bizygomatic breadth**	119.2
Cranial capacity*	118.8
Glabella thickness	118.2
Fossa length**	116.8
Glabella-basion**	116.0
Palate breadth**	114.9
Base width**	114.5
Outer biorbital breadth*	112.3
Length**	110.3
Inner biorbital breadth**	109.9
M 1-3**	107.9
Breadth	103.2
Minimum frontal breadth	101.0

*Statistically significant differences between female and male means at $P < 0.05$.
**Statistically significant differences between female and male means and no overlap between female and male ranges.

DISCUSSION

The study of natural selection has shown that morphological structures can be interpreted on the basis of function. Anatomical structures are adaptive in function which can be determined through the study of behavior. Males and females of a species share a basic core of similar behaviors. The real behavioral difference between males and females, beyond the basic core and aside from primary sexual ones, are those related to male aggression. This aggressive behavior can take place within the species, between two species, or can be predatory behavior. This major difference in male-female behavior is manifested by functional structures that can be seen as the anatomy of aggression. The behavior may be displayed in numerous ways through direct fighting, threat, or bluff and is

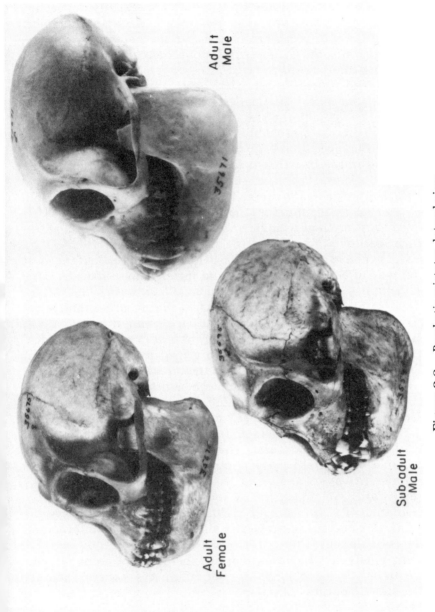

Figure 3.8. *Presbytis cristatus*, lateral view.

correlated with a number of specific structures. When the difference between males and females is understood to be aggressive behavior, a new way of examining many traits which are sexually dimorphic, and at first appear to be unrelated, is provided. Using this approach the description of a species must begin with the female as a baseline. By first describing the female anatomy one then can determine where the female-male differences occur and analyze how these may be correlated with aggressive behavior.

It can be seen that the smallest differences between female and male are to be found in the braincase and in the molar teeth. These slight differences are probably related directly to body size. The greatest differences are in the canine teeth, correlated part of the palate, and in the bony crests directly related to the origin of the temporal muscles. The degree of difference varies from species to species, but the general pattern of the differences is the same for all. The problem is to interpret this female-male pattern. Specific problems concern how to understand the way the pattern is modified in each species.

The hypothesis forming the basis for this study is that the most useful way of comparing females and males is to assume that the basic anatomy of the species is the female and that *all* the female-male differences (aside from the primary sexual ones) are anatomical expressions of fighting. This allows the female-male differences to be seen as parts of a single anatomical pattern (total morphological pattern, Le Gros Clark 1955). This also avoids the common anthropological practice of counting differences in individual features (browridges, minimum frontal diameter, sagittal crest, nuchal crest, etc.) as if they were functionally unrelated. It allows the skeletal differences to be related to manes, hair patterns, and threat displays, all important in bluffing and fighting. It permits the anatomy to be related to developmental and behavioral differences seen in play, dominance, territorial behavior, and predator defense. It suggests very different ways of analyzing fossils. The purpose, then, is to take a step toward developing a theory and a point of view that allows the combination of a wide variety of evidence and makes very specific predictions that can be proved, or disproved, as new information becomes available.

Obviously the basic assumption behind the point of view presented is that the major phenotypic differences discussed here are the results of natural selection. According to Cherry, Case, and Wilson (1978) and Wilson, Carlson, and White (1977), structural evolution seems to take place at rates remarkably different from biochemical evolution. Even if neutral mutations are evolutionarily important and evolution may take place in a clocklike manner, large

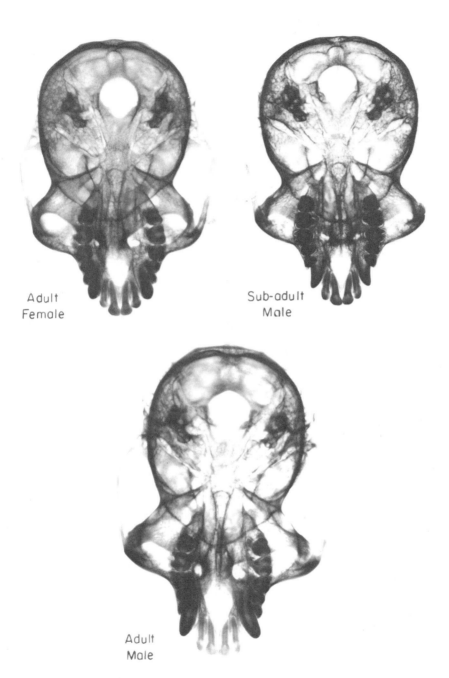

Figure 3.9.   *Presbytis cristatus*, x-ray, superior view.

phenotypic adaptive differences are probably due to natural selection as described by the conventional synthetic theory (Dobzhansky et al. 1977; Mayr 1970, 1972; and Simpson 1953, 1975).

The importance of female-male differences has recently been stressed in sociobiology (Wilson 1975; Barash 1977; and Trivers 1972). However, sociobiologists offer no methods for actually comparing the structural differences that underlie the behavioral differences to which they call attention. Among Old World monkeys and apes, sexual differentiation varies dramatically from almost zero in some gibbons to a very great degree in the mandrill (Schultz 1978).

As can be seen in the photographs and x-rays, the majority of cranial measurements are anatomically complex: for example, head length includes endocranial length (in which there is little sexual differentiation) and thickness at glabella and the nuchal region (which is much greater in males); palate length includes canine length; and bizygomatic breadth includes infratemporal fossa breadth. Correlations between measurements help in seeing the patterns of sexual differentiation. For example, it is no accident that the greatest sexual differentiation is in canine length, mastoid crest, interorbital breadth (solid bone in monkeys), and dimensions of the temporal fossa. These are the parts most directly related to the anatomy necessary for fighting.

It is of interest to compare the method presented here with the traditional method of analyzing males and females. As was stated previously, the traditional description of a species was of the male structure, and if the female structure was described it was usually expressed as a lesser percentage of the dimensions of the male. Primates in the first scientific collections were the largest and biggest trophies that could be obtained—usually males that visibly stood in the forefront of their group and thus were easily collected (Du Chaillu 1868; Owen 1835). The preponderance of males in current collections has been due to this accidental sampling and trophy hunting, and to the prevalent bias in the past that the male skull gives better information. The male, therefore, became the prototype; the female the derivative. Descriptions of these large males have become standardized in the literature for most species of Old World monkeys and apes (Savage 1847; Hooton 1931; Napier and Napier 1967; and Crook 1972).

Statements on sexual dimorphism in a species have usually stressed body size, but have also considered pelage, and other secondary characteristics. A summary of the most significant dimorphic features has been made by Crook (1972) as follows: (1) weight and muscular development; (2) body and cranial dimensions; (3) pelage color and markings; (4) specific anatomical features, such

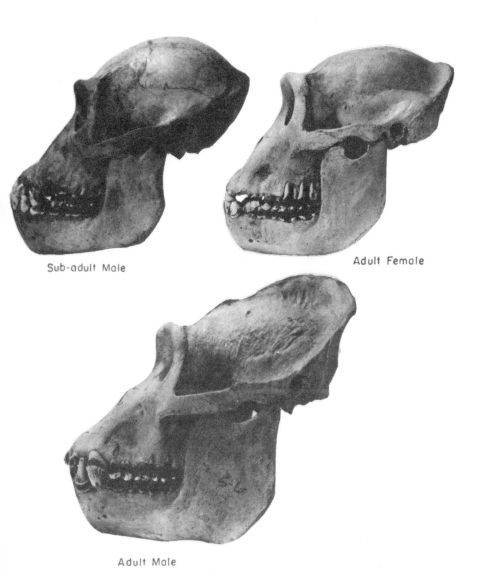

Sub-adult Male

Adult Female

Adult Male

Figure 3.10. *Gorilla gorilla beringei*, lateral view.

as length of canines, pouches, crests, and manes; and (5) maturational or seasonal changes.

Many theories have been put forward to explain these diverse
manifestations of sexual dimorphism (Martin 1980). One theory
attributes them to behavior or environmental factors such as: sexual
selection (Darwin 1871), mating systems (Alexander 1971; Alexander
et al. 1976; Selander 1972), social organization (Crook 1972), niche
utilization (Selander 1966), predation, defense, or the acquisition of
food (Barash 1977). Sociobiologists have attributed dimorphism to
inclusive fitness (Wilson 1975; Barash 1977; Harvey, Kavanagh, and
Clutton-Brock 1978), or parental investment (Trivers 1972) and seek to
develop general laws of the evolution and biology of social behavior,
ultimately extending these to human behavior. They contend that
polygamy, modified by territorial pressures, leads to increased sexual
selection and this, in turn, to increased sexual dimorphism (Wilson
1975).

These interpretations all serve to explain some part of the
observed morphological differences, but the one underlying cause, in
all instances, and the one predominant difference is the more
aggressive behavior displayed by the male.

The anatomy of aggression is exhibited in many other ways. For
example, threat displays are common (Guthrie 1970), and morphologic structures have developed centered around the face and neck to
enhance displaying. These features are more pronounced in, if not
exclusive to, the male, and are used in bluffing and aggression short
of fighting. Many primates have neck ruffs, manes, a great quantity
of facial hair or eccentric hair patterns on the head. Large ruffs are
seen on *Papio hamadryas, Mandrillus,* and *Macaca fascicularis*
(Napier and Napier 1967). *Theropithecus gelada* and *P. hamadryas*
males have bulky manes, and a hair crest or cap is seen in *Presbytis
cristatus*. These diverse hair patterns are seen as structures for
aggression and are used by males to intimidate other males as
piloerection is a common threat gesture. The large nose in the male
Nasalis larvatus may be erected and is a threat gesture. Laryngeal
pouches have developed to an extreme size in the males as a method of
increasing the males' ability to make loud vocal threats. Cheek pads
as well as laryngeal pouches are large and well developed in the male
orangutan. Howler monkeys have an elaborate laryngeal anatomy
with a vast resonant chamber larger in the male than in the female.

Distinct coloring of the hair around the mouth and the presence of
beards or whiskers tend to emphasize the area of the face that is used
in fighting. The bright skin color of the snout of the mandrill also
draws attention to the facial area and the large canines.

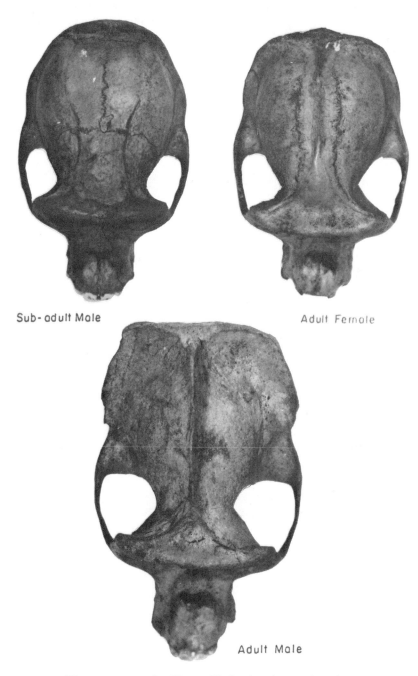

Sub-adult Male

Adult Female

Adult Male

Figure 3.11. *Gorilla gorilla beringei*, superior view.

In contrast, the female lacks these distinctive structures and morphological features. All of the secondary sexual characters involved in bluffing (pelage, voice, hair color, posture, gestures) as well as the morphological differences (body size, muscles, crests, teeth) can be considered part of the adaptive complex of the biology of fighting.

Body size as a major factor in aggression is well exemplified in the apes. Among the apes the most extreme sexual dimorphism in body size occurs in the orangutan and gorilla. The weight of an orangutan male is approximately 160 percent of the female and the gorilla male is 175 percent of the female (Napier and Napier 1967). In the gibbon, however, the male and female are almost identical in size. Body size does not seem to correlate either with an arboreal or a ground-living species—both the gibbon and the orangutan are arboreal yet exhibit opposite extremes of sexual dimorphism in body size. Body size, however, does appear to correlate with aggression. The male orangutan is extremely aggressive in contrast to the less aggressive female (Galdikas 1978), whereas both male and female gibbons are aggressive (Carpenter 1940). Lack of sexual dimorphism in the gibbon in body size and dentition can apparently be correlated with the degree of aggression and their type of social organization (one male, one female, and young) (Frisch 1963b). Both sexes in the gibbon have long sharp canines—adapted to eating of heavy husked fruits—but if these canines were used in intragroup fighting they would inflict serious damage on both sexes. The presence of one male and one female in each group avoids intragroup fighting and reinforces the social structure.

Frisch found no marked sexual dimorphism in the size or shape of the gibbon canine teeth, but found that many more males suffered fractures and loss of canines (41 percent) than did the females (19 percent) (Frisch 1963a,b). This indicates the male uses his canines in a more vigorous and aggressive manner than the female. Frisch ascribes this to male conflicts, in defense or attack, and this appears to be substantiated by the number of fractures found in the male canines. Dimorphism is not seen in the canine teeth: it would be interesting to speculate whether this could be demonstrated by the weights of the masseter and temporalis muscles, but these data are not available. Dimorphism might be evident also in the mastoid crest thickness.

Leutenegger and Kelly (1977) studied sexual dimorphism in body size and canine size in 34 species of anthropoids. They noted a wide range of interspecific differences in the degree of sexual dimorphism in both body size and canine size. The positive correlation between

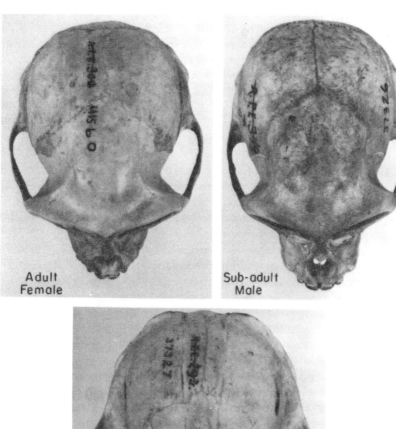

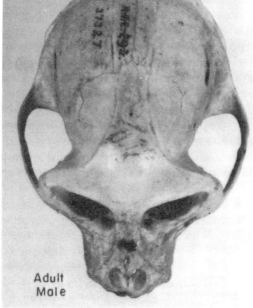

Figure 3.12. *Nasalis larvatus*, superior view.

body-size dimorphism and canine-size dimorphism that they found was determined primarily by female availability.

The increase in canine size in the male is due to the amount of intrasexual selection, and this, in turn, is related to social structure. Leutenegger believes the reason that the chimpanzee has developed only moderate body-size dimorphism and moderate canine size is because of its social structure, that is, the coexistence of male and females in a loose, sexually tolerant, related group, with little need for defense mechanisms. Chimpanzee size is also limited by their arboreal mode of living.

Gorillas, on the other hand, have developed extreme body and canine dimorphism. They are not extremely arboreal and there is, therefore, less constraint on male body size. Their social structure is age-graded with more intrasexual selection; this could account for the greater dimorphism.

The orangutan is very dimorphic in body size, yet only shows moderate dimorphism in canine size due to the large size of the canine in the female (James 1960). The absence of great dimorphism in the canines may be related to an increase in the male anatomy for aggressive bluffing, laryngeal pouches and cheek pads. This adaptation of aggressive behavior seems to be explained by orangutan social structure. Lone males engage in intense intrasexual selection, but, as they patrol large territories and are solitary much of the time, their aggressive competition can usually be minimized by calls and bluffing. When the males do contact each other in the forest, serious fighting usually occurs (Galdikas 1979). If the female were used as the norm in analyzing the great ape behavior and dimorphism, there could be a more exact determination of the female-male differences, and these dimorphic differences then could be more precisely related to the male aggressive anatomy.

Social behavior, social structure, and predatory behavior have all been linked with sexual dimorphism and, ultimately, in a feedback relation with male aggression. Predatory behavior is of importance in determining sexual dimorphism as shown by studies of baboons. Among Old World monkeys the baboon is one of the most dimorphic in body size; the male is almost twice the weight of the female (DeVore and Washburn 1963). The baboon also has developed pronounced dimorphism in the skull and canines, the males being extremely aggressive in intrasexual selection, in defense of territory and in repelling predators. In baboons the importance of the fighting ability of the large males is clearly shown in defensive actions against predators (dogs, hyenas, leopards), but male-male fighting is much more frequent and may be more important from an evolutionary point of view.

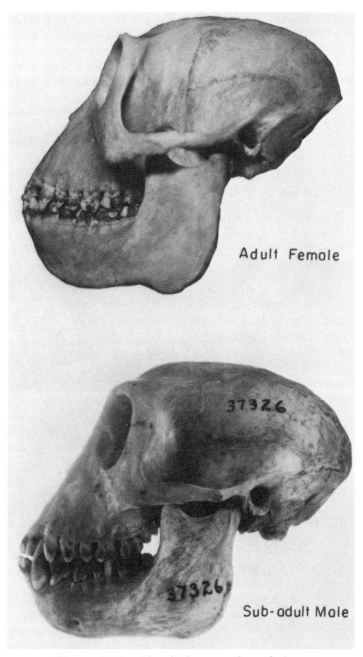

Figure 3.13. *Nasalis larvatus*, lateral view.

Protection from predators does not seem to be a major cause of female-male size differences. This is shown in the orangutan where there is great dimorphism, but no need for predator defense—and in some small monkeys (such as *C. aethiops*) where there is also great dimorphism and yet poor predator defense due to their small size. Therefore, to stress protection from predators as a major determinant of body size dimorphism seems unjustified.

The anatomy of aggression results from the necessity of the male being more aggressive than the female, whether centered around social structure, the access to females, territorial behavior, the access to food, or defense against predators. All factors that tend to make the male more aggressive than the female are reflected in the anatomy of aggression including sexual dimorphism and body size.

The incipient anatomy of aggression in the male can be seen in the early juvenile development of the male monkey (Dolhinow and Bishop 1972; Symons 1978). The behavior of the young male in play is different from that of the young female. The young male engages in aggressive and rough play, consisting of play fighting, play biting, and play chasing. The juvenile male initiates this type of play 2.5 to 3.5 times more frequently than does the female (Symons 1978). This early aggressive difference between the males and females is evident in their juvenile play behavior but is not yet reflected in the anatomy of the skull. It is at the time of the appearance of the canine teeth and the presumed increase in the production of testosterone that the male skull begins to differentiate from that of the female and acquire the characteristics of the adult monkey. As Washburn and Hamburg state (1968):

> The aggressive actions are practiced and brought to a high
> level of skill in play. . . . the whole practiced, skillful,
> aggressive complex is present before the canine teeth erupt.
> The really dangerous weapon is not present until the male
> monkey is a full adult, experienced member of the social
> group. As the canine teeth erupt, the temporal muscles more
> than double in size, and the male changes from a roughly
> playing juvenile to an adult that can inflict a very serious
> wound, even death, with a single bite. [P. 473]

Before the anatomy of aggression is evident the adult female skull and the subadult male skull are similar in size. Dimorphic cranial features appear suddenly, coinciding with the growth in the male skull at the time the canine teeth begin to erupt. Many descriptions of skulls of male and female apes have noted this fact. Ashton (1957) reports that male and female chimpanzee skulls exhibit few signifi-

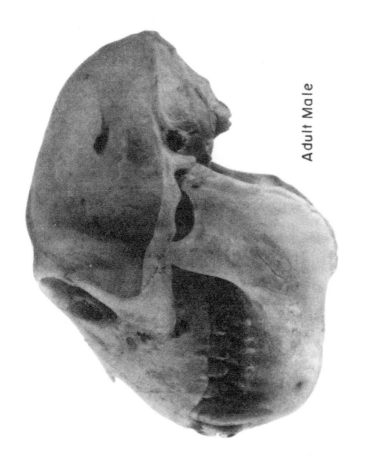

Adult Male

Figure 3.14. *Nasalis larvatus*, lateral view.

cant differences until the eruption of the canine and the third molar. Moore and Lavelle (1974) demonstrate that these differences occur at puberty and are greater in the facial skeleton than in the neurocranium. Schultz (1962) studied and correlated age changes and sex differences in the skulls in a number of primate species and found that the greatest sexual dimorphism occurred in dimensions that showed the most growth following infancy. These are all areas and measurements that reflect the anatomy of aggression and fighting in the male: facial height, bizygomatic, biorbital, and facial breadth. He found the least dimorphism in the braincase portion of the skull. These braincase measurements reflect the large primate brain that develops early and to a similar degree in both males and females, and that changes relatively little in size from the juvenile period to adulthood. These areas of the braincase are not involved directly with aggression. Dimensions concerned with the anatomy of aggression show greater age changes and more pronounced sexual dimorphism.

The growth spurt in the male at puberty—resulting in the anatomy of aggression—is, presumably, due to increased levels of testosterone. Goy has demonstrated that testosterone given to pregnant monkeys tends to masculinize a female fetus and produce more aggressive behavior in the female infant (Goy 1968). Hamburg (1971) has shown that an increase of testosterone is correlated with an increase in learning of aggressive behavior. This also has been discussed by Washburn and Hamburg (1968) in relation to baboon behavior. Testosterone and its connection to aggressive behavior can be seen in many male behaviors. Early rough-and-tumble play of juvenile male monkeys, early learning of aggressive techniques, types of male social behavior all are in contrast to female behaviors (Hamburg and van-Lawick Goodall 1974). Although the behaviors of subadult males reflect aggression, this is not obvious in any crania of the subadult males in these series—they are almost identical in size to those of the adult female. In monkeys aggressive behavior is present early. Perhaps by experimentation, sexual dimorphism could be demonstrated in muscular development, but no sexual dimorphism is seen in the juvenile skull at this time.

With this approach—that of using the female as a baseline—one can deal more successfully with many anatomical problems. Several features of the male which are additions to the basic form of the female, such as the form of the mental symphysis and the size of the simian shelf, can be related to behavior requiring the augmentation of bone in the male mandible. The simian shelf is recognized as a buttress for the canines and when the large male canines erupt they require an increase of bone in this area. If the augmentation of bone is

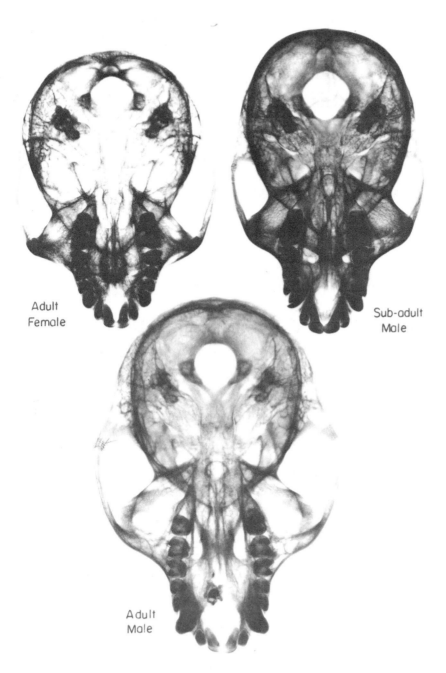

Figure 3.15. *Nasalis larvatus*, x-ray, superior view.

considered in terms of the anatomy of aggression, the shape becomes understandable. The huge male fighting canines predetermine a different shape for the simian shelf in males than in females. The size of the piriform aperture, in most species larger in males than in females, is related to the size of the teeth and falls in with the same pattern. One can examine the larger male orbits, larger zygomatic arches, mastoid process and the heavier interorbital region and understand how they interrelate with each other and how they form functional patterns. Assessing the anatomy of the female first ensures that the degree of variation between the male and female is not underestimated.

Among many birds and most mammals, males are generally larger than females and more aggressive; in situations where females are more aggressive they are also larger (Trivers 1972). Selective pressures related to pregnancy and lactation may have resulted in the female being larger than the male in some species (Ralls 1976). As has been shown, the degree of dimorphism varies with the dimension used for comparison—and the assumption that the female is merely a smaller version can be very deceptive. The data from the *Cercopithecus aethiops* series will illustrate this point.

When the *C. aethiops* series was collected by S. L. Washburn he also recorded body weights and measurements, and approximate weights of some specific muscles. The body weight of the male was 1.5 times that of the female (male 160 percent of female), whereas the average trunk length of the male was only slightly larger than the female (male 113 percent of female). These figures demonstrate the striking difference between the weight and length of the sexes and indicate the much larger muscle mass and strength of the male. But of more interest are the weights of the two muscles in the face, which were significantly larger in the male. The masseter of the male was 207 percent of that of the female and the temporalis was 275 percent of the female's. The greater strength of the temporalis in the male (assumed from its greater weight) indicates the power of the canine teeth. As demonstrated by Grant (1973) the anterior fibers of temporalis are thin red fibers that function predominantly during chewing, whereas the posterior fibers are close, hardpacked, long white fibers that function when the canine teeth are used for rapid powerful action as in fighting. There is a clearly marked difference in the size of the anterior and posterior portions of temporalis in the male and female (Grant 1973), and it can be assumed this is correlated with fighting and with the aggressive behavior of the male. These muscles are absolutely larger in the male of *C. aethiops* and are also relatively larger when compared with body weight. This anatomy can be interpreted as a reflection of differences in behavior.

The variation in the degree of sexual dimorphism in *C. aethiops* from slight in body size (male 113 percent of female), or body weight (male 160 percent of female), to tremendous in some muscle weight (male 275 percent of female), shows how easily the degree of difference can be underestimated if sexual dimorphism is summed up in a single statement referring to the "female as 70 percent of the male."

Using the female as a species model may be useful in the study of fossil species. It is realized that the differences seen in the male and female teeth of modern anthropoids form a pattern that is not applicable to the study of fossil man. The greatest sexual dimorphism in the dentition of monkeys and apes is in the canine tooth, but this model is not useful where there has been a reduction in the size of the canine as in the Hominidae. It is also true that the lack of sexual dimorphism in the length of M 1-3, as shown in these species, does not help in understanding the fossils, except to confirm that the sex of primate fossils cannot be determined from the molars.

Fleagle, Kay, and Simons (1980) have shown sexual dimorphism in three species of primates from the Oligocene of Egypt. In the early ape *Aegyptopithecus zeuxis* they have found the molar teeth to be uniform in size but there is a distinct bimodal distribution in the size of lower canines and premolars, with the larger canines presumably belonging to males and the smaller ones to females.

If some of the other measurements used in this study were obtainable on fossil specimens, such as the thickness of bone in certain areas, it might be possible to determine whether these dimensions—glabella, mastoid crest, or nuchal crest thickness—fall into bimodal distributions. If bimodal distributions can be determined for several critical dimensions within fossil populations it might suggest a male-female dichotomy.

The importance of the structural basis for fighting may be seen when considering such fossils as the large hominid *Australopithecus boisei* from east of Lake Turkana. The small incisors and canines suggest that these teeth were not used in fighting. This is confirmed by the form and size of the nuchal crest and by the position of the sagittal crest (which is high on the skull and does not extend to the nuchal region). The temporal muscles were large anteriorly in an optimum position for crushing and not posteriorly in the position for anterior biting (Grant 1973). The whole anatomy indicates that fighting had been transferred from teeth to weapons, and that sex differences were of the human kind (Washburn and Ciochon 1974; Washburn 1968b, 1971). Evidence for such differences is far more likely to be found in the crests and bony thicknesses associated with muscle origins than in the molar teeth which show minimum female-male differences even when males are much larger than females.

CONCLUSIONS

Several advantages result from utilizing the female structure as the baseline for a species description and from considering the increments in the male skull as due to the anatomy of aggression (bluff and actual fighting). It is possible to correlate anatomy and behavior, and so to combine understandings from field work, museum, and laboratory.

With this approach, the morphological patterns which differentiate male and female may be clearly distinguished and analyzed into their component parts. Differences are often much larger than might be suspected from traditional methods of comparison. Psychological and hormonal differences appear to be greater than osteological ones, probably because of their importance in aggressive behaivors. This study is an attempt to develop a general theory of sexual differentiation and to provide interpretation of dimorphism in contemporary primate forms.

APPENDIX: MEASUREMENTS

1. **Cranial length.** The maximum cranial length. Glabella to opisthocranion.
2. **Cranial breadth.** The maximum cranial breadth above the supramastoid crests at right angles to the mid-sagittal plane. Euryon to euryon.
3. **Minimum frontal breadth.** The minimum breadth on the frontal or sphenoid between the temporal crests. The minimum postorbital breadth.
4. **Maximum biorbital breadth.** The greatest distance between the outer edges of the lateral orbital border.
5. **Inner biorbital breadth.** The greatest width from the inner edge of one lateral orbital border to the other. Ectoconchion to ectoconchion.
6. **Interorbital breadth.** The minimum distance between the two orbits.
7. **Bizygomatic breadth.** The greatest breadth between the two zygomatic arches.
8. **Cranial base length.** The distance from glabella to basion.
9. **Face length.** The distance from glabella to prosthion.
10. **Palate length.** The distance from prosthion to a line tangent to the posterior border of the maxillary processes.
11. **Palate breadth.** The maximum distance on the outside of the maxilla from one external lateral alveolar margin to the other, at right angles to the mid-sagittal plane. Ectomalare to ectomalare.

12. **Base width.** The maximum width across the base postporion and at right angles to the mid-sagittal plane.
13. **Cranial capacity.** The skull is filled with mustard or hemp seed and this quantity then measured in a graduated cylinder.
14. **Glabella thickness.** The thickness of the bone at glabella in the midline.
15. **Mastoid crest.** The thickest part of the temporal bone on the supramastoid crest above petrous temporal and at right angles to the mid-sagittal plane.
16. **Nuchal crest.** The thickness of the nuchal crest in the midline parallel to the Frankfort Horizontal Plane.
17. **Fossa length.** The maximum length of the infratemporal fossa from the lower border of the maxilla to the lower border of the temporal bone (the approximate length of the zygomatic arch).
18. **Fossa breadth.** The breadth of the infratemporal fossa from the most lateral inferior point of the curve of the sphenoid to the zygomatic arch at right angles to the mid-sagittal plane.
19. **Malar depth.** The minimum height of the malar from the maxilla to lower edge of orbit.
20. **M 1-3.** The length measurement of all three upper molars. From the mesial side of M1 to the distal side of M3.
21. **Canine length.** The mesiodistal diameter of the upper canine.
22. **Bicanine breadth.** Maximum intercanine distance on the external border of the maxilla.
23. **Petrotemporal width.** The distance on the base of the skull from the point where the sphenosquamous suture crosses the petrotympanic fissure to the outside of the zygomatic arch at right angles to the mid-sagittal plane.
24. **Bimalar breadth.** The greatest width between the two malars taken at their most anterior lateral edge.
25. **Greatest length.** Maximum skull length, from prosthion to opisthocranium (only taken on *Gorilla gorilla berengei*.)

BIBLIOGRAPHY

Alexander, R. D. 1971. "The Search for an Evolutionary Philosophy of Man." *Proceedings of the Royal Society of Victoria*, 84:99-120.

Alexander, R.D., J. L. Hoogland, R. D. Howard, K. M. Noonan, and P. W. Sherman. 1976. "Sexual Dimorphism and Breeding Systems in Pinnipeds, Ungulates, Primates and Humans." Paper presented at meeting of the American Anthropological Association.

Ashton, E. H. 1957. "Age Changes in Dimensional Differences Between the Skulls of Male and Female Apes." *Proceedings of the Zoological Society of London*, 128:259-265.

Barash, D. P. 1977. *Sociobiology and Behavior*. New York: Elsevier North-Holland.

Carpenter, C. R. 1940. "A Field Study in Siam of the Behavior and Social Relations of the Gibbon (*Hylobates lar*)." *Comparative Psychology Monographs*, No. 48. Baltimore: John Hopkins.

Cherry, L. M., S. M. Case, and A. C. Wilson. 1978. "Frog Perspective on the Morphological Differences Between Humans and Chimpanzees." *Science*, 200:209-211.

Clutton-Brock, T. H., Paul H. Harvey, and B. Rudder. 1977. "Sexual Dimorphism, Socionomic Sex Ratio and Body Weight in Primates." *Nature*, 269:797-800.

Crook, J. H. 1972. "Sexual Selection, Dimorphism, and Social Organization in the Primates." In *Sexual Selection and the Descent of Man, 1871-1971*, edited by B. Campbell, pp. 231-281. Chicago: Aldine.

Damon, A., H. W. Stoudt, and R. A. MacFarland. 1966. *The Human Body in Equipment Design*. Cambridge, Mass.: Harvard University Press.

D'Andrade, R. G. 1966. "Sex Differences and Cultural Institutions." In *The Development of Sex Differences*, edited by E. Maccoby, pp. 174-204. Stanford, Calif.: Stanford University Press.

Darwin, C. 1871. *The Descent of Man, and Selection in Relation to Sex*. London: John Murray.

DeVore, I., and S. L. Washburn. 1963. "Baboon Ecology and Human Evolution." In *African Ecology and Human Evolution*, edited by F. C. Howell and F. Bourlière, pp. 335-367. Chicago: Aldine.

Dobzhansky, T. D., F. J. Ayala, G. L. Stebbins, and J. W. Valentine. 1977. *Evolution*. San Francisco: Freeman.

Dolhinow, P., and N. Bishop. 1972. "The Development of Motor Skills and Social Relationships Among Primates Through Play." In *Primate Patterns*, edited by P. Dolhinow, pp. 312-338. New York: Holt, Rinehart and Winston.

Du Chaillu, P. 1868. *Wild Life Under the Equator*. New York: Harper.

Elliot, D. G. 1913. "A Review of the Primates." *American Museum of Natural History Monographs*, Vol. 3, No. 1. New York: American Museum of Natural History.

Fleagle, John G., Richard F. Kay and Elwyn L. Simons. 1980. "Sexual Dimorphism in Early Anthropoids." *Nature*, 287:328-330.

Frisch, J. E. 1963a. "Dental Variability in a Population of Gibbons (*Hylobates lar*)." In *Dental Anthropology*, edited by D. Brothwell, pp. 15-28. Oxford: Pergamon Press.

———. 1963b. "Sex Differences in the Canines of the Gibbon (*Hylobates lar*)." *Primates*, 4:1-10.

Galdikas, B. 1979. "Orangutan Adaptation at Tanjung Puting Reserve: Mating and Ecology." In *The Great Apes, Perspectives on Human Evolution*, Vol. 5, edited by D. Hamburg and E. R. McCown, pp. 195-233. Menlo Park, Calif.: Benjamin-Cummings.

Goy, R. W. 1968. "Organizing Effects of Androgen on the Behavior of Rhesus Monkeys." In *Endocrinology and Human Behavior*, edited by R. Michael, pp. 12-31. London: Oxford University Press.

Grant, P. G. 1973. "Biomechanics of the Masticatory Apparatus of the Rhesus Macaque (*Macaca mulatta*)." Ph.D. dissertation, University of California, Berkeley.

Guthrie, R. D. 1970. "Evolution of Human Threat Display Organs." In *Evolutionary Biology*, Vol. 4, edited by T. Dobzhansky, M. K. Hecht, and W. C. Steere, pp. 257-302. New York: Appleton-Century-Crofts.

Hamburg, B. A. 1978. "The Biosocial Bases of Sex Difference." In *Human Evolution: Biosocial Perspectives, Perspectives on Human Evolution*, Vol. IV, edited by S. L. Washburn and E. R. McCown, pp. 155-213. Menlo Park, Calif.: Benjamin-Cummings.

Hamburg, D. A. 1971. "Recent Research on Hormonal Factors Relevant to Human Aggressiveness." *International Social Science Journal*, 23:36-47.

Hamburg, D. A., and J. van Lawick-Goodall. 1974. "Factors Facilitating Development of Aggressive Behavior in Chimpanzee and Humans." In *Determinants and Origins of Aggressive Behavior*, edited by J. de Wit and W. W. Hartup, pp. 59-84. The Hague: Mouton.

Harvey, Paul H., M. Kavanagh, and T. H. Clutton-Brock. 1978. "Sexual Dimorphism in Primate Teeth." *Journal of Zoology* (London), 186:475-485.

Hooten, E. A. 1931. *Up from the Ape*. New York: Macmillan.

James, W. W. 1960. *The Jaws and Teeth of Primates*. London: Pitman Medical.

Krogman, W. M., and A. H. Schultz. 1938. "Anthropoid Ape Materials in American Collections." *American Journal of Physical Anthropology*, 24:199-234.

Leakey, R. E. F., and R. Lewin. 1978. *Origins*. New York: E. P. Dutton.

Le Gros Clark, W. E. 1955. *The Fossil Evidence for Human Evolution*. Chicago: University of Chicago Press.

Leutenneger, W., and J. T. Kelly. 1977. "Relationship of Sexual Dimorphism in Canine Size and Body Size to Social, Behavioral, and Ecological Correlates in Anthropoid Primates." *Primates*, 18:117-136.

Martin, R. D. 1980. "Sexual Dimorphism and the Evolution of Higher Primates." *Nature*, 287:273-275.

Mayr, E. 1970. *Populations, Species, and Evolution*. Cambridge, Mass.: Belknap Press, Harvard University.

_____. 1972. "Sexual Selection and Natural Selection." In *Sexual Selection and the Descent of Man, 1871-1971*, edited by B. Campbell, pp. 87-104. Chicago: Aldine.

McCown, Elizabeth R. 1978. "Sex Differences: Cranial Anatomy of Old World Monkeys." Ph.D. dissertation, University of California, Berkeley.

Montagu, M. F. A. 1960. *An Introduction to Physical Anthropology*. 3rd ed. Springfield: Charles C Thomas.

Moore, W. J., and C. L. B. Lavelle. 1974. *Growth of the Facial Skeleton in the Hominoidea*. London: Academic Press.

Napier, J. R., and P. H. Napier. 1967. *A Handbook of Living Primates*. New York: Academic Press.

Owen, R. 1835. "On the Osteology of the Chimpanzee and Orangutan." *Transactions of the Zoological Society of London*, 1:343.

————. 1848. "On a New Species of Chimpanzee." *Proceedings of the Zoological Society of London*, 1848:27-35.

Ralls, K. 1976. "Mammals in Which Females are Larger than Males." *The Quarterly Review of Biology*, 51:245-276.

Savage, T. S. 1847. "Notice of the External Character and Habits of a New Species of Troglodytes (*T. gorilla*, Savage) Recently Discovered by Dr. Savage Near the River Gaboon, Africa." *Proceedings of the Boston Society of Natural History*, 2:245-247.

Schultz, A. H. 1962. "Metric Age Changes and Sex Differences in Primate Skulls." *Zeitschrift für Morphologie und Anthropologie*, 52:239-255. Reprinted in: *Yearbook of Physical Anthropology 1962*, Vol. 10.

————. 1978. "Illustrations of the Relation Between Primate Ontogeny and Phylogeny." In *Human Evolution: Biosocial Perspectives*, edited by S. L. Washburn and E. R. McCown, pp. 255-283. Menlo Park, Calif.: Benjamin-Cummings.

Selander, R. K. 1966. "Sexual Dimorphism and Differential Niche Utilization in Birds." *Condor*, 68:113-151.

————. 1972. "Sexual Selection and Dimorphism in Birds." In *Sexual Selection and the Descent of Man 1871-1971*, edited by B. Campbell, pp. 180-231. Chicago: Aldine.

Simpson, G. G. 1953. *The Major Features of Evolution*. New York: Columbia University Press.

————. 1975. "Recent Advances in Methods of Phylogenetic Inference." In *Phylogeny of the Primates*, edited by W. P. Luckett and F. S. Szalay, pp. 3-19. New York: Plenum Press.

Symons, D. 1978. *Play and Aggression: A Study of Rhesus Monkeys*. New York: Columbia University Press.

Tanner, J. M. 1962. *Growth at Adolescence*. Oxford: Blackwell Scientific Publications.

Trivers, R. L. 1972. "Parental Investment and Sexual Selection." In *Sexual Selection and the Descent of Man, 1871-1971*, edited by B. Campbell, pp. 136-179. Chicago: Aldine.

Washburn, S. L. 1968a. "On Holloway's 'Tools and Teeth'." *American Anthropologist*, 70:97-101.

————. 1968b. *The Study of Human Evolution*. Condon Lecture, Oregon State System of Higher Education, Eugene, Oregon.

————. 1971. "The Study of Human Evolution." In *Background for Man*, edited by P. Dolhinow and V. Sarich, pp. 82-117. Boston: Little, Brown.

Washburn, S. L., and D. A. Hamburg. 1968. "Aggressive Behavior in Old World Monkeys and Apes." In *Primates: Studies in Adaptation and Variability*, edited by P. C. Jay, pp. 458-478. New York: Holt, Rinehart and Winston.

Washburn, S. L., and R. L. Ciochon. 1974. "Canine Teeth: Notes on Controversies in the Study of Human Evolution." *American Anthropologist*, 76:765-784.

Weidenreich, F. 1943. *The Skull of Sinanthropus Pekinensis.* Palaeontologia Sinica 127. Geological Survey of China, Pehpei, Chungking. Lancaster, Pa.: Lancaster Press.

Wilson, A. C., S. Carlson, and T. J. White. 1977. "Biochemical Evolution." *Annual Review of Biochemistry,* 46:573.

Wilson, A. P., and R. C. Boelkins. 1970. "Evidence for Seasonal Variation in Aggressive Behavior by *Macaca mulatta.*" *Animal Behavior,* 18:719-724.

Wilson, E. O. 1975. *Sociobiology: The New Synthesis.* Cambridge, Mass.: Belknap Press, Harvard University.

Four

The Fossil Record of Sex

Grover S. Krantz

Many years ago during my first teaching job I was showing some casts of Neandertal skulls to the class and mentioned something about one of them being female. A student asked how this was known. Without thinking, I answered, "There are differences between the sexes, but I can't show them to you here." After the laughter died down I explained that what I meant was that the fine distinctions in the skulls were mostly too small to be seen by everybody in a classroom of that size. I went on to describe some of the sexual differences in the skull without direct reference to the specimens. Perhaps that was just as well because the criteria I mentioned actually did not apply very consistently to these fossils. So, what criteria do apply?

Sex determination in modern human skeletal material is one of the most extensively studied subjects in physical anthropology. (See Hamilton, Chapter 5 of this volume.) The practical applications of this knowledge are many and obvious. Descriptions of modern skeletal remains in terms of age, sex, race, and anomalies are essential for making individual identifications. Archeological analysis tells the investigator which sex certain grave goods are associated with, and if there was differential treatment of the bodies based on their sex in life. Prehistoric demographic studies depend as much on sex identification as on age to reconstruct population pyramids and differential mortality rates.

Prior to the appearance of modern human types, and before deliberate burials, most of these criteria do not apply. But for such periods we still need proper sex identification in order to answer the one question about those people that is well known for today: How did males and females differ from each other skeletally? There are more applications as will be seen shortly. By using modern sexing criteria we can divide a sample of early hominid remains into two groups. We can then look at these and conclude that their males and females differed in the same ways that ours do. This may in fact be true, but it is also circular reasoning. What we need are somewhat more objective procedures to help avoid the potential pitfall of assuming what we intend to prove.

As a first step we should recognize the different kinds of sexually dimorphic traits that are found in modern skeletons. These fall into essentially two groups, those based on size differences and those related to childbirth. In all human groups males average almost 1.1 times as tall as females and are correspondingly more massive. Disproportionate muscularity is needed to move such greater body bulk, and there is evidence for this in the markings for muscle attachment. Body weight increases with the cube of linear dimension, whereas muscle strength increases only with the square. Thus larger bodies require relatively larger muscles to perform the same actions as smaller bodies. Other allometric differences tend to occur as a result of increasing absolute size, such as longer power arms on many muscle levers, and relatively smaller braincases in relation to facial skeletons.

The requirements of childbirth are most conspicuous in the larger pelvic opening of the female. Largely as a consequence of the broader pelvic base, carrying angles in the knees and elbows of females are generally greater. Apparently related to the requirements of child care, the female has what might be called a "central emphasis" to the skeleton. Compared with the male, the trunk is a greater percentage of the body mass; the limbs are shorter, both absolutely and relative to the trunk; distal segments of the limbs are short relative to proximal ones; and hands and feet are especially small. The reverse of all these in the male can be called "peripheral emphasis."

Many of the female skeletal traits are reminiscent of those seen in the young—absolutely smaller body, less musculature, relatively larger braincase, and less size emphasis on the peripheral parts. This condition is called "pedomorphy," or childlike, as opposed to the male condition. Male gerontomorphy is often given as a trait in itself, but it appears to follow from the other factors, and is simply a descriptive term without explanatory value.

The application of these same criteria to fossil populations presupposes that sexual dimorphism followed the same pattern as today, but this is not necessarily so. The amount of size contrast between sexes must be determined empirically from the fossils; the pelvic dimorphism should be expected to show only to the degree that infant head size crowds the female pelvis; the central body emphasis in the female may not apply if social protection was not afforded and the females had to fend for themselves.

We necessarily have to base any sexual reconstructions on the actual fossils. A single specimen of an extinct species cannot be sexed with any certainty, so obviously some kind of population is needed. How many fossils would suffice is quite another matter, and we're often told the more the better and we never seem to have enough. (That this is partly a cop-out may be suspected when it is realized that we have more australopithecine remains than of any other fossil hominid type, and their sex diagnosis is one of the most disputed.)

POPULATION MODELS AND IDEAL TYPES

Modern biology teaches us to think in terms of population ranges instead of ideal types. The tendency now is to entirely abandon typological thinking—this is unfortunate. For any given population there is always an ideal type that is being selected for—all deviations from this type being selected against to varying degrees. The range of variation that exists in any population is not advantageous at that time and place, but rather it represents an insurance policy for the species in order to shift adaptations if and when conditions change. Individuals who are deviant in one generation may turn out to be the ideal type at a later time.

Any species with a wide geographical distribution will face different environmental conditions in different parts of its range. There will be different ideal types for each of these contrasting environments, and selection will act accordingly. A gradation of subspecies is the automatic result. In addition there will always be two ideal types, male and female, in every species and subspecies. Our mammalian ancestors have always been selected for two ideals based on the minimal fact that only one sex carries, births, and suckles the young.

Thinking in terms of fossil populations can lead to some particular errors. First is the pooling of many individuals into each category, whether of sex or species, in order to make statistical statements. The common error here is to pool specimens without first ascertaining the proper identity of every individual that is used in the sample. One cannot assume that all material from a particular site, time range, or body size belongs to one taxon without determining this membership objectively from each specimen itelf. Investigators have sometimes assumed (by sampling) the very correlations they set out to test. Australopithecine divisions by site and size in South Africa are the classic example of this error.

The second error that can arise from population thinking is the pooling of material from a taxon without giving equal weight to both sexes. One must assume that the two sexes occurred in about equal numbers in nature. If the fossil sample includes significantly fewer representatives of one sex, a description of the species must be adjusted to correct for this. For example, average dimensions of canine teeth for a highly dimorphic species will not be the mean of known specimens if these consist of one male and six females.

The third possible error is in arbitrarily quantifying the amount of difference between measurements of males and females where large and equal samples are available. Bimodal graphs of measurements will result from different, but overlapping, ranges of sexual values. The common error here is to choose a point between the two modes and to assume this to be the sexual dividing line—males on one side and females on the other. The averages of the two groups may then be calculated and compared, supposedly to show the difference between the sexes. Actually, in an overlapping distribution some males will have been below the size-dividing line and some females above it. Drawing such a line will include members of each sex in the wrong sample and will exaggerate the supposed difference. A more correct allocation would put a few small individuals back into the male sample, and some large ones in the female sample, thus reducing the amount of size dimorphism from what was found with the other method. If the specimens cannot all be sexed individually, then the closest measure of sexual contrast is the difference between the modes on the original graphing of the measurements. (Of course this all presupposes that only one taxon is being sampled, from the same time zone, and with similar representation of the two sexes.)

SOURCES OF VARIATION IN FOSSILS

When we actually examine the data on a set of fossil material that might belong to one species we expect to find a great deal of variation. The problem is to sort out these variations and to assign them to their correct sources. Sources of variation can be described in 12 categories. The first three on this list apply only to published sources and include potential problems with photographs and casts. (These can be important in those cases where the investigator is not a member of the elite group that has access to original specimens.)

1. Recording and typographical errors; wrong captions; mislabeled casts.
2. Measurement error by describer; incorrect instrument calibra-

tion; lack of photographic scale; loss of detail from repeated cast copying.

3. Differences in measuring techniques; subject posing and distance from camera; mold shrinkage depending on material used.
4. Specimen preparation including cleaning, repairing, reconstructing, and combining of parts to make up individuals; photographs and casts with reconstructions not clearly indicated.
5. Factors external to specimen before discovery (before or after fossilization), such as carnivore chewing, weathering, crushing or bending from earth pressure, surface erosion, and missing parts.
6. Original pathologies, such as healed fractures and diseases.
7. Original anomalies such as odd-number ribs, unusual sacral position on vertebral column, wormian bones, supernumerary teeth, etc.
8. Individual age at death.
9. Species identification if more than one is possible.
10. Geographical variations (race) and equivalent contrasts in a lineage over time.
11. Sexual dimorphism.
12. Individual variation, such as size, linearity, limb proportions, muscular development.

After this point it will be assumed that the first seven sources of variation on this list are under reasonable control, but the investigator should be wary of them at all times. Items 8 through 12 are of special concern here because variations in each of them can be confused with variations in the others. Although sex identification is the prinicipal concern here, there are four other factors that can be, and commonly are, confused with it. All five sources of variation can cause the same kinds of observed morphological contrasts. The study of sexual dimorphism depends on our ability to separate these causative factors. Some general rules-of-thumb for each category can be given first.

Individual Age

Individual age is usually the first of the five variables that can be determined and thus be removed from further consideration. For most studies of fossil populations, only adult remains are valid, but with due allowance for potential growth, increasing gerontomorphy, and allometric changes, juvenile specimens can sometimes be used. Raymond Dart was able to do this with the first *Australopithecus* skull when he assessed its taxonomic position.

The sex of a youthful specimen is generally not determinable (unless size dimorphism is extreme). But if adulthood is erroneously assumed, an incorrect sex or species identification may easily result. Young individuals are pedomorphic (by definition), females of any species tend to be more pedomorphic than males, and hominid evolution has included a trend toward pedomorphy in many traits over time. If a young individual is not recognized as such, it may be taken as an adult female, or as a representative of a type previously assumed to have lived at a much later date.

Obvious indications of individual age are tooth eruption and epiphyseal unions. When these are not available there are still many more criteria. Estimated body size is a good indication, but only if one knows for certain to which taxon the specimen belongs (including sex) and what size those adults really are. Porous surface is often an indication of youth, especially in postcranial bones.

It is not enough to say a skull "looks adult," or that there is "no reason to assume otherwise." One should check for more specific details to be sure. Fused sutures are not a dependable guide, especially with the small-brained australopithecines. In apes the sutures are fused endocranially by the time of second molar eruption, in modern humans not until well after the third molar is in place. Which pattern an extinct hominid followed is not readily apparent.

Young skulls have muscle attachment ridges that are less well marked than one would expect in an adult of comparable size. One should compare the nuchal crest with the size of the whole head, and the temporal lines with the jaw size. Lateral pterygoid origin borders also sharpen up only with maturity.

Species Identification

It is always possible that differences between fossils represent separate phyletic lines. (Whether these lines are to be classed as species, genera, or even higher categories is mainly a matter of taste and is not important here.) Such morphological separations may also be taken to represent successive species in a single phyletic line if temporal data are poorly known. The boundaries of contemporary or successive fossil species are not testable in terms of reproductive isolation, of course, so they are defined in terms of the morphological-gap concept. (The amount of difference between two similar living species is the amount used to separate fossil species.)

Because size differences automatically lead to differing degrees of pedomorphy versus gerontomorphy, it is desirable to compare specimens that are, as nearly as possible, of the same body sizes. Where these are not available, correction must be made. Small skulls, just like young ones, must be visualized as being more gerontomorphic when compared with larger ones. One cannot just use a visually enlarged version, but it must be supplied with exaggerated ridges and crests and only a slightly increased brain size. Likewise, a mental reduction from a large form should reduce crests the most, facial structures less, and brain size least, in order to make direct comparisons.

Given comparisons between like-sized individuals (real or allometrically adjusted), one should then look for actual morphological contrasts. Separate species are indicated when a set of such contrasts can be described that are not of the kind normally associated with sexual distinctions. Size alone might be the basis of species separation, but this is very unlikely without a clustering of other morphological contrasts going along with it.

Geographical and temporal positions may also be factors here. If two distinct morphotypes are fully separated in either time or space, then the possibility of subspecies or race must remain viable. Temporal race versus species can be an arbitrary distinction. Contemporary race versus species is a biological reality, but one that is often difficult to distinguish without geographical intermediaries. When the two (or more) morphotypes overlap in time and space then species separation is likely.

Ideally, species distinctions should include morphological contrasts in more than one trait complex. Body size and molarization alone are not enough because they can interrelate causally. If one adds to this some differences in skull design and a few dental details, as in the australopithecines, then valid contemporary species are indicated.

It is also desirable to show some ecological contrast to support a speciation model. By definition, there must be such a contrast, but it is understandable that we might not be able to see it in the fossil record. If such a contrast can be demonstrated the case is strong; if not, the issue remains open.

Geographical Variation

Racial distinctions, over space or through time in a single lineage, are mostly like species distinctions, but in lesser amounts. Often a single trait complex is the only contrast, such as size and its allometric consequences. Again, it is desirable to show an ecological basis for such a contrast. These subspecies separations differ in that they must be separated from each other either by space or in time; direct overlap is not possible. Racial variations should also involve traits that are not normally taken as sexual dimorphisms. In most cases a significant sample of specimens is needed to distinguish such subspecies contrasts from individual variations.

Sex Identification

Morphological differences between certain specimens usually can be referred to sex when age, species, and race have been ruled out. The differences noted should also be of the same kinds that are known to distinguish sexes in living forms. In higher primates, the two sexes almost always differ in pedomorphy versus gerontomorphy. These size-related contrasts, which also follow from differences in individual age, often distinguish races and species as well. With adult specimens of one lineage at one time level and in one geographical region, observed differences in degree of gerontomorphy will be sexual or individual variation. If sexual size dimorphism is minor, then confusion with individual variation is likely, and other criteria should be looked for. Even so, a bimodal distribution of any measurement will most likely represent the modes of the two sexes. The quantity of sexual size dimorphism should not be presupposed— see what the data suggest. Linear dimensions of skeletal parts may be nearly equal, or male lengths could be as much as one-third more, as in some living primate species. Some other mammals have even greater discrepancies.

Depending on bimodal distributions in samples—when age, race, and species are controlled for—is often the only workable method of determining sex differences. Under more fortunate circumstances, individual specimens can be sexed directly. Among the more recent hominids, enlarged brains have led to pelvic dimorphism that is usually recognizable. Among the smaller-brained pithecanthropines this dimorphism should be there, although much reduced, but this has not yet been demonstrated with actual specimens. In the australopithecines one should not expect pelvic dimorphism, other than size, just as with the living apes; their brain sizes at birth did not likely pose any serious problems.

In the earliest australopithecine, *A. afarensis*, dental dimorphism is quite obvious. Males have projecting canines, disproportionately large incisors, precanine disastemas, and nearly parallel tooth rows; female dentitions are more like the later australopithecines. This kind of dental dimorphism is typical of most higher primates where there is also a great body-size difference. In *afarensis* we see the last evidence among hominids of this degree of anterior dental emphasis in the males. One can safely presume that any earlier hominid ancestor, whether separate or joined with the African apes, would show the same dental dimorphism.

Hominid sexual dimorphism, other than size, can be divided into three temporal segments. During the last 100,000 years pelvic dimorphism was marked in much of the world, and probably was at least noticeable in all of the world for the last 1.5 million years. Prior to about 3 million years ago dental dimorphism was a major distinction. The middle period, from 3 up to 1.5 million, was without either of these morphological contrasts, and size dimorphism is almost all we have to go on in this time frame.

Individual Variation

This is the last catchall category for all differences between specimens that are not accounted for by age, species, race, or sex. Normally these variations should be confined to a single trait or trait complex in any one individual. If several unusual contrasts are found, then another explanation should be looked for, perhaps including pathologies and anomalies. Individual variation should be expected either to exaggerate or minimize any of the other kinds of differences in various instances. This is the source of the range of variation seen for almost any biological trait.

The preceding paragraphs are offered as some guidelines for separating the expressions of age, species, race, sex, and individual variations that may be encountered in the fossil record. There are a few other considerations that can be added, some of which were touched on above.

OTHER ISSUES IN DEFINING SEXUAL DIMORPHISM IN FOSSILS

Geographical distributions of contrasting types can often help to determine what they represent, provided sampling is sufficiently large. At a given time depth, nonoverlapping distributions suggest either separate races or allopatric species. Partial overlapping rules out races and makes sympatric species the most likely explanation. Full overlap may also be from separate species, but sex contrast then becomes more likely. The decision between species and sex should rest largely on whether the observed differences are of the same kind, regardless of degree, as are found to distinguish the sexes of other species in the same order. The nature of the geographical and ecological overlap can also be important—the closer the overlap, the more likely they are two sexes.

Postcranial remains are often little appreciated, apparently in large part because they are usually difficult to match with cranial material. When this is possible, and when they can be diagnosed with some certainty, they are potentially useful in two contrasting ways, either merging or splitting taxa that were previously based only on cranial and dental material. Miocene fossils of *Pliopithecus* had long been considered to be closely associated with gibbons, but their limbs and vertebrae are now known to contrast so markedly that putting them in the same family is no longer feasible. On the other hand, *Ramapithecus* is now on the verge of being combined with *Dryopithecus* (= *Sivapithecus*), in part because of the essential similarity of recently discovered postcranials (undescribed as of this writing).

Absolute body-size variations can also be important in ways other than their allometric effects on structural designs. Generally speaking, increasing size correlates with increasing longevity, with decreasing reproductive rate, with a higher survival rate among offspring, with lower selective pressure to prune out deviants, and, consequently, with greater morphological variability. Among higher primates this complex trend is carried to a high degree, and morphological variability within a single breeding population is often as great as that found in several species of other mammals. One should equally expect that in fossils of higher primates a comparable morphological diversity might well occur in what was then a single species.

Sexual dimorphisms should not be expected to be the same in all species. These are not consistent in living forms, and they could also follow unexpected patterns in the fossil record. Males are usually larger than females, but size dimorphism varies greatly in living hominoids. In gorillas and orangs, males outweigh females by 2:1; in chimps and humans, males outweigh females by only about 25 percent; and in gibbons, the sexes are nearly equal. It is not immediately evident from a fossil's affinities just what degree of size dimorphism ought to be present. Ecological circumstances may be important here, and it must be noted that the greatest size dimorphism among primates (2.5:1) is found in terrestrial quadrupeds like baboons.

Larger pelvic apertures in females might be presumed for human ancestors, but this is not notable with the other hominoids where infant brain size does not demand any special discrepancy. Thus it should be brain size, per se, not hominid affinity, that dictates pelvic dimorphism in the fossil record.

Emphasis on the anterior dentition is a standard male trait in most hominoids, although in gibbons and humans this distinction is negligible. Size equality appears to be the major factor for this in gibbons, while cultural behavior may be the critical one in ourselves.

One should not assume that the ancestors of each of the living hominoid species necessarily showed the same kind and degree of sexual dimorphism as their living descendants. Similarly, if sexual dimorphisms can be established in fossil forms, it does not automatically follow that their descendants (including living species) should all follow the same pattern.

We do not presently have a consensus in paleoanthropology as to just what are the sexual distinctions in all of our fossil ancestors. There is also much disagreement about the relative effects of age, race, species, and individual variation in explaining observed morphological contrasts. What little agreement there is tends to be concentrated toward the more recent end of the fossil record, and opinions become increasingly divergent and uncertain as one goes back in time. We can distinguish three general time zones, which correspond to the geological epochs of Pleistocene, Pliocene, and Miocene, where the agreements move from good to medium to poor, in that order.

PLEISTOCENE HOMINID SEXUAL DIMORPHISM

The last hominids prior to the modern type that are well known as fossils are the Neandertals. Here I am using Neandertal in the narrower sense of Late Pleistocene hominids of Europe and southwestern Asia, and not as a universal stage in human evolution. While they share most details of cranial anatomy with the preceding pithecanthropines, they also have large braincases (1500 cc) of the modern size. Their head sizes at birth would thus require the same quantity of pelvic dimorphism as is found today. Wolpoff (1980) has estimated Neandertal body-size dimorphism to be slightly less than is usual now, the females being 94 percent of male stature. In many ways the morphological distinctions that separate the sexes in modern skulls apply here as well. But projecting brow ridges and retreating foreheads are not diagnostic of males—the female Neandertals seem almost as extreme in these features. On the other hand, projecting occipital bulges do appear to distinguish the larger male skulls in a manner not noted in modern skulls.

Skeletal muscularity does not distinguish the Neandertal sexes nearly as much as it does today, according to Wolpoff. To some degree this may follow from the more nearly equal body sizes, assuming these skeletons are typical and have been properly identified. This may also indicate that females had to behave very much like the males, and that there was little economic division of labor between them. This would also make sense if they survived each winter primarily on their stored body fat (Krantz 1967). In order to carry 20 to 30 kg of extra weight in the autumn a powerfully built body would be needed. This would then apply to both sexes about equally, in proportion to their absolute body sizes.

Hominids of the Middle and Lower Pleistocene (*H. erectus*) had somewhat smaller brains, mostly about 1000 cc, or halfway between ape and Neandertal sizes. Their pelvic dimorphism would, expectably, be less marked in terms of birth-canal sizes, but in terms of total body size and muscularity their dimorphism was probably greater. This is evident from the great size spread seen in the crania and their superstructures, which indicates a sexual size dimorphism that is more than that found in either Neandertals or modern humanity. At the same time, the uncertainty in sexing a few of the individuals from the Solo and Peking series indicates a great amount of individual variation within one or (presumably) both sexes.

Identifying the sex of crania in an *H. erectus* series should be no great problem, provided both sexes can be presumed to be present. This is done by using modern criteria in the "three-part system." One first lines up the specimens in order of overall size and calls the largest one-third of them males and the smallest one-third females, with almost no chance of error. Next, one studies these extreme groups for all distinguishing traits that seem little affected by absolute size. These traits, and no others, are then presumed to be valid for sex distinction and are applied to the middle third for individual diagnosis. The point of this system is to discover the sexually diagnostic traits in the particular population under study. One may begin with a list of modern distinctions as clues for what to look for, but by testing against the two extremes, one finds out which do and which do not apply in the particular case. By this method it can be seen that projecting brow ridges and retreating foreheads do not work well with Neandertals and (as I class them) other *erectus*, but facial size, mastoid processes, and occipital bulges do tend to distinguish the sexes.

PLIOCENE HOMINID SEXUAL DIMORPHISM

The australopithecines date from about 1.5 to 3.7 million years ago, almost matching the marine faunal definition of the Pliocene, which is from 1.8 to 5 million. There is little agreement as to their sexual dimorphism except that most authorities think it is very great—equal to or more than that found in later *erectus* populations. One problem here is that neither the human pelvic contrasts nor the usual primate dental dimorphisms are evident. This is the difficult middle ground of hominid evolution where size difference is almost all we have to go on. Because of this limitiation it is especially difficult to separate the effects of sex from those of race and species.

My own interpretation of the data will be given here (from Krantz 1977), although most authorities (including myself) would not accept the following picture as being anywhere near proven. The first step in disentangling the different sources of size contrast is to rule out the time-honored equation of *africanus* = Sterkfontein = small, and *robustus* = Swartkrans = large. If this equation does not hold, then we must begin at virtually "ground zero" with a mass of disarticulated parts to arrange in any way we see fit. No reason has ever been given why each of these major South African sites should have included only one type. As it turns out, both types are found in both sites (Aguirre 1970), but the sites were labeled according to a few diagnostic specimens recognized in each.

The only safe way to begin sorting the australopithecine remains is to look for morphological types in definite adults based on criteria that are nowhere associated with sex. This easily appears in the form of relative molarization of the dentitions where two types have long been recognized. Combined crown areas of the anterior dentition (incisors and canines) can be compared with the posterior (premolars and molars). In *africanus* the anteriors are usually more than 25 percent of the size of the posteriors; in *robustus* the anteriors are 20 percent or less of the posteriors. The relative sizes of canines and premolars in a single jaw also serve to separate the two types. In *africanus* these three teeth have nearly the same crown areas in a given individual, while in *robustus* they ascend in size, each one being half-again larger than the tooth in front of it. Many other detailed morphological traits also serve to distinguish these dentitions (Robinson 1956).

These two types of dentitions contrast in a way resembling the usual primate sexual dimorphism in terms of relative canine size, but there are at least two problems with this idea. The *africanus* dentitions have the larger canines, but they are not notably larger in overall tooth size—if they were all males their molars should also be larger. In *africanus* the second premolar is unusually small (no larger than the first) and this is not consistent with known sexual contrasts. Also, the variety of other detailed distinctions is of the kind normally found in contrasting taxa, not between sexes. There are several cranial distinctions that are directly associated with the two kinds of dentitions, which again are not known to separate sexes.

Given these two kinds of skulls and jaws, the next step is to decide whether these are racial or species distinctions. The combination of several cranial and dental differences suggests species. The occurrence of both kinds in the same deposits also implies species (unless there were geographical shifts of the environment and the races shifted with them).

Up to this point I have deliberately ignored absolute size and allometric consequences. Now it may be noted that there are two major size categories of each dental type. The implication that this represents size dimorphism by sex is unavoidable. The amount of difference is enormous, but it includes no other contrasts except allometric adjustments in skull design. The indicated body-size contrast is on the order of 2:1, and perhaps more. A tentative body-weight schedule I find is:

Male *africanus*	68 kg
Male *robustus*	55 kg
Female *africanus*	36 kg
Female *robustus*	21 kg

One might note the reversal of body sizes by species; the two sexes of *africanus* average 52 kg, whereas in *robustus* they are just 38 kg. Previous thinking was based on comparisons of only male *robustus* with female *africanus* specimens.

This interpretation of the South African fossil remains allows us to make more sense out of a number of otherwise puzzling specimens. Most of the so-called "Telanthropus" material is from the very small female *robustus* that had previously gone almost unnoticed. Some very large *africanus* fragments (including Sk 27 and "Meganthropus") now make sense when classified as males of that species.

Both female *robustus* and male *africanus* are poorly represented, and their remains have often been misinterpreted as belonging to early *Homo*. Evidently some agency was concentrating australopithecine remains of the middle size range in the South African deposits. That agency has probably been identified by Brain (1970) as leopards whose kills fell from their feeding trees and into the caves.

There also appear to be racial variations in that the same two species are also found in East Africa. I cannot find any significant differences from the South African material, except for somewhat larger sizes for all categories, with corresponding allometric adjustments. In the East African material, the male *africanus* is so large that fragmentary specimens of young ones are regularly taken to be some kind of early *Homo* from their brain sizes. This should not be too surprising if these *africanus* did, in fact, evolve into *Homo* about 1.5 million years ago.

MIOCENE HOMINID SEXUAL DIMORPHISM

Here we are faced with the whole dryopithecine assemblage, including *Ramapithecus, Sivapithecus*, and *Proconsul*. These are all clearly allied with humans and apes on the basis of dentition, but how many lineages there are and who begat whom is still a wide-open controversy. My own interpretation is tight and simple and follows largely from a recognition of sexual and racial variations. It will be presented here with due caution to the reader that it is not yet widely accepted (Krantz 1973).

In order to focus on the dryopithecine problem it is first advisable to exclude a number of other fossil primates of similar times that are not closely related. *Oreopithecus* is a Miocene brachiator from Europe with no close relationship to any of the hominoids; its locomotor adaptations are a parallelism. *Pliopithecus* is a small European and African catarrhine of uncertain affinities with the hominoid groups. Most published opinion would classify this genus as an ancestral gibbon, but this can be ruled out with some certainty; gibbons show every evidence of having had much larger progenitors. *Gigantopithecus* of China and India is probably much later in time, and may, in fact, be a hominid; it is likely descended from dryopithecines. The remaining generic names that are sometimes used are probably all synonyms for those already mentioned here.

Proconsul may be retained, if one wishes, as the generic category for the earliest dryopithecines from Africa prior to 17 million years ago when that continent joined Eurasia. They are, no doubt, the ancestors of the main dryopithecine assemblage that later spread over all three continents.

The first question to ask of the dryopithecines, as delimited here, is: How many evolving lineages are represented? The answer I give is, just one. Because of the multiplicity of names given to the various specimens in the past, it used to be assumed that a major adaptive radiation occurred then. But more careful study shows that postulation of a single, highly dimorphic species, changing over time, and with many racial and individual variations, can easily account for all the fossils. This single species must then be the ancestor of all the living hominoids. This picture correlates well with the separation times indicated by serum protein evolution, more popularly known as the "biochemical clock" (Sarich 1971). Both morphological and molecular protein analysis would have the gibbons split off rather early in dryopithecine times; the orang-African split would occur at about the time they drop out of sight from the fossil record some 10 million years ago; and the human split would occur still later.

This interpretation stands in sharp contrast with that presented in almost every textbook since 1965 (prior to then, no clear picture of hominoid phylogeny had emerged). What most of us have read is that *Ramapithecus* was an already separated human ancestor, a true hominid, with fossils dating back to at least 14 million years ago. At the same time, various species of *Pliopithecus, Dryopithecus,* and perhaps *Sivapithecus* were claimed to be the separated ancestors of the different living apes (Simons 1967).

The biochemical clock was the first convincing piece of evidence arguing against this long separation of the hominoid lineages. Recognition of the range of racial, sexual, and individual differences began to prompt questions about the rigid phylogeny. Finally, some geographical considerations showed that more than one species could not reasonably have coexisted over such a great range with the same adaptations. What has yet to be generally accepted is that these Miocene "apes" were terrestrial quadrupeds. We are forced to this last conclusion from some of the postcranial remains, from their locations around the edges of the grasslands with no connecting forests, and from their wide geographical range that is so much greater than that of any arboreal species.

By identifying "Ramapithecus" as the female of the latest and largest stage of the dryopithecine lineage, its anatomy now makes complete sense. It was previously called a hominid because of its small anterior dentition, especially the short canines. In many other primates this kind of dimorphism in the anterior dentition is a sexual distinction. Among terrestrial, quadrupedal primates this dimorphism is carried to an extreme. Given the geographical argument for "Ramapithecus" being a grassland quadruped, sexual dimorphism of this kind and degree might well be expected. Given the close coincidence of distributions of "Ramapithecus" and late "Dryopithecus" (= "Sivapithecus"), the two dimorphic sexes would appear to be identified.

Attention has been called to other, supposedly hominid, traits of "Ramapithecus," including thick molar enamel, short muzzle, strong mandibular bodies, and other indications of powerful chewing adaptations. These are all found in the other late dryopithecines and have sometimes been used to distinguish "Sivapithecus" from the earlier "Proconsul." Savanna and woodland habitats provided an ecological niche with an emphasis on chewing small, tough food objects.

Still other hominid traits of "Ramapithecus" have proven to be incorrect with the recovery of additional specimens. It did not have especially vertical incisors; it did not have a closed tooth row—the diastema is clear; it did not have a bicuspid first lower premolar, but rather a fully sectorial one; and its canine fossa turned out not to be a hominid trait at all.

Perhaps the most elegant support for this interpretation comes in the form of geographical variations which ought to be evident in both males and females if this is indeed a single species. The large "Dryopithecus" and "Ramapithecus" of Asia are both noted for having more highly arched palates than those found elsewhere. The two forms from Africa both show greater development of cingulums. Molar crown heights suggest the same geographical contrast. These distinctions also set the stage for deriving orangs from the eastern forms, and African apes and man from the western ones, but that is another subject entirely (Greenfield 1979; Krantz 1981).

The variety seen in the dryopithecine fossil record is not just a reflection of sexual dimorphism combined with a high degree of individual variation. Changes over time also exist in the form of increasing body size as well as in the apparently early shift from a more arboreal to a more terrestrial way of life. These changes may have included increasing sexual dimorphism of size and morphology, as well as the redesigning of jaws and teeth for harder chewing. Given these temporal trends, combined with some uncertain datings, it is possible that more than just two types might appear to exist at one time and place. Another source of multiple types would follow from the geographical variations, especially where these involve size differences. When climatic or other major environmental factors change there can be geographical shifts of location by some of these races. This could include geographical overlapping of races within narrow time zones.

As noted earlier, this interpretation of the dryopithecines as being a single, highly dimorphic lineage has not met with general acceptance. Only a few of us have suggested the possibility (Eckhardt 1972; Frayer 1974), and we are prepared to back off from this extreme view at any time. When Simons and Pilbeam (1965) reduced the "radiation" of Miocene apes to just three genera, that was difficult enough to swallow. Taking this on down to just a single species is understandably hard to believe without very solid evidence. Thus far, the evidence continues to point in this direction.

OVERVIEW

Sexual dimorphism has been a conspicuous feature in at least 30 million years of human ancestry, apparently from the basic monkey *Aegyptopithecus* through *Dryopithecus* and *Australopithecus*, and declining to the usual mammalian degree only during the last 1.5 million years of the genus *Homo*. There is no obvious reason why the ancestral Oligocene monkey should have been as dimorphic as the later forms. Escape from predators should have been an equal problem for both sexes in the trees. The dryopithecine period makes full sense, by analogy with terrestrial baboons, where males are selected for fighting strength while females are selected for reproductive efficiency on limited food resources. Continuing dimorphism during our brachiating period is not obviously required (nor established), but it may be no disadvantage either, as long as overall size remains large.

Australopithecine dimorphism continued for perhaps obvious reasons with the return to savanna life. But here the loss of clear dental dimorphism leaves size alone as the major distinguishing trait to look for in the fossils.

By all evidence, size dimorphism began its reduction with the larger-brained pithecanthropines where infant head sizes caused selection for larger females. By late *erectus* times (Neandertal), the size discrepancy had declined to its modern, modest level. At about this same time, pelvic dimorphism also becomes modern and we have a mostly new, and highly dependable, method of distinguishing the sexes in fossil material.

In terms of morphological features, dimorphism has passed through three major phases in the fossil record. First, there were size and dental contrasts; then size alone; and finally pelvic contrasts with minor size differences. These phases correspond roughly to the geological epochs of Miocene, Pliocene, and Pleistocene. Interestingly, this does not accord fully with the degree of consensus about sex determination in the fossil record. Agreement is good for the Pleistocene, as might be expected, given the greater similiarity of the fossils to ourselves and the longer time that the matter has been studied. Agreement is medium for the Pliocene australopithecines where it ought to be least, considering we have only size contrasts to go on. Agreement is poorest for the Miocene where it ought to be at least medium, considering that we apparently have both size and dental dimorphisms.

The reduction of size dimorphism during the time of genus *Homo* would seem to call for some special explanation because this apparently corresponded with the time of increasing division of labor between the sexes. When communal food-foraging was replaced by a divided emphasis between male hunting and female collecting, one might think there should be a revived emphasis on anterior dentition in the males and an even stronger pressure to maintain the sexual size difference.

Explaining the continuing similarity in dentitions is simple. Wide cranial bases with broad jaws and divergent tooth rows prevent interlocking canines (Mills 1963). The use of hunting weapons and butchering tools makes specialized dentitions superfluous anyway.

It is possible that cultural behavior acted to reduce male body size in an interesting way, as suggested by Roger La Jeunesse (personal communication). He points out that male baboons achieve their larger size by extending the growth period at the expense of adult longevity. Given a cultural adaptation, to continue this adolescent growth stage to the same degree should effectively delay the males' entry into full cultural participation as adults. By cutting short the male growth period to more nearly that of the female, the males can then prolong their adult longevity simply by beginning it sooner. Only in a cultural setting, where cooperation is more important than physical prowess, would this become advantageous to a terrestrial primate.

A very different view also ties reduced size dimorphism to culture, but through the medium of increased brain size. The reasoning here is that larger infant head size caused selection for increased female body size without necessarily affecting the body size of males. There are two reasons for this, anatomical and physiological. Anatomically, the female pelvis can be made to accommodate increasing infant head size by simply making entire female bodies larger (Kjerstie Nelson, personal communication). Physiologically, the growing infant's brain is a fantastic consumer of nutrition because it must be built so rapidly. Both before and after birth the infant depends on its mother for nutrition, and the larger her body, the greater the reserves to draw upon (Krantz 1981).

Choosing between the above explanations would depend on identifying our specific australopithecine ancestors, correctly identifying them as to sex, and knowing the body size of each. It should then be a simple matter to observe whether males grew smaller or females grew larger. My interpretation of the australopithecine remains indicates clearly the latter is correct; females became larger. Of course this presupposes no other factors affected body-size changes. For instance, if there were a general body-size increase this could be combined with a relative male reduction and the first theory would fit with the observed skeletal data, as interpreted here. What is missing is a clear picture of the required general increase.

There are no easy solutions or simple formulas for sex identification in our fossil ancestors, contrary to what I thought those many years ago when I was up in front of my first class. A few of the notable precautions bear restating here. (1) Don't expect to find good pelvic dimorphism unless there is a large brain for the body size; (2) Look for allometric effects of body size, where small and young individuals will appear more modern and large ones more primitive; (3) The amount of sexual size dimorphism should not be presumed—find it in the data; and (4) Do not assume that erect posture automatically makes a fossil human with all that implies in terms of culture, division of labor, longevity, and reduced dimorphism.

Beyond this I can only urge the student to weigh carefully all the possible sources of variation, especially age, species, race, sex, and individual. These all can cause similar effects, and sorting them out can be difficult. The sortings I have given here for the australopithecines and dryopithecines may or may not turn out to be correct in the long run. What may be more important than answers are procedures; I hope I have offered some useful ones here.

BIBLIOGRAPHY

Aguirre, E. 1970. "Identificacion de 'Paranthropus' en Makapansgat." *Cronical del XI Congreso Nacional de Arqueologia, Merida, 1969*, pp. 98-124.

Brain, C. K. 1970. "New Finds at the Swartkrans Australopithecine Site." *Nature*, 225:1112-1119.

Eckhardt, R. B. 1972. "Population Genetics and Human Origins." *Scientific American*, 226:94-103.

Frayer, D. W. 1974. "A Reappraisal of *Ramapithecus*." *Yearbook of Physical Anthropology*, 18:19-30.

Greenfield, L. O. 1979. "On the Adaptive Pattern of '*Ramapithecus*'." *American Journal of Physical Anthropology*, 50:527-548.

Krantz, G. S. 1967. "Winter Survival of Classic Neanderthals." Paper presented at annual meeting of the American Anthropological Society, Washington, D.C.

————. 1973. "The Double Descent of Man." In *Paleoanthropology, Morphology and Paleoecology*, edited by R. Tuttle, pp. 131-152. The Hague: Mouton. [Published 1975.]

————. 1977. "A Revision of Australopithecine Body Sizes." *Evolutionary Theory*, 2:65-94.

————. 1981. *The Process of Human Evolution*. Cambridge, Mass.: Schenkman.

Mills, J. R. E. 1963. "Occlusion and Malocclusion in Primates." In *Dental Anthropology*, edited by D. Brothwell, pp. 29-51. Oxford: Pergamon Press.

Robinson, J. T. 1956. *The Dentition of the Australopithecines.* Pretoria: Transvaal Museum Memoir No. 9.

Sarich, V. M. 1971. "A Molecular Approach to the Question of Human Origins." In *Background for Man,* edited by P. Dolhinow and V. Sarich, pp. 60-81. Boston: Little, Brown.

Simons, E. L. 1967. "The Earliest Apes." *Scientific American,* 217:28-35.

Simons, E. L., and D. R. Pilbeam. 1965. "Preliminary Revision of the Dryopithecinae (Pongidae, Anthropoidea)." *Folia Primatologica,* 3:81-152.

Wolpoff, M. H. 1980. *Paleoanthropology.* New York: Alfred A. Knopf.

Five

Sexual Dimorphism
In Skeletal Samples

Margaret E. Hamilton

The current interest in sexual dimorphism originated a decade ago in efforts to explain a wide range of size and shape variation among the australopithecine fossil materials (Brace 1969). While most experts accepted the idea of assigning the material to two or more apparently sympatric genera (Robinson 1972) or species (Le Gros Clark 1967; Howell 1967), a few researchers argued for a single species interpretation based on the competitive exclusion principle (Wolpoff 1971). Instead of representing two or more hominid lineages, these researchers argued that the australopithecine collection represented one lineage of a highly dimorphic, polytypic hominid population sampled from several million years of the human fossil record (Brace 1969, 1973; Swedlund 1974; Wolpoff 1975, 1976a,b). Later discoveries (Leakey and Walker 1976) and interpretations (White and Harris 1977; Johanson and White 1979) essentially neutralized the debate, but the interest in sexual dimorphism persists.

As more osteologists and paleoanthropologists include an analysis of sexual dimorphism in their research, it is important to note the potential sources of error in such studies. Surprisingly, the control of error in such estimates has been rarely discussed in the past since the debate about sexual dimorphism focused chiefly on issues surrounding taxonomic procedure (Brace, Mahler, and Rosen 1973; Campbell 1974; Robinson 1965, 1967; Tobias 1966; Wolpoff 1974) and theories about speciation (Pilbeam and Zwell 1973; Swedlund 1974; Wolpoff 1971) without attempting to actually estimate the magnitude of dimorphism involved. A notable exception is the work of Wolpoff (1975, 1976a,b). What follows in this chapter applies chiefly to skeletal analysis, but some comments are also relevant to work with living populations. Error in the estimation of sexual dimorphism may originate from three major sources. First, errors in sex identification may exaggerate or underestimate sexual size differences in a skeletal series. Second, sampling errors from other sources, such as age, can affect the measured magnitude of size dimorphism. Finally, the failure to control for variables which influence sexual dimorphism at the genotypic or phenotypic level may also influence results and interpretation.

This chapter discusses problems in the study of sexual dimorphism in skeletal populations, including principles of interpretation, and illustrates the points made with a specific example from Lower Illinois River Valley populations.

SEX IDENTIFICATION

For a long time it has been generally acknowledged that the magnitude of size differences between the sexes can vary from one human population to the next. For example, in his discussion of sexing procedures Hrdlička commented (1939):

> It must therefore always be expected that in a series of skeletons or skulls or other body parts, a certain proportion of the specimens will offer a serious difficulty and even impossibility for a definite sex identification. Moreover, conditions in this respect vary somewhat among the different racial and functional groups, so that in some the sex identification of the skeletal parts is more difficult than in others. As a general rule the more cultured the groups of people from which the skeletal parts are derived, the more difficult will be the sex determination; and the same is true of human groups that have become physically weakened. [P. 112]

Because of this, skeletal studies of size dimorphism cannot begin by sexing the material on the basis of apparent overall size differences between the sexes. The use of size in sexing decisions, whether it be subjective evaluation or discriminant analysis, could potentially bias the outcome. The subjective evaluation of size can lead to what Weiss has shown to be as much as a 12 percent bias in favor of males in the sexing of robust skeletal fossils (Weiss 1972). Since the degree of size dimorphism is frequently low, an error of such magnitude could result in meaningless or erroneous conclusions.

When at all possible, a study aiming to define the magnitude of sexual dimorphism for size or other features in a skeletal series should establish sex identification upon other criteria than size. This is best achieved by using body proportions which are known to vary with sex, or the nonmetric innominate features identified by Phenice (1969).

The Phenice method of innominate evaluation for sex examines presence or absence of the ventral arc, the subpubic concavity, and the breadth of the ischiopubic ramus. The technique offers 96 percent accuracy when two out of the three variables are assessed unambiguously. A more recent evaluation of Phenice's technique confirmed its reliability (Kelley 1978). A review of the subpubic angle may also be added to the analysis. In addition, dorsal pitting at the pubic symphysis (parity trauma) and development of the preauricular sulcus may add weight to a female identification. Although a recent analysis questioned the association of parity and dorsal pitting of the pubic symphysis (Holt 1978), most researchers agree that the two are associated (Ashworth et al. 1976; Kelley 1979; Putschar 1976; Suchey et al. 1979). It has also been established that the preauricular sulcus is an even more reliable indicator of parity, and, therefore, sex (Houghton 1974; Kelly 1979).

The other method of sexing that seems to be free from size bias is the analysis of innominate proportions. This involves the use of indices in which one measure is typically larger in females (pubis length or sciatic notch depth) and the other measure is typically larger in males (ischial length or cotylosciatic breadth). The value of the ischialpubic index for sexing has been demonstrated by several authors (Hamilton 1975; Hanna and Washburn 1953; Thieme and Schull 1957; Washburn 1948, 1949). A. H. Schultz (1930) was one of the first to suggest comparing this relationship. He defined a landmark in the acetabulum from which both pubis and ischium lengths are taken. As several workers have pointed out, the acetabular landmark is difficult to identify in the mature innominate (Brothwell 1972; Stewart 1954). Observers may vary as to where they choose to locate this landmark (Hamilton 1975), but as long as all skeletons in the same series are measured consistently, the ischiopubic index will remain a valuable tool for sexing without size bias. In addition to the ischiopubic index, Olivier (1969) has suggested an index comparing cotylosciatic breadth (acetabulosciatic breadth) and sciatic notch depth which can be used in conjunction with the ischialpubic index to evaluate areas of overlap that will occur with the use of the first index. The two indices are not necessarily correlated because growth in the pubis and growth of the sciatic notch are controlled by apparently independent systems (Washburn 1949; Coleman 1969).

In the best of all possible worlds, skeletons are recovered complete and intact and provide the osteologist with extremely accurate sex identifications. In real life, skeletal material is often incomplete and fragmentary. However, with adequate sample sizes it is often possible to evaluate part of the sample using some or all of the nonmetric criteria plus one or several innominate proportions. This subsample can then be used to evaluate other measures of proportion shared by both the complete and incomplete subsamples.

This method of comparing subsamples may follow several steps, depending upon the nature of the sample to be sexed. If an adequate number of intact innominates is available they may be sexed using the nonmetric criteria. This accurately sexed subsample is then plotted for the ischiopubic and/or cotylosciatic index. For both indices there will be areas of overlap between males and females. In general, the area of overlap will fall between the means of the two sexes. In any case, the area of overlap is divided into quartiles and the percentage of males or females is calculated for each quartile (Hamilton 1975; Wolpoff 1975, 1976b). These percentages can then be used as probability statements for the likelihood of correctly sexing individuals from the subsample which cannot be evaluated using nonmetric criteria. In this situation, individual specimens that are still ambiguous after comparison with the sexed sample can be eliminated since the decision is based on ambiguous proportions rather than size. If proportions are not used to compare the sexed and unsexed subsamples, ambiguous individuals should be split evenly between male and female samples. This procedure introduces error, but an elimination of individuals ambiguous for size will only inflate the dimorphism estimate.

Frayer (1978) used morphological features of the cranium when postcranial material was not availale in his study samples. Discriminant function analysis suggested that several individuals were misclassified but Frayer kept the original sex identification and noted that probable error seemed to be equal in both directions (1978). In the case of Frayer's study, he double checked his results by calculating sexual dimorphism for his sexed sample based on the innominate, and compared this with his larger sample that included specimens sexed with cranial morphology. The smaller innominate sexed sample displayed more dimorphism than the larger sample. Thus, Frayer was able to demonstrate that his estimates for sexual dimorphism were conservative. Whenever it is necessary to use size-related variables to determine sex, the osteologist should avoid using the measurements that will be used to calculate dimorphism (Frayer

1978, 1980). In all cases some attempt should be made to estimate the magnitude of error in sexing, and estimates of dimorphism should be evaluated on this basis. This is especially important when using data collected by others from periods which predate the recent improvements in sexing techniques (Bass 1969, 1979).

If the condition of a sample is such that sexing cannot be achieved without the use of size-related information, then discriminant function analysis (Giles 1970), canonical analysis, or hierarchical grouping analysis (Alexander 1976) may be used with the accompanying statements of error probability. The major limitation associated with these procedures is the requirement that there be no missing variables. Sexing on the basis of size-related features alone is not nearly as satisfactory as the nonmetric innominate information. However, since the alternative is doing no analysis at all, most investigators would rather make the attempt, but their estimates should always be viewed as a degree more speculative than those based on nonmetric sexing criteria. In the use of discriminant analysis or other related statistical techniques, osteologists should attempt to use an array of measurements which do not repeat information about sex differences (Kowalski 1972).

Traditional statistical sexing has usually employed closely related traits, such as an array of cranial traits (Alexander 1976; Giles 1970) or femur traits (Pons 1955). Special attention should be paid to recent works that have identified sexually significant variation in the foot (Steele 1976), dental root lengths (Garn, Cole, and Van Alstine 1979) or mid-shaft femur circumferance (Black 1978; DiBennardo and Taylor 1979). Depending on the structure of the data set, the investigator may wish to retain the last measurement for the actual measure of dimorphism since it is a highly significant measurement (Hamilton 1975). Some authors have suggested that multivariate analysis should not be limited to a list of traits that have been traditionally chosen because of their significance in univariate statistical tests for male-female sex differences (Van Gerven 1972; Van Gerven and Oakland 1974). Through principal components analysis Van Gerven has demonstrated that such widely used measurements all have a tendency to separate out into a single eigenvector which can be characterized as size variation with a high positive correlation between size-dependent features (1972). Van Gerven enhances his analysis with the use of measurements that reflect shape variation in the femur (Van Gerven 1972; Van Gerven and Oakland 1974). This sexually significant shape variation reflects sex differences in the biomechanics of hip function, that, in turn, are directly related to wide female pelvis breadth and reproductive function. Mechanically significant measurements have also been taken from the pelvis (Gustav 1972). Since the collection of certain mechanically significant measurements may be time consuming, the size and condition of the data set may ultimately determine whether or not it is worth it.

In the worst of all possible worlds, a sample of skeletal material may be so fragmentary and incomplete that estimates of sexual dimorphism are theoretically impossible. Indeed, such a sample may be so small as to necessitate sexing the material on the basis of measurements that will also be used to estimate dimorphism (Wolpoff 1975; 1976a,b). There are very few situations where such a procedure might be justified, but the early hominid fossil record may be one such case. In most studies of australopithecine dimorphism, ranges of variation for samples of unknown sex ratio were compared with samples of living humans and nonhuman primates (Brace 1973; Tobias 1971; Zihlman 1976). This approach is safer than the actual estimation of sex and dimorphism but lack of knowledge about sex ratio may bias results. As usual, the results should always be considered tentative because new discoveries added to small sample sizes can change established ranges of variation for the fossil sample and thus conclusions about the magnitude of sex differences. A lack of consensus about genus and species identification also introduced doubt and resulted in different dimorphism estimates for early hominid populations. Thus, while Brace (1973) and Wolpoff (1976a,b) combined the australopithecine sample producing variation comparable to the most dimorphic nonhuman primates, Zihlman (1976) used samples from single sites or areas to evaluate variation comparable to the small magnitude of dimorphism in pygmy chimpanzees.

The boldest attempt to estimate dimorphism was done by Wolpoff (1976a,b). Wolpoff sexed a combined sample of australopithecine specimens on the basis of a bimodal distribution for canine breadth. Working first with chimpanzee and gorilla distributions for this measure Wolpoff demonstrated a low degree of error for a dimorphism estimate. Wolpoff validated the bimodal distribution by testing for normalcy and not finding it. In Wolpoff's work, the presence of bimodality is crucial to his sexing procedure but would not be applicable to more recent populations of Pleistocene human material (Wolpoff, 1975, 1976b). The validity of bimodality for Wolpoff's sample has been questioned by a number of authors who argued that the sample was simply highly skewed (Trinkaus 1976); that the apparent bimodal distribution was an artifact of the class intervals used (Siegel 1976); and that the bimodality may be attributable to the presence of more than one genus in the sample (Murad 1976). Recent revisions of the early fossil record have shown that the combined australopithecine sample has no taxonomic reality (White and Harris

1977; Johanson and White 1979; Leakey and Walker 1976). However, certain subsamples of this group, such as the Swartkrans sample, still show apparent bimodality (Robinson 1956). As fossil discoveries accumulate it may still be possible to estimate dimorphism for the Plio-Pleistocene genera and species using Wolpoff's approach, if bimodality is apparent and if it is reasonable to believe that sex is responsible for the bimodality. Since these estimates will still be speculative they will have to be supplemented with theoretical expectations about early hominid dimorphism based on evidence for factors that influence dimorphism, such as sexual competition, cultural practices, and predation in the fossil record (Hamilton 1981; Issac 1978; Tanner and Zihlman 1976; Zihlman and Tanner 1978).

One unresolved problem associated with a dental investigation of sexual dimorphism in fossil hominids is the assumption that sexual dimorphism measures in the teeth reflect sexual dimorphism for body size (Post, Goldstein, and Melnick 1978). A brief survey of the literature reveals considerable confusion on this point, and this area should be considered fertile ground for any interested graduate students looking for research topics!

To begin with, there is a growing awareness that dental size can be affected by such environmental variables as nutritional stress in the same manner that these forces affect growth in body size. Heritability of tooth size is lower than was traditionally assumed (Garn, Osborne, and McCabe 1979; Townsend and Brown 1978). Experiments with androgenized female monkeys have shown the role of androgens in male dental growth (Zingeser and Phoenix 1978), and sexual dimorphism in the dentition derives from prolonged enamel deposition in males (Moss and Moss-Salentijn 1977). Using data from the National Collaborative Perinatal Project, Garn, Osborne, and McCabe (1979) note that small dental size is associated with maternal hypertension, low birth weight, and small birth length, while maternal diabetes is associated with high birth weight and a large dentition. The dynamics of dental and body growth during environmental stress require further investigation.

More relevant to this discussion is the question of correlation between sexual dimorphism for the dentition and body size. This problem should not be confused with the question of correlation between tooth size and body size (Garn et al. 1967). For tooth and body size the results are mixed. Some studies show a low or insignificant relationship between dental size and body height in humans (Garn and Lewis 1958; Henderson and Corruccini 1976). Other studies have shown a significant correlation between long bone lengths (plus some diameter measurements) and dental size in macaques (Lauer 1975), and humans and apes (Lavelle 1977). For comparisons across species some have shown significant correlations between dental size and body weight for 6 species of hominoid primates (Gingerich 1977), and 29 species of ceropithecoids (Goldstein, Post, and Melnick 1978). In a sample of American Caucasians, Anderson, Thompson, and Popovitch (1977) showed a correlation between tooth size and body weight for only the males in their sample.

If it is possible to demonstrate a relationship between dental size, body weight, and possibly linear measurements, one would assume that sexual dimorphism for the dentition and body size would also correlate. However, the two could be correlated with a third variable producing an apparent relationship between the first two measurements (Post 1980). Thus while Garn et al. (1967) have shown a weak correlation between sexual dimorphism for dental size and stature in sister-brother pairs, Post, Goldstein, and Melnick (1978) found no relationship between body weight and dimorphism and either incisor width or postcanine area dimorphism in a sample of 29 cercopithecoid species. Instead, dietary class (folivore, frugivore, omnivore) explained more variability in dental dimorphism than did sexual dimorphism for body weight. In contrast, Brace and Ryan (1980) dismiss the role of diet in the expression of dental dimorphism in humans, noting the lack of data in an area which needs to be investigated for human populations. Post, Goldstein, and Melnick (1978) suggest that the higher degree of dental dimorphism in omnivores feeding on a wider variety of food items could indeed be attributable to a greater opportunity for intersexual feeding-niche separation. These authors caution against immediate acceptance of this speculation noting the paucity of data documenting sex difference in food preference (i.e., Post 1978) and the need for more studies. They also point to problems in assigning dietary class and of relating high dental dimorphism in large animals with omnivory or large size. The work of Post and his colleagues should be considered mandatory for anyone wishing to investigate this area further.

AGE AT DEATH

Age may influence estimates of dimorphism in two ways. First, measurements of dimorphism may show a tendency to change in a secular manner with each generation. It is most unlikely that secular trend would be discernible within skeletal groups since such samples are usually limited in numbers and temporally diffuse. However, it is possible, in theory at least, that an archaeological site might contain enough information to identify subsamples of skeletal material associated with limited time periods. In such a situation, it would be prudent to compare the subsamples for significant differences before lumping them together. Although it is most often impossible to control for secular trend within skeletal collections, it should not be ignored when temporal subsamples are defined within a single site.

The second age influence derives from the change in skeletal dimensions with aging in each individual. Continuing bone remodeling after 20 years of age and throughout life has been demonstrated for the cranium and face (Israel 1973, 1977), the mandible (Hunter and Garn 1972), the femur (Smith and Walker 1964), and the second metacarpal (Garn et al. 1967, 1968, 1972). Examining 41 roentgenographic measurements, Israel (1973) demonstrated increases in craniofacial dimensions ranging from 0 percent to 22 percent. He did not test specifically for sex differences in this change, but his data demonstrate a definite increase in size with a tendency for females to gain slightly more on the basis of the few anthropometric measurements compared by sex (Israel, 1977). Ruff (1980) has also documented this change for Indian Knoll males. Hunter and Garn (1972) have demonstrated changes in the pattern of sexual dimorphism for the mandible with aging. There is no consistent pattern of one sex declining or increasing relatively more when each of 10 roentogenographic and anthropometric measurements is considered. However, the overall pattern involves an increase in dimorphism with age, particularly in the gonial area (Hunter and Garn 1972). Garn and his co-workers have demonstrated continuing subperiosteal apposition in the second metacarpal, with females gaining relatively more as they age (Garn et al. 1967, 1968, 1972). A six-decade period adds up to a 4 percent increase in metacarpal diameter for females. For the same time period, males average about 1.5 percent (Garn et al. 1968). When the data are broken into decades it can be seen that this process starts in the twenties and continues throughout life. It is not an exclusively postmenopausal phenomenon (Garn et al. 1968). Smith and Walker (1964) demonstrated an 11 percent gain in periosteal femoral diameter in a female sample aged 45-90. There is no male-female comparison in this study, but other sources imply that the pattern of sex difference found in the second metacarpal may be repeated in other long bones (Garn et al. 1972).

There are two sorts of errors which might result from such an influence. First, within a population, males and females should have similar age distributions. Since females apparently gain relatively more long bone diameter than males with age, they are essentially gaining on males in certain measurements. This type of change does not affect long bone lengths (Garn et al. 1972). A comparison of male and female samples in which there was an excessive number of very young or very old females could, theoretically, distort the estimate of dimorphism. Long bone diameters and circumferences can be highly significant in dimorphism comparisons (Hamilton 1975). Since estimates are likely to employ these measurements, researchers should test for such effects when using them. An example from my own work (Hamilton 1975) is the Indian Knoll collection housed at the University of Kentucky. The data set collected included a female sample which consisted of 69 percent in the decade aged 21 to 30 compared to 43 percent in the male sample. Table 5.1 shows a comparison of dimorphism calculations using the formula:

$$\frac{\text{Male mean} - \text{Female mean}}{\text{Female mean}} \times 100$$

Several types of measurements are compared for the original unbalanced sample and a balanced sample in which 25 percent of the younger female skeletons were randomly deleted.* For size and length measures (such as ischial length, humerus length, or humerus head diameter) the difference is minor, while the femur diameter and clavicle circumference show larger differences which might reflect this effect. The differences in dimorphism between the two samples are small, but since the ultimate comparisons of

TABLE 5.1

Percent Sexual Dimorphism Scores Influenced by Continuing Subperiosteal Apposition.

Measurements	Sample Unbalanced for Age by Sex	Sample Balanced for Age by Sex	Difference
Ischial length	8.91	8.68	0.23
Humerus length	8.65	8.65	0
Humerus head diameter	14.58	14.06	0.52
Midshaft femur diameter (anterior-posterior)	16.66	15.96	0.70
Clavicle circumference	22.08	21.04	1.04

Note: Percent sexual dimorphism scores for selected measurements comparing an unbalanced sample, heavily weighted with very young females, with an age-balanced sample from which 25 percent of the younger female skeletons have been randomly deleted. The circumference measurements are more affected by continuing subperiosteal apposition than are width and length measurements.

*An appendix lists descriptions and sources for all measurements used in this study.

interpopulation differences in dimorphism are also small, every attempt should be made to eliminate noise from the data.

Another age effect which might appear in archaeological samples is a tendency for size to increase or decrease by decade (Pfeiffer 1980). This may be attributable to secular influences in temporally limited samples or it may reflect a pattern of larger or smaller individuals selectively surviving into their later decades. The archaeological context rarely allows for a detailed interpretation of such a pattern, but balancing the samples for age distribution will also control for such influences.

Just as continuing bone remodeling or secular patterns may distort the estimate of intrapopulation sex differences, so too it may affect interpopulation comparisons. Populations that are to be compared with each other for differences in the magnitude of dimorphism should be examined for similarities in age distributions. It is not always possible to match archaeological samples precisely for age, but observers should be alert for such an influence if the samples are markedly different from each other.

MEASUREMENTS

Studies of sexual dimorphism have employed a diverse array of measurements. In many cases the choice of measurements will be determined by the fragmentary nature of the skeletal sample. Thus, studies that include Pleistocene samples invariably use dental dimensions (Brace 1973; Brace and Ryan 1980; Frayer 1978, 1980; Wolpoff 1975, 1976a,b) or perhaps measurements of the mandibular corpus (Wolpoff 1975, 1976b).

When the skeletal sample allows a choice, several factors should be considered. While studies of living nonhuman primates and humans employ weight (Crook 1972; Post 1980) or body length (stature in humans) (Crook 1972; Eveleth 1975; Hall 1978), these dimensions are not readily available to the osteologist. A reconstruction of stature using long bone lengths may introduce error inherent in the estimate (Trotter and Gleser, 1958). Variation in stature may originate from any component of the body and may conceal variation of interest in a dimorphism study. Hall has also noted that stature incorporates numerous genotypic and phenotypic influences making the results more difficult to interpret (Hall 1978). Stature estimates may be interesting because they give a perspective on overall physical size when compared to our own, but they are not appropriate for studies of dimorphism in skeletal samples.

Within the skull, facial and mandibular measurements are usually more dimorphic than cranial dimensions, but there are several problems which may present themselves with craniofacial measurements. Related to aging, attention should be paid to the potential influence of tooth loss and consequent remodeling in the mandible and maxilla. Also related to remodeling in the craniofacial skeleton is the practice of cranial deformation. This practice has the potential of influencing facial and mandibular growth as suggested by an analysis of cranial deformation and facial height measurements by Schendel, Walker, and Kamisugi (1980). Some have avoided the problem of cranial deformation by simply not using craniofacial measurements (Hamilton 1975). Since methods of cranial deformation differ from one population to the next (Moss 1958) and the practice may vary with social class (Briggs and Sancho 1952), it may be best to avoid using such material until we are able to fully assess the impact of this cultural practice on craniofacial growth.

Within the postcranial skeleton long bone lengths will yield significant differences (Hamilton 1975; Key 1980) but articular surfaces, bone diameters, and circumferences are usually more significant, as Table 5.1 demonstrates (Dorsey 1897; Dwight 1905; Hamilton 1975). As noted above, most studies of sexual differences in the skeleton have focused on size variables and have ignored highly significant shape differences (Van Gerven 1972; Van Gerven and Oakland 1974). Femoral angles and articulated pelvis measurements are time consuming but they may provide significant information.

Another approach to the postcranial skeleton which has worked well is the use of subjective evaluations of muscle robusticity for structures like the deltoid tuberosity (Hamilton 1975). Figure 5.1 presents five grades for variation in the deltoid tuberosity as I have observed it in nine different populations of precontact Amerindian groups who range in subsistence activity from maritime hunter-gatherers to lower-class urban merchants. Only the most complete samples are used in detail for this chapter. In addition to the Indian Knoll collection and the four groups in Tables 5.2 to 5.6, I scored deltoid tuberosities for a collection of maritime hunters from British Columbia, early agriculturalists from Tlatilco, an early urban site at Cuicuilco, and urban residents of Tlatelolco (adjacent to Tenochititlán). The last three collections are all from the Valley of Mexico (Hamilton 1975). Tables 5.2 through 5.5 present deltoid tuberosity score distributions by sex for four sequential samples from the Lower Illinois River Valley, and associated chi-square values (see Table 5.6 for archaeological information on these populations). Mean scores for males and females were calculated by treating the ordinal values as an interval scale, with values of 1 to 5. For each site a ratio of male to

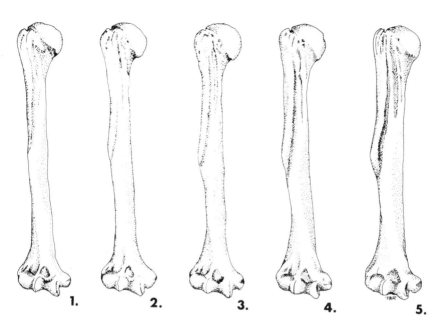

Figure 5.1.   Five grades for robusticity of the deltoid tuberosity. Grade 1: Line of muscle attachment for m. deltoideus and m. pectoralis major is visible without a raised surface. Lateral border of the humerus approximates a straight line. Grade 2: Line of muscle attachment is a slight raised ridge and lateral border shows slight protuberance. Grade 3: Ridge of muscle attachment shows medium relief with a noticeable protrusion of the lateral border. Grade 4: Ridge of muscle attachment shows marked roughness with marked protrusion of the lateral border. Grade 5: Relief of muscle attachment and lateral protrusion is highly developed to the point of giving the shaft an appearance of extreme torsion.

TABLE 5.2
Robusticity of the Deltoid Tuberosity at Gibson-Klunk by Sex.

	Females $N = 56$	Males $N = 41$
1-slight	11	0
2-medium	26	9
3-large	17	15
4-marked	2	16
5-extreme	0	1

Note: Percent sexual dimorphism for 12 metric measurements: 11.93; male score = 3.22; female score = 2.18; ratio = 1.48; chi-square = 29.7; $df = 4$; significance = P 0.001.

TABLE 5.3
Robusticity of the Deltoid Tuberosity at Koster by Sex.

	Females $N = 33$	Males $N = 29$
1-slight	1	0
2-medium	11	0
3-large	12	10
4-marked	8	16
5-extreme	1	3

Note: Percent sexual dimorphism for 12 metric measurements: 10.19; male score = 3.76; female score = 2.91; ratio = 1.29; chi-square = 15.6; $df = 4$; significance = P 0.001.

TABLE 5.4
Robusticity of the Deltoid Tuberosity at Late Woodland Schild by Sex.

	Females $N = 29$	Males $N = 20$
1-slight	1	0
2-medium	11	2
3-large	10	6
4-marked	7	9
5-extreme	0	3

Note: Percent sexual dimorphism for 12 metric measurements: 12.27; male score = 3.65; female score = 2.79; ratio = 1.31; chi-square = 10.2; $df = 4$; significance = P 0.04.

TABLE 5.5
Robusticity of the Deltoid Tuberosity at Mississippian Schild by Sex.

	Females $N = 43$	Males $N = 39$
1-slight	0	0
2-medium	14	4
3-large	18	16
4-marked	10	15
5-extreme	1	4

Note: Percent sexual dimorphism for 12 metric measurements: 9.48; male score = 3.49; female score = 2.95; ratio = 1.18; chi-square = 8.3; $df = 4$; significance = $P < 0.05$.

TABLE 5.6
Illinois River Valley Sample.

Site and Location	Archaeological Level and Approximate dates	Subsistence	Average Sample Sizes	
Gibson & Pete Klunk mounds; Calhoun County, Illinois	Middle Woodland 160 B.C.-A.D. 400 (Buikstra 1972; Crane & Griffin 1963; Tainter 1975)	Hunting plus "intensive harvesting and collecting" (Montet-White 1968; Parmalee, Paloumpis, & Wilson 1972; Struever & Vickery 1973)	Females = 55 Males = 40	
Koster mound group; Greene County, Illinois	Late Woodland A.D. 630-670 (Crane & Griffin 1966; Tainter 1975)	Hunting plus "intensive harvesting and collecting" (Ford 1974; Munson 1973; Parmalee, Paloumpis, & Wilson 1972; Struever & Vickery 1973)	Females = 28 Males = 26	
Schild mound group; Greene County, Illinois	Late Woodland A.D. 720-840 (Tainter 1975)	Early maize-squash agriculture and continued hunting and gathering (Asch & Asch 1977; Ford 1974; Munson 1973; Tainter 1975)	Females = 27 Males = 19	
Schild cemetery; Greene County, Illinois	Mississippian A.D. 940-1190 (Crane & Griffin 1966; Perino 1971)	Maize-beans-squash agriculture and selective hunting and gathering (Asch & Asch 1977; Griffin 1967; Smith 1974, 1975)	Females = 42 Males = 39	

female average robusticity scores was calculated for comparison with average percent sexual dimorphism of metric traits. These data are included in the tables. In some cases there is agreement. The Mississippian Schild group has the lowest average metric dimorphism and lowest ratio of male and female deltoid score. For both types of measurement this is brought about by an increase in female size relative to the previous sample (Late Woodland Schild) and a decrease in male size (see Table 5.7). In other cases, such as the transition from Koster to Late Woodland Schild, male and female deltoid scores show approximately the same decline resulting in similar ratios at both sites. At the same time, metric changes (Table 5.8) show an increase in dimorphism relative to Koster brought about chiefly by a decline in female size. Like sexual dimorphism in the dentition, changes in dimorhism of muscularity do not always correlate with changes in dimorphism of skeletal size. The dynamics of sexual differences in phenotypic responses to environmental influences for dental, skeletal, and muscular systems require further investigation.

The deltoid tuberosity score and other evaluations of muscularity could offer insights into activity patterns. For this sample, changes in female arm muscle mass may be related to changes in food preparation while male changes may be related to weapons use. Both of these speculations require corroboration from the archaeological record which is not currently available. Sampling problems may also

TABLE 5.7

A Summary of Change in Percent Sexual Dimorphism and Male and Female Size in the Transition from Late Woodland Schild to Mississippian Schild.

Measurement	Change in Percent Sexual Dimorphism	Change in Female Size	Change in Male Size
Ischial length	−4.6	+1.3	−2.3
Cotylosciatic width	−1.7	+0.1	−0.5
Bicondylar femur length	−4.6	+14.0	−4.0
Humerus length	+0.7	−3.0	−1.0
Clavicle length	−0.7	−1.0	−2.0
Humerus epicondylar width	−2.9	+0.7	−0.8
Humerus head diameter	−2.4	+0.3	−0.6
Humerus articular width	−3.7	−0.3	−1.8
Femur head diameter	−2.8	+0.4	−0.7
Clavicle circumference	−3.4	+0.5	−0.5
Ant./post. femur shaft diameter	−1.9	+0.2	−0.3
First metatarsal circumference	−5.5	+0.5	−1.7

TABLE 5.8

A Summary of Change in Percent Sexual Dimorphism and Male and Female Size in the Transition from Koster to Late Woodland Schild.

Measurement	Change in Percent Sexual Dimorphism	Change in Female Size	Change in Male Size
Ischial length	+2.2	−0.4	+1.3
Cotylosciatic width	−1.0	−0.4	−0.8
Bicondylar femur length	+3.5	− 5.0	+9.0
Humerus length	+0.3	−2.0	−1.0
Clavicle length	+0.4	0	+0.5
Humerus epicondylar width	+2.3	−1.4	−0.3
Humerus head diameter	+2.0	−1.5	−0.9
Humerus articular width	+2.0	−1.0	+0.1
Femur head diameter	+3.5	−1.1	+0.2
Clavicle circumference	+3.6	−1.0	0
Ant./post. femur shaft diameter	−0.3	+0.4	+0.4
First metatarsal circumference	+5.4	−0.8	+1.3

be associated with this data set and these are discussed in the section on specific examples in interpretation.

STATISTICS

Just as dimorphism studies have varied in the choice of measurements, so they also vary in their approach to statistical analysis. Most studies include a percent sexual dimorphism score. This score may represent the female mean as a percentage of the male mean (Crook 1972; Wolpoff 1975, 1976a,b); the male mean as a percentage of the female mean (Wolpoff 1975, 1976b); or the difference between the means weighted by the mean of one sex (Frayer 1978; Hamilton 1975, this chapter; Zihlman 1976), the sum of the two sexual means (Key 1980), or the mean of the combined sample (Wolpoff 1975, 1976b). For any one data set comparing different subsamples, each type of percentage score will rank the subsamples from least to most dimorphic the same way (Hamilton 1975). When the samples to be compared for differences in dimorphism have significantly different variances, the difference between male and female means may be weighted by the standard deviation of the combined sample (Hamilton 1975; Himes and Malina 1977; Wolpoff 1975, 1976b). It is often helpful to present percentage scores or scores weighted by variance in a visual manner as illustrated in Figures 5.2 through 5.13.

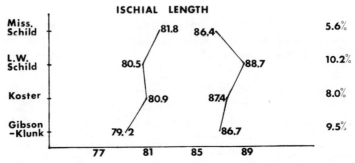

Figure 5.2. Ischial length. A comparison of female means (left) and male means (right) between four skeletal samples from the Lower Illinois River Valley. Percent sexual dimorphism is at the far right.

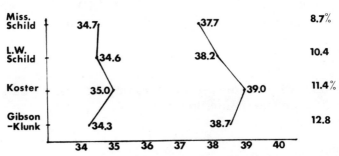

Figure 5.3. Cotylo-Sciatic width. A comparison of female means (left) and male means (right) between four skeletal samples from the Lower Illinois River Valley. Percent sexual dimorphism is at the far right.

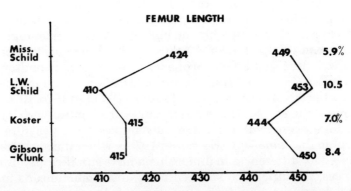

Figure 5.4. Femur length. A comparison of female means (left) and male means (right) between four skeletal samples from the Lower Illinois River Valley. Percent sexual dimorphism is at the far right.

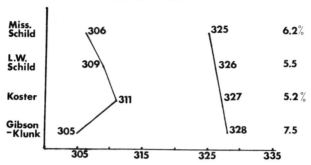

Figure 5.5. Humerus length. A comparison of female means (left) and male means (right) between four skeletal samples from the Lower Illinois River Valley. Percent sexual dimorphism is at the far right.

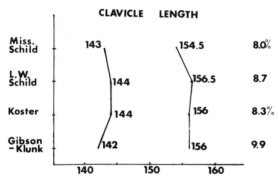

Figure 5.6. Clavicle length. A comparison of female means (left) and male means (right) between four skeletal samples from the Lower Illinois River Valley. Percent sexual dimorphism is at the far right.

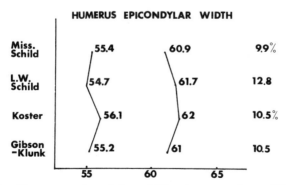

Figure 5.7. Humerus epicondylar width. A comparison of female means (left) and male means (right) between four skeletal samples from the Lower Illinois River Valley. Percent sexual dimorphism is at the far right.

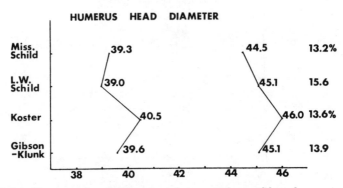

Figure 5.8. Humerus head diameter. A comparison of female means (left) and male means (right) between four skeletal samples from the Lower Illinois River Valley. Percent sexual dimorphism is at the far right.

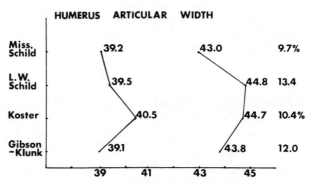

Figure 5.9. Humerus articular width. A comparison of female means (left) and male means (right) between four skeletal samples from the Lower Illinois River Valley. Percent sexual dimorphism is at the far right.

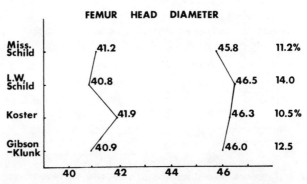

Figure 5.10. Femur head diameter. A comparison of female means (left) and male means (right) between four skeletal samples from the Lower Illinois River Valley. Percent sexual dimorphism is at the far right.

126

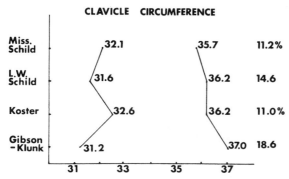

Figure 5.11. Clavicle circumference. A comparison of female means (left) and male means (right) between four skeletal samples from the Lower Illinois River Valley. Percent sexual dimorphism is at the far right.

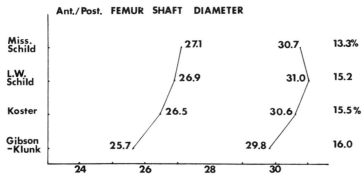

Figure 5.12. Anterior/posterior femur shaft diameter. A comparison of female means (left) and male means (right) between four skeletal samples from the Lower Illinois River Valley. Percent sexual dimorphism is at the far right.

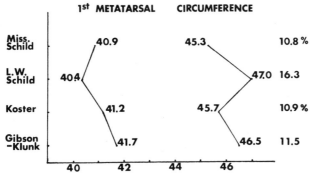

Figure 5.13. First metatarsal circumference. A comparison of female means (left) and male means (right) between four skeletal samples from the Lower Illinois River Valley. Percent sexual dimorphism is at the far right.

127

In addition, Simpson (1941) developed a ratio diagram which can also be used to illustrate sexual dimorphism (Thieme and Schull 1957). Table 5.9 and Figure 5.14 show the differences between the logarithms of the means of males and females in four populations. One sex is arbitrarily assigned a value of zero (in this case males) and the difference of the logarithms of the means is plotted against the standard zero. If females were simply scaled-down males with similar proportions, the line representing variation in their measurements would be vertical or nearly so. To the degree that the line departs from verticality there are sexual differences in the proportions of the

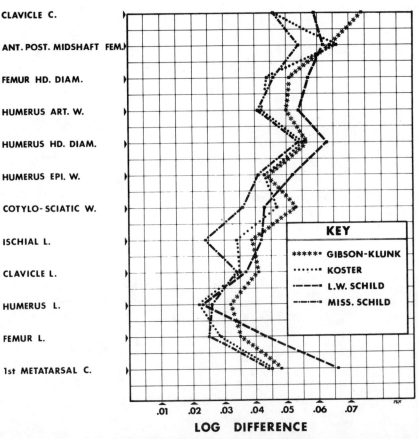

MEASUREMENTS

CLAVICLE C.

ANT. POST. MIDSHAFT FEM.

FEMUR HD. DIAM.

HUMERUS ART. W.

HUMERUS HD. DIAM.

HUMERUS EPI. W.

COTYLO-SCIATIC W.

ISCHIAL L.

CLAVICLE L.

HUMERUS L.

FEMUR L.

1st METATARSAL C.

KEY

***** GIBSON-KLUNK
.... KOSTER
— — — L.W. SCHILD
—·—·— MISS. SCHILD

.01   .02   .03   .04   .05   .06   .07

LOG DIFFERENCE

Figure 5.14.   Log differences between the means of males and females for 12 measurements in four skeletal samples from the Lower Illiois River Valley. Difference in logarithms of the means are plotted against the standard zero arbitrarily assigned to males (see text and Table 5.7).

TABLE 5.9

Sample Table Showing Measurement Means, Common Logarithms (Base 10), and Log Differences for Twelve Measurements Shown in Figure 5.14 from the Gibson-Klunk Mound Group.

Measurement	Male Mean	Female Mean	Log Male Mean	Log Female Mean	Log Difference
Clavicle circumference	37.0	31.2	1.568	1.494	0.074
Ant./post. femur shaft diameter	29.8	25.7	1.474	1.410	0.064
Femur head diameter	46.0	40.9	1.663	1.612	0.051
Humerus articular width	43.8	39.1	1.642	1.592	0.050
Humerus head diameter	45.1	39.6	1.654	1.598	0.056
Humerus epicondylar width	61.0	55.2	1.785	1.742	0.043
Cotylosciatic width	38.7	34.3	1.588	1.535	0.053
Ischial length	86.7	79.2	1.938	1.899	0.039
Clavicle length	156.0	142.0	2.193	2.152	0.041
Humerus length	328.0	305.0	2.516	2.484	0.032
Bicondylar femur length	450.0	415.0	2.653	2.618	0.035
First metatarsal circumference	46.5	41.7	1.668	1.620	0.048

measurements used. Simpson developed this technique to compare different paleontological samples for probable species differences, but it also works well for sexual comparisons (Thieme and Schull 1957). Simpson provides a more detailed description of the method (1941).

Beyond the tabular and visual presentation of within population sex differences some studies have attempted to test for statistical significance. In some cases the student's t-test or the Mann-Whitney U are used to confirm sex differences within each group compared (Almquist 1974; Frayer 1978; Hamilton 1975; Wolpoff 1975, 1976b).

To test whether demonstrated differences in the magnitude of dimorphism are statistically significant between populations there are a number of univariate and multivariate techniques. Eveleth (1975) used regression analysis to compare sex differences in height means on sex average of height means for a large number of populations sampled from five different ethnic groups defined by continent. The regression lines for each ethnic group were tested for parallelism and coincidence in order to examine the significance of differences in the pattern of sexual dimorphism for stature between each ethnic group. Eveleth's "ethnic groups" are quite large and probably conceal significant variation within each class. However, the statistical technique is interesting and could probably yield more meaningful results using data that had more biological reality with better control over genotypic and phenotypic factors which influence sexual dimorphism. Hall also used regression analysis comparing differences between male and female means with male mean, female mean, and the midpoint between the two averages. Hall's purpose was not to test for significant population differences but to examine the relative contributions of males and females to variation in sexual dimorphism (Hall 1978). Key (1980) used percent sexual dimorphism scores from 101 European skeletal samples and regressed them on the sample dates ranging from Mesolithic to late Medieval periods. While his linear regression of the index of sexual dimorphism on site data was highly significant, an analysis of variance of index of dimorphism means by cultural period approached but did not achieve significance (Key 1980).

I have also used analysis of variance to test for the significance of sex differences between populations. For a data set composed of several populations represented by both sexes, the variance of all the observations is partitioned into parts and each part represents variance originating in a specific source. Analysis of variance examines variance with each cell (population #1 females, #1 males, #2 females, etc.) plus variance due to sex and population effects. There is also a sum of squares value for interaction which measures a lack of additivity of sex and population effects. The interaction value is the focus of interest in tests for significant dimorphism differences. The hypothesis being tested is that the sex and population effects are additive, i.e., that there is no interaction. If the effects are additive, it means that each cell has a mean to which is added an effect due to sex identification and an effect due to population identification. This should account for all variability. If it does not, the sex and population effects have synergistic interaction. A significant F ratio is obtained for the interaction value and we reject the hypothesis that there is no interaction. In other words, the population an individual is placed in does have an effect on the magnitude of sex differences.

Analysis of variance comparing the four populations listed in Table 5.6 for 12 measurements yielded very few statistically significant F ratios for interaction. While it may be prudent to test for statistically significant differences in the magnitude of dimorphism between populations, the actual differences are often very small and the quality of the analysis may be limited further by small sample sizes. In such cases the *consistency* of change in dimorphism between the populations compared for a number of different measurements may be all that supports the contention that the demonstrated differences are real (Figures 5.2 through 5.13).

The past decade has witnessed an ongoing debate over the usefulness and misapplication of multivariate statistical techniques (N. A. Campbell 1978; Corruccini 1975; Howells 1969; Kowalski 1972; Rightmire 1969; Van Gerven 1972; Van Gerven and Oakland 1974; Vark 1976). In favor of multivariate approaches Howells (1969) argues:

> If you measure an individual (or a skull) in N measurements, you have . . . mathematically speaking a vector of measurements to represent him. If then each of the N measurements is simply used by itself . . . the individual vector is dismembered. . . .Nor is a population vector created in the process. The statistics are simply those of . . . a vector for measurement x determined by m individuals. . . . This is the fundamental limitation of univariate statistics: There is no real vector or profile representing either individuals or populations. [P. 312]

In response to Howells, Kowalski (1972) has remarked:

> Test statistics often turn out to be complicated functions which do not have intuitive value as summaries of the informational content of the data from which they are computed. [P. 120]

Individual observers will ultimately have to decide for themselves whether or not to use multivariate precedures and the characteristics of their data must be considered in this decision.

The use of multivariate techniques requires high quality data. Most statistical experts agree that the main problem associated with multivariate analyses in biological anthropology derives from a failure to consider certain features of the data set that may affect the quality of the results. Skeletons with missing variables cannot be used, and therefore individuals may be lost from the sample. Measurements to be used in the analysis must be chosen with care. As Kowalski points out "the inclusion of 'noise' variables in the analysis can have a deleterious effect on the sensitivity of the procedure" (Kowalski 1972, p. 121). Van Gerven made this point when he improved the sexual discrimination of a sample from 86.6 to 92.8 percent by first running a test of principal components to select variables with separate information about sex differences (Van Gerven 1972; Van Gerven and Oakland 1974). If statements of statistical significance are sought, the samples should be checked for normality (Campbell 1978). Perhaps even more important, the samples to be compared should be checked for homogeneity of covariance or dispersion (Campbell 1978; Corruccini 1975). Skeletal data are particularly vulnerable to these flaws.

Multivariate statistics rarely have been used to describe sexual dimorphism but there are a few examples. Frayer (1980) used average discriminant function scores to illustrate sexual distance in samples from the European Upper Paleolithic, Mesolithic, and Neolithic. Another distance statistic, the D^2 of Mahalanobis, may also be used to describe the magnitude of sexual difference. Reyment (1969) has used this approach in the analysis of sexual dimorphism in paleontological samples.

It would be convenient if students of sexual dimorphism could agree on a program of standard statistical description, but even if this were possible it would not be practical because of the nonstandard nature of skeletal samples. Each data set presents its own peculiarities and individual researchers must use their judgment following the basic guide of Gnanadesikan and Wilk reminding us that "the main business of statistical data analysis is the description and communication of the informational content of a body of data" (1969, p. 624).

GENERAL PRINCIPLES OF INTERPRETATION

Sexual dimorphism for size is a complex feature which demands multiple levels of explanation covering both selective factors affecting the genotype and environmental influences on the phenotype. While many studies have focused on a single influence, it is better to think of sexual dimorphism as resulting from different selective factors operating on each sex individually plus similar selective factors which may affect the sexes differentially. The summation of genetic and environmental influences affecting males, or females, or both in different ways, will result in the magnitude of dimorphism measured.

Most anthropological studies of sexual dimorphism have also been narrowly focused in the sense that they tend to concentrate on selection affecting males (Alexander et al. 1979; Brace 1970, 1973; Brace and Ryan 1980; DeVore 1963; Frayer 1978, 1980; Wolpoff 1975, 1976b). As I argue later, it is also important to consider selection affecting females (Hamilton 1975; Post 1979). Returning to males, one of the most basic influences that must be considered is sexual selection. Trivers developed a general model which predicts the basic pattern of sexual competition in many species (1972). When care of the young is undertaken unequally by the two sexes, the sex that contributes the most becomes a limiting reproductive resource and the opposite sex competes for this resource. Since care of the young is defined by Trivers as any activity which precludes care of additional young, females in most species are defined as the limiting reproductive resource (Trivers 1972; Wilson 1975). Since human females have a long pregnancy and period of lactation, they are prevented from reproducing additional young during that time while males are theoretically free to seek additional matings. Over the course of human evolution, cultural innovation has created means for male contributions to offspring above and beyond that found in most mammalian species (Hamilton 1981). This change has modulated male competition to some degree and in certain situations it has created female competition for males, but male competition generally persists alongside these changes (Hamilton 1981).

In many species male competition creates selection favoring large male size. This is particularly true when competition takes place largely in the physical realm. For primates in general and humans in particular, male competition may be more subtle and involve psychological interaction, alliance formation, and efforts to develop skills that do not always involve physical size. In most human societies it is often advantageous for males to cooperate in defense and hunting activities and this factor works to discourage outright male competition. Competition may also take place through alliances of male kin where the strength of the group may be more important than the size of individual participants (Chagnon 1979).

Despite these modifications of the basic mammalian pattern, it is still possible to cite examples of apparent reproductive advantage associated with large male size; however, the connection is not as clear as some would like to think. Reproductive success of males in human societies is greatly influenced by the ability of males to control resources or accumulate wealth. Such an ability seems to be chiefly dependent on intelligence and social skill, but there are instances cited where size may facilitate this effort. Sometimes the connection between reproductive success and success in hunting or warfare is quite explicit. Chagnon (1979) cites Yanomamo men who state that they go to war for women. Siskind and Kensinger cite examples in which men are motivated to hunt and share meat with women for sex (Kensinger 1975; Siskind 1975). What is not explicit in these examples is the connection between male physique and success in these activities. It is important to remember that a wide range of physical ability may be associated with any given body size (Parizkova and Merhaustova 1970). Nevertheless, we may imagine some connection between the two, as Laughlin (1968) suggests:

> It is possible to generalize on headmen from the existing literature. As a rule they appear to be well informed, to have better memories, more equipment or material goods, more wives including access to women who may not formally be their wives, to be above average in physical constitution, and—directly as a consequence of their superior hunting abilities—to have a better food supply than those less well endowed. A multitude of consequences follow. The wife, or wives, of a headman are better fed and more likely to carry a pregnancy to full term, and any infants are likely to be better fed and therefore more likely to survive to reproductive age than those infants that are less well fed. [Pp. 317-318]

Of course Laughlin's comment ignores the importance of women and kin networks in the production and distribution of food in many societies. Yet for the purpose of interpreting sexual dimorphism it seems reasonable to acknowledge selection associated with hunting and warfare favoring at least an adequate male physique.

Alexander et al. (1979) claim to have documented population variation in the magnitude of sexual dimorphism associated with different degrees of male competition. The degree of male competition that takes place in any society is theoretically influenced by the degree of polygyny which is realized. When polygyny occurs, fewer males than females contribute genetically to the next generation and males display wide variance in their reproductive success. When male success is based on size, the resulting selection produces varying degrees of sexual dimorphism. For cross-species comparisons, monogamy is associated with little sexual dimorphism whereas extreme polygyny is correlated with extreme dimorphism (Ralls 1977). For populations between the two extremes, other factors may disrupt the correlation between the degree of polygynous mating and dimorphism. As Ralls has pointed out, extreme sexual dimorphism is a very good predictor of polygyny but polygyny is not a good predictor of sexual dimorphism (Ralls 1977).

Within the human species Alexander et al. (1979) still suggest a significant relationship between the mating system and dimorphism (1979). They classified 93 human societies as either practicing polygyny ($N = 46$), socially imposed monogamy ($N = 31$), or ecologically imposed monogamy ($N = 16$). A Mann-Whitney U comparison showed no significant differences in dimorphism for stature between the polygynous and socially imposed monogamous societies. Both of these groups were significantly different from the ecologically imposed monogamists ($P = 0.03$) (Alexander et al. 1979). In the comparison of different osteological samples with different magnitudes of dimorphism it may be tempting to use variance in mating systems to explain variance in dimorphism, but researchers should examine the data of Alexander et al.—as well as their conclusions—since each mating category displays a full range of sexual dimorphism for stature. Other factors clearly are contributing to the variation, and indeed the authors acknowledge that since ecologically imposed monogamous societies frequently live in marginal habitats, nutritional stress may contribute to the slightly lower degree of average dimorphism for this group (Alexander et al. 1979).

This last point illustrates the importance of considering factors that limit male size. Stress, particularly nutritional stress, may affect adult size and this selective force usually affects the two sexes differentially. In some populations of the modern world, undernutrition and malnutrition have been suggested as causes of decreased sexual dimorphism (Hiernaux 1968; Stini 1969, 1972; Tobias 1962, 1972). A diet which is deficient in protein, calories, or both, is known to affect all members of a population, but especially young children and adolescents (Scrimshaw and Behar 1965; Stini 1971). Chronic or temporary nutritional stress can cause long-term or temporary growth lag of height and weight, delay in maturation and onset of puberty, delay in attainment of adult muscle mass, prolongation of growth, and in severe, chronic cases it may cause cessation of growth and loss of cortical bone (Acheson 1960; Dreizen et al. 1953; Dreizen, Spirakis, and Stone 1964, 1967; Ellis 1945; Frisancho, Garn, and Ascoli 1970a,b; Garn et al. 1964; Greulich 1951; Laporte 1946; Scrimshaw and Behar 1965; Stini 1969, 1971, 1972; Tanner 1962; Wolff 1940; Young and Scrimshaw 1971). The presence of disease and parasites can further aggravate a situation of nutritional stress by mobilizing labile protein for the production of antibodies and decreasing the absorption of nutrients (Jelliffe 1966; Scrimshaw and Behar 1965; Scrimshaw, Taylor, and Gordon 1968). Lag in growth of height and weight, delay in maturation, and anemia may occur even when nutritional stress is not severe (Acheson 1960; Birkbeck and Lee 1973; Dreizen, Spirakis, and Stone 1967; Ellis 1945; Laporte 1946; Wolff 1940). In certain instances these studies have shown that exposed adolescents may experience growth prolongation and catch-up growth at least in stature (Birkbeck and Lee 1973; Greulich 1951; Stini 1971; Wolff 1940). Yet chronic stressful conditions do not always allow for catch-up growth and maturation appears to be less affected than actual growth in size. Thus, Frisancho, Garn, and Ascoli (1970a,b) have shown that while growth in body size is delayed from infancy through adolescence, skeletal maturation is not as retarded during adolescence as it is in childhood. Even though the period of growth in their malnourished Central American sample had been prolonged by about 7 percent, adult stature appeared to be reduced by 7 to 10 percent compared to American standards (Frisancho, Garn, and Ascoli 1970a,b). In other words, "Malnourished individuals and groups enter into puberty small, and end it relatively smaller still. They 'catch-up' in timing but not in size" (Garn 1972, p. 134). Other researchers have also noted this effect (Acheson 1960; Martorell et al. 1979; Scrimshaw and Behar 1965).

In addition to documenting the adverse effects of nutritional stress on the growth of children, many workers have also noted that males appear to be more severely affected than females (Ashcroft, Heneage, and Lovell 1966; Dreizen et al. 1953; Dreizen, Spirakis, and Stone 1964; Frisancho et al. 1973; Frisch and Revelle 1969; Greulich 1951, 1957; Greulich, Crismon, and Turner 1953; Hewitt, Westropp, and Acheson 1955; Laporte 1946; Prader, Tanner, and von Harnack 1963; Stini 1969, 1972; Sutow, Conrad, and Griffith 1965; Tanner 1962; Widdowson 1968). This phenomenon has been further clarified by Garn, Frisancho, and co-workers, who have shown that in percent delay and percent dimensional reduction, boys and girls are equal, but on an absolute basis the male is more affected (Frisancho, Garn, and Ascoli 1970a,b; Garn and Frisancho 1971; Garn et al. 1973). The reasons for this observed difference in response to nutritional and other stresses are not clear, although higher male metabolic rate (Tanner 1970) and the role of testosterone (Hamilton 1948) have been implicated in male vulnerability. What does seem clear is that those individuals who have small bodies and require less of the environment during growth and adulthood have a better chance of survival under poor nutritional conditions (Frisancho, Garn, and Ascoli 1970a,b;

Frisancho et al. 1973; Garrow and Pike 1967; Graham and Adrianzen 1971; Malcolm 1969, 1970; Stini 1972; Thomson 1966; Widdowson 1968). It is this effect which is used to explain reduced sexual dimorphism in populations exposed to chronic stress or frequent periods of growth arrest. If males are more susceptible to chronic nutritional stress and disease, their growth may be retarded enough to preclude the achievement of full adult size. If females are less affected by this stress, the resulting adult population should be less dimorphic. This is exactly the kind of interpretation which has been used to explain the decline in sexual dimorphism documented for several Mesoamerican skeletal samples associated with increasing maize dependency and correlated dietary stress (Hamilton 1975; Haviland 1967; Saul 1972).

For male size the selective pattern is stabilizing or normalizing. It is important to note that the action of selection is not necessarily operating directly on the genotype for size. Adult size is established during growth in childhood and adolescence while certain selective factors, such as those favoring male physical performance, occur during adulthood. In this case the traits under selection are the extremes of phenotypic response. If a young boy fully responds to stress by growth arrest and reduced adult size, he may not do as well during adult competition with peers who responded with less growth arrest. Likewise, if a young boy responds to plentiful nutrition with rapid growth and achievement of large adult size for his population, he may not survive as well as his peers who grew less rapidly if the population is subjected to stress during their adulthood. This model of stabilizing selection for size may also be applied to females, but the selective factors operating at the two extremes of phenotypic expression are slightly different.

Female size may also be limited by environmental stresses experienced during childhood growth, but the most powerful selective factor favoring small female size is lactation. Both pregnancy and, especially, lactation produce increased caloric need (W.H.O. 1965a,b, 1973). Estimates of increased caloric need vary. The World Health Organization has declined to make specific recommendations, but it does list suggested allowances for pregnancy ranging from 0 to 600 extra calories per day plus 5 to 55 extra grams of protein per day during the latter stages (1965b, 1973). The higher figures usually come from countries with larger body sizes and colder climates. Lactation demands even more calories. Part of the increase covers the metabolic costs of producing milk while the rest covers the actual calories contained in the milk (Gopalan and Belavady 1961). Both increased metabolic rate and milk output are difficult to estimate but most agree that the *minimum* increase in demand during the first 6 months of lactation amounts to 500 extra calories per day with some estimates approaching 1000 extra calories (W.H.O. 1965b, 1973). Since the state of lactation accounts for most of a woman's reproductive life span in nontechnological societies, it represents a selective force that has operated throughout human evolution to limit female size. If females started off with the body size, muscle mass, and caloric needs of males, it would be difficult (discounting present conditions in the Western world) to obtain those extra calories. With smaller female stature and less muscle mass, fewer calories are normally required relative to males. Post (1979) has also emphasized this selective factor for analyzing variation in sexual dimorphism among nonhuman primates.

As with males, selection that determines female size is stabilizing and operates against both extremes of the phenotypic range of response during growth. If the caloric demands of reproduction limit female size, there are other factors related to reproduction which limit how small a female may be. Stini argues that there is a limit to how much reduction in muscle mass may take place during growth under stressful conditions. Since skeletal muscle functions as a storage depot for amino acids, it may be drawn upon if daily protein intake is not adequate during lactation (Stini 1975). Most researchers agree that the needs of the human fetus and infant are usually met regardless of the intake of the mother in all but the most extreme conditions (Bagchi and Bose 1962; Gopalan and Belavady 1961; Gunther 1952; Janz, Demayer, and Close 1957; Senecal 1959; Thomson 1959; W.H.O. 1965b). This means that females who display the most extreme phenotypic response in growth reduction under stress would have fewer personal resources to draw upon during adulthood. A depletion of personal tissue resources could adversely affect all subsequent reproductive attempts as well as mothering activities. These factors usually result in a balance between too much and too little muscle mass and the same is true of skeletal size (Mueller 1979).

Skeletal size as measured through stature or the biomechanically correlated pelvic dimensions is important during childbirth. Women on the lower range for their population's variation in stature have more difficulty during birth. Several studies have demonstrated that the frequencies of cephalopelvic disproportion, abortions, stillbirths, prematurity, caesarean sections, forceps deliveries, and perinatal loss all go up with decreasing maternal height (Baird 1945, 1949; Baird and Illsley 1953; Bernard 1952; Bresler 1962; Friedman 1967; Kaltreider 1963; Niswander and Jackson 1974; Seibert 1940; Thomson 1959). Bernard (1952) demonstrated that 34 percent of his sample of women under five feet in height had flattened pelvic shapes compared with 7 percent of women over five feet five inches. In his study a majority of the small women were also members of the lower classes; this demonstrates that it is difficult to separate the effects of small stature from those of poor nutrition and health (Baird 1945, 1949; Baird and Illsley 1953; Bernard 1952; Thomson 1959). Yet even when data are broken down by classes or racial groups there is still a gradient of decreasing success in childbirth with decreasing stature within each class or race (Baird 1945; Baird and Illsley 1953; Kaltreider 1963; Niswander and Jackson 1974; Thomson and Belewicz 1963). As with lactation, the physical requirements of birth create selective forces that limit the extremes of phenotypic response to stress and favor larger women in the absence of dietary limitations. For each population the actual size that marks the balance between selective forces favoring large and small females will differ, but for each population range in size these selective forces may work to limit the extremes of phenotypic response to environmental conditions.

SPECIFIC EXAMPLES IN INTERPRETATION

The analyst of sexual dimorphism in skeletal samples should be aware of all potential influences, although in particular comparisons one selective factor may dominate the contrast in dimorphism between groups. For instance, Frayer (1978, 1980) has demonstrated a marked decline in craniofacial and dental dimorphism between the Upper Paleolithic and Mesolithic. This change is clearly attributable to a more precipitous decline in male size (Frayer 1978, 1980). Frayer emphasizes Upper Paleolithic and Mesolithic contrasts in hunting technology (spears versus bow and arrows) and prey size (social megafauna versus smaller, less social forms) to explain the difference (1978, 1980). While Frayer may be correct in emphasizing the demands of hunting large game with spears as a selective factor maintaining large male size in the Upper Paleolithic, he tends to ignore the importance of diet. Large male size cannot be maintained without dietary support. Since the transition involved a marked reduction in prey size and therefore in meat supply, the decline in dimorphism could just as well be attributed to a decline in dietary support for large males manifested in less rapid growth of males during childhood. Frayer's explanation also fails to account for a second smaller decline in dimorphism between the Early and Late Mesolithic samples in which females gain relatively more in size than males (Frayer 1978). This type of change is not unknown. Greulich documented greater female response during secular increases in stature among native Japanese in the first half of this century

(Greulich 1957). The same pattern is also evident in the contrasts between the Gibson-Klunk and Koster samples and Late Woodland and Mississippian Schild samples illustrated in Figures 5.2 to 5.13. Tobias has observed that this sort of population response is probably more characteristic of groups which experience improvement of tolerable conditions (Tobias 1972). It is doubtful that one generalization will be able to explain all instances of this type of change. It would be helpful to determine the earlier conditions of the two sexes and particularly the question of whether or not such a change was preceded by differential access to resources. Favoritism toward males under harsh conditions could depress female size relatively more and result in greater female response as conditions improve. In contrast to the Japanese example, a study of secular trend in Poland comparing same-sexed parents and offspring shows secular increases with males gaining more in both stable and advancing educational status families (Bielicki and Charzewski 1977). Tobias has shown increases in stature dimorphism among Bushmen populations due to relatively greater responses by males making the transition from extremely poor to merely poor environmental circumstances. The pattern of females gaining more than males during secular increase appears less common, and each example will probably require a special explanation. Nevertheless, cultural factors that control access to improving resources by sex may sometimes influence the eventual expression of dimorphism.

ANALYSIS OF
LOWER ILLINOIS RIVER VALLEY POPULATIONS

Data from the Lower Illinois River Valley show several fluctuations which take place over a relatively short period of time and therefore probably fall within the realm of phenotypic response to fluctuating environmental circumstances. Table 5.6 summarizes archaeological information for each sample. The Gibson and Pete Klunk mound groups are close in location, temporally overlapping, biologically similar, and can be combined as one sample (Buikstra 1972, 1976). This group represents a period in the Lower Illinois River Valley that is characterized by an elaborate burial tradition and artifacts and participation in a trade network for exotic raw materials and products made from them (Buikstra 1972, 1976; Dragoo 1976; Griffin 1967; Struever 1968; Tainter 1977). It is now generally agreed that these groups and their contemporaries in the area had established a subsistence system that involved the exploitation of natural resources as well as native cultigens, squash, and gourd (Chomko and Crawford

1978; Cleland 1976; Struever and Vickery 1973; Yarnell 1969, 1976). Although maize pollen has been identified in this area from an earlier time (Schoenwetter 1979), the evidence has been questioned (Chomko and Crawford 1979) and maize use has still not been verified through flotation analysis (Struever and Vickery 1973). The accessible ecological diversity present in this area (Zawacki and Hausfater 1969) and the abundance of projectile points and animal bones attest to the diversity of resource exploitation for this period (Montet-White 1968; Parmalee, Paloumpis, and Wilson 1972). The overall impression is that this period was reasonably prosperous (Dragoo 1976) and can be characterized by a highly favorable relationship between estimated population levels and wild food abundance (Asch 1976). Despite this, there is some evidence for intermittent environmental stress from disease and diet (Cook and Buikstra 1979). Chronic infectious disease processes have been identified in this area (Cook 1972) and periodic seasonal shortages may have interacted with disease to produce episodic skeletal stress responses. As Garn (1972) has noted:

> Amerindian nutritional diversity was such as to make seasonal caloric malnutrition more likely than classic protein-caloric malnutrition. Even the maize eaters did not achieve the yellow maize exclusiveness of post-contact Central America. [P. 136]

When intermittent growth retardation occurred at Gibson-Klunk, the ability to catch up may have been influenced by status.

There are clear indications of ascribed status differences in this Middle Woodland sample and others, as evidenced from the distribution of burials in the mounds and associated artifacts (Buikstra 1972, 1976; Tainter 1975, 1977). Status is assumed to be ascribed because a number of infants and children were buried using the most elaborate mortuary rituals and their graves were located in the high status central tombs (Buikstra 1972, 1976; Tainter 1975, 1977). Individuals (usually male) buried in the highest status tombs are taller (Buikstra 1976). However, an analysis of trace elements in the skeleton from three status classes at the Gibson mound group shows no significant differences between the two upper classes, which account for a majority (76.5%, $N = 65$) of the individuals (Lambert, Szpunar, and Buikstra 1979). A combined sample of the two upper groups was significantly different from the lowest status group of burials (23.5%, $N = 20$) (Lambert, Szpunar, and Buikstra 1979). This finding introduces potential error into the remaining analysis since equivalent information is not available for the other samples presented here. However, some information is available on the distribution of status at Koster and Late Woodland Schild (Tainter 1975, 1977) and this will have to serve instead. Trace element analysis is designed to reveal differential access to animal protein (Brown 1973; Lambert, Szpunar, and Buikstra 1979; Schoeninger 1979; Szpunar, Lambert, and Buikstra 1978). If trace element analysis does not show significant differences between the taller, highest status individuals at Gibson and the second status class, it is still possible that there may have been differential access during childhood growth, but this has yet to be established (Buikstra 1976). Interestingly enough, a comparison of males and females at Gibson showed no significant differences (Lambert, Szpunar, and Buikstra 1979). Trace element analysis is clearly a valuable tool in the study of dimorphism in skeletal samples, and researchers should make every effort to supplement their data with this kind of information.

Summarizing the Gibson-Klunk sample, the level of sexual dimorphism is apparently not influenced by sex differences in access to animal protein, but the proportion of high status individuals may ultimately be an important influence in comparison with other groups. Since status is ascribed the association between competition and male reproductive success is not clearly connected with long-term selection for large size and physical performance. Over the short term there was probably very little selection *against* large male size during this time. That the highest status males are taller could be attributable to better nutrition undetected by trace element analysis or perhaps to the taller height of their ancestors who established their social position at the onset of stratified social systems.

The Koster and Late Woodland Schild samples represent the following Late Woodland stage in this region. There is general agreement that the Late Woodland period represents a major transition in subsistence strategy accompanied by social change and increased environmental stress (Cleland 1976; Cook 1972, 1978; Cook and Buikstra 1979; DeRousseau 1973; Dragoo 1976; Tainter 1975, 1977; Whatley and Asch 1975). There is a shift away from earthwork construction, elaborate burial practices, a decline in the trade networks, and a decrease in status differentiation (Cleland 1976; Dragoo 1976; Ford 1974; Tainter 1975, 1977). There is also an increase in habitation site density with new sites filling in previously unoccupied zones and moving into the uplands of tributary stream valleys. These changes are believed to indicate an increase in population density (Asch 1976; DeRousseau 1973; Dragoo 1976; Farnsworth 1973; Perino 1962; Tainter 1975, 1977; Whatley and Asch 1975).

The early Late Woodland is characterized as "the culmination of forest efficiency" in which "virtually all edible resources of any consequence were hunted or collected in quantity" (Ford 1974, p. 403). With the breakdown of regional integration, village populations apparently became more isolated and established local resource territories in which there was a focus on food available in the immediate area (Cleland 1976; Dragoo 1976; Ford 1974; Tainter 1975; Whatley and Asch 1975). Ford suggests that this localization led to an increasing dependence on agricultural production (Ford 1974). As the Late Woodland progressed there was increasing pressure on natural resources as suggested by a gradual decline in the proportion of deer to fish remains (Parmalee, Paloumpis, and Wilson 1972; Whatley and Asch 1975). The introduction of the bow and arrow at the beginning of this period (Ford 1974) may have increased hunting efficiency, but local decreases in deer density would have made them more difficult to find. The limitation to smaller local resource territories within the immediate area would also affect availability (Whatley and Asch 1975). The importance of land for cultivation, the pressure on natural resources, and the apparent lack of regional authority may have led to increased conflict during this time (Dragoo 1976; Ford 1974; Tainter 1975). The increasing strain culminated in a commitment to more extensive maize cultivation beginning about A.D. 800 (Asch and Asch 1977; Ford 1974; Munson 1973; Whatley and Asch 1975). Beans were not introduced into the area until at least 100 years later, after A.D. 900 (Asch and Asch 1977; Dragoo 1976; Ford 1974). Without the beans to revitalize the soil and form a protein complement to maize, soil exhaustion and nutritional stress may have persisted after the onset of increased maize use (Ford 1974).

Sexual dimorphism in the context of the Late Woodland in the Lower Illinois River Valley is difficult to interpret because the details of these various changes are still being worked out. The generalization that the late Woodland period was stressful would lead us to predict a decline in the physical size of the population with males affected more than females resulting in decreased dimorphism. So far, the data do not show this.

In the Koster sample (Figures 5.2 to 5.13 summarized in Table 5.10) there is a consistent increase in physical size among the females relative to the Gibson-Klunk sample. Rather than stress, this change suggests a maintenance of earlier subsistence conditions or a slight improvement. The shift in the distribution of deltoid tuberosity grades (Tables 5.2 and 5.3) also suggests adequate or improved nutrition. Males also show an upward shift in the range of deltoid tuberosity, but no consistent change in physical size that the female shift would lead us to expect. Introduction of the bow and arrow may have favored greater arm, pectoral, and back muscle mass without skeletal size increases; however, this explanation does not account for the female

TABLE 5.10

A Summary of Change in Percent Sexual Dimorphism and Male and Female Size in the Transition from Gibson-Klunk to Koster.

Measurement	Change in Percent Sexual Dimorphism	Change in Female Size	Change in Male Size
Ischial length	−1.5	+1.7	+0.7
Cotylosciatic width	−1.4	+0.7	+0.3
Bicondylar femur length	−1.4	0	−6.0
Humerus length	−2.3	+6.0	−1.0
Clavicle length	−1.6	+2.0	0
Humerus epicondylar width	0	+0.9	+1.0
Humerus head diameter	−0.3	+0.9	+0.9
Humerus articular width	−1.6	+1.4	+0.9
Femur head diameter	−2.0	+1.0	+0.3
Clavicle circumference	−7.6	+1.4	−0.8
Ant./post. femur shaft diameter	−0.5	+0.8	+0.8
First metatarsal circumference	−0.6	−0.5	−0.8

increase. This discrepancy among males may also be due to sampling error. Cremation was more common in the Late Woodland than in the Middle Woodland (Asch 1976). Tainter notes that there may be an unexcavated crematory at Koster mounds (Tainter 1977). Since cremation was a more elaborate burial practice involving chiefly persons of the highest status (Tainter 1977) and since in the previous period this highest status involved mostly males (Buikstra 1976), the Koster sample may be lacking in proportional representation of this group. If they were physically larger as analysis of the high status Gibson males suggests (Buikstra 1976) then skeletal size dimorphism measured for Koster may not be accurate. The maintenance of significant sex differences for deltoid tuberosity (Table 5.3) suggests that Koster males increased as much as Koster females and the real change in size dimorphism may have been very little relative to the Gibson-Klunk sample.

   The true nature of size dimorphism in the early Late Woodland of this area may never be known, but additional skeletal material and archaeological information from Koster or other nearby sites of similar age should improve our understanding of this sample and its interpretation. For the present it appears that the subsistence conditions of the Middle Woodland carried over into the early Late Woodland and stress did not become significant until later (Cook 1978; Ford 1974).

The comparison of Koster and the later Late Woodland Schild samples shows some striking changes (Figures 5.2 to 5.13 summarized in Table 5.8). There is an increase in size dimorphism brought about by a consistent decrease in female physical size while males generally increase or maintain size relative to the Koster sample. The increases in male size may be more apparent than real because of the sampling problem at Koster. The Late Woodland Schild does not seem to be as affected by this error since the sample includes 12.5 percent of the graves in the highest status category while Koster's proportion is only 1.9 percent (Tainter 1977). While the apparent increase or maintenance of male size may be an artifact, the decline in female size seems very real. Arm muscle as measured by deltoid tuberosity grades does not really help to illuminate this change (Tables 5.3 and 5.4). Relative to Koster there are slightly fewer females in the upper grades with greater male variability resulting in an apparent decrease of dimorphism in this measurement. The small sample sizes may be a problem here (Table 5.6).

If the changes at Late Woodland Schild are real, they go against the biological models developed in the previous section. Decline in size would be predicted for this time period, which is believed to have been especially stressful (Cook 1978; Cook and Buikstra 1979). This is the period discussed above which marks increased utilization of maize without the benefit of beans. Cook (1978) has analyzed stress indicators in children through the time periods covered by this Lower Illinois River Valley data set. She notes that the combined pathological configuration for later Late Woodland groups suggests chronic stress and growth failure rather than the acute interruptions and resumptions of growth evident for other periods in this area. Cook emphasizes that the stress is not necessarily attributable to corn, per se, since maize-use correlates, such as poor weaning foods, continue into the Mississippian period while health and nutrition improve. Instead Cook cites short-term dislocations in the balance between population size, subsistence base, and subsistence technology (Cook 1978).

If females show evidence of this stress it should appear at the same or greater degree in males. Since it does not, we may hypothesize differential treatment of males and females, possibly encouraged by the warfare and conflict evident from this period (Dragoo 1976; Ford 1974; Tainter 1975). On the surface this suggestion seems fanciful, and sampling error may ultimately illuminate this disparity. However, there is some evidence from another later Late Woodland site in this area which supports this interpretation. Trace element analysis at the Ledders site shows that males had a higher animal protein intake than females (Lambert, Szpunar, and Buikstra 1979). This difference could have been brought about by a hunting pattern in which males had to travel longer distances for game (relative to earlier periods) and ate more at the kill site, hence returning with less. Emphasis on male children as potential warriors may also have occurred. Both scenarios would provide support for adequate male size while favoring smaller female size. More skeletal data are needed to clarify this Late Woodland pattern by confirming the results and trace element analysis for all skeletal samples. Another approach which would also improve our understanding of phenotypic shifts in dimorphism is an analysis of sexual dimorphism in skeletal pathology. Adult sex differences in pathological indicators of stress incurred during growth and adulthood could help confirm or refute the speculations presented here about sex differences in stress experience. The sophistication of paleopathological analysis has improved over the last decade (Armelagos, Goodman, and Bickerton 1980; Buikstra and Cook 1977; Cook 1976, 1978; Cook and Buikstra 1979; Doyle and Johnson 1977; Merchant and Ubelaker 1977; Perzigian 1977; Rose, Armelagos, and Lallo 1978), and the possibility of application to Plio-Pleistocene hominid samples should not be ignored either (White 1978).

The final group presented here comes from the beginning of the Mississippian period. The Mississippian is characterized by agriculture employing a full range of cultigens that include maize, beans, and squash. Selective faunal exploitation of fish, migratory water fowl, deer, raccoon, and turkey on a seasonal basis has also been documented (Smith 1974, 1975). The reestablishment of extensive trade networks indicates a stabilization of intervillage relations and a decline in localized focus (Ford 1974; Dragoo 1976). Ford (1974) suggests a level of regional authority reinforced by kinship ties and ceremony involving high ranking officials responsible for redistribution and storage of some food, ritual knowledge, and long-distance trade. Probably the most important changes in terms of human well-being were the establishment of beans to complement the animo-acid deficiency of maize, and the political and economic stabilization brought about by alliances and a level of regional organization.

The magnitude of sexual dimorphism for the Mississippian Schild sample shows a decline relative to the Late Woodland Schild. In 9 out of the 12 measurements presented, there is an increase in female physical size relative to the previous sample while males decline slightly. This is a more extreme expression of the pattern observed at Koster, and some of the same problems may occur in this sample. The burials in the Schild Mississippian cemetery include high status individuals (of unknown proportion) but there is also evidence for cremation activity which probably focused on the highest ranking class (Goldstein 1975). Beyond this, it is not possible at this time to evaluate the influence of sampling error for status.

The change in females relative to Late Woodland Schild suggests improving conditions and this is supported by the evaluation of pathological stress indicators in children (Cook 1978). There is still stress present, particularly from weaning trauma and disease, but the indicators of chronic growth retardation from the previous period are not as well represented (Cook 1978). While uncertainty remains about the representation of the males in the metric measurements, the deltoid tuberosity grades agree with the metric results; this was not so at Koster (Tables 5.3 and 5.5). Females show a slight shift into the upper grades and males show a slight decline. Deltoid grades for males at Koster showed increases despite the sampling bias toward the lower ranks, while deltoid grades for Mississippian Schild males show declines in spite of potential bias. If the changes are real we may hypothesize a more equal distribution of more stable food supplies resulting in dietary support for larger females based on long-term selection for the upper range of phenotypic response in the absence of dietary limitation. The males may or may not have decreased depending on the validity of this sample. Decline in size does not necessarily indicate that unusual stress was limited to males. An adequate diet could have led to moderate growth in the absence of what appears to be cultural intervention for large male size in the previous period. It is also possible that both sexes experienced intermittent stress episodes with males being affected more than females. As noted above, speculations about short-term phenotypic influences could be greatly enhanced with trace element analysis and information about sexual dimorphism in stress pathology. Another potential influence, which is still being evaluated, is the possibility of migration in and out of the area with sex differences in mobility, but preliminary analyses do not reveal significant changes in the biological continuity of populations in this area over the time covered by these data (Buikstra 1976; Droessler 1975).

CONCLUSIONS

Sexual dimorphism is not a simple trait controlled by a single selecive factor. Long-term selection on the genotype and short-term fluctuation of the phenotype are components of any estimation of sexual dimorphism for a particular population. The temporal scope and characteristics of the data set will determine the emphasis in interpretation. For long-term changes in the fossil record covering several taxonomic transitions a discussion of selection at the genotypic level seems more appropriate. Phenotypic fluctuations are probably hidden by the sampling conditions of fossil hominid collections. In spite of this, analysts of sexual dimorphism in the hominid fossil record should be prepared to assess short-term influences since obvious perturbations of growth do appear in fossil specimens as White (1978) has described. For recent samples covering shorter time spans as presented above, an analysis of phenotypic change is more important.

In either case, the analysis of sexual dimorphism in skeletal samples presents special problems not usually encountered with analysis of living groups. Error in sex identification is the most obvious of these. In many cases, estimates should also include an assessment of sampling errors particularly with regard to status and age distributions. It is also imperative that biological theory, archaeological information, and ecological reconstructions be used to their fullest in order to estimate the social and nutritional environments that may influence sexual dimorphism. Attention should be paid to both sexes since they clearly do not respond equally to the same conditions and are influenced by different selective forces as well. When appropriate and available, additional biological information from the skeleton may improve precision of interpretation.

Understanding sexual dimorphism in skeletal samples requires more analysis than many of us originally anticipated (Hamilton 1975), but without the requisite attention to detail and control of error, the estimate of skeletal dimorphism risks reduction to a meaningless exercise yielding questionable results.

APPENDIX: OSTEOLOGICAL MEASUREMENTS

1. *Ischial length* follows the directions of Schultz (1930) as modified by Hamilton (1975). The acetabular landmark is cited approximately 10 mm lateral to the fusion point of ischium, ilium, and pubis at the border of the articular and nonarticular surfaces of the acetabulum.

2. *Pubis length* for the ischiopubic index follows Schultz (1930) with modification of the acetabular landmark as described above (#1).

3. *Cotylosciatic width* follows Oliver (1969) measuring the breadth of the ischium superior to the ischial spine from the acetabular border to the greater sciatic notch border.

4. *Sciatic notch depth* for the cotylosciatic index follows Olivier (1969) with modification by Hamilton (1975). Depth of the notch was measured from the inferior posterior iliac spine to the inferior base of the ischial spine (Hamilton 1975).

5. *Bicondylar femur length* follows Martin (1928, p. 1037) #2.

6. *Maximum humerus length* follows Martin (1928, p. 1010) #1.

7. *Maximum clavicle length* follows Martin (1928, p. 1005) #1.

8. *Humerus epicondylar width* follows Martin (1928, p. 1011) #4a.

9. *Humerus head diameter* follows Martin (1928, p. 1011) #10.

10. *Humerus articular width* measures the breadth of trochlea and capitulum following Martin (1928, p. 1012) #12a.

11. *Femur head diameter* follows Martin (1928, p. 1041) #18.

12. *Clavicle circumference* at midshaft follows Martin (1928, p. 1006) #6.

13. *Anterior posterior midshaft femur diameter* follows Martin (1928, p. 1040) #6.

14. *First metatarsal circumference* was taken from the diaphysis at midshaft.

BIBLIOGRAPHY

Acheson, R. F. 1960. "Effects of Nutrition and Disease on Human Growth." In *Human Growth. Symposium of the Society for the Study of Human Biology*, edited by J. M. Tanner, 3:73-92. Oxford: Pergamon Press.

Alexander, R. D., J. L. Hoogland, R. D. Howard, K. M. Noonan, and P. W. Sherman. 1979. "Sexual Dimorphism and Breeding Systems in Pinnipeds, Ungulates, Primates, and Humans." In *Evolutionary Biology and Human Social Behavior*, edited by Napoleon A. Chagnon and William Irons, pp. 402-435. North Scituate, Mass.: Duxbury Press.

Alexander, R. W. 1976. "Hierarchial Grouping Analysis and Skeletal Materials." *American Journal of Physical Anthropology*, 45:39-43.

Almquist, A. J. 1974. "Sexual Differences in the Anterior Dentition of African Primates." *American Journal of Physical Anthropology*, 40:359-367.

Anderson, D. L., G. W. Thompson, and F. Popovich. 1977. "Tooth, Chin, Bone and Body Size Correlations." *American Journal of Physical Anthropology*, 46:7-12.

Armelagos, G. J., A. Goodman, and S. Bickerton. 1980. "Determining Nutritional and Infectious Disease Stress in Prehistoric Skeletal Populations." Paper read at the Forty-Ninth Annual Meeting of the

American Association of Physical Anthropologists, Niagara Falls, New York.

Asch, D. 1976. *The Middle Woodland Population of the Lower Illinois Valley: A Study in Paleodemographic Methods.* Evanston, Ill.: Northwestern University Archaeological Program Scientific Papers, No. 1.

Asch, D. L. and N. B. Asch. 1977. "Chenopod as Cultigen: A Re-evaluation of Some Prehistoric Collections from Eastern North America." *Midcontinental Journal of Archaeology*, 2:3-45.

Ashcroft, M. T., P. Heneage, and H. G. Lovell. 1966. "Heights and Weights of Jamaican School Children of Various Ethnic Groups." *American Journal of Physical Anthropology*, 24:35-44.

Ashworth, Joel Thomas, Jr., M. J. Allison, E. Gerszten, and A. Pezzia. 1976. "The Pubic Scars of Gestation and Parturition in a Group of Pre-Columbian and Colonial Peruvian Mummies." *American Journal of Physical Anthropology*, 45:85-90.

Bagchi, K., and A. K. Bose. 1962. "Effect of Low Nutrient Intake During Pregnancy on Obstetrical Performance and Offspring." *American Journal of Clinical Nutrition*, 11:586-592.

Baird, D. 1949. "Social Factors in Obstetrics." *Lancet*, I:1079-1083.

_____. 1945. "The Influence of Social and Economic Factors on Stillbirths and Neonatal Deaths." *Journal of Obstetrics and Gynecology of the British Empire*, 52:339-366.

Baird, D., and R. Illsley. 1953. "Environment and Childbearing." *Proceedings of the Royal Society of Medicine*, 46:53-59.

Bass, William M. 1979. "Recent Developments in Human Identification." *American Journal of Physical Anthropology*, 51:555-562.

_____. 1969. "Recent Developments in the Identification of Human Skeletal Material." *American Journal of Physical Anthropology*, 30:459-461.

Bernard, R. M. 1952. "The Shape and Size of the Female Pelvis." *Transactions of the Edinburgh Obstetrical Society* published with *Edinburgh Medical Journal*, 59:1-16.

Bielicki, T., and J. Charzewski. 1977. "Sex Differences in the Magnitude of Statural Gains of Offspring over Parents." *Human Biology*, 49:265-277.

Birkbeck, J. A., and M. Lee. 1973. "Growth and Skeletal Maturation in British Columbia Indian Populations." *American Journal of Physical Anthropology*, 39:727-738.

Black, Thomas K., III. 1978. "A New Method for Assessing the Sex of Fragmentary Skeletal Remains: Femoral Shaft Circumference." *American Journal of Physical Anthropology*, 48:227-231.

Brace, C. L. 1973. "Sexual Dimorphism in Human Evolution." *Yearbook of Physical Anthropology 1972*, 16:31-49.

_____. 1970. "The Origin of Man." *Natural History*, 79 (1):46-49.

_____. 1969. "The Australopithecine Range of Variation," *American Journal of Physical Anthropology*, 31:255.

Brace, C. L., P. E. Mahler, and R. B. Rosen. 1973. "Tooth Measurements and the Rejection of the Taxon 'Homo habilis'." *Yearbook of Physical Anthropology 1972*, 16:50-68.

Brace, C. L., and A. S. Ryan. 1980. "Sexual Dimorphism and Human Tooth Size Differences." *Journal of Human Evolution*, 9:417-435.

Bresler, J. B. 1962. "Maternal Height and the Prevalence of Stillbirths." *American Journal of Physical Anthropology*, 20:515-517.

Briggs, L. C., and D. Sancho. 1952. "Cranial Deformation in Minorca, Balearic Islands." *American Journal of Physical Anthropology*, 10:371-372.

Brothwell, D. R. 1972. *Digging up Bones*, 2nd ed. London: British Museum of Natural History.

Brown, A. B. 1973. "Bone Strontium Content as a Dietary Indicator in Human Skeletal Populations." Ph.D. dissertation, University of Michigan. Ann Arbor: University Microfilms.

Buikstra, J. E. 1976. *Hopewell in the Lower Illinois Valley*. Evanston, Ill.: Northwestern University Archaeological Program Scientific Papers, No. 2.

―――. 1972. "Hopewell in the Lower Illinois River Valley: A Regional Approach to the Study of Biological Variability and Mortuary Activities." Ph.D. dissertation, University of Chicago.

Buikstra, J. E., and D. C. Cook. 1977. "Pre-Columbian Tuberculosis: an Epidemiological Approach." Paper read at the Forty-Sixth Annual Meeting of the American Association of Physical Anthropologists, Seattle, Washington.

Campbell, B. 1974. "A New Taxonomy of Fossil Man." *Yearbook of Physical Anthropology 1973*, 17:194-201.

Campbell, N. A. 1978. "Multivariate Analysis in Biological Anthropology: Some Further Considerations." *Journal of Human Evolution*, 7:197-203.

Chagnon, N. A. 1979. "Mate Competition, Favoring Close Kin, and Village Fissioning Among the Yanomamo Indians." In *Evolutionary Biology and Human Social Behavior*, edited by N. A. Chagnon and W. Irons, pp. 86-132. North Scituate, Mass.: Duxbury Press.

Chomko, S. A., and G. W. Crawford. 1979. "Reply to Schoenwetter." *American Antiquity*, 44:601-602.

―――. 1978. "Plant Husbandry in Prehistoric Eastern North America: New Evidence for Its Development." *American Antiquity*, 43:405-408.

Cleland, C. E. 1976. "The Focal-Diffuse Model: An Evolutionary Perspective on the Prehistoric Cultural Adaptations of the Eastern United States." *Midcontinental Journal of Archaeology*, 1:59-76.

Coleman, W. H. 1969. "Sex Differences in the Growth of the Human Bony Pelvis." *American Journal of Physical Anthropology*, 31:125-152.

Cook, D. C. 1978. "Age at Death, Bone Lesions and Disturbed Growth: The Meaning of Stress Indicators in Paleonutrition." Paper read at the Forty-Seventh Annual Meeting of the American Association of Physical Anthropologists, Toronto, Canada.

―――. 1976. "Pathologic States and Disease Process in Illinois Woodland Populations: An Epidemiologic Approach." Ph.D. dissertation, University of Chicago.

―――. 1972. "Subsistence Base and Growth Rate in Four Illinois Woodland

Populations." Paper read at the Forty-First Annual Meeting of the American Association of Physical Anthropologists, Lawrence, Kansas.

Cook, D. C., and J. E. Buikstra. 1979. "Health and Differential Survival in Prehistoric Populations: Prenatal Dental Defects." *American Journal of Physical Anthropology*, 51:649-659.

Corruccini, R. S. 1975. "Multivariate Analysis in Biological Anthropology: Some Considerations." *Journal of Human Evolution*, 4:1-19.

Crane, H. R., and J. B. Griffin. 1966. "University of Michigan Radiocarbon Dates XI." *Radiocarbon*, 8:256-285.

_____ . 1963. "University of Michigan Radiocarbon Dates VIII." *Radiocarbon*, 5:228-253.

Crook, J. H. 1972. "Sexual Selection, Dimorphism, and Social Organization in the Primates." In *Sexual Selection and the Descent of Man*, edited by B. Campbell, pp. 231-281. Chicago: Aldine.

DeRousseau, C. J. 1973. "Mortuary Site Survey and Paleodemography in the Lower Illinois River Valley." Paper read at the Seventy-Second Annual Meeting of the American Anthropological Association, New Orleans, Louisiana.

DeVore, I. 1963. "A Comparison of the Ecology and Behavior of Monkeys and Apes." In *Classification and Human Evolution*, edited by S. L. Washburn, pp. 301-319. *Viking Fund Publications in Anthropology*, No. 37. New York: Wenner-Gren Foundation for Anthropological Research.

DiBennardo, R., and J. V. Taylor. 1979. "Sex Assessment of the Femur: A Test of a New Method." *American Journal of Physical Anthropology*, 50:635-637.

Dorsey, G. A. 1897. "A Sexual Study of the Size of the Articular Surfaces of the Long Bones in Aboriginal American Skeletons." *Boston Medical Surgical Journal* [now *New England Journal of Medicine*], July 22, 1897.

Doyle, W. J., and O. Johnston. 1977. "On the Meaning of Increased Fluctuating Dental Asymmetry: A Cross Populational Study." *American Journal of Physical Anthropology*, 46:127-134.

Dragoo, D. W. 1976. "Some Aspects of Eastern North American Prehistory: A Review 1975." *American Antiquity*, 41:3-27.

Dreizen, S. C., C. Currie, E. J. Gilley, and T. D. Spies. 1953. "The Effect of Nutritive Failure on the Growth Patterns of White Children in Alabama." *Child Development*, 24:189-202.

Dreizen, S., C. N. Spirakis, and R. E. Stone. 1967. "A Comparison of Skeletal Growth and Maturation in Undernourished and Well-nourished Girls before and after Menarche." *Journal of Pediatrics*, 70:256-263.

_____ . 1964. "Chronic Undernutrition and Postnatal Ossification." *American Journal of Diseases of Children*, 108:44-52.

Droessler, J. G. 1975. "Cultural Interaction: Biological Change at the Late Woodland-Mississippian Interface." Paper read at the Forty-Fourth Annual Meeting of the American Association of Physical Anthropologists, Denver, Colorado.

Dwight, T. 1905. "The Size of Articular Surfaces of the Long Bones as Characteristic of Sex: an Anthropological Study." *American Journal of Anatomy*, 4:19-32.

Ellis, R. W. B. 1945. "Growth and Health of Belgian Children during and after the German Occupation (1940-1944)." *Archives of Disease in Childhood*, 20:97-109.

Eveleth, P. B. 1975. "Differences between Ethnic Groups in Sex Dimorphism of Adult Height." *Annals of Human Biology*, 2:35-39.

Farnsworth, K. B. 1973. *An Archaeological Survey of the Macoupin Valley.* Illinois State Museum Reports of Investigations, No. 26, Illinois Valley Archaeological Program Research Papers, Vol. 7. Springfield: Illinois State Museum.

Ford, R. I. 1974. "Northeastern Archeology: Past and Future Directions." In *Annual Review of Anthropology*, edited by B. J. Siegel, pp. 385-413. Palo Alto, Calif.: Annual Reviews, Inc.

Frayer, D. W. 1980. "Sexual Dimorphism and Cultural Evolution in the Late Pleistocene and Holocene of Europe." *Journal of Human Evolution*, 9:399-415.

_____. 1978. *Evolution of the Dentition in Upper Paleolithic and Mesolithic Europe.* Lawrence: University of Kansas Monographs in Anthropology, No. 10.

Friedman, E. A. 1967. *Labor. Clinical Evaluation and Management.* New York: Appleton-Century-Crofts.

Frisancho, A. R., S. M. Garn, and W. Ascoli. 1970a. "Childhood Retardation Resulting in Reduction of Adult Body Size due to Lesser Adolescent Skeletal Delay." *American Journal of Physical Anthropology*, 33:325-336.

_____. 1970b. "Unequal Influence of Low Dietary Intakes on Skeletal Maturation during Childhood and Adolescence." *American Journal of Clinical Nutrition*, 23:1220-1227.

Frisancho, A. R., J. Sanchez, D. Pallardel, and L. Yanez. 1973. "Adaptive Significance of Small Body Size under Poor Socioeconomic Conditions in Southern Peru." *American Journal of Physical Anthropology*, 39:255-261.

Frisch, R., and R. Revelle. 1969. "Variation in Body Weights and the Age of the Adolescent Growth Spurt among Latin American and Asian Populations in Relation to Calorie Supplies." *Human Biology*, 41:185-212.

Garn, S. M. 1972. "Biological Correlates of Malnutrition in Man." In *Nutrition, Growth, and Development of North American Indian Children*, edited by W. M. Moore, M. M. Silverberg, and M. S. Read, pp. 129-138. Department of Health, Education, and Welfare Publication No. (NIH) 72-76, U.S. Government Printing Office.

Garn, S. M., P. E. Cole, and W. I. Van Alstine. 1979. "Sex Discriminatory Effectiveness Using Combinations of Root Lengths and Crown Diameters." *American Journal of Physical Anthropology*, 50:115-117.

Garn, S. M., and R. Frisancho, 1971. "Effects of Malnutrition on Size and

Skeletal Development." In *Proceedings of a Workshop on Problems of Assessment and Alleviation of Malnutrition in the United States*, edited by R. G. Hansen and H. N. Munro, pp. 84-93. Washington, D.C.: U.S. Government Printing Office.

Garn, S. M., R. Frisancho, S. T. Sandusky, and M. B. McCann. 1972. "Confirmation of the Sex Difference in Continuing Subperiosteal Apposition." *American Journal of Physical Anthropology*, 36:377-380.

Garn, S. M., and A. B. Lewis. 1958. "Tooth-size, Body-size and 'Giant' Fossil Man." *American Anthropologist* 60:874-880.

Garn, S. M., A. B. Lewis, D. R. Swindler, and R. Kerewsky. 1967. "Genetic Control of Sexual Dimorphism in Tooth Size." *Journal of Dental Research*, 46:963-972.

Garn, S. M., R. H. Osborne, and K. D. McCabe. 1979. "The Effect of Prenatal Factors on Crown Dimensions." *American Journal of Physical Anthropology*, 51:665-678.

Garn, S. M., C. G. Rohmann, M. Behar, and M. A. Guzmann. 1964. "Compact Bone Deficiency in Protein-calorie Malnutrition." *Science*, 145:1444-1445.

Garn, S. M., C. G. Rohmann, B. Wagner, and W. Ascoli. 1967. "Continuing Bone Growth throughout Life: A General Phenomenon." *American Journal of Physical Anthropology*, 26:313-317.

Garn, S. M., S. T. Sandusky, N. N. Rosen, and F. Trowbridge. 1973. "Economic Impact on Postnatal Ossification." *American Journal of Physical Anthropology*, 38:1-4.

Garn, S. M., B. Wagner, C. G. Rohmann, and W. Ascoli. 1968. "Further Evidence for Continuing Bone Expansion." *American Journal of Physical Anthropology*, 28:219-222.

Garrow, J. S., and M. C. Pike. 1967. "The Long Term Prognosis of Severe Infantile Malnutrition." *Lancet*, I:1-4.

Giles, E. 1970. "Discriminant Function Sexing of the Human Skeleton." In *Personal Identification in Mass Disasters*, edited by T. Dale Steward, pp. 99-109. Washington, D.C.: Smithsonian Institution.

Gingerich, P. D. 1977. "Correlation of Tooth Size and Body Size in Living Hominoid Primates, with a Note on Relative Brain Size in *Aegyptopithecus* and *Proconsul*." *American Journal of Physical Anthropology*, 47:395-398.

Gnanadesikan, R., and M. B. Wilk, 1969. "Data Analytic Methods in Multivariate Statistical Analysis." In *Multivariate Analysis–II*, edited by P. R. Krishnaiah, pp. 593-638. New York: Academic Press.

Goldstein, L. G. 1975. "Mississippian Social Organization in the Lower Illinois Valley: Regional Manifestations of a Complex Society." Paper read at the Forty-Fourth Annual Meeting of the American Association of Physical Anthropologists, Denver.

Goldstein, S., D. Post, and D. Melnick. 1978. "An Analysis of Cercopithecoid Odontometrics. I. The Scaling of the Maxillary Dentition." *American Journal of Physical Anthropology*, 49:517-532.

Gopalan, C., and B. Belavady. 1961. "Nutrition and Lactation." *Federation*

Proceedings 20 (Suppl. 7):177-184.

Graham, G. G., and B. Adrianzen. 1971. "Growth, Inheritance, and Environment." *Pediatric Research*, 5:691-697.

Greulich, W. W. 1957. "A Comparison of the Physical Growth and Development of American-born and Native Japanese Children." *American Journal of Physical Anthropology*, 15:489-516.

―――. 1951. "The Growth and Development Status of Guamanian School Children in 1947." *American Journal of Physical Anthropology*, 9:55-70.

Greulich, W. W., C. S. Crismon, and M. L. Turner. 1953. "The Physical Growth and Development of Children Who Survived the Atomic Bombing of Hiroshima and Nagasaki." *Journal of Pediatrics*, 43:121-145.

Griffin, J. B. 1967. "Eastern North American Archaeology: A Summary." *Science*, 156:175-191.

Gunther, M. 1952. "Composition of Human Milk and Factors Affecting It." *British Journal of Nutrition*, 6:215-219.

Gustav, B. L. 1972. "Sexual Dimorphism in the Adult, Bony Pelvis of a Prehistoric Human Population from Illinois." Ph.D. dissertation, University of Massachusetts.

Hall, R. L. 1978. "Sexual Dimorphism for Size in Seven Nineteenth Century Northwest Coast Populations." *Human Biology*, 50:159-171.

Hamilton, J. B. 1948. "The Role of Testicular Secretions as Indicated by the Effects of Castration in Man and by Studies of Pathological Conditions and the Short Lifespan Associated with Maleness." *Recent Progress in Hormone Research*, 3:257-322.

Hamilton, M. E. 1981. "Female Competition in the Evolution of Human Female Sexuality." Manuscript. Submitted to *American Anthropologist*.

―――. 1975. "Variation Among Five Groups of Amerindians in the Magnitude of Sexual Dimorphism of Skeletal Size." Ph.D. dissertation, University of Michigan. Ann Arbor: University of Michigan. Order No. 76-9410.

Hanna, R. E., and S. L. Washburn. 1953. "The Determination of the Sex of Skeletons as Illustrated by a Study of Eskimo Pelves." *Human Biology*, 25:21-27.

Haviland, W. A. 1967. "Stature at Tikal, Guatemala: Implications for Ancient Maya Demography and Social Organization." *American Antiquity*, 32:316-325.

Henderson, A. M., and R. S. Corruccini. 1976. "Relationship between Tooth Size and Body Size in American Blacks." *Journal of Dental Research*, 55:94-96.

Hewitt, D., C. K. Westropp, and R. M. Acheson. 1955. "Oxford Child Health Survey: Effect of Childish Ailments on Skeletal Development." *British Journal of Preventive and Social Medicine*, 9:179-186.

Hiernaux, J. 1968. "Variabilitié du Dimorphism Sexuel de la Stature en Afrique Subsaharienne et en Europe." In *Anthropologie and Humangenetik*, pp. 42-50. Stuttgart: Gustav Fischer Verlag.

Himes, J. H., and R. M. Malina. 1977. "Sexual Dimorphism in Metacarpal Dimensions and Body Size of Mexican School Children." *Acta Anatomica*, 99:15-20.

Holt, C. Adams. 1978. "A Re-examination of Parturition Scars on the Human Female Pelvis." *American Journal of Physical Anthropology*, 49:91-94.

Houghton, P. 1974. "The Relationship of the Pre-Auricular Groove of the Ilium to Pregnancy." *American Journal of Physical Anthropology*, 41:381-390.

Howell, F. 1967. "Review of Man-Apes or Ape-Men?" *American Journal of Physical Anthropology*, 27:95-101.

Howells, W. W. 1969. "The Use of Multivariate Techniques in the Study of Skeletal Populations." *American Journal of Physical Anthropology*, 31:311-314.

Hrdlička, A. 1939. *Practical Anthropometry*. Philadelphia: Wistar Institute.

Hunter, W. S., and S. M. Garn. 1972. "Disporportionate Sexual Dimorphism in the Human Face." *American Journal of Physical Anthropology*, 36:133-138.

Isaac, G. 1978. "The Food-Sharing Behavior of Protohuman Hominids." *Scientific American*, 238(4):90-108.

Israel, H. 1977. "The Dichotomous Pattern of Craniofacial Expansion during Aging." *American Journal of Physical Anthropology*, 47:47-51.

──────. 1973. "Age Factors and the Patterns of Change in Craniofacial Structures." *American Journal of Physical Anthropology*, 39:111-128.

Janz, A. J., E. M. Demayer, and J. Close. 1957. "Nutrition et Lactation chez la Femme." *Annales de la Nutrition et de l'Alimentation*, 11:A33-A81.

Jelliffe, D. B. 1966. *The Assessment of the Nutritional Status of the Community*. Geneva: World Health Organization Monograph Series No. 53.

Johanson, D. C., and T. D. White. 1979. "A Systematic Assessment of Early African Hominids." *Science*, 203:321-330.

Kaltreider, D. F. 1963. *Effects of Height and Weight on Pregnancy and the Newborn*. Springfield, Ill.: C. C. Thomas.

Kelley, Marc A. 1979. "Parturition and Pelvic Changes." *American Journal of Physical Anthropology*, 51:541-546.

──────. 1978. "Phenice's Visual Sexing Technique for the *Os Pubis*: A Critique." *American Journal of Physical Anthropology*, 48:121-122.

Kensinger, K. M. 1975. "Studying the Cashinahua." In *The Cashinahua of Eastern Peru*, edited by J. P. Dwyer, pp. 9-85. *Studies in Anthropology and Material Culture*, Vol. 1. Providence, Rhode Island: The Haffenreffer Museum of Anthropology, Brown University.

Key, P. 1980. "Evolutionary Trends in Femoral Sexual Dimorphism from the Mesolithic to the late Middle Ages in Europe." Paper read at the Forty-Ninth Annual Meeting of the American Association of Physical Anthropologists, Niagara Falls, New York. Published Abstract: *American Journal of Physical Anthropology*, 52: 244.

Kowalski, C. J. 1972. "A Commentary on the Use of Multivariate Statistical Methods in Anthropometric Research." *American Journal of Physical*

Anthropology, 36:119-131.

Lambert, J. B., C. B. Szpunar, and J. E. Buikstra. 1979. "Chemical Analysis of Excavated Human Bone from Middle and Late Woodland Sites." *Archaeometry*, 21:115-129.

Laporte, M. 1946. "The Effect of War Imposed Dietary Limitations." *American Journal of Diseases of Children*, 21:244-247.

Lauer, C. 1975. "The Relationship of Tooth Size to Body Size in a Population of Rhesus Monkeys (*Macaca mulatta*)." *American Journal of Physical Anthropology*, 43:333-340.

Laughlin, W. S. 1968. "Hunting: An Integrating Biobehavior System and Its Evolutionary Importance." In *Man the Hunter*, edited by Richard B. Lee and Irven DeVore, pp. 304-320. Chicago: Aldine.

Lavelle, C. L. B. 1977. "Relationship between Tooth and Long Bone Size." *American Journal of Physical Anthropology*, 46:423-426.

Leakey, R. E. F., and A. C. Walker. 1976. "Australopithecus, Homo Erectus and the Single Species Hypothesis." *Nature*, 261:572-574.

Le Gros Clark, W. E. 1967. *Man-Apes or Ape-Men*. New York: Holt, Rinehart and Winston.

Malcolm, L. A. 1970. "Growth and Development of the Bundi Child of the New Guinea Highlands." *Human Biology*, 42:293-328.

――――. 1969. "Growth and Development of the Kaiapit Children of the Markham Valley, New Guinea." *American Journal of Physical Anthropology*, 31:39-51.

Martin, R. 1928. *Lehrbuch der Anthropologie*, 2nd ed. (3 vols.). Jena: Gustav Fischer.

Martorell, R., C. Yarborough, R. E. Klein, and A. Lechtig. 1979. "Malnutrition, Body Size, and Skeletal Maturation: Interrelationships and Implications for Catch-up Growth." *Human Biology*, 51:371-389.

Merchant, V. L., and D. H. Ubelaker. 1977. "Skeletal Growth of the Protohistoric Arikara." *American Journal of Physical Anthropology*, 46:61-72.

Montet-White, A. 1968. *The Lithic Industries of the Illinois Valley in the Early and Middle Woodland Period*. Anthropological Papers, Museum of Anthropology, No. 35. Ann Arbor: University of Michigan.

Moss, M. L. 1958. "The Pathogenesis of Artificial Cranial Deformation." *American Journal of Physical Anthropology*, 16:269-286.

Moss, M. L., and L. Moss-Salentijn. 1977. "Analysis of Developmental Processes Possibly Related to Human Dental Sexual Dimorphism in Permanent and Deciduous Canines." *American Journal of Physical Anthropology*, 46:407-414.

Mueller, W. H. 1979. "Fertility and Physique in a Malnourished Population." *Human Biology*, 51:153-166.

Munson, P. J. 1973. "The Origins and Antiquity of Maize-beans-squash Agriculture in Eastern North America." In *Variation in Anthropology: Essays in Honor of John C. McGregor*, edited by Donald W. Lathrop and Jody Douglas, pp. 107-135. Urbana: Illinois Archaeological Survey.

Murad, T. A. 1976. "Comments." *Current Anthropology*,17:598.
Niswander, K., and E. C. Jackson. 1974. "Physical Characteristics of the Gravida and their Association with Birth Weight and Perinatal Death." *American Journal of Obstetrics and Gynecology*, 119:306-313.
Olivier, G. 1969. *Practical Anthropology*. Springfield, Ill.: Charles C Thomas.
Parizkova, J., and J. Merhaustova. 1970. "The Comparison of Somatic Development, Body Composition and Functional Characteristics in Tunisian and Czech Boys of 11 and 12 Years." *Human Biology*, 42:391-400.
Parmalee, P. W., A. A. Paloumpis, and N. Wilson. 1972. *Animals Utilized by Woodland Peoples Occupying the Apple Creek Site, Illinois*. Illinois State Museum Reports of Investigations, No. 23. Springfield: Illinois State Museum.
Perino, G. 1971. "The Mississippian Component at the Schild Site (No. 4), Greene County, Illinois." In *Mississippian Site Archaeology in Illinois I*, edited by James A. Brown, pp. 1-148. Springfield: Illinois Archaeological Survey Bulletin No. 8.
_____. 1962. "A Review of Calhoun County, Illinois, Prehistory." *Wisconsin Archeologist*, 43:44-51.
Perzigian, A. J. 1977. "Fluctuating Dental Asymmetry: Variation among Skeletal Populations." *American Journal of Physical Anthropology*, 47:81-88.
Pfeiffer, S. 1980. "Age Changes in the External Dimensions of Adult Bone." *American Journal of Physical Anthropology*, 52:529-532.
Phenice, T. W. 1969. "A Newly Developed Visual Method of Sexing the Os Pubis." *American Journal of Physical Anthropology*, 30:297-301.
Pilbeam, D. R., and M. Zwell. 1973. "The Single Species Hypothesis, Sexual Dimorphism, and Variability in Early Hominids." *Yearbook of Physical Anthropology 1972*, 16:69-79.
Pons, J. 1955. "The Sexual Diagnosis of Isolated Bones of the Skeleton." *Human Biology* 27:12-21.
Post, D. G. 1979. "Sexual Dimorphism in Primates: Some Thoughts on Causes and Correlates." Paper read at the Forty-Eighth Annual Meeting of the American Association of Physical Anthropologists, San Francisco, California. Published Abstract: *American Journal of Physical Anthropology*, 50: 471-472.
_____. 1978. "The Feeding and Ranging Behavior of the Yellow Baboon (*Papio cynocephalus*)." Ph.D. dissertation, Yale University.
Post, D., S. Goldstein, and D. Melnick. 1978. "An Analysis of Cercopithecoid Odontometrics. II. Relations between Dental Dimorphism, Body Size Dimorphism and Diet." *American Journal of Physical Anthropology*, 49:533-544.
Prader, G. P., J. M. Tanner, and J. A. von Harnack. 1963. "Catch-up Growth following Illness or Starvation." *Journal of Pediatrics*, 62:646-659.
Putschar, W. G. J. 1976. "The Structure of the Human Symphysis Pubis with Special Consideration of Parturition and Its Sequelae." *American*

Journal of Physical Anthropology, 45:589-594.

Ralls, K. 1977. "Sexual Dimorphism in Mammals: Avian Models and Unanswered Questions." *American Naturalist*, 11:917-938.

Reyment, R. A. 1969. "Statistical Analysis of Sexual Dimorphism in Some Groups of Living Animals." In *Sexual Dimorphism in Fossil Metazoa and Taxonomic Implications*, edited by G. E. G. Westerman, pp. 21-27. Stuttgart: Nagele and Obermiller.

Rightmire, G. P. 1969. "On the Computation of Mahalanobis' Generalized Distance (D^2)." *American Journal of Physical Anthropology*, 30:157-160.

Robinson, J. T. 1972. *Early Hominid Posture and Locomotion*. Chicago: University of Chicago Press.

————. 1967. "Variation and the Taxonomy of the Early Hominids." In *Evolutionary Biology Vol. 1*, edited by T. Dobzhansky, M. K. Hecht, and W. C. Steere, pp. 69-100. New York: Appleton-Century-Crofts.

————. 1965. *Homo habilis* and the Australopithecines." *Nature*, 205:121-124.

————. 1956. *The Dentition of the Australopithecinae*. Transvaal Museum, Memoir No. 9, Pretoria, South Africa.

Rose, J. C., G. J. Armelagos, and J. W. Lallo, 1978. "Histological Enamel Indicator of Childhood Stress in Prehistoric Skeletal Samples." *American Journal of Physical Anthropology*, 49:511-516.

Ruff, C. B. 1980. "Age Differences in Craniofacial Dimensions among Adults from Indian Knoll, Kentucky." *American Journal of Physical Anthropology*, 53:101-108.

Saul, F. P. 1972. *The Human Skeletal Remains of Altar de Sacrificios. An Osteobiographic Analysis*. Papers of the Peabody Museum of Archaeology and Ethnology, Harvard University, Vol. 63, No. 2, the Peabody Museum, Cambridge, Mass.

Schendel, S. A., G. Walker, and A. Kamisugi. 1980. "Hawaiian Craniofacial Morphometrics: Average Mokapuan Skull, Artificial Cranial Deformation, and the 'Rocker' Mandible." *American Journal of Physical Anthropology*, 52:491-500.

Schoeninger, M. J. 1979. "Diet and Status at Chalcatzingo: Some Empirical and Technical Aspects of Strontium Analysis." *American Journal of Physical Anthropology*, 51:295-309.

Schoenwetter, J. 1979. "Comment on 'Plant Husbandry in Prehistoric Eastern North American'." *American Antiquity*, 44:600-601.

Schultz, A. H. 1930. "The Skeleton of the Trunk and Limbs of Higher Primates." *Human Biology*, 2:303-438.

Scrimshaw, N. S., and M. Behar. 1965. "Malnutrition in Undeveloped Countries." *New England Journal of Medicine*, 272:137-144.

Scrimshaw, N. S., C. E. Taylor, and J. E. Gordon. 1968. *Interactions of Nutrition and Infection*. Geneva: World Health Organization Monograph Series No. 57.

Seibert, H. C. 1940. "Observations on the Somatic Constitution of Mothers with and without Infant Mortality among Their Progeny." *Human Biology*, 12:232-246.

Senecal, J. 1959. "Alimentation de L'Enfant dans les Pays Tropicaux et Subtropicaux." *Courrier*, 9:1-22.

Siegel, M. I. 1976. "Comment." *Current Anthropology*, 17:600.

Simpson, G. G. 1941. "Large Pleistocene Felines of North America." *American Museum Novitates*, No. 1136.

Siskind, J. 1975. "Tropical Forest Hunters and the Economy of Sex." In *Peoples and Cultures of Native South America*, edited by D. R. Gross, pp. 226-240. Garden City, New York: Doubleday/The Natural History Press.

Smith, B. D. 1975. *Middle Mississippi Exploitation of Animal Populations*. Museum of Anthropology Anthropological Papers, No. 57. Ann Arbor: University of Michigan.

_____. 1974. "Middle Mississippi Exploitation of Animal Populations: A Predictive Model." *American Antiquity*, 39:274-291.

Smith, R. W., Jr., and R. R. Walker. 1964. "Femoral Expansion in Aging Women: Implications for Osteoporosis and Fractures." *Science*, 145:156-157.

Steele, D. G. 1976. "The Estimation of Sex on the Basis of the Talus and Calcaneus." *American Journal of Physical Anthropology*, 45:581-588.

Stewart, T. D. 1954. "Sex Determination in the Skeleton by Guess and by Measurement." *American Journal of Physical Anthropology*, 12:385-392.

Stini, W. A. 1975. *Ecology and Human Adaptation*. Dubuque, Iowa: William C. Brown.

_____. 1972. "Reduced Sexual Dimorphism in Upper Arm Muscle Circumference Associated with Protein Deficient Diet in a South American Population." *American Journal of Physical Anthropology*, 30:341-352.

_____. 1971. "Evolutionary Implications of Changing Nutritional Patterns in Human Populations." *American Anthropologist*, 73:1019-1030.

_____. 1969. "Nutritional Stress and Growth: Sex Difference in Adaptive Response." *American Journal of Physical Anthropology*, 31:417-426.

Struever, S. 1968. "Woodland Subsistence-settlement Systems in the Lower Illinois Valley." In *Perspectives in Archeology*, edited by S. R. Binford and L. R. Binford, pp. 285-312. Chicago: Aldine.

Struever, S., and K. D. Vickery. 1973. "The Beginnings of Cultivation in the Midwest-Riverine Area of the United States." *American Anthropologist*, 75:1197-1220.

Suchey, J. Myers, D. V. Wiseley, R. F. Green, and T. T. Noguchi. 1979. "Analysis of Dorsal Pitting in the *Os Pubis* in an Extensive Sample of Modern American Females." *American Journal of Physical Anthropology*, 51:517-540.

Sutow, W. W., R. A. Conrad, and K. M. Griffith. 1965. "Growth Status of Children Exposed to Fallout Radiation on Marshall Islands." *Pediatrics*, 36:721-730.

Swedlund, A. C. 1974. "The Use of Ecological Hypothesis in Australopithecine Taxonomy." *American Anthropologist*, 76:515-529.

Szpunar, C. B., J. B. Lambert, and J. E. Buikstra. 1978. "Analysis of Excavated Bone by Atomic Absorption." *American Journal of Physical Anthropology*, 48:119-202.

Tainter, J. A. 1977. "Woodland Social Change in West-Central Illinois." *Midcontinental Journal of Archaeology*, 2:67-98.

————. 1975. "The Archaeological Study of Social Change: Woodland Systems in West-central Illinois." Ph.D. dissertation, Northwestern University. Ann Arbor: University Microfilms.

Tanner, J. J. 1970. "Physical Growth." In *Carmichael's Manual of Child Psychology*, Vol. 1, 3rd ed., edited by P. H. Mussen, pp. 77-155. New York: Wiley.

————. 1962. *Growth at Adolescence*. Oxford: Blackwell Scientific Publications.

Tanner, N., and A. Zihlman. 1976. "Women in Evolution. Part I: Innovation and Selection in Human Origins." *Signs: Journal of Women in Culture and Society* (3, Part 1):585-608.

Thieme, F. P., and W. J. Schull, 1957. "Sex Determination from the Skeleton." *Human Biology*, 29:242-273.

Thomson, A. M. 1966. "Adult Stature." In *Somatic Growth of the Child*, edited by J. J. van der Werff, T. Bosch, and A. Hask, pp. 197-204. Springfield, Ill.: Charles C. Thomas.

————. 1959. "Diet in Pregnancy. 3. Diet in Relation to the Course and Outcome of Pregnancy." *British Journal of Nutrition*, 13:509-529.

Thomson, A. M., and W. Z. Belewicz. 1963. "Nutritional Status, Maternal Physique, and Reproductive Efficiency." *Proceedings of the Nutritional Society*, 22:55-60.

Tobias, P. V. 1972. "Growth and Stature in Southern African Populations." In *Human Biology of Environmental Change*, edited by D. J. M. Vorster, pp. 96-104. London: International Biological Programme.

————. 1971. "The Distribution of Cranial Capacity Values among Living Hominoids." *Proceedings 3rd International Congress of Primatology*, Zurich, 1970. Vol. 1: 18-35. Basel: Karger.

————. 1966. "The Distinctiveness of *Homo habilis*." *Nature*, 209:953-957.

————. 1962. "On the Increasing Stature of the Bushmen." *Anthropos*, 57:801-810.

Townsend, G. C., and T. Brown. 1978. "Heritability of Permanent Tooth Size." *American Journal of Physical Anthropology*, 49:497-504.

Trinkaus, E. 1976. "Comments." *Current Anthropology* 17:600-601.

Trivers, R. L. 1972. "Parental Investment and Sexual Selection." In *Sexual Selection and the Descent of Man 1871-1971*, edited by Bernard C. Campbell, pp. 136-179. Chicago: Aldine.

Trotter, M., and G. C. Gleser. 1958. "A Re-evaluation of Estimation of Stature Taken during Life and of Long Bones after Death." *American Journal of Physical Anthropology*, 16:79-123.

Van Gerven, D. P. 1972. "The Contribution of Size and Shape Variations to Patterns of Sexual Dimorphism of the Human Femur." *American Journal of Physical Anthropology*, 37:49-60.

Van Gerven, D. P., and G. B. Oakland. 1974. "Univariate and Multivariate Statistical Models in the Analysis of Human Sexual Dimorphism." *The Statistician*, 22:256-268.

Vark, G. N. van. 1976. "A Critical Evaluation of the Application of Multivariate Statistical Methods to the Study of Human Populations from Their Skeletal Remains." *Homo*, 27:94-114.

Washburn, S. L. 1949. "Sex Differences in the Pubic Bone of Bantu and Bushman." *American Journal of Physical Anthropology*, 7:425-532.

_____. 1948. "Sex Differences in the Pubic Bone." *American Journal of Physical Anthropology*, 6:199-207.

Weiss, K. 1972. "On the Systematic Bias in Skeletal Sexing." *American Journal of Physical Anthropology*, 37:239-249.

Whatley, B. L., and N. B. Asch. 1975. "Woodland Subsistence: Implications for Demographic and Nutritional Studies." Paper read at the Forty-Fourth Annual Meeting of the American Association of Physical Anthropologists, Denver, Colorado.

White, T. D. 1978. "Early Hominid Enamel Hypoplasia." *American Journal of Physical Anthropology*, 49:79-83.

White T. D., and J. M. Harris. 1977. "Suid Evolution and Correlation of African Hominid Localities." *Science*, 198:13-21.

Widdowson, E. M. 1968. "The Place of Experimental Animals in the Study of Human Malnutrition." In *Calorie Deficiencies and Protein Deficiencies*, edited by R. A. McCance and E. M. Widdowson, pp. 225-234. Boston: Little, Brown.

Wilson, E. O. 1975. *Sociobiology: The New Synthesis*. Cambridge, Mass.: Harvard University Press.

Wolff, G. 1940. "A Study on the Trend of Weight in White School Children from 1933-1936. Material Based on the Examination of Pupils of the Elementary Schools in Hagerstown, Maryland." *Child Development*, 11:159-180.

Wolpoff, Milford H. 1976a. "Primate Models for Australopithecine Sexual Dimorphism." *American Journal of Physical Anthropology*, 45:497-510.

_____. 1976b. "Some Aspects of the Evolution of Early Hominid Sexual Dimorphism." *Current Anthropology*, 17:579-606.

_____. 1975. "Sexual Dimorphism in the Australopithecines." In *Paleoanthropology Morphology and Paleoecology*, edited by Russell H. Tuttle, pp. 245-284. The Hague: Mouton.

_____. 1974. "The Evidence for Two Australopithecine Lineages in South Africa." *Yearbook of Physical Anthropology 1973*, 17:113-139.

_____. 1971. "Competitive Exclusion among Lower Pleistocene Hominids: The Single Species Hypothesis." *Man*, 6:601-614.

World Health Organization. 1973. *Energy and Protein Requirements*. W.H.O. Technical Report Series No. 522. F.A.O. Nutrition Meetings Report Series No. 52. Rome.

_____. 1965a. *Protein Requirements*. W.H.O. Technical Report Series No. 301. [Issued also as F.A.O. Meetings Report Series, No. 37, Geneva.]

_____. 1965b. *Nutrition in Pregnancy and Lactation*. W.H.O. Technical

Report Series No. 302. Geneva.

Yarnell, R. A. 1976. "Early Plant Husbandry in Eastern North America." In *Culture Change and Continuity*, edited by Charles E. Cleland, pp. 265-273. New York: Academic Press.

———. 1969. "Contents of Human Paleofeces." In *The Prehistory of Salts Cave, Kentucky*, edited by Patty Jo Watson, pp. 41-54. Springfield: Illinois State Museum Reports of Investigations, No. 16.

Young, V. R., and N. S. Scrimshaw. 1971. "The Physiology of Starvation." *Scientific American*, 225(4):14-21.

Zawacki, A. A., and G. Hausfater. 1969. *Early Vegetation of the Lower Illinois Valley*. Illinois State Museum Reports of Investigations, No. 17; Illinois Valley Archaeological Program Research Papers, Vol. 1. Springfield: Illinois State Museum.

Zihlman, A. L. 1976. "Sexual Dimorphism and Its Behavioral Implications in Early Hominids." Paper prepared for IXe Congres, Union Internationale des Sciences préhistoriques et protohistoriques, Colloque IV "Les plus anciens hominides"; organized by P. V. Tobias and Y. Coppens for publication in Congress Proceeding, CNRS.

Zihlman, A., and N. Tanner. 1978. "Gathering and the Hominid Adaptation," in *Female Hierarchies*, edited by Lionel Tiger and M. Fowler, pp. 53-62. Chicago: Aldine.

Zingeser, M. R., and C. H. Phoenix. 1978. "Metric Characteristics of the Canine Dental Complex in Prenatally Androgenized Female Rhesus Monkeys (*Macaca mulatta*)." *American Journal of Physical Anthropology*, 49:187-192.

Six

Sexual Dimorphism and Settlement Pattern in Middle Eastern Skeletal Populations

David J. Finkel

General trends toward a reduction in human sexual dimorphism from the Lower Pleistocene to recent times have been reported for a number of different populations (Brace 1973; Frayer 1977; Olivier 1969; Wolpoff 1973, 1976). Considerable discussion has been presented to explain the reduction. Campbell (1966) as well as others (e.g., Brace 1973) have suggested that the increasing size of both sexes throughout the Pleistocene along with the increased social roles of women may have operated to reduce sexual dimorphism. The use of tools has also been a factor, compensating for size differential (DeVore and Washburn 1963). The loss of estrus in females, the corresponding evolution of the human family to replace the dominance hierarchy, and the development of a more permanent male-female relationship are also hypothesized to have reduced selection for secondary sexual characteristics (Campbell 1966).

These explanations of reductions in sexual dimorphism of early man (pre-*Homo sapiens* of the postglacial period) are generally bio-behavioral in nature and may be summarized:

1. Loss of estrus led to a reorganization of the social unit; females increased in size due to their social role as protector of the family.
2. Change to a high protein diet and the availability of such resources during the Pleistocene as humans developed hunting skills eliminated the advantage of small size for females, such as DeVore and Washburn (1963) postulated for baboons.

3. Reduction in sexual competition eliminated, at least to some extent, the advantage of secondary sexual characteristics.
4. There was an advantage to large size for both sexes in terms of survival on the savannah; the advantage of a large birth canal for female bipeds with large headed fetuses intensified the general advantage to increased size (Campbell 1966).

Studies in sexual dimorphism of more recent *Homo sapiens* sapiens have stressed socioeconomic factors as associated with a general reduction in sexual dimorphism and, possibly, as causal. Frayer (1978) explained dimorphism differences by noting differences in sex roles between hunter-gatherers, where division of labor by sex is more rigidly demarcated, and agricultural groups, where sharing of economically based activities tends to occur (Murdock and Provost 1973). Gracilization of males occurred because of the continued improvement in tool technology and the change in the types of animals hunted; for example, a reduction in the generally strenuous economic lifeways of males took place between the Upper Paleolithic and Mesolithic in Europe. Further reduction in dimorphism occurred in the European Neolithic, possibly because of the greater degree of shared economic activities by males and females engendered by the agricultural way of life. Continued reduction in relative sexual dimorphism of dental measurements occurred between Neolithic and modern groups; yet, unexplained increases in percent sexual dimorphism occurred for cranial and postcranial measurements (Frayer 1978).

Sexual dimorphism in cranial measurements in skeletal populations from the Middle East and Mediterranean Europe over a 3500-year span at a time when rapid technological and associated sociocultural change was taking place was analyzed to determine whether similar increases in relative sexual dimorphism occurred as observed by Frayer (1978). Analysis of sexual dimorphism was carried out on a regional basis as well as over time, but it was hypothesized that the greatest changes in relative sexual dimorphism of the cranium would occur in association with historically and archaeologically documented sociocultural and technological change. It was further hypothesized that economic and nutritional differences between skeletal populations of similar technological and demographic levels would also be associated with differences in sexual dimorphism.

SAMPLES TO BE ANALYZED

Finkel (1978) used osteometric variables of the cranium and mandible to describe 48 skeletal samples of males from Mediterranean Europe and the Middle East, ranging in time from 3100 B.C. to A.D. 200. A model of population and group divergence, based on geographic separation and ancient cultural boundaries, satisfactorily described the spatial and temporal relationships of the samples. That is, statistically significant F-ratios were obtained when single classification analysis of variance was performed between samples. The cranial and mandibular measurements within a group were significantly more similar to each other than to skeletal samples in other groups. The skeletal samples are described in Table 6.1, according to the nine groups into which they had previously been divided. These include groups from coastal Turkey and Northern Cyprus, Southern Cyprus and the Amuq Valley in Syria, Anatolia, Israel, Greece and Crete, Italy, the Nile Valley, the Tigris-Euphrates Valley, and Iran.

Seven of the archaeological sites contained samples from different time levels, so that it was possible to compare samples from different time periods while holding the spatial dimension constant. Results showed nonsignificant (P greater than 5 percent) statistical differences over time at all sites except one, Lachish, where in 25 percent of the variables tested mean values showed significant differences. This finding may be attributed to historically and archaeologically documented migration (Kenyon 1960).

Sample means for all 48 samples correlated with time were nonsignificant for all but two of 16 variables. The largest r value, 0.456, while statistically significant, explains less than 21 percent of the variance. The following conclusions were drawn:

1. Skeletal samples closest together in space are most likely to represent interbreeding units and, therefore, to resemble each other morphologically.
2. Ancient cultural boundaries, confirmed through historic, archaeological, and linguistic sources, possibly represent interbreeding boundaries as well.
3. Populations of postglacial *Homo sapiens* are more likely to show significant statistical differences when compared spatially as opposed to temporal comparisons at the same site or regionally.

Beyond the boundaries of each of the nine groups, the phenotypes, as represented by cranial and mandibular measurements, had mean values that were significantly different statistically from those within the group. Although composed of availability samples, as is the case with virtually all archaeological material, the groups represent points of population divergence even though rates of change at individual sites were slow. Tests of significance between sample means from different time levels at the seven sites discussed

TABLE 6.1
Local Populations in Time and Space by Nine Group Cultural Spatial Model.

Site (N)	Dating	Settlement Type	Source
Group 1–Coastal Turkey and Northern Cyprus			
Ephesus (74)	300-100 B.C.	Urban	Schümacher (1926)
Karatash (142)	*ca.* 2400 B.C.	Village agr.	Angel (1966, pers. comm.)
Lapethos			
a (19)	*ca.* 2500 B.C.	Village agr.	Buxton (1920)
b (50)	1800-1600 B.C.	Proto-urban	
Sardis (86)	*ca.* A.D. 100	Urban	Bostanci (1963, 1967, 1969)
Troy			
a (26)	*ca.* 2600 B.C.	Village agr.	Angel (1951)
b (28)	*ca.* 500 B.C.	Proto-urban	
Group 2–Anatolia			
Alisharhuyuk			
a (18)	2500-2300 B.C.	Proto-urban	Krogman (1933, 1937)
b (16)	1000-800 B.C.	Village agr.	
c (18)	500-300 B.C.	Village agr.	
Kultepe (15)	*ca.* 1900 B.C.	Proto-urban	Senyurek (1952)
Group 3–Southern Cyprus and the Amuq Valley, Syria			
Sotira (62)	3200-3000 B.C.	Village agr.	Angel (1953)
Tell-al-Judaidah (24)	1400-1200 B.C.	Proto-urban	Krogman (1949)
Group 4–Israel			
Gezer (88)	*ca.* 1450 B.C.	Village agr.	Finkel (1974)
Lachish			
a (79)	2400-2200 B.C.	Proto-urban	Risdon (1939)
b (863)	*ca.* 700 B.C.	Urban	
Megiddo			
a (18)	*ca.* 2900 B.C.	Proto-urban	Hrdlička (1940)
b (14)	1600-1400 B.C.	Urban	
Group 5–Greece and Crete			
Athens			
a (31)	*ca.* 2400 B.C.	Village agr.	Angel (1944, 1945, 1946)
b (26)	1400-1200 B.C.	Proto-urban	
c (52)	1100-1000 B.C.	Proto-urban	
d (33)	900-700 B.C.	Urban	
e (15)	500-300 B.C.	Urban	
f (50)	300-100 B.C.	Urban	

TABLE 6.1. (continued)

Site (N)	Dating	Settlement Type	Source
Olynthus (16)	*ca.* 400 B.C.	Urban	Angel (1942)
Zakro (22)	*ca.* 1500 B.C.	Urban	Dawkins (1900-1901)
Group 6–Italy			
Etruria (28)	700-500 B.C.	Urban	Sergei (1901)
Rome (70)	*ca.* A.D. 100	Urban	Brothwell (pers. comm.)
Group 7–Nile Valley			
Abydos (48)	*ca.* 2900 B.C.	Urban	Morant (1925)
Sedment (71)	*ca.* 2100 B.C.	Urban	Woo (1930)
Group 8–Tigris-Euphrates Valley			
Kish			
a (47)	*ca.* 2500 B.C.	Urban	Buxton & Rice
b (60)	*ca.* 500 B.C.	Urban	(1931)
Nippur (32)	700-500 B.C.	Urban	Swindler (1956)
Nuzi (46)	*ca.* A.D. 200	Urban	Ehrich (1939)
Group 9–Iran			
Tepe Hissar (336)	*ca.* 2000 B.C.	Urban	Krogman (1940)

above showed only nine cases of significance. The average change per generation for those significant cases, assuming a 20-year generational span, was 0.055 mm. Further, absence of statistically significant deviations from a normal distribution for all samples, plotted by probit analysis, suggested that population equilibrium was rarely disturbed during the time period under consideration.

Finkel (1978) inferred that migration was insufficient to prevent group divergence. The absence of major fluctuations in the morphological attributes between geographically as well as temporally similar samples allowed the inference that genetic drift was not a major factor in the population evolution of the region over the rather short time period represented by the skeletal samples. Disturbances in population equilibrium, such as observed at Lachish, appeared to result from migration rather than from mutation, selection, or drift.

Since a statistically and culturally significant model of spatial and temporal relationships exists for these samples, they are ideal for analysis of sexual dimorphism. Female skeletal samples were available for 35 of the 48 groups. Male and female samples were used to determine percent sexual dimorphism of the skull and its components, cranial vault, face, and mandible. It was possible to

1. Determine whether differences exist in the degree of percent sexual dimorphism of the several components of the skull.
2. Determine the extent of differences in percent sexual dimorphism between these samples, which represent agriculturally based populations, and the European hunting-gathering populations of previous time periods.
3. Determine the extent of differences in percent sexual dimorphism among the samples of the study, i.e., to ask whether skeletal samples assort by degree of percent sexual dimorphism in the same way they have been shown to cluster by the absolute value of the osteometric variables of the skull (Finkel 1978).
4. Determine the extent and direction, if any, of changes in percent sexual dimorphism over time.
5. Suggest factors associated with increases or decreases in percent sexual dimorphism, whether biobehavioral or socioeconomic. For example, Table 6.1 describes the settlement type of each skeletal sample. While all populations are agricultural in their method of subsistence, those populations practicing village agriculture may be expected to exhibit sex roles and degrees of economic sharing different from urban and proto-urban settlements where food comes into the settlement from the countryside in return for crafts and services (Trigger 1972; Wheatley 1972). Although ethnographic evidence is not readily available for these populations, historical and archaeological evidence, in most cases, allows the inference of economic status.

MATERIALS AND METHODS

Twenty-two osteometric variables of the cranium and mandible were selected to reflect the dimensions of the cranial vault, the face, and the mandible. The material was measured, and observations on pathology and nutritional status were made by the author, when possible, to reduce variance due to different measurement techniques and to ensure consistency of observation. When this was impossible, measurements of individual crania from published studies were utilized. Measurements (Martin's number in parentheses) are listed in Table 6.2. For the 35 skeletal samples, the median sample size, males and females combined, is 33.

The extent of sexual dimorphism for any variable may be expressed conveniently as a percent, i.e., the difference between

TABLE 6.2

Mean Percent Sexual Dimorphism in the Skull of European Upper Paleolithic (UP), Mesolithic (Meso) and Neolithic (Neo) Samples and 35 Middle Eastern and Mediterranean European (ME) Samples with the Number of Significant F-Ratios Between Male and Female Variances of the Middle Eastern and Mediterranean European Samples.

	Percent Dimorphism[a]				
Variable (Martin's N)	UP	Meso	Neo	ME(35)	F (N samples)
Maximum length (1)	6.3	5.3	3.9	4.6	1 (34)
Basion-nasion (5)	6.4	6.9	5.4	4.2	2 (22)
Maximum width (8)	1.9	2.8	3.0	2.7	1 (33)
Max. frontal width (10)	5.1	3.6	2.7	3.0	0 (21)
Biasterionic breadth (11)	4.5	4.0	4.1	4.4	1 (8)
Basion-bregma (17)	—	—	—	4.1	2 (22)
Occipital arc (28)	3.7	6.3	2.6	4.4	1 (6)
Basion-prosthion (40)	7.6	4.9	5.4	5.4	0 (16)
Biorbital breadth (44)	—	—	—	4.3	1 (15)
Bizygomatic width (45)	3.7	5.2	6.4	6.3	1 (23)
Nasion-prosthion (48)	7.8	7.5	6.4	5.7	0 (25)
Interorbital width (50)	—	—	—	5.1	1 (17)
Orbital width (51)	—	—	—	3.8	1 (25)
Orbital height (52)	—	—	—	1.2	3 (26)
Nasal width (54)	7.2	2.4	4.5	5.6	2 (26)
Nasal height (55)	7.6	7.5	6.3	5.5	0 (24)
Bicondylar width (65)	6.4	6.0	6.7	5.8	1 (9)
Bigonial width (66)	4.2	7.4	6.3	7.8	1 (13)
Mandibular length (68)	4.6	1.4	2.9	4.1	0 (12)
Symphyseal height (69)	—	—	—	9.0	0 (15)
Asc. ramus height (70)	—	—	—	10.4	0 (9)
Asc. ramus breadth (71)	—	—	—	4.7	1 (16)
Mean cranial variables	5.6	5.1	4.6	4.4	(4.7)[b]
Mean mandibular variables	5.1	4.9	5.3	7.0	(5.9)[b]

[a]Data are from Frayer (1978).
[b]Mean, based in the table only on those variables used by Frayer (1978).

male and female means, divided by the male mean, multiplied by 100. While literally a percentage, the result represents a standardization of the male and female values for a particular variable so that sexual dimorphism of different variables may be combined and compared.

Since skeletal samples represent availability samples of the original populations, F-ratios were calculated between male and female variances of each variable for each skeletal sample. Statistical significance of two-tailed F-ratios was determined at the 0.05 level of significance. Table 6.2 shows that the number of significant *F*-ratios is quite small, often zero, for each variable, allowing the conclusion that male and female variances are not significantly different and that population means may be compared without heterogeneous variance distorting results. Individuals from different sites were not combined nor were individuals at the same site at different time levels, so that the use of samples in this study seems justified. Mean percent sexual dimorphism was calculated for all samples and is presented in Table 6.2 as well.

Comparison of percent sexual dimorphism of cranial and mandibular variables between the skeletal samples of this study and skeletal samples of the European Upper Paleolithic, Mesolithic, and Neolithic (after Frayer 1978) appear in Table 6.2. Cranial and mandibular variables of the sample means of this study were averaged for all variables and for only those variables used in Frayer's (1978) study and are presented in Table 6.2.

Mean percent sexual dimorphism of the variables of the cranial vault and base (4.10) and that of the face (4.67) for the skeletal samples of this study differ considerably less than both differ from mean mandibular percent sexual dimorphism (6.98). Since mandibular variables are unavailable for 19 of the 35 skeletal samples, their inclusion with variables of the face and vault in the remaining 16 samples would bias considerably the resulting mean percent sexual dimorphism of these samples. There are only six skeletal samples where variables of the face were unobtainable: Lapethos a, Kultepe, Alisharhuyuk b, Megiddo a, Megiddo b, and Olynthus. Only Lapethos a, Alisharhuyuk b, and Megiddo a show mean percent sexual dimorphism considerably below the combined mean percent sexual dimorphism of variables of the vault and face (4.39), so that the combination of variables of the cranial vault and face for all samples will not result in the distortion of percent sexual dimorphism.

Table 6.3 presents the mean percent sexual dimorphism of cranial and mandibular variables separately for each skeletal sample, arranged in a time sequence, beginning with the earliest. Because percent sexual dimorphism appears to decline over time in previous periods (see Table 6.2) and because this decline is often attributed to changes in tool technology (Brace 1973; Frayer 1978), skeletal samples are grouped according to traditional time divisions of Mediterranean Europe and the Middle East, which are based largely on changes (improvements) in tool material, manufacture, and efficiency as well as other similar kinds of cultural innovation. While these traditional divisions may vary greatly with regard to time over a geographical area, an approximate chronology may be suggested for this region.

TABLE 6.3

Mean Percent Sexual Dimorphism of Skeletal Samples in Time Sequence.

Sample	Dating	Percent Dimorphism Cranium	Mandible
Early Bronze I	3200-2700 B.C.	3.31	4.82
Sotira	3200-3000 B.C.	2.59	4.82
Abydos	*ca.* 2900 B.C.	4.14	—
Megiddo a	*ca.* 2900 B.C.	3.20	—
Early Bronze II	2600-2200 B.C.	3.70	6.60
Troy a	*ca.* 2600 B.C.	3.88	8.25
Kish a	*ca.* 2500 B.C.	3.72	3.03
Lapethos a	*ca.* 2500 B.C.	1.67	—
Athens a	*ca.* 2400 B.C.	4.49	—
Karatash	*ca.* 2400 B.C.	2.96	8.53
Alisharhuyuk a	2500-2300 B.C.	5.61	—
Lachish a	2400-2200 B.C.	3.57	—
Middle Bronze	2100-1600 B.C.	4.91	6.79
Sedment	*ca.* 2100 B.C.	5.34	6.81
Tepe Hissar	*ca.* 2000 B.C.	4.62	6.77
Kultepe	*ca.* 1900 B.C.	4.59	—
Lapethos b	1800-1600 B.C.	5.10	—
Late Bronze	1500-1200 B.C.	4.69	12.95
Megiddo b	1600-1400 B.C.	5.77	—
Zakro	*ca.* 1500 B.C.	2.88	—
Gezer	*ca.* 1450 B.C.	1.76	—
Athens b	1400-1200 B.C.	5.12	—
Tell-al-Judaidah	1400-1200 B.C.	7.94	12.95
Iron	1100-600 B.C.	3.84	8.62
Athens c	1100-1000 B.C.	3.87	8.76
Alisharhuyuk b	1000-800 B.C.	2.95	—
Athens d	900-700 B.C.	5.63	8.51
Lachish b	*ca.* 700 B.C.	3.53	—
Etruria	700-500 B.C.	1.96	—
Nippur	700-500 B.C.	5.07	8.59
Greco-Persian	500-300 B.C.	4.27	4.41
Kish b	*ca.* 500 B.C.	5.97	4.73
Troy b	*ca.* 500 B.C.	—	4.08
Alisharhuyuk c	500-300 B.C.	4.11	—
Athens e	500-300 B.C.	1.53	—
Olynthus	*ca.* 400 B.C.	5.45	—
Roman	200 B.C.-A.D. 200	4.26	6.39
Athens f	300-100 B.C.	2.08	5.86
Ephesus	300-100 B.C.	3.60	—
Rome	*ca.* A.D. 100	6.56	6.16
Sardis	*ca.* A.D. 100	3.21	9.28
Nuzi	*ca.* A.D. 200	5.85	4.27

RESULTS AND DISCUSSION

From Table 6.3, it can be seen that the range for cranial variables of percent sexual dimorphism is from 7.94 at Tell-al-Judaidah to 1.53 at Athens e, with a mean for all samples of 4.13 (median is 4.00); the variance of this distribution is 4.14 ($s = 2.04$). While the variance and coefficient of variation of a distribution developed from sample means may not have the same exact statistical meaning as one developed from individual measurements, percent sexual dimorphism can certainly be regarded as a standardized measurement of the extent of sexual dimorphism of a variable or series of variables. As such, the variance of the distribution is an indication of its variability and can be useful for comparative purposes.

The range of mandibular percent sexual dimorphism is from 12.95, again at Tell-al-Judaidah, to 3.03 at Kish a, with a mean of 6.96 for all samples (median is 6.79) and a variance of 6.41 ($s = 2.53$). Coefficient of variation for percent sexual dimorphism of the cranial variables is 49.39 and 36.35 for the mandibular variables, indicating high variability for both groups.

In order to determine the influence of spatial relationships on percent sexual dimorphism of the cranium and mandible, the values of percent sexual dimorphism of the cranial and mandibular variables were assorted into the groups listed in Table 6.1. Single classification analysis of variance was carried out separately on cranial and mandibular variables. The among group/within group variance ratio for cranial variables is $F = 0.094$ ($P > 0.5$), and for mandibular variables it is $F = 0.120$ ($P > 0.5$). The spatial relationship which was observed to be statistically significant for the osteometric variables of both cranium and mandible (Finkel 1978) does not even approach statistical significance for percent sexual dimorphism of both cranial and mandibular variables. Geographic proximity, then, is not predictive of degree of sexual dimorphism.

In order to determine whether a correlation exists between time and percent sexual dimorphism, the product-moment correlation coefficient was calculated. For cranial variables, $r = 0.044$ (slope $= 0.009$); for mandibular variables, $r = 0.023$ (slope $= 0.005$). Neither is statistically significant.

While there is no linear correlation between time and percent sexual dimorphism for the entire period, it was considered possible that statistically significant differences exist between the traditional cultural subdivisions presented in Table 6.3 (Early Bronze I through Roman periods). Single classification analysis of variance was carried out on the seven time subdivisions for cranial and mandibular variables separately. Neither F-ratio was significant; for cranial variables, $F = 0.124$ ($P > 0.5$); for mandibular variables, $F = 2.29$ ($0.2 > P > 0.1$).

The Student-Newman-Keuls test, carried out on the seven group means for percent sexual dimorphism of cranial variables only (sample size was insufficient for mandibular variables) shows only one statistically significant difference: between Early Bronze I and Middle Bronze where $t = 3.658$ ($0.02 > P > 0.01$). This calls attention to a minor trend; values of percent sexual dimorphism increase steadily from 3100 B.C. to 1600 B.C. and then stabilize; slight declines and increases may be observed after this. A consideration of mandibular percent sexual dimorphism shows a similar trend for the seven time subdivisions. Here, there is an increase in percent sexual dimorphism from 3100 B.C. to 1200 B.C., followed by a stabilization although, again, there are slight increases and decreases after 1200 B.C. There is, then, a general trend toward increase in percent sexual dimorphism for both cranial and mandibular variables during the first half of the time period under consideration, followed by a stabilization of these values.

More definite time trends were noted for periods prior to that of this study (Frayer 1978). Moderate reduction in percent sexual dimorphism of cranial variables occurred between Upper Paleolithic and Mesolithic through Neolithic samples; yet, there was virtually no difference in percent sexual dimorphism between Neolithic samples and those of this study. A different trend is noted for mandibular percent sexual dimorphism; moderate increases occur between the European Neolithic and the samples of this study. However, values remain relatively stable between Upper Paleolithic and Neolithic periods, contrasted with a substantial decline in cranial percent sexual dimorphism during this period.

Rates of Males and Female Morphological Change

Testing for statistically significant differences in cranial and mandibular variable means between skeletal samples from the same archaeological site, but from different time levels, was carried out on males for the sites of Alisharhuyuk, Athens, Kish, Lachish, Lapethos, Megiddo, and Troy (Finkel 1978). As many of the 16 variables used in that study as were obtainable for these samples were analyzed by the Student-Newman-Keuls test for males and females separately. Additionally, the six variables not used in that study, but used here, maximum frontal diameter, occipital arc, biorbital breadth, nasal width, bicondylar width and height of the ascending ramus, were also tested in the male and female samples separately, where available, again using the Student-Newman-Keuls test.

Comparison of rates of change per generation for male and female samples, using only those variable means showing statistically significant differences, demonstrates that the rate of change for females is almost twice that of the rate for males. None of the factors discussed thus far would adequately account for such a difference.

Only Lachish, where 15 variables were tested between two levels, showed a substantial number and percentage (5-33.3%) of statistically significant comparisons for males. Three sites, Kish, Megiddo, and Troy, showed no significant differences. At Athens where 22 variables were tested for six levels, only four significant differences (1.0%) were noted. Similarly at Alisharhuyuk (2-5.1%) and Lapethos (2-2.4%) the number and percentage of statistically significant differences were not notable. For all seven sites, a total of 582 tests of significance on male samples were carried out; only 13 showed significant differences (2.2%). For females, 16 of 247 tests of significance showed significant differences (6.5%). For male variables showing significant differences, the average rate of change per generation, assuming a 20-year generational span, was 0.066 mm. For female variables showing significant differences the average rate of change per generation, also assuming a 20-year generational span, was 0.113 mm.

Female samples from the same archaeological sites were tested for statistically significant differences in variable means, using the same methodology that was used for the male samples (see Table 6.4). Due to the smaller number of comparisons, the importance of a single significant difference at Kish (of 12), Megiddo (of 5), and Troy (of 5) is difficult to assess. No significant differences were found at Alisharhuyuk (of 12) or Lapethos (of 9). At Lachish, three significant differences were observed (27.3%), and the three variables also show statistical significance for the male sample from Lachish. Clearly both male and female samples reflect phenotypic change between earlier and later populations from this site. As discussed above, migration is suggested as the primary causal factor for the observed differences.

Although only 5.2 percent of the 193 tests of significance between the six levels at Athens showed significant differences, 8 of the 10 cases involve Athens f. In the absence of historical or archaeological evidence, it may be suggested tentatively that this latest sample from Athens represents the accumulated effects of mutation, selection, and drift, as well as previous migration, and was, therefore, able to be differentiated statistically from earlier samples.

TABLE 6.4
Variables and Populations Showing Significant Difference.

Site	Variable	Difference in Means (mm)	Number of Generations	Rate per Generation	Also in Males
Athens d, e	Maximum length	6.09	20	0.134	no
Athens d, f	Maximum width	8.74	30	0.291	no
Athens c, f	Maximum width	8.41	42.5	0.198	no
Athens a, f	Bizygomatic width	8.61	110	0.078	no
Athens c, f	Bizygomatic width	6.26	42.5	0.147	no
Athens b, f	Nasion-prosthion	6.71	55	0.122	no
Athens b, c	Nasion-prosthion	3.76	12.5	0.301	no
Athens d, f	Nasal width	4.10	30	0.137	no
Athens a, f	Nasal width	2.68	110	0.024	no
Athens c, f	Nasal width	1.99	42.5	0.047	no
Kish a, b	Maximum length	8.20	100	0.082	no
Lachish a, b	Maximum length	4.40	80	0.055	yes
Lachish a, b	Orbital width	1.23	80	0.015	yes
Lachish a, b	Nasal width	2.00	80	0.025	yes
Megiddo a, b	Bizygomatic width	9.00	75	0.120	no
Troy a, b	Asc. ramus width	2.80	105	0.027	no
Female average				0.113	
Male average				0.066	

Sexual Dimorphism and Cultural Selection

Similarity in percent sexual dimorphism, especially for cranial variables, between Neolithic and later samples may be based on similarity of male and female economic roles. Herchelheim (1958) stated that the agricultural life, based on job sharing between males and females, continued into the Bronze Age, in some areas virtually unchanged from Neolithic times. The model described by Murdock and Provost (1973) included such activities as gathering, crop planting, preparation of skins, harvesting, and crop tending as likely to be performed by both males and females. More strenuous activities, such as hunting, ore smelting and metal working, lumbering and wood working, butchering, land clearing and soil preparation, and house building, would be likely to be male dominated.

With the development of proto-urban and, especially, urban societies, certain activities previously carried out by males and females, e.g., distillery, baking, and pottery making (Herchelheim 1958), began to be carried out primarily by men, possibly because these activities represented a primary source of economic livelihood. As simple artifacts and processes were replaced by more complex ones, male domination of the activity increased (Murdock and Provost 1973). For example, the introduction of the plow increased male participation in all aspects of agricultural activity, not just soil preparation. So, too, as the degree of occupational specialization in crafts became more complex, males assumed roles as potters and weavers.

In the absence of any clearly defined temporal or spatial trends in percent sexual dimorphism in these skeletal samples, I have investigated the relationship between sexual dimorphism and biological and sociocultural factors such as nutrition, disease, complexity of social organization, cultural lifeways, and economic status for those sites where such information was available.

However, the relationship between increasing cultural complexity and technological improvement and biometric change is often difficult to analyze. While differences have been observed among hunter-gatherer groups of the Upper Paleolithic and Mesolithic and early agriculturalists of the Neolithic (Frayer 1978), these changes may result from large-scale cultural changes, such as the introduction of agriculture. In such cases, shifts to new life-styles may have greatly affected male and female social roles and, possibly, morphological and metric variables.

In the time period considered in this study, trends may be particularly difficult to interpret since biosocial change is generally in the form of increased food production, leading to the possibility of better nutritional status and increased population size and density (increased urbanization). These changes are hard to document archaeologically. Yet, certain variables generally are available for testing, such as settlement type; economic status of the individuals of each sample, as indicated either historically or by the quality of grave goods; nutritional status and disease, as indicated by observation of the skeletal material and various postcranial indices.

Settlement type often indicates the degree of social complexity and the role sharing taking place in the society. Agricultural activity, especially as practiced by the village agricultural societies of this sample, is likely to be engaged in equally by males and females. Frayer (1978) considers equivalent sex roles in farming to be one of the major causes in the reduction of percent sexual dimorphism from hunting and gathering societies to the early agricultural ones. The present study includes village farming sites but also contains skeletal samples from proto-urban communities, generally able to be characterized as market towns or distribution centers, where crafts, trade, and redistribution of agricultural products have promoted the division of labor. Increased food supply and increased population density have resulted in nonagricultural occupations for a majority of the population, not only in crafts and trade, but in administrative, military, and religious positions as well. These social factors usually produce differential distribution of wealth and, consequently, different social roles for women, depending on class and occupation. These processes are intensified in urban societies, which are generally supported by an agricultural base outside the urban area. Urban societies tend to be highly stratified with regard to class and wealth. Assuming division of labor is most intensified in upper socioeconomic classes, it is expected that class differences in the extent of sexual dimorphism would exist within an urban society, as females in lower economic classes would be expected to play a far greater role in subsistence. Greater percent sexual dimorphism would be expected, then, in upper classes.

Nutrition and disease are closely associated with settlement type. In a discussion of treponematosis, Hudson (1965) emphasized the gap in cleanliness, public health, nutritional intake, and resistance to disease between villages and towns. Anderson (1974) noted that economic factors are the major determinant of infant mortality; differences were cited between rural village communities and urban areas. The impedance of growth and development by disease and malnutrition has been well documented (Cohen and Hansen 1962; Frisch and Revelle 1969). Some agricultural populations provide examples of malnutrition resulting from protein deficiency (Stini 1971). Stini (1969) has demonstrated in one such agricultural population that growth retardation, resulting from malnutrition, is greater in males than in females. This results in less sexual dimorphism in this group than would be present otherwise.

Table 6.1 lists those skeletal samples from populations believed to have practiced village agriculture. Some of the sites have indicated fortifications (Karatash); most have not. They were basically nonstratified farming communities exhibiting poor public health facilities; a generally poor nutritional base, as evidenced by extreme long bone curvature and dental wear and caries; and high percentages of occurrence of debilitating diseases, demonstrated by osteoarthritis and porotic hyperostosis (Angel 1966; Finkel 1974). Infant mortality is high; infant and juvenile skeletal material is the majority found at these sites. At Karatash (Angel 1966) and Sotira (Angel 1953) the samples appear to be somewhat better off than the other skeletal samples with regard to health and nutrition. Mean percent sexual dimorphism for cranial variables of this group is 3.05 ($N = 8$), 30.5 percent below the average of 4.39 for cranial variables from all samples; mean percent sexual dimorphism for mandibular variables is 7.20 ($N = 3$), about average (3.2% above). Variance for cranial variables equals 1.10 ($s = 1.05$); the coefficient of variation is 34.43 percent. For mandibular variables, variance equals 4.27 ($s = 2.07$); the coefficient of variation is 28.68 percent.

Proto-urban communities represent transitional development between village agriculture and high population density urban areas. The samples listed here as proto-urban may be regarded as simple stratified societies, often composed largely of merchants (e.g., Athens c, Kultepe) and artisans, or they may simply represent societies where population density and building have advanced the status of the community (e.g., Lachish a, Megiddo a). Evidence of nutrition and disease suggests high variation in this group. Some samples, such as Troy b and Athens b, exhibit poor health as evidenced by extensive curvature in long bones and very high infant mortality (Angel 1945, 1951). Others, such as Kultepe and Athens c (Angel 1945), exhibit much better health; long bone indices demonstrated flattening, and the skeletal material showed a population in generally good health. Archaeologically and historically, improved public health facilities were present (Angel 1945).

Mean percent sexual dimorphism of cranial variables ($N = 8$) for the proto-urban samples is 4.88; variance equals 2.23 ($s = 1.49$); coefficient of variation is 30.53 percent. Student's t-test carried out between the average of cranial percent sexual dimorphism of the proto-urban group and that of the village agricultural group was statistically significant, $t = 2.836$ ($0.02 > P > 0.01$). For mandibular variables, mean percent sexual dimorphism is 8.60 ($N = 3$), variance is 19.69 ($s = 4.44$), and coefficient of variation is 51.63 percent. Confidence in mandibular calculations is small because of the small sample size and high coefficient of variation. When Student's t-test was calculated between mean mandibular percent sexual dimorphism of proto-urban groups and that of village agricultural ones, $t = 0.495$ ($P > 0.5$). While the difference in percent sexual dimorphism for mandibular variables from village agricultural societies to proto-urban ones was 19.4 percent, the difference in percent sexual dimorphism for cranial variables between these two groups was 60.0 percent.

Eighteen skeletal samples were from densely populated urban areas. They exhibit complex stratification of economic and social class, allowing inferences of differential nutritional intake, differential access to public and private health facilities, and differential role behavior of males and females. As discussed above, it was assumed that male and female economic cooperation and sharing diminishes with the increase in socioeconomic level. The economic, nutritional, and health status of the individuals comprising the skeletal samples of these societies was estimated from the quality and nature of grave goods and from analysis of the skeletal material itself (carried out at Athens d, Athens e, Athens f, Olynthus, Lachish b, Sardis, Abydos, Rome, Kish a, Kish b, Nippur, and Sedment). Athens e, Athens f, Ephesus, Lachish b, and Sardis are sites where the individuals were considered to have belonged in the lower economic class, generally exhibiting poor nutritional and health characteristics (Ephesus was placed in this category because of the location of skeletal material in a poor section of the city and the poor quality of grave goods). Grave goods of superior quality and, where observable, good health and nutritional status, were found at Athens d, Megiddo b, Olynthus, Abydos, Sedment, Etruria, Rome, Kish a, Kish b, Nippur, Nuzi, Zakro, and Tepe Hissar.

Mean percent sexual dimorphism of cranial variables for all urban samples was 4.52, similar to that for the proto-urban groups. A Student's t-test between urban and proto-urban groups for cranial variables showed nonsignificant differences ($t = 0.557$; $P > 0.5$). Statistically significant diferences were found between urban and village agricultural groups, however ($t = 2.455$; $0.05 > P > 0.02$).

Mean percent sexual dimorphism of mandibular variables for all urban samples was 6.42 ($N = 10$). Variance was 4.10 ($s = 2.02$) as opposed to variance of 2.35 for cranial variables. Coefficient of variation for mandibular variables was 31.46 percent, similar to that for cranial variables, 33.85 percent. No significant differences were observed in average mandibular percent sexual dimorphism between urban samples and proto-urban ones or between urban and village agricultural samples. In the former, $t = 1.258$ $(0.4 > P > 0.2)$; and, in the latter, $t = 0.583$ $(P > 0.5)$.

The mean percent sexual dimorphism of cranial variables for samples, designated as upper-class, with grave goods of precious metals, well-made polychrome pottery, and/or skeletal material indicating a good nutritional and public health base, was 4.84. Variance equaled 1.78 $(s = 1.33)$; coefficient of variation was 27.48 percent. Mean percent sexual dimorphism of cranial variables for lower-class samples, denoted by poorly made grave goods and/or skeletal material showing a poor public health and nutritional base, was 2.79. Variance was 0.87 $(s = 0.93)$; coefficient of variation was 33.33 percent. Regrettably, insufficient sample size of lower-class populations prevented a similar comparison of mean mandibular percent sexual dimorphism; however, a t-test between upper- and lower-class cranial variables showed statistical significance $(t = 3.127; P < 0.01)$. The data appear to confirm that sexual dimorphism is reduced when the economic role behavior is similar in males and females, is increased as role behavior differentiates, and that it is greater in societies showing a higher standard of public health and a more substantial nutritional base.

CONCLUSIONS

The skeletal samples analyzed in this study have been described separately with regard to percent sexual dimorphism. Within a sample, average percent sexual dimorphism of the cranium and mandible differ considerably. The skeletal samples show no tendency to vary in dimorphism by geographical subregion, as was the case for the osteometric variables themselves, or by time, although some short-term trends have been noted. The skeletal samples show less percent sexual dimorphism of cranial variables than similar samples from the European Upper Paleolithic and Mesolithic, but their percent sexual dimorphism is similar to that of European Neolithic samples. Mandibular percent sexual dimorphism increases between Mesolithic and Neolithic and between Neolithic and the samples of this study, although the increases are small.

It is suggested that similarity in percent sexual dimorphism between Neolithic and later periods is due to the retention, by village agricultural populations of the Bronze Age, of male-female economic cooperation and sharing of tasks. At the same time, comparison of male and female rates of phenotypic change in osteometric variables shows that the female rate is almost double that of males.

Associations exist among settlement pattern, nutrition and health status of the society, and percent sexual dimorphism. A definite increase in percent sexual dimorphism was found in communities adopting settlement patterns (proto-urban and urban) that produced differences in male and female behavior, especially with regard to economic activity. Further, statistically significant differences in sexual dimorphism exist between urban samples of upper economic class that show evidence of a strong nutritional and health base and samples of urban lower economic class with evidence of poor nutritional and health base. As hypothesized in other studies (Stini 1971), greater percent sexual dimorphism is found in the upper-class samples.

In conclusion, this study has found that settlement type and economic base are better predictors of sexual dimorphism in cranial attributes than spatial or temporal factors.

BIBLIOGRAPHY

Anderson, J. G. 1974. "Effects of Social and Cultural Processes on Health." *Sociological-Economic Planning Sciences*, 8:9-22.

Angel, J. L. 1942. "Classical Olynthians." In *Necrolynthia: Excavations at Olynthus*, edited by D. M. Robinson, Vol. 2, pp. 211-240. Baltimore: Johns Hopkins University Press.

––––––. 1944. "A Racial Analysis of the Ancient Greeks: An Essay on the Use of Morphological Types." *American Journal of Physical Anthropology*, 2:329-376.

––––––. 1945. "Skeletal Material from Attica." *Hesperia*, 14:279-363.

––––––. 1946. "Social Biology of Greek Culture Growth." *American Anthropologist*, 48:493-533.

––––––. 1951. *Troy, the Human Remains. Supplemental Monograph Number 1.* Princeton: Princeton University Press.

––––––. 1953. "Neolithic Crania from Sotira." In *Excavations at Sotira*, edited by P. Dikaios. Philadelphia: Museum Monographs, University Museum, University of Pennsylvania Press.

––––––. 1966. "Human Remains at Karatash." In "Excavations at Karatash-Semayük in Lycia, 1965," edited by M. J. Mellink. *American Journal of Archaeology*, 72:260-263.

Bostanci, E. 1963. "An Examination of Some Human Skeletal Remains from the Sardis Excavations." *Antropoloji* 1:17-36.

––––––. 1967. "Morphological and Biometrical Examination of Some Skulls from the Sardis Excavations." *Belleten, Turk Tarih Kurumu* 31:1-48.

––––––. 1969. "Sardis Kazarilinda Çikan Kafatashlarin Incelenmesi ve Eski Anadolu Halklari ile olan Munasebetleri." *Ankara Universitesi Dil ve Tarih-Cografya Fakultesi*, 185:1-98.

184   Sexual Dimorphism in *Homo Sapiens*

Brace, C. L. 1973. "Sexual Dimorphism in Human Evolution." *Yearbook of Physical Anthropology 1972*, 16:31-49.

Buxton, L. H. D. 1920. "The Anthropology of Cyprus." *Journal of the Royal Anthropological Institute*, 50:183-235.

Buxton, L. H. D., and D. T. Rice. 1931. "On the Human Remains Excavated at Kish." *Journal of the Royal Anthropological Institute*, 61:57-119.

Campbell, B. G. 1966. *Human Evolution*. Chicago: Aldine.

Cohen, S., and J. D. L. Hansen. 1962. "Metabolism of Albumin and Gamma Globulin Kwashiorkor." *Clinical Science*, 23:351-359.

Dawkins, W. B. 1900-1901. "Skulls from Cave Burials at Zakro." *Annual of the British School at Athens*, 7:150-155.

DeVore, I., and S. L. Washburn. 1963. "Baboon Ecology and Human Evolution." In *African Ecology and Human Evolution*, edited by F. C. Howell and F. Bourlière. Chicago: Viking Fund Publications in Anthropology No. 36, Aldine.

Ehrich, R. W. 1939. "Late Cemetery Crania." In *Nuzi*, edited by R. F. S. Starr. Cambridge, Mass.: Harvard University Press.

Finkel, D. J. 1974. "Human Remains at Tell Gezer." In *Gezer IV, the Field I Caves*, edited by J. Seger. Jerusalem: Keter.

———. 1978. "Spatial and Temporal Dimensions of Middle Eastern Skeletal Populations." *Journal of Human Evolution*, 7:217-229.

Frayer, D. W. 1977. "Dental Sexual Dimorphism in the European Upper Paleolithic and Mesolithic." *Journal of Dental Research*, 56:871.

———. 1978. *Evolution of the Dentition in Upper Paleolithic and Mesolithic Europe*. University of Kansas, Publications in Anthropology, 10. Lawrence, Kansas: University of Kansas Press.

Frisch, R., and R. Revelle. 1969. "Variation in Body Weights and the Age of the Adolescent Growth Spurt among Latin American and Asian Populations in Relation to Calorie Supplies." *Human Biology*, 41:185-212.

Herchelheim, F. M. 1958. *An Ancient Economic History*. Leiden: A. W. Sijthoft's UitGeversmaatschaatschappij.

Hrdlička, A. 1940. "Skeletal Remains." In *Megiddo Tombs*, edited by P. L. O. Guy and R. M. Engberg. *Oriental Institute Publications*, 33:192-208.

Hudson, E. H. 1965. "Treponematosis and Man's Social Evolution." *American Anthropologist*, 67:885-901.

Kenyon, K. 1960. *Archaeology in the Holy Land*. New York: Praeger.

Krogman, W. M. 1933. "The Cranial Types." In *The Alishar Huyuk, Seasons of 1928 and 1929, Part 2*, edited by E. F. Schmidt. *Oriental Institute Publications* 20:122-128.

———. 1937. "Cranial Types from Alishar Huyuk and Their Relations to Other Racial Types, Ancient and Modern, of Europe and Western Asia." In *The Alishar Huyuk, Seasons of 1930-32, Part 3*, edited by H. H van der Osten. *Oriental Institute Publications* 30:213-293.

———. 1940. "Racial Types from Tepe Hissar, Iran, from the Late Fifth to the Early Second Millenium B.C." *Verhandelingen der Koninklijk Nederlandsche Akademie van Wetenschappen Afdeeling Natuurkunde*, 39:1-87.

————. 1949. "Ancient Cranial Types at Chatal Huyuk and Tell-al-Judaidah, Syria, from the Late Fifth Millenium B.C. to the Mid-Seventh Century A.D." *Belleten, Turk Tarih Kurumu* 13:407-477.

Morant, G. M. 1925. "A Study of Egyptian Craniology from Prehistory to Roman Times." *Biometrika*, 17:1-52.

Murdock, G. P., and C. Provost. 1973. "Factors in the Division of Labor by Sex: A Cross Cultural Analysis." *Ethnology*, 12:203-225.

Oliver, G. 1969. "L'Evolution Séculaire des Populations Subfossiles et Récentes." In *Evolutionary Trends in Fossil and Recent Hominids*, edited by J. Nemeskéri and G. Deszó. *Symposia Biologica Hungarica*, 9:65-72.

Risdon, D. L. 1939. "A Study of the Cranial and Other Human Remains from Palestine Excavated at Tell Duweir (Lachish) by the Wellcome-Marston Archaeological Research Expedition." *Biometrika*, 31:99-166.

Schümacher, O. 1926. "Über Alt-Griechische Schädel von Myrina und Ephesus." *Zeitschrift für Morphologie und Anthropologie*, 25:435-463.

Şenyurek, M. S. 1952. "A Study of the Human Skeletons from Kultepe, Excavated under the Auspices of the Turkish Historical Society." *Belleten, Turk Tarih Kurumu*, 16:323-343.

Sergei, G. 1901. "Note upon the Skulls of Erganos." *American Journal of Archaeology*, 5:315-328.

Stini, W. A. 1969. "Nutritional Stress and Growth: Sex Difference in Adaptive Response." *American Journal of Physical Anthropology*, 31:417-426.

————. 1971. "Evolutionary Implications of Changing Nutritional Patterns in Human Populations." *American Anthropologist*, 73:1-12.

Swindler, D. R. 1956. *A Study of the Cranial and Skeletal Material Excavated at Nippur*. Philadelphia: Museum Monographs, University Museum, University of Pennsylvania Press.

Trigger, B. 1972. "Determinants of Urban Growth in Preindustrial Societies." In *Man, Settlement and Urbanism*, edited by P. J. Ucko, R. Tringham, and G. W. Dimpleby. Cambridge, Mass.: Schenkman.

Wheatley, P. 1972. "The Concept of Urbanism." In *Man, Settlement and Urbanism*, edited by P. J. Ucko, R. Tringham, and G. W. Dimpleby. Cambridge, Mass.: Schenkman.

Wolpoff, M. H. 1973. "Sexual Dimorphism in the Australopithecines." In *Paleoanthropology: Morphology and Paleoecology*, edited by R. H. Tuttle. The Hague: Mouton.

————. 1976. "Some Aspects of the Evolution of Early Hominid Sexual Dimorphism." *Current Anthropology*, 17:579-606.

Woo, T. L. 1930. "A Study of 71 Ninth Dynasty Egyptian Skulls from Sedment." *Biometrika*, 22:65-93.

Two

Studies in
Modern Populations

Seven

Unit of Analysis

Roberta L. Hall

All researchers in human biology must deliberate and decide what unit of analysis to use. Not only is *Homo sapiens* polymorphic and polytypic, it is the most widespread mammal, both climatically and geographically; cultural differences intensify the capacity for local differentiation as well as the capacity for worldwide uniformity. For these reasons, no single sample can stand unequivocally for the species in any variable attribute, human sexual dimorphism included. Even the range of variation may not prove constant across human populations.

It can be shown that average values for male and female size differ on a regional basis, as do many other phenotypic traits. It also appears that the average value for size differences between the sexes differs regionally yet may not be related to average size values in a simple, proportional manner (i.e., may be independent of size or may be allometrically related). A nonsuperficial analysis of size sexual dimorphism will require a sophisticated research design as well as a more complex theoretical formulation than any offered so far.

At this point, two theoretical postures have been struck to interpret interpopulational differences in size sexual dimorphism. The first posits that sexual dimorphism tends to be increased or exaggerated in populations that have an abundance of food and tends to be decreased or depressed in populations experiencing under-nourishment. Underlying this position is the premise, which has some empirical support, that male growth patterns respond more sensitively to deprivation or abundance of food and that females appear to more canalized or buffered against nutritional fluctuations (Stini 1969; Bielicki and Charzewski 1977; Tobias 1975; Greulich 1951).

A second theoretical posture is that the degree of sexual dimorphism, unlike total size, is fairly insensitive to the nutritional base of a population. Rather, this position is that size dimorphism reflects the action of genetic tendencies that differ among populations. Presumably, the genetic attributes arise from natural selection acting either in the distant or the immediate past. A traditional theory suggests that sexual dimorphism for size, along with other morphological and metric traits, emerged in the distant past of each population and has proved resistant to change. A more dynamic as well as more contemporary model, that of sociobiology, predicts that the degree of sexual dimorphism for size responds to changes in courtship and marital patterns. According to this perspective, we should expect sexual dimorphism to be reduced in populations in which little competition for mates exists and to be exaggerated in those in which males compete for mates and where there is a great deal of variance in male reproductive success.

However, these theoretical postures do not encompass all of the possible factors that could cause variation in size sexual dimorphism. For example, they do not accord a role to climate or to activity pattern, both of which may interact with the nutritional environment and the genotype to affect growth (Roberts 1973). Since growth results as an interaction between the genotype and the environment, and is affected by behavior, there are systematic factors, which affect all individuals who possess given genes or who experience given environments; and there also are unique factors, which arise from the timing of particular events and their interactions. In other words, variability is inherent in human growth, and phenotypes are not perfectly predictable. Neither are they random—the task of the human biologist is to discern the patterns in a variable set of arrays. The purpose of this chapter is not to develop a multifactorial model of size sexual dimorphism but to discuss the appropriate units within which to apply such a model. What unit is most likely to elucidate the effects of genotype, environment, climate, and activity patterns on human sexual dimorphism? I will examine the advantages and disadvantages of three: the major continental race, the local population, and the stratified subpopulation.

MAJOR CONTINENTAL RACE

This unit has one major advantage: traditional name-familiarity. Almost everyone knows in a general way what is meant by a term such as Amerindian, Mongoloid, Causcasian, etc. The problems come when specific samples are treated. For example, to what group do the

Bushmen belong? the Ainu? North Africans? Morphological as well as climatic-geographic diversity within each of the continents makes the unity of this category questionable. Additionally, there is the very real possibility that the major geographic race will be further divested of meaning by confusion with what Wagley calls the "social race concept" (Wagley 1965) or what I prefer to term the "folk taxonomy of race." Wagley shows that within the Americas three kinds of criteria are used—but used differently in the various societies and nations—to define "races." The three criteria are phenotype, ancestry, and sociocultural status. For example, in Mexico, education and socio-cultural status seem to weigh more than genealogy or phenotype in folk classifications of "race"—mestizo, Indian, or white. In the United States, certain phenotypic traits, chiefly skin color and hair type, are accorded more importance than ancestry or socio-economic status in classifying individuals as "black" or "white." In neither example are populations defined or classifications made according to accepted taxonomic principles in which the first rule is to define the breeding populations and the second step is to describe the distribution of genetic and morphological traits. Folk taxonomies do not correspond to biological taxonomies.

The concept of the major continental race harks back to the early development of human diversity studies when the concept of major stocks was commonly accepted. According to this view, hominids evolved in continental clusters with geographical isolation between major units. Due to population expansion and migration, it was thought, the groups began to interact at borders and produced a blurring of morphological traits. It should be pointed out that this model assumes a general conservativeness of traits and it de-emphasizes micropopulational adaptation to specific environments or evolutionary pressures.

Not all investigators who use the concept of the major race identify the same number of units. For example, Garn (1965) identifies nine, some being more populous and more widespread than others. However many are identified, most of the units encompass populations that are quite varied in a number of ways: culturally, climatically, nutritionally, morphologically, and metrically. They are considered as units by custom or convention. Convention is involved, for example, when it is decided that a trait such as the Mongoloid eyefold is a crucial population identifier (Mongoloid), or absence of the B-gene is a classificatory key (Amerindian). The point is that the groups are not inductively or empirically defined—even though empirical traits are utilized as keys.

Weiss and Maruyama (1976) thoroughly examined the question of whether modern human populations are the end-points of races that have a great antiquity or whether they represent more recent local variations of an expanding *Homo sapiens* population. One of their conclusions was that the evidence does not allow a final determination. Additionally, and more critically, they concluded that the traditional "major races" are cultural constructs of our society and do not represent a major biological event in human evolution. If Weiss and Maruyama are correct—and I believe they are—can major races be used in sexual dimorphism studies to test whether size dimorphism is genetically controlled? Has anyone tried to do so?

The answer to the first question would appear to be an emphatic "no" but the answer to the second question is "yes." Eveleth (1975) attempted to test whether sexual dimorphism for height is genetically or nutritionally controlled by investigating whether the amount of difference between male and female average heights varied among five groups of populations. The study was marred by a number of methodological and statistical errors, among them: use of mean of means—a significant problem intensified here by the absence of a measure of variation; regression of sex difference in height on the mid-point between male and female average height rather than on each sex's average height; printing of regression lines without data points; publication of regression formulae without confidence intervals; confusion of statistical significance with biological significance—regressions were produced with correlation coefficients of 0.21 and 0.22, which differ statistically from zero but as they explain only 0.04 of the variance cannot be considered biologically meaningful; inclusion of data in tables that did not correspond with data in the text; and inadequately interpreted methodology.

These statistical, interpretive, and editorial flaws are perhaps less important than the conceptual ones, however. Eveleth dealt with five "ethnic groups," namely, Europeans (76 samples), Negroes (58), Amerindians (67), Asiatics (36), and New Guineans (27). An ethnic group was defined as "a number of populations that is morphologically more alike than another group of populations" (Eveleth 1975, p. 37). The groups were not affiliated culturally—ethnically as the term is commonly used—so one must conclude that "ethnic" was a euphemism for "race." On inspection, the groups appear to be the old major continental races, or at least four of them are; the fifth, the New Guinean group, is a minor variant on the old theme.

As indicated earlier, the sex difference in height correlations with the sex mid-point of height explained only 0.04 of the variance in the large European, Negro, and Amerindian groups; in none of these groups is there an intense predictive relationship between the two variables. In the two smaller samples, correlation coefficients accompanying the regression were 0.43 and 0.47 and accordingly more deserving of interest. However, the author seemed at a loss to explain the higher correlations and did not investigate whether greater commonalities in culture, climate, nutrition, or genealogy and genetic affinity were responsible.

Unfortunately, in this study, as in many of the early sexual dimorphism studies, the report terminated just at the point that it became interesting; and incorrect conclusions were drawn. For example, the report claimed to demonstrate that low sexual dimorphism for height does not indicate that a population is malnourished; in fact, the analysis did not really address the question. Nor did the study indicate that sexual dimorphism in height is genetically determined, as it also stated. Both of these propositions may be true, or may be false, but this study did not test them. The one point that the data indicate is that larger and possibly less clearly delimited groups of populations are more heterogeneous in the way average sex differences in height vary with the mid-point for male-female average stature. The constructs "Europeans," Negroes," and "Amerindians" in fact were shown to be counterproductive in the purpose for which they were used.

LOCAL POPULATION

Ernst Mayr (1966, p. 138) presents the local population ("the community of potentially interbreeding individuals at a given locality") as the crucial unit for the study of natural selection and genetic variation. Ideally, the local population is panmictic; it would be difficult to argue that this ideal normally is met in human groups in which there usually are at least several dimensions of mating rules. Still, the local population is the unit in which environment and genetic structure react to form individual phenotypes. Looked at from a slightly different perspective, natural selection acts in specific environments upon phenotypes and, through them, selects appropriate genotypes. For single-gene traits the borders around local populations can be very steep, if selection differs on either side of the border (Endler 1973). Borders are less well-marked and clines are more gradual when selection varies continuously or when traits are polygenic and/or affected by environmental factors.

Though Garn (1965) recognizes major geographic races, he considers that unit at the highest level of abstraction and implies that the local population is the unit of most importance to the human biologist studying the forces of evolution. Lewontin (1972) has shown that at the genetic level the greatest amount of variation occurs between individuals within the local population, rather than between populations of one traditionally defined race, or group of populations that share a recognized geographical region, or between such races. Where does the study of size sexual dimorphism fit into this picture? The analysis is admittedly complex because in one sense size sexual dimorphism is "caused" by a simple genetic difference—possession of two X chromosomes by females and one X and one Y by males. But attributes considered for size, whether composed of skeletal, muscular, or fatty tissue, must be multifactorial and must include both genetic and environmental components. Variability exists within both sexes, with considerable overlap in size ranges between them. A given local population may be characterized by an average value and specific range for each size measure, yet each individual has a unique set of values for phenotypic traits.

Analysis of sexual dimorphism, then, offers all the complexities and challenges of the study of any other multifactorial trait. How can the use of the local population as a unit of description and analysis make it possible to analyze the effects of genetics, environment, and activity patterns? A hypothetical example may serve to illustrate.

Suppose we identify two local populations in Peru existing within a reasonable proximity but one is at 2000 feet altitude and the other at 10,000 feet. Suppose further that we have a like situation in Tibet— two almost proximate local populations, again separated by 8000 feet altitude. (And if we were lucky and could find and afford additional samples, we would add them.) In all locales we would want to sample indigenous adults, for the same age range, for a number of size attributes. We would want to calculate average values and variances for both sexes, all samples, and compute measures of intersex differences, both in raw figures and as a ratio to male and female average values. We would want to compare group variances also. Our purpose would be to determine whether the several high altitude samples differed from their respective low altitude populations in the same manner, if indeed they varied at all.

This example is simplified but it illustrates a method of attack. To add complexity to this example, it would be ideal to determine the nutritional, climatic, and activity pattern attributes of each population. If it could be argued justifiably that they are similar between samples and that each sample is genuinely homogeneous, we should be fortunate indeed, for then the controls would be built-in. It is more likely that the populations would be found to differ at least between regions so that sexual dimorphism differences among the populations could not be ascribed only to the genetic base or to altitude.

Oversimplified and idealistic as it is, the example demonstrates that the local population may be an appropriate unit to sample in studies of size sexual dimorphism. It works best in what might be termed "anthropological" populations; that is, relatively small, isolated cultural groups who have restricted mobility and relative homogeneity of life-styles and activity patterns. These may still be found in many modern nations due to isolation by geography, culture, religion, or, in some cases, by poverty and lack of opportunity.

In complex societies the dimensions that affect human growth, and hence affect sexual dimorphism within an interbreeding unit, include (at the minimum) wealth, work styles, activity patterns, mobility, parental ancestry, and fluctuating sex roles. The local population may not be sufficiently complex by itself to discriminate factors controlling size sexual dimorphism in modern societies.

STRATIFIED SUBPOPULATIONS
AND RESEARCH STRATEGIES

Human biological studies in modern populations shift from the local population, tied closely to a specific environoment and life-style, to the individual, whose ancestry and life-style are heterogeneous and determined by cultural background, idiosyncratic factors, and personal choice. Studies of size sexual dimorphism in modern populations require large samples so that a large number of independent variables can be surveyed and analyzed by the regression technique. An alternative methodology would be to test a specific hypothesis by selecting a sample according to one criterion, for example, vegetarian feeding practices from infancy on, or intense training as a gymnast during childhood. In this method, the values for size measures by sex would be matched between the specialized sample and a general sample unclassified, for example, by nutrition or activity patterns. The latter research strategy has the advantage of permitting smaller samples and a more explicit hypothetical framework, but at this point the depth of our ignorance is great enough that the more descriptive "broadcast" strategy may also be recommended. The purpose of this chapter, in any case, is not to outline all possible research strategies or to weigh their value, but to review conceptual problems that must be confronted.

SUMMARY

In this chapter I have discussed the pitfalls of attempting to use traditional but meaningless major race categories as units of analysis in size sexual dimorphism studies. I have also argued that sexual dimorphism for size may not be entirely accounted for by genetic or nutritional factors: The old "nature-nurture" dichotomy oversimplifies a complex and interacting set of phenomena. In relatively isolated or traditional societies the local population still may provide the best unit for study of size dimorphism. In complex societies, a more sophisticated research strategy or set of strategies must be applied. In such populations, the genetic structure of the interbreeding unit changes rapidly due to migration and individual mobility. Environmental influences on growth are also highly individualized, dynamic, and heterogeneous. Failure to take account of these factors renders description of sex dimorphism invalid and genuine analysis impossible.

BIBLIOGRAPHY

Bielicki, T., and J. Charzewski. 1977. "Sex Differences in the Magnitude of Statural Gains of Offspring over Parents." *Human Biology*, 49:265-277.

Endler, J. A. 1973. "Gene Flow and Population Differentiation." *Science*, 179:243-250.

Eveleth, P. B. 1975. "Differences between Ethnic Groups in Sex Dimorphism of Adult Height." *Annals of Human Biology*, 2:35-39.

Garn, S. 1965. *Human Races*, 2nd ed. Springfield: Charles C Thomas.

Greulich, W. W. 1951. "The Growth and Developmental Status of Guamanian School Children in 1947."*American Journal of Physical Anthropology*, 9:44-53.

Lewontin, R. C. 1972. "The Apportionment of Human Diversity." *Evolutionary Biology*, 6:381-398.

Mayr, E. 1966., *Animal Species and Evolution*. Cambridge: Belknap Press.

Roberts, D. F. 1973. *Climate and Human Variability*. Addison-Wesley Module in Anthropology No. 34:1-38.

Stini, W. A. 1969. "Nutritional Stress and Growth: Sex Difference in Adaptive Response." *American Journal of Physical Anthropology*, 31:417-426.

Tobias, P. V. 1975. "Anthropometry Among Disadvantaged Peoples: Studies in Southern Africa." In *Biosocial Interrelations in Population Adaptation*, edited by E. S. Watts, F. E. Johnston, and G. W. Lasker. The Hague: Mouton.

Wagley, C. 1965. "On the Concept of Social Race in the Americas." In *Contemporary Societies of Latin America*, edited by D. B. Heath and R. N. Adams, pp. 531-545.

Weiss, K. M., and T. Maruyama. 1976. "Archaeology, Population Genetics and Studies of Human Racial Ancestry." *American Journal of Physical Anthropology*, 44:31-50.

Eight

A Cross-Cultural Investigation into the Sexual Dimorphism of Stature

Linda D. Wolfe
J. Patrick Gray

While in all human societies, males are on the average taller than females, societies vary in the degree to which mean societal male height is greater than mean societal female height. The causes of intersocietal variability in the sexual dimorhism of stature have been the subject of much debate in the last 10 years, with participants usually advancing either a nutritional or a genetic hypothesis. The nutritional perspective holds that the anatomical, physiological, and metabolic demands of pregnancy and lactation have resulted in females evolving hormonal mechanisms to mediate the influence of nutritional stress on body size (see Greulich 1951; Stini 1975; Thomson 1954). In contrast, the height attained by males is assumed not to be mediated by these hormonal mechanisms and therefore fluctuates as a function of the quality and quantity of the food resources of a society to a greater extent than female height. As a result of this sex difference, societies with inadequate nutritional resources will be characterized by short males and short females and low sexual dimorphism in stature. With improved nutrition both males and females are taller, but the male gain is greater than the female gain, creating a greater dimorphism in stature than exhibited by poorly nourished groups (see Hall 1978; Hamilton 1975; Tobias 1962, 1975; Stini 1969). As the nutritional perspective on sexual dimorphism is reviewed elsewhere in this volume we will not discuss the relevant studies here.

The genetic perspective suggests that there is a strong genetic component to sexual dimorphism of height and, therefore, no systematic relationship between the degree of stature dimorphism and level of nutrition. Eveleth (1975), for example, arrived at this conclusion after analyzing mean stature data for adults from 264 populations (see, however, Hall, this volume, for a statistical and methodological critique of Eveleth's study). The genetic perspective, if correct, is only a partially adequate explanation of intersocietal variability in the sexual dimorphism of stature, for it is still necessary to delineate the evolutionary factors that resulted in the differential distribution of genotypes responsible for this variability. This second step has been taken recently by sociobiologists exploring human sexual dimorphism from the perspectives of sexual selection and parental investment theory.

THE SOCIOBIOLOGICAL HYPOTHESIS

Alexander et al. (1979), for example, presented data on sexual dimorphism of body length and breeding systems for various species of pinnipeds, ungulates, and primates. They tested the hypothesis that interspecies differences in sexual dimorphism are correlated with differences in breeding systems. In polygynous species, hoarding of females by a few males results in great variability in male reproductive success with some males fathering a disproportionate number of offspring while other males do not reproduce at all. Since males with larger bodies are able to compete successfully with smaller bodied males for access to females, they will contribute more genes for body size to the next generation than do the smaller males, resulting in selection for larger males. Unless other factors are concurrently selecting for larger females, this situation leads to a high degree of sexual dimorphism. In contrast, monogamous breeding systems are characterized by less male-male competition for mates (given an equal sex ratio) and a much smaller degree of variance in male reproductive success. Since larger males are not being selected for in such systems, these populations are characterized by low degrees of sexual dimorphism unless factors other than male-male competition select for larger males or smaller females.

The data presented by Alexander et al. generally support their hypothesis, as indicated by the following results:

1. For the pinnipeds and the nonhuman primates, when polygynous species are placed in one category and compared with a

category composed of monogamous species, the former exhibit greater sexual dimorphism.

2. For pinnipeds, ungulates, and nonhuman primates, as maximum harem size characteristic of a species increases (indicating more intense male-male competition), so does the degree of sexual dimorphism.

3. For each of the groups, as the mean harem size increases, so does the degree of sexual dimorphism.

In another section of their paper Alexander et al. treat intersocietal variation in human sexual dimorphism of stature as analogous to interspecies variability. Their measure of human sexual dimorphism is the ratio of mean societal male height to mean societal female height. They note that mean "harem" size is not available for human societies for which degrees of sexual dimorphism of stature are known (but see below) and, therefore, restrict their comparison to the categories of polygynous societies and monogamous societies. When the category of polygynous societies (mean dimorphism ratio = 1.078) was compared to the monogamy category (mean dimorphism ratio = 1.078) no significant difference in stature dimorphism was found.

Alexander et al. then argue that their failure to find support for the sexual selection hypothesis stems from lumping into one category two breeding systems that are actually quite different, i.e., ecologically imposed monogamy and socially imposed monogamy. The former is defined as the breeding system present when the ecological situation is such that individual males are unable to gain reproductive success by trying to provide for the offspring of more than one female at a time. It is predicted to occur in marginal environments and is seen as the true analogue to what is labeled as monogamy in the nonhuman animal world. In contrast, socially imposed monogamy is unique to humans and exists when a system of laws prevents polygyny even though the ecological situation is such that males could increase their reproductive success by providing for the offspring of more than one female at a time. The authors suggest that such a system is characteristic of the European and Asian states and of previously polygynous societies now dominated by such states.

These two types of monogamy are hypothesized to have different effects on male-male competition and variance in male reproductive success. Ecologically imposed monogamy results in almost all males obtaining wives and this small variance in male reproductive success results in low degrees of sexual dimorphism. Socially imposed monogamy, however, is seen by Alexander et al. not to be real monogamy at all. They suggest there is actually intense male-male competition for mates due to high levels of mortality for young males in warfare. Thus, even though each male is restricted by law or custom to a single mate, there is actually great variation in male reproductive success, with the result that socially imposed monogamy should have the same effect on degree of sexual dimorphism as polygyny. When the authors retested the relationship between human marriage systems and sexual dimorphism of stature, they found some support for their position. Societies classified as exhibiting ecologically imposed monogamy had a statistically significant lower mean dimorphism ratio, 1.068 ($N = 16$), than either polygynous societies, 1.078 ($N = 46$), or societies classified as exhibiting socially imposed monogamy, 1.078 ($N = 31$).

At this point, however, Alexander et al. note that the differences in the degree of sexual dimorphism between societies classified as ecologically imposed monogamous and societies with the other two marriage systems may not reflect a differential distribution of genotypes responsible for sexual dimorphism in stature. They suggest (1979, p. 409) that it is possible that the lower degree of sexual dimorphism of stature characteristic of societies with ecologically imposed monogamy may be the result of previously polygynous societies entering marginal environments and mean societal male height subsequently decreasing as a result of poor food resources. This would, of course, lower the degree of sexual dimorphism in the manner suggested by the nutritional perspective. In the summary of their paper, however, this possibility is not mentioned and the impression is given that the results of the human data support conclusions drawn from the studies of other animals (1979, p. 435).

We have discussed the methodological shortcomings of the Alexander et al. analysis in another paper (Gray and Wolfe 1980). Some of these problems confront any study attempting to link human sexual dimorphism with sociological variables and we will deal with these in the following sections of this chapter. Other problems, however, are specific to the Alexander et al. paper and result from violating standard cross-cultural research procedures (see Naroll, Michik, and Naroll 1976). For example, it appears that the individual (i.e., K. Noonan for Alexander et al. 1979, p. 409) who collected the data on human sexual dimorphism was acquainted with the socio-biological perspective. Further, it appears that the persons who classified societies as to marriage systems were aware of the hypothesis to be tested. In normal cross-cultural research both these tasks would have been done by two or more coders unaware of the purpose of the research; this is done to prevent bias from influencing the classification procedure. The use of two or more coders also allows for a check of coding reliability, a crucial issue in the Alexander et al. paper due to the creation of a new concept: socially imposed monogamy.

The possibility for bias in the study arises at two points in the classification procedure. First, Alexander et al. note (1979, p. 408) that they excluded societies whose marriage systems they decided could not be classified reliably. However, since no criteria for reliability are presented it is possible that societies not in agreement with the hypothesis were unconsciously excluded. This possibility is important because of the second source of potential bias, the fact that the classification criteria are quite subjective and do not serve to define mutually exclusive categories. For example, all the criteria for poor habitat are either subjective or questionable. Ethnographers might, for example, reject the idea that either the Semang or the Pygmies, two societies classified as ecologically imposed monogamous by Alexander et al., inhabit marginal environments. It also appears that several groups classified as exhibiting socially imposed monogamy have features (small band size, marginal environment, etc.) that could result in their being classified as cases of ecologically imposed monogamy (e.g., Andamese, Choco, Toba). Other methodological flaws that make the results of the Alexander et al. study difficult to interpret include their inclusion of questionable stature data (Gray and Wolfe 1980) and failure to consider the influence of male and female height on the degree of sexual dimorphism exhibited by a society.

Gray and Wolfe (1980) used marriage system codes published by Murdock (1967) and mean height measurements for 140 human societies to test for a relationship between marriage system and degree of sexual dimorphism in stature as measured by the ratio of mean societal male height to mean societal female height. Murdock classified societies as exhibiting monogamy, limited polygyny, or general polygyny and we recommended this classification as a crude ordinal scale of intensity of male-male competition for females. It should be noted that Murdock's classifications as we used them are not adequate to deal with the problem of socially imposed monogamy raised by Alexander et al. Our results indicated that while there is a statistically significant positive relationship between a high mean male societal height and the practice of polygyny, there is no corresponding association between sexual dimorphism of stature and marriage practices.

Another sociobiological approach to the problem of sexual dimorphism utilizes Trivers' (1972) parental investment hypothesis. Parental investment, which Trivers defines as "any investment by the parent in an individual offspring that increases that offspring's chance of surviving (and hence reproductive success) at the cost of the parent's ability to invest in other offspring" (1972, p. 139), is hypothesized as the link between sexual selection and sexual dimorphism rather than mating systems per se. In other words, there is generally a discrepancy between the sexes with regard to the extent each invests in offspring, with males usually investing less than females in most species of mammals. This being the case, males can maximize reproductive success by inseminating as many females as possible. Females, therefore, become a limited resource for which males compete, and this competition is believed to be won by males with the largest body size. The result would be greater sexual dimorphism than in species where males invest heavily in offspring.

There is some support for this hypothesized relationship between parental investment and sexual dimorphism. Kleiman (1977), for example, found that among the monogamous primates (e.g., gibbons, marmosets), where the parental investment of both sexes is nearly equal, there is little or no sexual dimorphism in body size. On the other hand, the primate species with the greatest degree of sexual dimorphism in body size are the polygynous and/or promiscuous species (e.g., baboons, orangutans) where the male invests little after insemination (Clutton-Brock and Harvey 1978).

Recently, both Crook (1980) and Gaulin (1980) have argued that there is a relationship between the degree of male parental investment and human sexual dimorphism, although neither tests the proposition. At first consideration there seems to be little reason to test the hypothesis since sex bias in parental investment tendencies correlates highly with mating systems for most animals. That is, species where males invest heavily in offspring tend to be monogamous, whereas low male parental investment is positively correlated with promiscuous or polygynous mating systems. Thus, a test of the relationship between human marriage systems and sexual dimorphism of stature provides an indirect test of the parental investment hypothesis. Although the logic of this argument is compelling for nonhuman animals, it overlooks the fact that human marriage practices are not the exact equivalents of the nonhuman animal mating systems labeled with the same term. Social, historical, symbolic, and ecological factors operate together to shape the marriage practices of a society and these factors have resulted in a "loosening" of the relationship between male parental investment tendencies and marriage systems. Evidence that this is indeed the case is provided by the fact that the passing of real and movable property (Gaulin's measure of male parental investment) from husband to wife's (or wives') offspring is found both in monogamous societies, which a nonhuman animal analogy would lead one to expect, and in polygynous societies, which runs counter to the expectations of the analogy. Because of this evidence that suggests that human systems of male parental investment are independent of marriage practices, we designed an investigation to explore the relationship between inter-societal variability in the sexual dimorphism of stature and human patterns of male parental investment. The hypothesis we tested predicted that low male societal patterns of parental investment were associated with a high degree of societal sexual dimorphism of stature. The null hypothesis was that societal male parental investment practices have no significant influence on the degree of societal sexual dimorphism of stature. We also included marriage practices and nutritional variables in the investigation because of research, cited above, suggesting that these variables can have an influence on mean societal male height and the sexual dimorphism of stature. Results of the investigation are reported in this chapter.

MATERIALS AND METHODS

The first step in our investigation—the location of data on mean societal male and female height for various societies—turned out to be more difficult than anticipated. There is no one single source that contains data for both simple and complex societies. Because we were interested in obtaining as many measurements taken before 1945 as possible (see below) we first turned to the societies in the Human Relations Area Files (HRAF). We found that although the files contain a category for anthropometric data, HRAF was a rather poor source of data. Part of the problem occurs because the files usually contain ethnographic sources, and references relating solely to physical anthropology have not yet been incorporated into the files of most societies. Another aspect of the problem is that early ethnographers often did not measure the people they observed and when they did so they only rarely measured females. Data from the HRAF sources often contain no information on the number or ages of the subjects measured and means are usually reported without the standard deviation statistic.

Our poor success with the HRAF system forced us to search journals and anthropological serials for additional data. Although we tried to be comprehensive, we do not claim our sample is exhaustive. There are several references which summarize data for major geographic regions: Salzano (1971) for Latin and South America, Field (1970) for India, Hierneaux (1968) for Africa, Hrdlička (1909, 1931, 1935) for North American Indians, Gifford (1926) for California Indians, Steggerda (1950) for South America Indians.

Alexander et al. present height ratios and references for the 93 societies in their sample but do not report male and female heights. Casey and Downey (1970) list height data for males only, but their references can be used to locate sources with information on female height. Meredith (1976) contains height data on females for 300 groups, but is generally restricted to measurements taken after 1945. Eveleth and Tanner (1976) is invaluable, but lacks data from smaller societies. There are many other sources dealing with single societies scattered throughout the literature. Our list of sources and height data is available upon request.

The following rules guided our selection of data. First, a society was not included in the final sample unless the means for both sexes had been calculated on heights of at least five individuals of each sex. Second, no sources were accepted where the ethnographer took no measurements but only guessed at mean heights. Third, if there were more than one source for a society we selected the source providing measurements taken before 1945. If all sources for a society were published before that date we selected the source that presented the most measurements on the sex least represented (usually females). Fourth, large cross-national surveys were included as data for several societies even though the exact number of individuals measured was not presented in the source. Finally, when age distributions were given in a source, measurements of individuals under 18 years of age were excluded from the calculation of the dimorphism statistic.

After the mean societal male and female height data were assembled, a mean societal measure of sexual dimorphism of stature was calculated for each society by dividing the mean societal male height by the mean societal female height. For 90 percent of the samples, the means were based on at least 15 individuals representing each sex. Statistical tests showed that societies where means for one or both of the sexes were calculated on from 5 to 14 individuals did not differ on any variable from the 90 percent of the sample where means were based on over 15 measurements; therefore we included these societies in the final sample. Statistical tests also showed that the 20 percent of the societies where the means were based on data collected after 1945 did not differ on any variable from the societies where data was collected before 1945 (minimizing to some extent the influence of recent secular trend in height) and therefore these were also included in the final sample. All told, acceptable data on height were obtained for 252 societies, with the following geographic distribution: 47 African, 30 circum-Mediterranean, 22 East Eurasian, 37 Insular Pacific, 59 North American, and 57 Central and South American. This sample corrects the severe underrepresentation of African societies reported in our earlier study (Gray and Wolfe 1980). In order to minimize the secular trend in height and to include a wide range of marriage practices, the sample is biased toward nonindustrial, smaller-scale traditional societies.

Holocultural Codes

The second step of the investigation was to locate published holocultural codes which could be used as measures of our independent variables. We found or constructed eight such measures, three dealing with marriage systems, two with nutrition, and three with parental investment. We will describe each of these measures briefly, noting how it was coded, the theoretical reasons for its use, and the problems involved in its use. For ease of reference we will often refer to the measures by the name it was given for computer classification.

1. *EAMARY* Marriage codes taken from Murdock's *Ethnographic Atlas* (1967). In column 14 of the *Atlas*, Murdock (1967) scores a society as exhibiting monogamy (his symbol "M"), occasional polygyny ("N"), or general polygyny ("P" to "S"). We interpret this as a crude ordinal scale of the degree of differential male reproductive success. This interpretation is based on the assumption that in most cases increasing degrees of polygyny indicate increasing male-male competition and increased numbers of males being excluded from reproducing. If the Yanomamo (Chagnon 1979) are typical of polygynous societies, this assumption is valid. Obviously a direct measure of numbers of males excluded from reproductive activity would allow a better test of the sociobiological hypothesis relating marriage systems to sexual dimorphism, but such a measure is not available in the ethnographic literature for most societies. Marriage practice codes for several of the societies from Africa were taken from *African Cultural Summaries* (Murdock 1956). The summaries were also used for information on protein availability and inheritance practices for some African societies not listed in the *Ethnographic Atlas*.

The use of Murdock's codes presents three problems that are unavoidable and should be kept in mind when evaluating the results of our research. First, many of the societies in the sample had been in contact with Western culture long before ethnographers recorded marriage practices. Such factors as depopulation resulting from warfare or disease, economic change, or the influence of missionaries or government officers may have been responsible for major changes in the marriage practices of these societies by the time the ethnographers arrived on the scene. Although researchers usually tried to recreate the original patterns (the "ethnographic present") they were not always successful. It should also be noted that factors such as disease or warfare may have disrupted the population so much that the distribution of height observed by the ethnographers no longer duplicated the distribution characteristic of precontact time.

The second problem with the EAMARY codes is that they are a mixture of cognized cultural rules, normative statements, and observed behavioral regularities. The scores for some societies were derived from informant statements on the "correct" aboriginal patterns, while in other cases the scores result from statistical descriptions of observed practices. The problem with this procedure is that cultural rules and behavior may not always be in agreement, in which case only the latter allows a proper test of the sociobiological hypothesis.

The final problem is that in many cases the heights used to calculate the sexual dimorphism of stature were derived from measurements taken many years after the marriage system of a society had been recorded. If the marriage system had changed in the intervening time period it is possible that the selective forces operative under the old system had been so relaxed that the distribution of height had changed.

2. *ALEXMARY*   Marriage system codes taken from Alexander et al. (1979). For purposes of comparison with our other two measures of marriage systems we included the societies classified as Alexander et al. as exhibiting ecologically imposed monogamy, socially imposed monogamy, and polygyny. After verifying the references cited by the authors we excluded some societies because the measure of sexual dimorphism was not reliable or because the tribal designation of the group measured was questionable. In cases where we found sources either earlier in time or with a greater number of measurements than those cited by Alexander et al. we substituted the new data. Thus, the ALEXMARY codes are not the precise equivalent to the sample presented by Alexander et al.

The three problems with the utilization of the EAMARY codes in this research are applicable also to the ALEXMARY codes and to the NEWMARY codes described next.

3. *NEWMARY*   Murdock's codes manipulated to deal with the problem of socially imposed monogamy.   As noted earlier, the EAMARY codes do not allow us to deal adequately with the distinction between ecologically imposed and socially imposed monogamy. Alexander et al. note that the latter is usually found in societies on the state level of organization and operates to produce

differential male reproductive success on the order of that exhibited by polygynous societies only if there is high male mortality in warfare. We question whether all the societies classified by Alexander et al. as exhibiting socially imposed monogamy actually have warfare intense enough to produce this situation, but we will accept their position on this question for the moment. We, therefore, examined all the societies scored as monogamous by Murdock and if a society had a score in column 33 indicating that it was a state level society (scores 3 and 4), we classified the society with the general polygyny societies. The NEWMARY codes are not a perfect solution to the problem of socially imposed monogamy, but they do provide a better test of the sociobiological hypothesis suggested by Alexander et al. than the EAMARY codes.

4. *PROTEIN*   Level of protein availability as coded by Whiting (1964). There are, unfortunately, no codes available that measure level of general nutrition for a large sample of societies. We, therefore, were forced to resort to a measure of level of protein availability as an indirect indicator of general nutritional status. Our scoring procedure was the one outlined by Whiting (1964) and utilized columns 7 and 29 in the *Ethnographic Atlas*. If the scores in column 7 indicated that a society obtains over half of its food from any combination of gathering, hunting, fishing, or animal husbandry, it was classified as having high protein availability. If a society obtains half or more of its food from agriculture and its principal crop was a cereal grain (column 29), the group was classified as having medium protein availability. If agriculture provides half or more of a society's food and the principal crops were roots or tubers, tree fruits, or vegetables, a society was classified as having low protein availability.

5. *NEWTEIN*   PROTEIN codes manipulated to deal with industrial societies. A number of the societies classified as medium protein societies are modern industrial groups in which average protein consumption may be higher than indicated by our scoring procedure. To see if this problem influenced our results, we examined the societies as medium protein availability groups and if column 31 of the *Ethnnographic Atlas* indicated that the society had one or more indigenous cities with more than 50,000 inhabitants, we placed the society in the high protein availability category for the NEWTEIN codes.

6. *NEARNESS*   Father-infant proximity as coded by Barry and Paxson (1971). Our search of the literature on cross-cultural codes revealed no codes that directly rate societies on the degree of male

parental investment. This lack of codes is partly due to the fact that ethnographers rarely had a theoretical orientation in which the problem of male parental investment was of central concern and therefore rarely collected data on this problem. In almost every human society adult males engage in some form of parental investment in that they provide more than sperm to the child. However, the variations in the form of investment (i.e., protection, interpersonal interaction, training, food, property after death, etc.) are so great that it is difficult to construct a measure which will be a good analogue to the measurement of male parental investment in nonhuman animal species.

As one measure of human male parental investment we chose the father-infant proximity codes published by Barry and Paxson (1971). These codes were constructed using standard cross-cultural research techniques, and the authors believe them to be highly reliable (1971, pp. 485-487). The codes score the degree of contact between males and their presumed offspring during infancy, the period between birth and, usually, 1 year of age. Barry and Paxson rate societies on a five-point ordinal scale ranging from 1 ("no close proximity") to 5 ("regular, close relationship or companionship"). In order to use analysis of variance techniques in our study we collapsed this scale into a dichotomous contrast between low male parental investment (scores 1 through 3) and high male parental investment (scores 4 and 5).

It is obvious that the Barry and Paxson codes are, at best, an indirect measure of human male parental investment and their use in this research is based on several assumptions. First, we assume that in most societies proximity of the father to the offspring increases to some degree the child's chances of survival. Second, the time the father spends with any one particular child usually reduces the amount of time he can spend with other children, especially if the other children belong to women other than the mother of the first child. Third, time spent with children reduces the amount of time the father can spend in pursuit of other females in attempts to create still more offspring. Although Trivers (1972) does not count time away from pursuit of other females to be part of the cost of male parental investment, we believe this is an important aspect of male parental investment for humans and see it as analogous to the concept of "promiscuity cost" of parental care among nonhuman animals recently discussed by Werren, Gross, and Shine (1980).

7. *REALPROP*   Inheritance of real property as coded by Murdock (1967). A uniquely human trait by which a father can assist his offspring is through allowing them to inherit his real or movable

property. Gaulin (1980) and Hartung (1976) have suggested that inheritance practices constitute the proper measure of male parental investment for human beings and both have used the scores in column 74 (real property) and column 76 (movable property) of the *Ethnographic Atlas* to test sociobiological hypotheses relevant to the problem of male parental investment. We decided to follow suit and include these codes in our research.

We did so, however, with great reluctance. Unlike the codes of Barry and Paxson, the inheritance codes in the *Ethnographic Atlas* are not reliable and Murdock has cautioned that they must be used only with great circumspection (1967, p. 59). Further, we believe inheritance may not be a good measure of male parental investment since it is possible for males to give away most or all of their property and thus actually transmit very little of it to their offspring according to the rules of society. Finally, the coding decisions necessary to utilize the inheritance codes result in most of the societies being excluded from tests of the male parental investment hypothesis. That is, each column has seven possible scores, with symbols "C," "D," and "P" indicating that a male usually passes his property on to his wife's offspring (high male parental investment) and symbols "M," "N," and "Q" indicating that a male normally gives property to individuals other than the offspring of his wife (low male parental investment). The main coding problem involves the use of the symbol "O," which indicates that a society either has no individually owned real or movable property, or, if there is individually owned property, there is no rule as to its transmission to other people. The "O" symbol is thus ambiguous. It does not differentiate societies where males invest time and effort in children, but cannot give them property because the group lacks property, from those societies where there is individually owned property but males do not necessarily invest it in their wife's offspring. In order to avoid this ambiguity we excluded societies scored as "O" from our sample (*see also* Gray and Wolfe, 1981, for other problems with these codes).

8. *MOVEPROP* Inheritance of movable property as coded by Murdock (1967). The problems of the REALPROP codes are also applicable to the MOVEPROP codes, with the additional ambiguity that a score of "O" may indicate that a man's movable property is destroyed, buried, or given away upon his death.

The overlap of societies with data for height and each of the independent variables is as follows: EAMARY, NEWMARY, PROTEIN, NEWTEIN each with 174 societies; ALEXMARY with 83 societies; NEARNESS with 62 societies; REALPROP with 89 societies; and MOVEPROP with 102 societies.

Variable Independence

To determine if the independent variables in our study are independent of one another, we calculated chi-square statistics for all possible combinations of the eight measures. Table 8.1 presents Cramer's *V* and *phi* statistics of the association for the variable pairs. As expected, the three measures of marriage practices are highly associated with one another as are the two measures of protein availability. The two measures of inheritance practices were strongly associated with each other; however, neither is associated with the measure of father-offspring contact. The inheritance of movable property is associated with EAMARY codes: Societies classified as exhibiting general polygyny were more likely to allow males to transmit property to individuals other than wives' offspring than societies with monogamy or limited polygyny. Still, the majority of general polygyny societies exhibited transmission of movable property to wives' offspring. The other measures of marriage systems were not significantly associated with either of the measures of inheritance. Protein availability as measured by the PROTEIN codes is associated with marriage systems: Low protein is more often found in polygynous societies than in societies with alternative marriage systems. However, the NEWTEIN recoding of protein availability is significantly associated only with the NEWMARY codes. Finally, parental investment as measured by the NEARNESS codes is significantly associated with the ALEXMARY and the NEWMARY codes. The NEWMARY codes indicate that high father-offspring contact tends to occur in polygynous societies more often than in societies with other forms of marriage. In contrast, the ALEXMARY codes indicate that high father-offspring contact is most often found in societies with ecologically imposed monogamy.

Although in the remainder of this chapter we analyze the effects of the eight measures as if there were no associations between them, the results of these chi-square tests should be kept in mind.

RESULTS

Figures 8.1 and 8.2 illustrate the regression equations on the relationship between societal sexual dimorphism of stature and the mean societal male and female height, respectively; linear correlation is low (0.17 and 0.15) but statistically significant, i.e., non-zero. The figures agree with the research of Hall (1978) on humans and Clutton-Brock, Harvey, and Rudder (1977) on nonhuman primates in suggesting that sexual dimorphism in body size is greatest in groups

TABLE 8.1
Statistics of Association Between the Eight Measures of Independent Variables.

	EAMARY	ALEXMARY	NEWMARY	PROTEIN	NEWTEIN	NEARNESS	REALPROP	MOVEPROP
EAMARY	—							
ALEXMARY	0.55[a]	—						
NEWMARY	0.85[a]	0.37[a]	—					
PROTEIN	0.23[a]	0.34[a]	0.19[b]	—				
NEWTEIN	0.15	0.16	0.19[b]	0.89[a]	—			
NEARNESS	0.24	0.61[a]	0.35[b]	0.05	0.10	—		
REALPROP	0.18	0.18	0.12	0.02	0.16	0.37[c]	—	
MOVEPROP	0.29[d]	0.25	0.18	0.05	0.18	0.20[c]	0.77[c,a]	—

[a] $P < 0.01$.
[b] $P < 0.05$.
[c] Phi coefficients; other figures are Cramer's V statistic.
[d] $P < 0.10$.

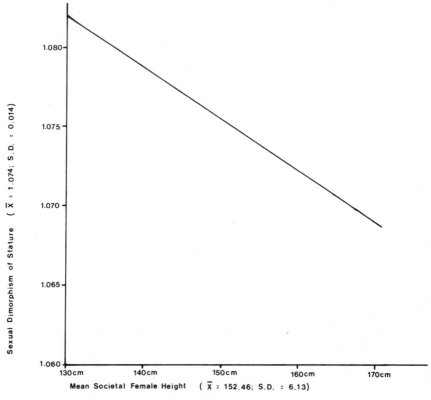

Figure 8.1.   Relationship of male height to sexual dimorphism of stature. Y = 1.014 + 0.000368X ± 0.0138; N = 252; r = 0.17.

with the largest males. Figure 8.3 presents the regression line for mean societal male and female height and indicates the high correlation (0.95) between these two variables. Average height of one sex is associated with that of the other to a much greater extent than to intersex differences. Allometry is present—but feeble.

In Table 8.2 we present the results of various *t*-tests exploring the relationships between male and female height, sexual dimorphism of stature, and our three measures of human marriage practices (all tests were duplicated using the Mann-Whitney U statistic; as the results were the same as with the *t*-test we report only the *t*-test here). In spite of our elimination of 10 cases, the ALEXMARY codes in our sample generally repeat the findings of the original Alexander et al. study. That is, the mean sexual dimorphism of stature for ecologically imposed monogamous societies is significantly lower than the mean for polygynous societies. The contrast between the mean sexual

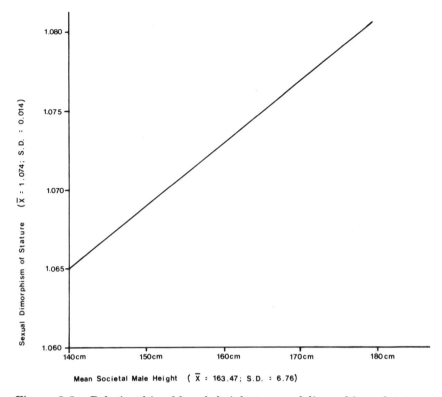

Figure 8.2. Relationship of female height to sexual dimorphism of stature. $Y = 1.126 - 0.000337X \pm 0.0139$; $N = 252$; $r = -0.15$.

dimorphism of stature in ecologically imposed monogamous societies and socially imposed monogamous societies is in the predicted direction and the t-test score falls only just outside the 0.05 level of statistical significance. Finally, the difference between the sexual dimorphism of stature of polygynous societies and societies exhibiting socially imposed monogamy is not significant.

Relationships between male and female height and the categories of the ALEXMARY codes suggest that the results of the tests relating marriage practices to sexual dimorphism of stature may be explained by the relationship of marriage practices to the mean societal height of males. We will test this possibility later and for now will only note that a comparison of societies classified as polygynous with those classified as ecologically imposed monogamous indicates that both mean societal male and female height are significantly greater in the former than in the latter. Also, mean societal male height is less in ecologically imposed monogamous societies than in groups where

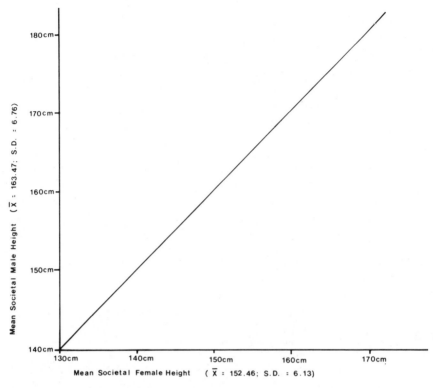

Figure 8.3. Relationship between female height and male height. $Y = 8.023 + 1.022X \pm 2.1088$; $N = 252$; $r = 0.95$.

monogamy is socially imposed, although the difference falls just outside the 0.05 level of significance.

The use of the EAMARY codes to classify marriage practices of societies results in basically the same conclusions reported in Gray and Wolfe (1980). When societies classified as exhibiting limited polygyny are compared with those exhibiting general polygyny, male and female mean societal heights are found to be significantly greater in the general polygyny groups than in the groups exhibiting limited polygyny. The difference in the sexual dimorphism of stature between the two categories does not quite reach statistical significance. Interestingly, the difference is in the direction opposite to that predicted by sociobiological theory, since the category indicative of less intense male-male competition for mates (i.e., limited polygyny) has a higher mean sexual dimorphism of stature than the category indicating more intense competition (i.e., general polygyny). Comparison of monogamous societies with the other two marriage systems reveals no significant differences in either mean societal height or sexual dimorphism.

We noted above that the EAMARY codes are not adequate to deal with the concept of socially imposed monogamy raised by Alexander et al. and proposed the NEWMARY codes as a solution to this problem. Table 8.2 indicates that classifying monogamous societies on the state level of organization as general polygyny rather than monogamy does indeed give us a clearer picture of the relationships between the variables than the EAMARY codes. For both male and female mean societal height, there are significant differences between the means of each category when compared to the other two categories although the comparison between monogamy and limited polygyny for mean societal female height is just above the 0.05 significance level. Comparison of the three categories for the sexual dimorphism of stature variable indicates that there are no significant differences. However, the comparison between monogamy and limited polygyny results in a t-test score significant at just below the 0.10 level. Further, the mean sexual dimorphism of stature of the limited polygyny societies is greater than that of the general polygyny societies, thereby repeating the finding using the EAMARY codes.

The results of t-tests for relationships between our two measures of nutrition, societal height and sexual dimorphism of stature, are presented in Table 8.3. In general, the findings suggest that the level of protein availability is not a strong predictor of the level of sexual dimorphism of stature. Utilization of the PROTEIN codes results in the discovery of a significant difference in mean societal male height between low protein availability societies and medium availability groups. Comparison of the same two categories on the level of sexual dimorphism indicates that the sexual dimorphism of stature is lower in low protein groups than in medium availability societies. This result, which is predicted by the nutritional perspective, does not quite reach the 0.05 level of significance, however. The fact that comparison of the low protein availability category with the high protein category yields no significant differences for male or female height or for sexual dimorphism is difficult to explain from the nutritional perspective.

Moving societies with medium protein availability and cities over 500,000 inhabitants from the medium availability category into the high availability category (NEWTEIN) eliminates the significant difference in mean male societal height observed when low availability groups are contrasted with medium availability societies. However, a difference in mean male societal height when high availability groups are compared with low availability groups is suggested but not significant. With the NEWTEIN codes, the

TABLE 8.2
Marriage Practices, Height, and Sexual Dimorphism of Stature.

	N	Mean	S.D.	Groups	t	1-Tailed Probability
ALEXMARY CODES						
Mean societal male height						
Ecological monogamy	12	160.69	8.34	1 vs. 2	−1.44	0.079
Social monogamy	30	164.49	7.47	1 vs. 3	−2.13	0.019
Polygyny	41	165.18	5.76	2 vs. 3	−0.44	0.330
Mean societal female height						
Ecological monogamy	12	149.95	6.36	1 vs. 2	−1.13	0.133
Social monogamy	30	152.50	6.72	1 vs. 3	−1.62	0.055
Polygyny	41	152.85	5.17	2 vs. 3	−0.25	0.402
Sexual dimorphism of stature						
Ecological monogamy	12	1.071	0.018	1 vs. 2	−1.46	0.076
Social monogamy	30	1.078	0.012	1 vs. 3	−2.02	0.024
Polygyny	41	1.081	0.012	2 vs. 3	−0.76	0.224
EAMARY CODES						
Mean societal male height						
Monogamy	39	164.94	6.98	1 vs. 2	0.91	0.182
Limited polygyny	74	163.73	6.59	1 vs. 3	−1.06	0.146
General polygyny	61	166.32	5.52	2 vs. 3	−2.49	0.007
Mean societal female height						
Monogamy	39	153.45	6.28	1 vs. 2	1.16	0.124
Limited polygyny	74	152.07	5.87	1 vs. 3	−1.36	0.088
General polygyny	61	155.01	5.07	2 vs. 3	−3.07	0.001
Sexual dimorphism of stature						
Monogamy	39	1.075	0.014	1 vs. 2	−0.62	0.267
Limited polygyny	74	1.077	0.014	1 vs. 3	0.60	0.275
General polygyny	61	1.073	0.015	2 vs. 3	1.42	0.079
NEWMARY CODES						
Mean societal male height						
Monogamy	22	161.15	5.86	1 vs. 2	−1.86	0.033
Limited polygyny	74	163.73	6.59	1 vs. 3	−4.50	0.000
General polygyny	78	167.09	5.35	2 vs. 3	−3.29	0.000
Mean societal female height						
Monogamy	22	150.36	5.68	1 vs. 2	−1.38	0.085
Limited polygyny	74	152.07	5.87	1 vs. 3	−4.14	0.000
General polygyny	78	155.54	5.04	2 vs. 3	−3.76	0.000
Sexual dimorphism of stature						
Monogamy	22	1.072	0.015	1 vs. 2	−1.42	0.080
Limited polygyny	74	1.077	0.014	1 vs. 3	−0.65	0.258
General polygyny	78	1.074	0.014	2 vs. 3	1.11	0.134

TABLE 8.3
Protein, Height, and Sexual Dimorphism of Stature.

	N	Mean	S.D.	Groups	t	1-Tailed Probability
PROTEIN CODES						
Mean societal male height						
Low	38	163.75	5.70	1 vs. 2	−1.87	0.032
Medium	69	165.90	5.65	1 vs. 3	−0.66	0.254
High	67	164.61	6.77	2 vs. 3	1.20	0.116
Mean societal female height						
Low	38	152.70	5.56	1 vs. 2	−1.26	0.105
Medium	69	154.13	5.66	1 vs. 3	−0.34	0.365
High	67	153.10	5.80	2 vs. 3	1.05	0.148
Sexual dimorphism of stature						
Low	38	1.073	0.011	1 vs. 2	−1.54	0.063
Medium	69	1.076	0.015	1 vs. 3	−1.02	0.154
High	67	1.075	0.015	2 vs. 3	0.49	0.313
NEWTEIN CODES						
Mean societal male height						
Low	38	163.75	5.70	1 vs. 2	−0.93	0.177
Medium	50	164.87	5.53	1 vs. 3	−1.48	0.070
High	86	165.60	6.68	2 vs. 3	−0.65	0.258
Mean societal female height						
Low	38	152.70	5.56	1 vs. 2	−0.29	0.385
Medium	50	153.05	5.63	1 vs. 3	−1.21	0.114
High	86	154.06	5.85	2 vs. 3	−0.98	0.164
Sexual dimorphism of stature						
Low	38	1.073	0.011	1 vs. 2	−1.70	0.047
Medium	50	1.078	0.016	1 vs. 3	−0.86	0.195
High	86	1.075	0.014	2 vs. 3	0.99	0.162

difference in the sexual dimorphism of stature between low and medium availability categories does reach the 0.05 level of significance and is in the direction predicted by the nutritional hypothesis.

In Table 8.4 we present the results of the t-tests for the relationships between our three measures of male parental investment, mean societal height, and the sexual dimorphism of stature. The inheritance of real property (REALPROP) is not significantly related to mean societal male or female height or to sexual dimorphism. However, societal rules for the transmission of movable property (MOVEPROP) are related to sexual dimorphism of stature: Societies where males usually pass on movable property to the offspring of their wife (i.e., high male parental investment societies) are characterized by a greater degree of societal sexual dimorphism of stature than societies where males tend to leave property to

TABLE 8.4
Male Parental Investment, Height, and Sexual Dimorphism of Stature.

	N	Mean	S.D.	Groups	t	1-Tailed Probability
REALPROP CODES						
Mean societal male height						
Wife's offspring	72	165.98	5.15	1 vs. 2	0.18	0.430
Other	17	165.73	5.13			
Mean societal female height						
Wife's offspring	72	154.21	4.86	1 vs. 2	−0.43	0.335
Other	17	154.77	4.86			
Sexual dimorphism						
Wife's offspring	72	1.076	0.015	1 vs. 2	1.33	0.093
Other	17	1.071	0.014			
MOVEPROP CODES						
Mean societal male height						
Wife's offspring	88	165.59	5.16	1 vs. 2	0.41	0.343
Other	14	164.96	6.58			
Mean societal female height						
Wife's offspring	88	154.02	4.97	1 vs. 2	−0.30	0.383
Other	14	154.46	6.05			
Sexual dimorphism						
Wife's offspring	88	1.075	0.014	1 vs. 2	1.70	0.046
Other	14	1.068	0.013			
NEARNESS CODES						
Mean societal male height						
Low proximity	43	164.87	6.03	1 vs. 2	2.76	0.004
High proximity	19	160.05	7.04			
Mean societal female height						
Low proximity	43	153.10	5.42	1 vs. 2	2.57	0.006
High proximity	19	148.99	6.59			
Sexual dimorphism						
Low proximity	43	1.077	0.014	1 vs. 2	0.68	0.248
High proximity	19	1.074	0.018			

individuals other than to their wife's offspring (i.e., low male parental investment societies). This result is in opposition to the parental investment theory discussed above which predicted that low societal male parental investment practices would be associated with a high degree of societal sexual dimorphism of stature. The degree of contact between father and infant as measured by the NEARNESS codes is not statistically related to sexual dimorphism of stature but is strongly related to both mean societal male and female height. The fact that societies where contact is low tend to be societies with a greater mean male height than societies where contact is high is in agreement with the parental investment hypothesis. However, the fact that there is a high mean societal female height associated with low contact societies is unexpected.

In summary, the results of t-tests indicate weak support for the existence of a link between human marriage practices and human mean societal height and/or societal sexual dimorphism of stature. We phrase this conclusion in an ambiguous manner because the three measures of marriage practices do not provide the same conclusions on these relationships. The classification of marriage practices as offered by Alexander et al. produces a statistically significant relationship between marriage practices and degree of sexual dimorphism. However, neither the EAMARY codes nor the NEWMARY codes produce the same relationship. The NEWMARY codes indicate that the degree of sexual dimorphism is not related to marriage practices, but that mean male and female societal height are related to marriage practices and both increase as one moves from monogamy to general polygyny. The codes NEARNESS, REAL-PROP, and MOVEPROP provide no support for the parental investment hypothesis. However, NEARNESS is significantly associated with both male and female mean societal height. Finally, some support is found for the nutritional perspective as the jump from low to medium protein availability results in a statistically significant increase in the degree of sexual dimorphism of stature.

Of course t-tests do not provide information on how much of the variation in a given dependent variable can be explained by changes in a specific independent variable. We therefore performed one-factor analysis of variance for each of our independent measures and the dependent variables of mean male and female societal height and sexual dimorphism of stature. The summary statistics for these ANOVAs are presented in Table 8.5.

The most interesting result in Table 8.5 is that marriage practices, as classified by the ALEXMARY codes, actually explain very little of the variation in degree of human sexual dimorphism of stature ($r^2 = 0.053$). Surprisingly, the ALEXMARY codes also explain little of the variance for both male and female height. However, the results also indicate that while the NEWMARY codes explain little of the variance in human sexual dimorphism of stature ($r^2 = 0.013$), they do account for a somewhat larger proportion of the variance in mean societal male ($r^2 = 0.114$) and female ($r^2 = 0.116$) height.

Neither of the protein measures explains much of the variation in height or sexual dimorphism and the same is true of the two measures of the transmission of property. Finally, father-infant proximity explains little of the variation in sexual dimorphism, but explains about 11 percent ($r^2 = 0.112$) of the variance in male height and 9 percent ($r^2 = 0.099$) of female height.

TABLE 8.5
Summary Statistics for One-Way Analysis of Variance.

	F	Significance of F	r	r^2
ALEXMARY CODES				
Sexual dimorphism	2.234	0.114	0.230	0.053
Mean male height	2.033	0.138	0.220	0.048
Mean female height	1.128	0.329	0.166	0.027
EAMARY CODES				
Sexual dimorphism	1.007	0.367	0.108	0.012
Mean male height	2.892	0.058	0.181	0.033
Mean female height	4.438	0.013	0.222	0.049
NEWMARY CODES				
Sexual dimorphism	1.157	0.317	0.116	0.013
Mean male height	10.896	0.000	0.337	0.114
Mean female height	11.202	0.000	0.341	0.116
PROTEIN CODES				
Sexual dimorphism	0.885	0.415	0.102	0.010
Mean male height	1.647	0.196	0.138	0.019
Mean female height	0.940	0.393	0.105	0.011
NEWTEIN CODES				
Sexual dimorphism	1.282	0.280	0.122	0.015
Mean male height	1.189	0.307	0.117	0.014
Mean female height	0.930	0.397	0.104	0.011
NEARNESS CODES				
Sexual dimorphism	0.469	0.469	0.088	0.008
Mean male height	7.598	0.008	0.335	0.112
Mean female height	6.628	0.013	0.315	0.099
REALPROP CODES				
Sexual dimorphism	1.775	0.186	0.141	0.020
Mean male height	0.031	0.861	0.019	0.000
Mean female height	0.183	0.670	0.046	0.002
MOVEPROP CODES				
Sexual dimorphism	2.898	0.092	0.168	0.028
Mean male height	0.164	0.686	0.040	0.002
Mean female height	0.089	0.766	0.030	0.001

Our final series of statistical tests involved two-way ANOVAs for sexual dimorphism of stature using the following practices with each measures of protein availability. Each ANOVA was run three times, once with no covariant, once with male height as a covariant, and once with female height as a covariant. The numerous tables produced by this procedure exhibited results which are summarized below.

Table 8.6 presents the results of analysis of variance and covariance when the ALEXMARY codes are paired with the NEWTEIN codes. The simple ANOVA indicates that the two variables explain about 9 percent (0.094) of the variance in sexual dimorphism, with the betas indicating that marriage practices are more important than level of protein availability in explaining the variation. When male height is added to the analysis, over 22 percent (r^2 = 0.224) of the intersocietal variance in sexual dimorphism of stature is explained, but the betas indicate that protein may be having a slightly greater influence on the variation than the marriage practices variable. Finally, adding mean societal female height as a covariant does little to the results obtained from the simple ANOVA, indicating that the effect of marriage practices and protein availability on sexual dimorphism is mediated mainly through the influence each has on male height. An ANOVA pairing ALEXMARY codes and NEWTEIN codes and examining their influence on the variation in mean societal male height suggests that the two variables explain about 10 percent of the variance with marriage practices (beta = 0.28) having a greater influence than protein availability (beta = 0.20). The two variables explain about 8 percent of the variance in female height, with each having about equal influence (betas = 0.22).

Since the ALEXMARY codes produce results contradictory to those produced when either the EAMARY or the NEWMARY codes are utilized, we present the pairing of the latter with the NEWTEIN codes in Table 8.7. In contrast to the results suggested by use of the

TABLE 8.6
Analysis of Variance and Covariance for Explaining Sexual Dimorphism of Height (ALEXMARY X NEWTEIN).

	F Statistic for Explained	Significance of F Statistic	ALEXMARY Beta	NEWTEIN Beta	r	r^2
No covariant	1.680	0.129	0.26	0.18	0.307	0.094
Mean male height as covariant	2.763	0.011	0.15*	0.19*	0.473	0.224
Mean female height as covariant	1.452	0.193	0.24*	0.18*	0.312	0.098

*Beta figures when adjusting for covariant.

TABLE 8.7
Analysis of Variance and Covariance for Explaining Sexual Dimorphism
of Height (NEWMARY × NEWTEIN).

	F Statistic for Explained	Significance of F Statistic	NEWMARY Beta	NEWTEIN Beta	r	r^2
No covariant	1.114	0.356	0.15	0.14	0.182	0.033
Mean male height as covariant	1.638	0.108	0.16*	0.14*	0.267	0.071
Mean female height as covariant	1.684	0.097	0.15*	0.15*	0.247	0.061

*Beta figures when adjusting for covariant.

ALEXMARY codes, these two variables have little influence on
sexual dimorphism of stature and both variables seem to have about
the same degree of influence. However, the two variables do explain
over 12 percent of the variance in both male and female height, with
marriage practices having greater influence in both cases (male beta
for protein = 0.10, for marriage = 0.33; female beta for protein = 0.09,
for marriage = 0.34).

Finally, Table 8.8 presents the ANOVA and analysis of covariance for the variable pairs NEARNESS and NEWTEIN. Again, the
variables have little influence on the degree of sexual dimorphism.
When male height is added as a covariant, only about 9 percent ($r^2 =$
0.094) of the intersocietal variance in sexual dimorphism of stature is
explained, with the parental investment variable (beta = 0.01) having
far less influence than protein availability (beta = 0.18). The two
variables explain about 14 percent of the variance in mean societal
male height, with father-infant proximity (beta = 0.37) more
influential than protein availability (beta = 0.03). The 12 percent of
the intersocietal variance in societal female height explained by the
two variables is also more influenced by the father-infant proximity
variable (beta = 0.34) than the protein availability variable (beta =
0.04).

It is clear that relationships between marriage practices and
dependent variables of mean societal adult height and sexual
dimorphism of stature are complex and that the situation is
complicated by the fact that marriage practices are statistically
associated with levels of protein availability. These complications
can be simplified to some extent by examining the interactions
between one independent variable and the dependent variables at

TABLE 8.8
Analysis of Variance and Covariance for Explaining Sexual Dimorphism
of Height (NEARNESS X NEWTEIN).

	F Statistic for Explained	Significance of F Statistic	NEARNESS Beta	NEWTEIN Beta	r	r^2
No covariant	0.942	0.461	0.10	0.19	0.220	0.048
Mean male height as covariant	1.220	0.310	0.01*	0.18*	0.306	0.094
Mean female height as covariant	0.992	0.440	0.15*	0.18*	0.258	0.067

*Beta figures when adjusting for covariant.

each level of another independent variable. Unfortunately, there are
not enough societies in the sample to do this for the ALEXMARY or
the NEARNESS codes. However, Table 8.9 presents such an analysis
using the NEWMARY codes and the NEWTEIN codes. At each level
of protein availability, monogamous societies are characterized by
males and females who are significantly shorter than those found in
societies where general polygyny is practiced. Also, limited polygyny
societies exhibit significantly shorter males and females than general
polygyny groups at all levels of protein availability, although the
difference for both sexes is above the 0.05 level of significance at the
low protein availability level. The differences in degree of sexual
dimorphism of stature between the marriage practice categories are
extremely small, in no consistent direction, and do not reach
statistical significance at either the low or medium protein availability levels. At the level of high protein availability, a pattern
emerges that clarifies the picture to some degree. As one moves from
the low protein level to the medium protein level, there is increase in
male and female height for comparable marriage practices and this
increase continues at the high protein level for both limited polygyny
and general polygyny. However, the five societies in the high protein
monogamy category exhibit the lowest male and female heights on
the chart. It is only this sharp drop in male and female height that
produces the significant differences in the degree of sexual dimorphism observed at the high protein level.

It is extremely difficult to interpret these last findings. A possible
explanation is suggested if the sexual selection perspective and the
nutritional perspective are combined as follows. Perhaps the five
societies are ecologically monogamous as defined by Alexander et al.;

TABLE 8.9
Influence of Marriage Systems (NEWMARY) on Height and Sexual Dimorphism at Each Level of Protein Availability (NEWTEIN).

	N	X̄	S.D.	Groups	t	1-Tailed Probability
Low Protein Availability						
Mean male height						
Monogamy	5	160.9	5.63	1 vs. 2	−0.57	0.288
Limited polygyny	17	162.8	6.59	1 vs. 3	−1.93	0.035
General polygyny	15	165.6	4.37	2 vs. 3	−1.40	0.086
Mean female height						
Monogamy	5	150.2	6.05	1 vs. 2	−0.46	0.325
Limited polygyny	17	151.7	6.42	1 vs. 3	−1.76	0.048
General polygyny	15	154.4	4.08	2 vs. 3	−1.39	0.087
Sexual dimorphism of stature						
Monogamy	5	1.072	0.009	1 vs. 2	−0.30	0.382
Limited polygyny	17	1.073	0.011	1 vs. 3	−0.22	0.414
General polygyny	15	1.073	0.012	2 vs. 3	0.09	0.463
Medium Protein Availability						
Mean male height						
Monogamy	12	163.0	5.15	1 vs. 2	−0.15	0.441
Limited polygyny	13	163.4	5.79	1 vs. 3	−2.13	0.020
General polygyny	24	166.9	5.06	2 vs. 3	−1.92	0.031
Mean female height						
Monogamy	12	151.5	4.88	1 vs. 2	0.05	0.479
Limited polygyny	13	151.4	5.33	1 vs. 3	−1.83	0.038
General polygyny	24	155.0	5.70	2 vs. 3	−1.89	0.033
Sexual dimorphism of stature						
Monogamy	12	1.076	0.017	1 vs. 2	−0.48	0.316
Limited polygyny	13	1.079	0.012	1 vs. 3	−0.05	0.479
General polygyny	24	1.077	0.018	2 vs. 3	0.44	0.333
High Protein Availability						
Mean male height						
Monogamy	5	156.8	6.47	1 vs. 2	−2.57	0.007
Limited polygyny	43	164.6	6.40	1 vs. 3	−3.89	0.000
General polygyny	38	167.9	5.90	2 vs. 3	−2.36	0.010
Mean female height						
Monogamy	5	147.8	7.44	1 vs. 2	−1.84	0.036
Limited polygyny	43	152.7	5.54	1 vs. 3	−3.41	0.000
General polygyny	38	156.4	5.00	2 vs. 3	−3.06	0.001
Sexual dimorphism of stature						
Monogamy	5	1.062	0.014	1 vs. 2	−2.25	0.014
Limited polygyny	43	1.078	0.015	1 vs. 3	−1.92	0.031
General polygyny	38	1.073	0.013	2 vs. 3	1.32	0.094

and although there is indeed a relationship between marriage practices and sexual dimorphism of stature, it is only at the high protein level that the increase in mean societal male height associated with polygyny finally "outstrips" the increase in female height, which we have found to be associated with increased polygyny. This interpretation runs into at least two problems. First, the degrees of sexual dimorphism associated with marriage practices at the high level of protein availability do not conform to the predictions of the sexual selection perspective; societies with limited polygyny were found to have a greater degree of sexual dimorphism than societies with general polygyny. Second, although Alexander et al. list four (Copper Eskimo, Vedda, Toda, Lapps) of these five societies as ecologically monogamous (the fifth, the Andamanese, are listed as socially imposed monogamy), Textor (1966) lists three of them (Copper Eskimo, Lapps, Andamanese) as having both secure and plentiful food supplies (there were no scores in Textor for the Vedda or Toda on these two points). Certainly the five societies are a heterogenous group, located in various climates and obtaining their subsistence in different ways (herding or hunting). One characteristic in common is that the mean size of the local community is less than 50 people. Thus, for these five societies, the data would seem to indicate that there is a strong intrinsic component to mean societal male and female height.

DISCUSSION

The goal of this investigation was to examine evidence bearing on the sociobiological explanations of intersocietal variation in human sexual dimorphism of stature. The nutritional hypothesis was also included in the research because it is an alternative to genetic explanations of human sexual dimorphism. To simplify our discussion we will examine each perspective by presenting a simple prediction derived from the perspective and noting how our results relate to that prediction.

SEXUAL SELECTION: As the number of polygynous marriages in a society increases so does the degree of sexual dimorphism.

Overall, the results of our research do not support this prediction. Two measures (EAMARY and NEWMARY) of the degree of polygynous marriage argue there is no relationship between the number of polygynous marriages and the degree of sexual dimorphism of stature. The ALEXMARY codes disagree on this point, and we believe this may be due more to the nature of their sample and the manner in which the societies were coded than to any actual relationship between degree of polygyny and degree of dimorphism. Regardless, analyses of variance using all three measures of marriage practices indicate that the marriage systems explain very little of the variation in human sexual dimorphism of stature. In contrast, there does seem to be a relationship between increasing degrees of polygyny and increased male and female height at all levels of protein availability. Thus, polygyny seems to select both for taller males, as predicted by sociobiology, and for taller females, which is not predicted by the sociobiological perspective.

The mechanism which unites polygyny with taller males and females does not appear to be clear at present. We will examine the situation for males first. Since there is little evidence of actual physical combat between human males for mates, an analogy of humans with certain baboon groups, seals, or ungulates does not seem in order. There are a number of other possibilities, however. Perhaps taller males have greater "presence of being" than shorter males and this gives them an advantage in seducing females or negotiating for extra wives with the male relatives of females. If people in other societies look to taller individuals for leadership, it is possible that these leaders may be able to accumulate and support more wives during their life than shorter males who are not leaders. Another possible mechanism would be demonstrated if it could be shown that shorter males have higher mortality in warfare than taller males. Such a demonstration would be of special interest with reference to the suggestion of Alexander et al. that socially imposed monogamy is a form of hidden polygyny. Finally, if taller males were perceived by females or the male relatives of females as being healthier or more capable providers than short males it might be possible that such males could accumulate more wives or impregnate more females than shorter males. It should be emphasized that none of these mechanisms have been demonstrated in human societies.

The association between female height and marriage systems is even more difficult to explain than the relationship between male height and polygyny. Given the low number of females who are never married in most societies it would seem necessary to suggest that taller women in polygynous societies produce more surviving offspring than shorter women. There is some support for the idea that taller women produce more viable offspring than shorter women (Bresler 1962; Thomson 1954) but this has not been related to marriage systems and the topic has not been studied in a large number of societies. Of course, statistical associations do not necessarily result from cause-effect relationships and it is possible that female height and male height are related to some third factor not investigated in this research (e.g., climate, diet) which is also causally related to marriage practices.

Thus, our conclusion is that the sexual selection perspective does not explain much of the intersocietal variation in human sexual dimorphism, although the relationships between marriage practices and the mean societal height for both sexes are significant and require further research.

PARENTAL INVESTMENT: The lower the degree of male parental investment, the greater the degree of sexual dimorphism of stature.

The tests of this prediction produced results that were generally negative, although the low number of societies in our sample and the inadequacy of the codes for inheritance practices prevent a conclusive test of the prediction. Of the three measures of male parental investment only the transmission of movable property was associated with significant differences in the degree of sexual dimorphism of stature; significantly, this association was in the opposite direction to that predicted by the hypothesis. As we argued above, we do not believe the transmission of movable property is an adequate measure of male parental investment, since males may be able to distribute large amounts of movable property in attempts to secure more opportunities to reproduce and thus end up leaving their heirs with only a minimal amount of property. Another reason the movable property codes are not a good measure of male parental investment is that the *Ethnographic Atlas* does not specify the exact forms of property that are transmitted and it is possible that some movable property may have no relationship to reproductive success (e.g., simple weapons, clothing, magical objects, etc.). Finally, the use of inheritance of movable property as a male parental investment measure is an invalid analogy for the concept of male parental investment in nonhuman animal breeding systems. In the nonhuman animal situation the choice of the male is whether to provide care for infants or not. In contrast, in the human inheritance system the choice for a male is not usually whether or not to "care" for offspring by giving them property, but whether to give his property to children of his wife, his sister, or someone else. Thus we would argue that the human species exhibits high male parental investment and that intersocietal variation in the targets of that investment are not equivalent to interspecies variation in male parental investment in the rest of the primate order.

The use of father-infant proximity as a measure of male parental investment is a better analogy to nonhuman animal breeding systems than that provided by the use of inheritance practice codes. However, the proximity variable shows no relationship with differences in the degree of human sexual dimorphism of stature. There is a significant association between increased proximity and lower mean societal male and female height, but this is probably the result of the correlation between the proximity variable and marriage practices (Table 8.1).

NUTRITION: The higher the level of nutrition, the greater the degree of sexual dimorphism of stature.

While our results are somewhat ambiguous and the use of protein availability is not an exact measure of the level of nutrition in a society, there is some support for the nutritional hypothesis. An interesting pattern calling for further research is that societies with medium levels of protein availability exhibit the greatest degree of sexual dimorphism of stature even though the tallest males and females are found in societies with high protein availability. Our findings do not invalidate the use of increasing degrees of sexual dimorphism as a measure of improving nutrition in a society over time. They do, however, suggest that such a perspective cannot account for the synchronic intersocietal variation in degrees of sexual dimorphism.

We are forced to conclude this chapter with the same thoughts found at the end of most papers on human sexual dimorphism. The causes of intersocietal variation of stature and sexual dimorphism of height are many and the relationships among the causes are complex. A complete model will have to include the variables of nutrition, climate, marriage practices, and assortive mating; and it is still far too early in the research to award primacy to any one of these factors. In addition to this general conclusion, we believe this chapter has accomplished two purposes. First, we have demonstrated that the sociobiological model advanced by Alexander et al. to explain human sexual dimorphism is not adequate to the task. Second, we have elaborated the difficulties in conducting cross-cultural research combining anthropometric and cultural variables. Some of these difficulties are unavoidable and others can be dealt with by careful consideration of the limitations of the data. In either case great care must be taken with this type of research.

BIBLIOGRAPHY

Alexander, R. D., J. L. Hoogland, R. D. Howard, K. M. Noonan, and P. W. Sherman. 1979. "Sexual Dimorphism and Breeding Systems in

Pinnipeds, Ungulates, Primates, and Humans." In *Evolutionary Biology and Human Social Behavior: An Anthropological Perspective*, edited by N. A. Chagnon and W. Irons, pp. 402-435. North Scituate, Mass.: Duxbury Press.

Barry, H., and L. M. Paxson. 1971. "Infancy and Early Childhood: Cross-Cultural Codes 2." *Ethnology*, 10:466-508.

Bresler, J. B. 1962. "Maternal Height and the Prevalence of Stillbirths." *American Journal of Physical Anthropology*, 20:515-517.

Casey, A. E., and E. L. Downey. 1970. *Compilation of Common Physical Measurements on Adult Males of Various Races*. Birmingham, Alabama: Amite Knocknagree Historical Fund.

Chagnon, N. A. 1979. "Mate Competition, Favoring Close Kin, and Village Fissioning among the Yanomamo Indians." In *Evolutionary Biology and Human Social Behavior: An Evolutionary Perspective*, edited by N. A. Chagnon and W. Irons, pp. 86-132. North Scituate, Mass.: Duxbury Press.

Clutton-Brock, T. H., and P. H. Harvey. 1978. "Mammals, Resources and Reproductive Strategies." *Nature*, 273:191-195.

Clutton-Brock, T. H., P. H. Harvey, and B. Rudder. 1977. "Sexual Dimorphism, Socionomic Sex Ratio and Body Weight in Primates." *Nature*, 269:797-800.

Crook, J. H. 1980. *The Evolution of Human Consciousness*. Oxford: Clarendon Press.

Eveleth, P. B. 1975. "Differences between Ethnic Groups in Sex Dimorphism of Adult Height." *Annals of Human Biology*, 2:35-39.

Eveleth, P. B., and J. M. Tanner. 1976. *World-wide Variation in Human Growth*. Cambridge: Cambridge University Press.

Field, H. 1970. *Contributions to the Physical Anthropology of the Peoples of India*. Coconut Grove, Florida: Field Research Projects.

Gaulin, S. J. C. 1980. "Sexual Dimorphism in the Human Post-reproductive Life-span: Possible Causes." *Journal of Human Evolution*, 9:227-232.

Gifford, E. W. 1926. "California Anthropometry." *University of California Publications in American Archaeology and Ethnology*, 22:217-390.

Gray, J. P., and L. D. Wolfe. 1980. "Height and Sexual Dimorphism of Stature among Human Societies." *American Journal of Physical Anthropology*, 53:441-456.

————. 1981. "Parental Certainty, Subsistence, and Inheritance Revisited." *Journal of Human Evolution*, 10:277-280.

Greulich, W. W. 1951. "The Growth and Developmental Status of Guamanian School Children in 1947." *American Journal of Physical Anthropology*, 9:55-70.

Hall, R. L. 1978. "Sexual Dimorphism for Size in Seven Nineteenth Century Northwest Coast Populations." *Human Biology*, 50:159-171.

Hamilton, M. E. 1975. "Variation among Five Groups of Amerindians in the Magnitude of Sexual Dimorphism of Skeletal Size." Ph.D. dissertation, University of Michigan.

Hartung, J. 1976. "On Natural Selection and the Inheritance of Wealth." *Current Anthropology*, 17:607-622.

Hierneaux, J. 1968. "Variabilité du Dimorphism Sexuel de la Stature en

Afrique Subsaharienne et en Europe." In *Anthropologie und Humangenetik*, pp. 42-50. Stuttgart: Gustav Fischer Verlag.

Hrdlička, A. 1909. "On the Stature of the Indians of the Southwest and of Northern Mexico." *Putnam Anniversary Volume*, pp. 405-426.

_____. 1931. "Anthropology of the Sioux." *American Journal of Physical Anthropology*, 16:123-170.

_____. 1935. "The Pueblos: With Comparative Data on the Bulk of the Tribes of the Southwest and Northern Mexico." *American Journal of Physical Anthropology*, 20:235-460.

Kleiman, D. G. 1977. "Monogamy in Mammals." *Quarterly Review of Biology*, 52:39-69.

Meredith, H. V. 1976. "Worldwide Somatic Comparisons among Contemporary Human Groups of Adult Females." *American Journal of Physical Anthropology*, 34:89-132.

Murdock, G. P. 1956. *African Cultural Summaries*. New Haven: Human Relations Area Files.

_____. 1967. *Ethnographic Atlas*. Pittsburgh: University of Pittsburgh Press.

Naroll, R., G. Michik, and F. Naroll. 1976. *Worldwide Theory Testing*. New Haven: Human Relations Area Files.

Salzano, F. M., editor. 1971. *The Ongoing Evolution of Latin American Populations*. Springfield, Ill.: Charles C Thomas.

Steggerda, M. 1950. "Anthropometry of South American Indians." *Handbook of South American Indians*, 6:57-70.

Stini, W. A. 1969. "Nutritional Stress and Growth: Sex Difference in Adaptive Response." *American Journal of Physical Anthropology*, 31:417-426.

_____. 1975. "Adaptive Strategies of Human Populations under Nutritional Stress." In *Biosocial Interrelations in Population Adaptation*, edited by E. S. Watts, F. E. Johnson, and G. W. Lasker, pp. 19-41. The Hague: Mouton.

Textor, R. 1966. *A Cross-cultural Summary*. New Haven: Human Relations Area Files.

Thomson, A. M. 1954. "Maternal Stature and Reproductive Efficiency." *Eugenics Review*, 51:157-162.

Tobias, P. V. 1962. "On the Increasing Stature of the Bushmen." *Anthropos*, 57:801-810.

_____. 1975. "Anthropometry among Disadvantaged Peoples: Studies in Southern Africa." In *Biosocial Interrelationships in Population Adaptation*, edited by E. S. Watts, F. E. Johnson, and G. W. Lasker, pp. 287-305. The Hague: Mouton.

Trivers, R. L. 1972. "Parental Investment and Sexual Selection." In *Sexual Selection and the Descent of Man, 1871-1971*, edited by B. H. Campbell, pp. 136-179. Chicago: Aldine.

Werren, J. H., M. R. Gross, and R. Shine. 1980. "Paternity and the Evolution of Male Parental Care." *Journal of Theoretical Biology* 82:619-631.

Whiting, J. 1964. "Effects of Climate on Certain Cultural Practices." In *Explorations in Cultural Anthropology*, edited by W. H. Goodenough, pp. 511-544. New York: McGraw-Hill.

Nine

Sexual Dimorphism for Size in Seven Nineteenth-Century Northwest Coast Populations*

Roberta L. Hall

An animal's size is an important morphological component upon which natural selection operates. As Gould (1974) illustrated, a strong argument can be made that *Homo sapiens* has evolved to the only appropriate size that would permit it to maintain the functions and behavior of its niche. Within the species, local populations vary slightly in norms for size. Infants with birthweights deviating from the norm are subject to a higher risk of mortality (Cavilli-Sforza and Bodmer 1971) and adults who are anthropometrically average appear to enjoy superior longevity as well as relatively high fitness (Damon 1971). Anthropologists have discussed body size and shape as adaptations to various environments (Newman 1953; Roberts 1973). On the assumption that the two sexes respond similarly to selective and environmental pressures, many studies of size variation are based only on one sex, usually the male, probably because more anthropometric data are available for males than for females. More recently, interest has focused on the degree of sexual dimorphism for size, as human biologists have become aware that populations not only vary in average size but in the average degree of male-female size differences (Eveleth 1975; Tobias 1975; Stini 1975; Hamilton 1975). Size sexual dimorphism in mammals has been viewed as a part of the species' total adaptive system, with energetics and behavioral as

*Reprinted from *Human Biology*, May 1978, Vol. 50(2):159-171, by permission of the Wayne State University Press. The author also wishes to acknowledge the help of Kathy White, Gerry Brush, and the Oregon State University Computer Center.

well as purely physical or mechanical components (DeVore and Washburn 1963; Coelho 1974). Brace (1973) postulated a relatively greater sexual dimorphism for size in australopithecines, based on the expectation of greater role differentiation in early hominids as opposed to modern humans. Also working with prehistoric populations, Hamilton (1975) investigated the hypothesis that in anatomically modern, prehistoric populations the degree of sexual dimorphism depends, in part, on the food economy, and, hence, the nutritional base. In her study of three Eastern and two Mexican prehistoric samples, the two populations most committed to agricultural subsistence also showed the least dimorphism. Stabilizing selection, involving many factors and affecting one or both sexes, may be responsible for existing patterns of sexual dimorphism. The average size of each sex is affected in part by selection, probably at the genetic level, but phenotypic fluctuations, which affect each sex independently, complicate analysis and interpretation.

The most crucial question concerning size sexual dimorphism in contemporary *Homo sapiens* is whether relatively low sexual dimorphism indicates a depression in food resources, possibly including a general condition of malnourishment, or whether the degree of dimorphism is a genetically based characteristic that is essentially nonadaptive. Basing his argument chiefly on data from African populations, Tobias (1975) showed that recent secular trends have produced an increase in sexual dimorphism. Further, he suggested that relatively low sexual dimorphism is itself an index of nutritionally deprived conditions. Central to this model is the concept that males are more sensitive to nutritional changes than are females. In a Colombian study, Stini (1972b) found no patterned differences. Greulich (1976) found that Japanese girls participated in the secular trend to increased stature more than Japanese boys, over the period from 1900 to 1970, and suggested that this is due to the "superior biological efficiency of the human female as compared with the male" (Greulich 1976, p. 568). Bielicki and Charzewski (1977) found that Polish boys exceeded the stature of their fathers to a larger extent than girls surpassed their mothers and suggested that males are more sensitive to environmental fluctuations.

Using data on mean stature in adult men and women from 264 populations, Eveleth (1975) stratified the samples by traditional continental racial categories. For each of the five groups she computed regressions of the difference between average male and female stature on the mid-point between the male and female means. Because the five slopes were not identical, Eveleth concluded that genetic factors explained variation in sexual dimorphism better than nutritional or other environmental factors. The regression slopes, however, did not explain much of the variance in the regressions; r^2 ranged from 0.0441 in her European group of 76 populations to 0.2209 in her New Guinean set of 27 samples.

One of the problems with using stature as a measure of sexual dimorphism is that stature is known to be affected by environmental changes (Wolański and Kasprzak 1976). In populations that are experiencing increase in average stature, age group norms may differ greatly (Hall 1972). Secular changes are compounded by age-related decreases in stature due to compression of the vertebral discs (Miall et al. 1967) and special statistical measures must be taken to separate the two effects (Himes and Mueller 1977). Stature has been used as a measure of general size because it is an obvious size attribute and because more data are available on stature than on other anthropometric measures, not because it is the most representative or most interpretable measure.

The study of sexual dimorphism, then, includes a study of growth and of the factors that modify growth patterns. An appropriate study of sexual dimorphism must include a study of many measures of size and an analysis of cultural, nutritional, and populational background data on the subjects sampled. The effect of various environmental factors on size norms must be analyzed for each sex, since it is apparent that selectional pressures as well as environmental factors do not affect growth patterns and size norms in the two sexes identically.

MATERIALS AND METHODS

Anthropometric data collected by Franz Boas (Boas 1891, 1895, 1898) in the late nineteenth century from Northwest and Northwest Coast Amerindians were analyzed in respect to sexual dimorphism. Along with data on 12 anthropometric traits, published data included not only the subjects' anthropometric values but also their age, village of birth of both parents, and presence or absence of artificial cranial deformation. In a study examining the statistical validity of Boas' classification of Northwest Amerindians, Hall and McNair (1972) analyzed the published data, eliminating individuals with artificially produced cranial morphologies and individuals for whom data were incomplete. Testing the local populations and the Boas categories by the Mahalanobis D^2 statistic, they found that the local populations had morphological integrity as classificatory units. In a further analysis of Boas' large sample from interior British Columbia, a pronounced secular trend for increased size was noted (Hall 1972). Occurring in both sexes, it was most pronounced in males and affected some, but not all, measures of the head and some transverse measures of size as well as several measures of linear height.

In addition to stature, 10 of the other traits recorded by Boas were analyzed for sexual dimorphism in local populations. As noted by Hall and McNair (1972), the trait arm length was not analyzed because preliminary analysis indicated unreliability. A twelfth trait, subischial height, was created as the difference between stature and sitting height; the importance of subischial height is that it is a statural measure that excludes the vertebral column, which is subject to age-related decrement (Himes and Mueller 1977). Of the 20 local population samples identified in the Boas British Columbia data, only seven samples met the criterion of a sample number of 10 or more for both sexes (Table 9.1). Descriptive statistics for the 12 traits were prepared and analyzed to assure normality of the data. In all cases, kurtosis and skewness did not vary greatly from values expected from statistically normal data. Coefficients of variation values also were produced.

Differences between male and female mean values were calculated for the 12 traits in the seven samples. The value obtained was then regressed on three other values: male average, female average, and the mid-point between the two averages. Eveleth (1975) used the same technique but regressed differences only on the mid-point between male and female averages, since her purpose was to determine whether five major groups of populations differed in degree of dimorphism. In this study the purpose of computing regression slopes was to determine whether variation in male or female average size contributed more to variation in the degree of sexual dimorphism.

Associated with the regressions, the correlation coefficient (r) and the correlation coefficient squared (r^2) were produced. No attempt was

TABLE 9.1

Sample Sizes and Average Ages for Local Populations Analyzed for Sexual Dimorphism.

	Males		Females	
Local Population	N	Average Age	N	Average Age
Lower Fraser-Harrison Lake	13	42	12	29
Nass Tsimshian	20	39	19	33
Lower Thompson	22	40	13	33
Upper Thompson	38	46	34	41
Shuswap Fraser	42	44	30	38
Lillooet	34	41	42	37
Chilcotin	33	34	18	41

made to generalize beyond the seven British Columbia samples themselves; since probability statements about the statistical significance of the correlation coefficients give estimates of whether generalizations to a larger universe of data are reasonable, probability statements are of little use here. The significance of the regressions is obtained by assessing the r^2 values. Since the correlation coefficient squared (r^2) is interpretable as a measure of the percentage of variation in the dependent variable that is explained by variation in the independent variable, only an r^2 score considerably greater than zero indicates a biologically meaningful regression. An attempt is being made to determine "biological significance" of the results, in the sense in which it is discussed by Simpson, Roe, and Lewontin (1960, p. 173), and not merely statistical significance. Questions asked of the regression data were: Does variation in either the male or female average explain a nontrivial amount of the variation in the average degree of sexual dimorphism? Which sex contributes most? What conclusions about differences in the way the two sexes respond to environmental variation can be drawn from these results?

RESULTS AND DISCUSSION

Tables 9.2 and 9.3 show that during the course of the nineteenth century, average size of both males and females in the native population of interior British Columbia changed notably, but in general greater effects occurred in males than in females. The tables also indicate that problems are involved in separating secular changes from age-related effects of size in samples that include adults of all ages. All measures that include the vertebral column may be expected to show an age-related effect due to disc-compression, whether or not secular changes from environmental effects are present. Since the vertebral column is its major component, the measurement sitting height expressed longitudinal age-effects particularly intensely. Predictably it is sitting height that, in both sexes, showed the highest value of r^2 (Table 9.2).

Nasal height and maximum nasal breadth showed high r^2 values in females. In these two traits the age-related relationship was reversed, and the oldest people had the highest values. Presumably age-related effects rather than secular, morphological changes are responsible for this relationship; Israel (1977) showed in longitudinal studies that systematic craniofacial expansion occurs throughout adulthood, in both sexes. It is possible that the lower relationship for the nasal measurements in the male sample resulted because effects

TABLE 9.2

Correlation Coefficient (*r*) and Percentage of Variance Explained (*r²*) for Relationship of Age and Eleven Anthropometric Traits, by Sex, for B.C. Interior Samples.

Trait	Male Sample: $N = 213$		Female Sample: $N = 182$	
	r	*r²*	*r*	*r²*
Stature	−0.5274*	0.278	−0.3741*	0.139
Shoulder height	−0.4623*	0.214	−0.3522*	0.124
Span	−0.4987*	0.249	−0.3472*	0.121
Sitting height	−0.6341*	0.402	−0.4883*	0.238
Subischial	−0.2634*	0.069	−0.0920	0.008
Shoulder width	−0.5018*	0.252	−0.3684*	0.136
Head length	−0.0913	0.008	−0.0941	0.009
Head breadth	−0.2762*	0.076	−0.1072	0.011
Facial height	−0.2813*	0.079	+0.0644	0.004
Facial breadth	−0.0059	0.000	+0.0385	0.001
Nasal height	+0.1950**	0.038	+0.4625*	0.214
Nasal breadth	+0.1765	0.031	+0.3940*	0.155

*Statistically significant at the 0.01 level.
**Statistically significant at the 0.05 level.

of the secular trend and aging both occurred but affected different age groups. Older males showed the age-related effect of enlargement of the nasal region, and the younger males expressed a secular change toward increased body size, including the face to some degree. Secular effects in females were weaker; hence, the aging effect appeared more pronounced.

Though linear regression is a powerful tool that can be used effectively to screen for systematic changes, it has to be used cautiously since it can mask curvilinear or other nonlinear patterns. It is clear from Table 9.2 that in the female sample age and stature do not fit a linear model very well, since this model explains only 13.9 percent of the variance. The pattern of female age and stature relationships is clarified in Table 9.3 in which mean stature of age-group subsamples is shown. Females and males were classed in seven decade-groups (ages 18-19, 20-29, 30-39, through 70-79). Examination of this table indicates that though in both sexes the oldest individuals on the average were also the shortest, the similarity in age-height patterns between the sexes ends there. Male means increase slowly by age, whereas in the females all those above 50 belong in one average height category; those between 40 and 59 do not differ significantly among themselves according to age; and the 18 to 39 age category of females also appears undifferentiated. The female secular trend is not linear.

TABLE 9.3

Average Stature in Seven Age Groups, by Sex, in an Interior British Columbian Sample.

Age		Male			Female	
	N	Mean Height	Standard Deviation	N	Mean Height	Standard Deviation
18-19	2	171.7	7.6	19	155.4	6.5
20-29	38	168.2	5.9	37	154.0	4.5
30-39	32	164.2	5.3	28	155.2	3.9
40-49	31	163.0	5.2	21	153.9	5.2
50-59	33	161.6	6.4	25	153.1	4.9
60-69	25	159.3	4.9	19	147.8	6.3
70-79	7	155.1	5.9	4	144.2	7.3

A scrutiny of coefficients of variation yielded no obvious patterns though a few generalizations may be made (Table 9.4). Male samples tended to have coefficients of variation slightly higher than those of female samples from the same populations in most linear traits related to body size (stature, shoulder height, span, sitting height, subischial height, head length), and the female samples tended to have larger coefficients of variation in the other traits (head breadth, facial height, facial breadth, nasal height, and nasal breadth). In no trait, however, did all seven of the paired samples show the same sex with higher values, and the minimal differences may be trivial. The data are recorded here so that they may be compared with other studies.

Table 9.5 lists the correlation coefficients for male and female means from the 7 samples, along with r and r^2 values obtained in correlations of the differences between male and female averages and the three values: male average, female average, and their mid-point. In all traits except three—nasal height, sitting height, and subischial height—higher r and r^2 values were obtained from the correlation between male averages and intersex differences than between female averages and intersex differences. If these correlations had been equal, the difference correlated with the mid-point would also be equivalent; since they differ, the mid-point-difference correlations fell between the correlations with male and female averages and showed no interesting patterns. They are recorded for comparison with other studies (Eveleth 1975).

In the case of nasal height, variation in the female average values explained 0.66 of the variation in the difference between means for the sexes; hence, it is potentially important. As noted previously, nasal height in females varied with age and increased as part of the

TABLE 9.4
Coefficient of Variation for Twelve Traits for Seven Local Populations, by Sex.

Traits	Lower Fraser-Harrison Lake M	F	Nass Tsimishian M	F	Lower Thompson M	F	Upper Thompson M	F	Shushwap Fraser M	F	Lillooet M	F	Chilcotin M	F
Stature	6.1	4.7	2.5	1.9	4.3	3.2	4.3	4.1	3.1	3.3	4.1	3.9	3.8	2.0
Shoulder	5.9	4.8	3.1	2.3	4.1	3.9	4.7	4.4	3.7	3.4	4.3	4.8	4.0	2.6
Span	5.6	4.8	3.6	2.8	4.9	3.9	4.4	5.1	3.6	3.7	4.4	4.1	4.5	2.8
Sitting height	6.9	5.3	4.1	2.2	5.3	4.0	4.2	4.9	4.2	3.4	4.5	5.0	3.8	3.5
Subischial height	5.6	5.9	5.3	4.4	4.7	4.7	5.6	5.1	4.5	5.2	6.0	4.9	5.9	3.3
Shoulder width	8.8	5.4	3.8	4.2	6.7	3.9	5.6	5.8	5.6	5.2	4.8	—	5.2	4.8
Head length	2.8	2.8	3.3	2.5	3.1	2.9	3.1	3.3	2.5	3.2	3.4	3.3	2.4	5.0
Head breadth	3.2	3.6	2.6	2.5	3.4	2.6	3.1	2.5	3.0	2.9	4.0	3.0	2.5	3.3
Facial height	5.6	5.5	4.3	4.0	6.5	4.2	4.7	4.9	4.6	4.7	4.7	6.2	5.0	5.1
Facial breadth	4.1	2.8	4.5	2.2	2.8	3.1	2.6	3.1	2.6	3.3	3.1	4.5	2.7	3.1
Nasal height	6.5	10.9	4.8	7.8	7.9	5.7	6.3	8.0	6.0	7.9	5.8	8.5	5.2	10.9
Nasal breadth	9.9	6.1	8.8	6.4	5.5	7.4	6.8	9.5	5.8	6.7	6.5	7.8	5.6	7.3

TABLE 9.5

Correlation (*r*) of Male and Female Sample Means, Correlation (*r*) and r^2
Values Obtained in a Regression of the Difference Between Male and
Female Sample Means on Male Means, Female Means, and the Mid-
point Between Male and Female Means, for Twelve Traits, in Seven
Local Populations.

Trait	Male-Female Correlation (*r*)	Difference Correlated with Male Mean		Difference Correlated with Female Mean		Difference Correlated with Mid-point	
		r	r^2	*r*	r^2	*r*	r^2
Stature	0.90*	0.77*	0.59	0.42	0.18	0.64	0.41
Shoulder height	0.88*	0.70	0.50	0.29	0.08	0.54	0.30
Span	0.77*	0.76*	0.57	0.17	0.03	0.55	0.30
Sitting height	0.70	0.33	0.11	−0.44	0.19	−0.07	0.01
Subischial height	0.92*	0.18	0.03	−0.22	0.05	−0.02	0.00
Shoulder width	0.66	0.84*	0.71	0.15	0.02	0.65	0.42
Head length	0.97*	0.63	0.39	0.42	0.17	0.53	0.29
Head breadth	0.81*	0.60	0.37	0.02	0.00	0.36	0.13
Facial height	0.84*	0.65	0.43	0.13	0.02	0.44	0.20
Facial breadth	0.87*	0.60	0.36	0.14	0.02	0.41	0.17
Nasal height	0.72	−0.18	0.03	−0.81*	0.66	−0.62	0.37
Nasal breadth	0.36	0.78*	0.60	−0.31	0.10	0.41	0.17

*Statistically significant at the 0.05 level, with 5 *d.f.*

craniofacial expansion in aging; dimorphism was greatest in those
samples in which women had, on the average, the shortest noses. A
similar pattern held for sitting height, which also was strongly age-
related. Neither of these traits was particularly useful for interpreting
sexual dimorphism in this study; large age-stratified samples would
be required in order to investigate their patterns of variation further.
The third case is quite different. The r^2 values for correlation of sex
differences with all three values for subischial height were neither
biologically nor statistically significant: 0.03, 0.05, and 0.004. The
sample averages for subischial height were not related in any
systematic way to sexual dimorphism in these samples. This is a

surprising result, since other linear measures of size appeared to show such relationships.

For the remaining nine traits, the table indicates that variation in the male average value explained a significant degree of variation in sexual dimorphism, with r^2 values from 0.36 for facial breadth through 0.71 for shoulder width. Correlations of the average sexual dimorphism values with the female averages, by contrast, varied from 0.00 for head breadth to 0.18 for stature. This array of traits includes variables that appeared not to have participated in the secular trend—such as head length and facial breadth—as well as those such as span and shoulder width that had significant secular trends and may therefore be considered environmentaly malleable (see Table 9.2). Within the samples and the traits analyzed here, variation in sexual dimorphism appeared to be controlled to a much larger extent by variation in average male size than by variation in female size.

CONCLUSIONS

As is true of any other investigation that tries to explain variation in growth patterns, this investigation of sexual dimorphism produced no simple conclusions. However, the analysis has demonstrated that sexual dimorphism is not constant, probably because the two sexes respond differently to environmental changes. Furthermore, and perhaps more importantly, separate parts of the body respond differently. Whereas sexual dimorphism existed in all of the measures studied—that is, male averages tended to be higher than female averages—these differences varied according to a number of variables which as yet are not interpretable.

The purpose of this inquiry was to indicate some of the controls that will need to be exercised in a more extensive study of sexual dimorphism for size. It is undoubtedly correct, as Wolański and Kasprzak (1976) and Tobias (1975) have shown, that stature is environmentally sensitive but it is also clear that it is not the only measure nor perhaps the best measure of size sexual dimorphism (Stini 1975). Measures of muscle size and of body fat also should be included along with standard anthropometrics such as were recorded by Boas and analyzed in this study. Further research is required before any group of anthropometric measures can be rejected as of no use in measuring variation in sexual dimorphism and before any definitive list of the most useful measures can be produced.

With the qualifications stated, the results of this study still indicate that for the samples surveyed variation in males contributed more to the degree of sexual dimorphism than did variation in females. The results support the contentions of Tobias (1975), Stini (1975), and Hamilton (1975). It has been hypothesized that, in respect to size, males tend to be somewhat less canalized in their development than females (Bielicki and Charzewski 1977). Hamilton (1975) provided an excellent summary of the natural selective factors that may be responsible for this effect. Central to her model is the concept that successful reproduction makes more exacting physiological demands on female size than is the case for males for whom size— except for its relationship to survival and to sexual selection—can be considered irrelevant to the reproductive process.

In a summary table appended to his module on climate and human variability, Roberts (1973) presented data on correlations between temperature and several physiological anthropometric traits. Though most samples were male, several female samples were included, and for the female samples significantly stronger relationships were found between anthropometric traits and temperature. In a thorough study of size sexual dimorphism in *Homo sapiens* it is essential to include climatic variables and to determine to what extent climatic adaptation, whether genetic or developmental, differs between the sexes and to what extent it affects sexual dimorphism. Though genetic factors may be responsible, in part, for the degree of sexual dimorphism (Eveleth 1975), many environmental factors including climate as well as nutrition (Roberts 1973; Tobias 1975), and also including the culture's economic base (Hamilton 1975), should be investigated.

BIBLIOGRAPHY

Bielicki, T., and J. Charzewski. 1977. "Sex Differences in the Magnitude of Statural Gains of Offspring over Parents." *Human Biology*, 49:265-277.

Boas, F. 1891. "Physical Characteristics of the Tribes of the North Pacific Coast." In *Report of the 61st Meeting of the British Association for the Advancement of Science*, pp. 424-449.

———. 1895. "Physical Characteristics of the Tribes of the North Pacific Coast." In *Report of the 65th Meeting of the British Association for the Advancement of Science*, pp. 524-551.

———. 1898. "Summary of the Work of the Committee in British Columbia." In *Report of the 68th Meeting of the British Association for the Advancement of Science*, pp. 667-688.

Brace, C. L. 1973. "Sexual Dimorphism in Human Evolution." *Yearbook of Physical Anthropology 1972*, 16:31-49.

Cavilli-Sforza, L. L., and W. F. Bodmer. 1971. *The Genetics of Human Populations*. San Francisco: W. H. Freeman.

Coelho, A. M. 1974. "Socio-bioenergetics and Sexual Dimorphism in Primates." *Primates*, 15:263-269.

Damon, A. [with the collaboration of F. L. Stagg and E. A. Hooton]. 1971. "Physique, Longevity and Number of Offspring: Possible Stabilizing Selection in Man." *American Journal of Physical Anthropology*, 35:276.

DeVore, I., and S. Washburn. 1963. "Baboon Ecology and Human Evolution." In *Human Evolution*, edited by N. Korn and F. Thompson, pp. 136-160. New York: Holt, Rinehart and Winston.

Eveleth, P. B. 1975. "Differences Between Ethnic Groups in Sex Dimorphism of Adult Height." *Annals of Human Biology*, 2:35-39.

Gould, S. J. 1974. "Sizing Up Human Intelligence." *Natural History*, 83(2):10-14.

Greulich, W. W. 1976. "Some Secular Changes in the Growth of American-born and Native Japanese Children." *American Journal of Physical Anthropology*, 45:553-568.

Hall, R. L. 1972. "Secular Changes in Anthropometric Measurements of Indigenous Populations of British Columbia" (abstract). *American Journal of Physical Anthropology*, 37:439.

Hall, R. L., and P. McNair. 1972. "Multivariate Analysis of Anthropometric Data and Classification of British Columbian Natives." *American Journal of Physical Anthropology*, 37:401-410.

Hamilton, M. E. 1975. *Variations Among Five Groups of Amerindians in the Magnitude of Sexual Dimorphism of Skeletal Size*. Unpublished Ph.D. dissertation, University of Michigan.

Himes, J. H., and W. J. Mueller. 1977. "Aging and Secular Change in Adult Stature in Rural Colombia." *American Journal of Physical Anthropology*, 46:275-280.

Israel, H. 1977. "The Dichotomous Pattern of Craniofacial Expansion During Aging." *American Journal of Physical Anthropology*, 47:47-52.

Miall, W. E., M. T. Ashcroft, H. G. Lovell, and F. Moore. 1967. "A Longitudinal Study of the Decline of Adult Height with Age in Two Welsh Communities." *Human Biology*, 39:445-454.

Newman, M. T. 1953. "The Application of Ecological Rules to the Racial Anthropology of the Aboriginal New World." *American Anthropologist*, 55:311-327.

Roberts, D. F. 1973. "Climate and Human Variability." Addison-Wesley Module in Anthropology, No. 34:1-38.

Simpson, G. G., A. Roe, and R. C. Lewontin. 1960. *Quantitative Zoology*. New York: Harcourt, Brace and World.

Stini, W. A. 1969. "Nutritional Stress and Growth: Sex Difference in Adaptive Response." *American Journal of Physical Anthropology*, 31:417-426.

_____ . 1972a. "Reduced Sexual Dimorphism in Upper Arm Muscle Circumference Associated with Protein-Deficient Diet in a South American Population." *American Journal of Physical Anthropology*, 36:341-352.

————. 1972b. "Malnutrition, Body Size and Proportion." *Ecology of Food and Nutrition*, 1:121-126.

————. 1975. "Adaptive Strategies of Human Populations Under Nutritional Stress." In *Biosocial Interrelations in Population Adaptation*, edited by E. S. Watts, F. E. Johnston, and G. W. Lasker, pp. 19-41. The Hague: Mouton.

Tobias, P. V. 1975. "Anthropometry Among Disadvantaged Peoples: Studies in Southern Africa." In *Biosocial Interrelations in Populational Adaptation*, edited by E. S. Watts, F. E. Johnston, and G. W. Lasker, pp. 287-305. The Hague: Mouton.

Wolański, N., and E. Kasprzak. 1976. "Stature as a Measure of Effects of Environmental Change." *Current Anthropology*, 17:548-552.

Ten

Size Sexual Dimorphism
and Secular Trend:
Indicators of Subclinical Malnutrition?*

Gerhard W. Brauer

Recognizing that the impact of environmental improvement on a population may be reflected in secular trends toward both increased stature and increased sexual dimorphism of stature, Tobias (1972) observes that

> Such effects may be an even subtler measure of environmental amelioration than the usual tests for the presence or absence of overt clinical signs of poor nutrition . . . [and] they have shed light on virtually subclinical modifications in the physical well-being of people. [P. 102]

Sexual dimorphism of both stature and muscle size has been demonstrated to be influenced under conditions of such long-term and/or severe malnutrition as chronic protein-calorie malnutrition (e.g., Stini 1969, 1972; Himes et al. 1976), acute food shortages due to war (e.g., Markowitz 1955), the stress and starvation resulting from the atomic bombing of Hiroshima and Nagasaki (e.g., Greulich, Crismon, and Turner 1953), and chronic socioeconomic deprivation (e.g., Acheson and Hewitt 1954). However, the usefulness of size

*The support of Dr. Ian Prior, Director of the Wellington Hospital Epidemiology Unit, the Wellington Hospital Board, the Tokelau Project Committee of the Medical Research Council of New Zealand, the Cardiovascular Unit of the World Health Organization, and the Tokelau communities in New Zealand and in Tokelau are acknowledged with gratitude.

sexual dimorphism as an indicator of *short-term* nutritional insufficiency has not yet been demonstrated.

The following is intended to demonstrate that the approach suggested by Tobias *can* be usefully applied to populations which are not severely (either chronically or acutely) malnourished. The findings presented here suggest that, if the relationship between sexual dimorphism and secular trend is carefully and explicitly recognized, their *combined* assessment may indeed provide a subtle measure of "subclinical modifications" in the growth patterns of a population.

SEXUAL DIMORPHISM, SECULAR TREND, AND NUTRITIONAL STATUS

The basic rationale linking variation in sexual dimorphism to nutritional status in a population relies on the hypothesis that, due to their size-sensitive childbearing role, females have, via evolutionary mechanisms, become buffered against environmental change in terms of their growth and development. Under conditions of both nutritional improvement *and* nutritional deterioration, it has been observed that females tend to respond less and more slowly than males in terms of their growth response. Given that females are, in terms of most anthropometric measures of size, smaller than males, it is predicted that sexual dimorphism will tend to increase in situations of improving nutrition and decrease in situations of nutritional shortfall. This indeed is the general expectation and theoretical position expressed in most papers on the topic.

It turns out, however, that this idea frequently is presented in a somewhat simplistic and static manner, i.e., the dynamic aspects of sexual dimorphism and secular trend are frequently underplayed. The observation that females respond *not only less but also more slowly* could result in seemingly paradoxical findings if measurements should happen to be taken during the period when the responses in growth have not yet stabilized. For instance, if improving nutritional conditions promote an increase in long-bone growth and males respond not only more but also more rapidly than do females, it is possible that the male secular trend may cease some years earlier than the female. Measurements at two periods in time *following* the stabilization of male stature might thus reveal a *decreasing* sexual dimorphism for size in the face of an improving nutritional environment. The fact that, after female size has stabilized as well, the degree of sexual dimorphism might be greater than that prior to the nutritional improvement may not be ascertained. Such findings have indeed been reported by Greulich (1957, 1976) and Froelich (1970), but they have not been interpreted as suggested above. More will be said about this, as the present chapter reports a similar finding from the South Pacific. The point that needs to be made here is that change in sexual dimorphism is too often discussed without at the same time considering the nature and timing of the secular trends that define such change.

The purpose of this report is to demonstrate how basic anthropometric data (even those collected at one point in time) can be used to describe secular trends and sexual dimorphism for size as indicators of subclinical malnutrition. Correction for the effect of age is discussed, as is the desirability of not restricting the study of size sexual dimorphism to measures of stature. The need for considering both secular trend and sexual dimorphism at the same time is the key point which this chapter seeks to make. The data presented here are from an anthropometric study in a Polynesian population which underwent a brief period of acute food shortages from 1966 to 1968.

THE TOKELAU ISLAND MIGRANT STUDY

The New Zealand dependency of Tokelau, situated about 300 miles north of Western Samoa, consists of three tiny coral atolls, Atafu, Fakaofo, and Nukunonu, separated by just enough Pacific Ocean to put them out of sight and ready contact with one another. The demographic history of Tokelau and the Polynesian people who call these islands home has been described (Hooper and Huntsman 1973).

In 1966, a hurricane severely damaged the islands' coconut and breadfruit food resource base. Following the subsequent establishment of a New Zealand government resettlement scheme, a large-scale, longitudinal epidemiological and anthropological study was developed in order that the effects of migration (to New Zealand) on physical health and social change might be assessed and monitored. The Tokelau Island Migrant Study (TIMS) has also been described elsewhere in detail (e.g., Prior et al. 1977). In 1976 the TIMS protocol was broadened to include the collection of an extensive series of serological, haematological, and physical measures from a sample of Tokelauan children and adults. This was to permit investigations into genetic aspects of (primarily) cardiovascular risk factors. The material presented here is part of the anthropometric data collected for the genetics section of TIMS by Dr. Maria Ramirez and the author (who received his training in anthropometry from Dr. Ramirez) in 1976 and 1977.

The population sample selected for this investigation of sexual dimorphism consists of the 845 Tokelauan adults (pregnant females were excluded) for whom anthropometric data were available and who were born in the four decades following January 1, 1921. Four 10-year birth cohorts are the basis for analysis, with ages ranging from 16 to 56. Due to very small numbers in the next older birth cohort and the need to exclude children, these age cutoffs were considered appropriate. The demographic characteristics of the sample studied are given in Table 10.1.

Island of residence (or affiliation) was included as the third independent variable (besides birth cohort and sex) because of the variation among the atolls in terms of the severity of the hurricane's impact on food resources. This variation will be described and discussed following an examination of the overall sexual dimorphism and secular trends for selected measurements.

The measurements selected for study in this investigation of secular trend and size sexual dimorphism are those which are directly related to overall body height: (a) standing height, (b) sitting height, (c) height of the anterior-superior iliac spine (iliac spine height), (d) height of *tibiale*, and (e) height of the medial malleolus. In addition, the length of the femur and that of the tibia were estimated as follows:

$$\text{Femur Length} \ = \ \frac{(a - b - d) + (c - d)}{2};$$

$$\text{Tibia Length} \quad = \ d - e.$$

The latter estimation is straightforward and requires no explanation. The estimate of femur length takes advantage of the fact that the two components of the numerator of the estimate (i.e., stature minus sitting height minus height of *tibiale* [a − b − d], and iliac spine

TABLE 10.1
Age, Sex, and Home Island Characteristics of Study Populations.

| | Home Island | | | | | | | |
| | Atafu | | Fakaofo | | Nukunonu | | Total | |
Birth Cohort	Male	Female	Male	Female	Male	Female	Male	Female
(1) 1921-1930	16	15	22	21	17	14	55	50
(2) 1931-1940	32	32	36	41	25	17	93	90
(3) 1941-1950	31	36	50	67	29	29	110	132
(4) 1951-1960	56	51	66	55	42	45	164	151
All cohorts	135	134	174	184	113	105	422	423

height minus height of *tibiale* [c — d]) respectively underestimate and overestimate femur length by roughly the same amount.*
    One index, the skelic index, was calculated according to Krogman and Snodgrasse (1947) as

Skelic Index = 100 (a — b)/b

This index, a measure of "leggedness," gives the subischial height (mainly leg length) as a percentage of sitting height. Measurements were taken in accordance with the recommendations by Krogman and Snodgrasse (1947) and Tanner, Hiernaux, and Jarman (1969).

STATURE AS THE SOLE BASIS FOR DESCRIBING SEXUAL DIMORPHISM

Considering primarily the figures for the total population, it is evident that the six variables do not present a consistent picture. In terms of standing height (Figure 10.1A) males seem to show a secular trend to a decrease in size, while females seem to be stable in height. When, however, one looks at variables which represent purely long-bone growth, such as femur and tibia length (Figure 10.1E, F), it becomes apparent that something quite different is taking place. Long-bone growth in males seems to be more or less stable over the four 10-year birth cohorts, while a secular trend to increased length of these bones seems to be the case for females. The apparent decrease in male standing height is thus largely due to the decrease in sitting height (Figure 10.1 B). As the latter variable has a less clear relationship to nutritional status, influenced as it is by posture, than is the case for the long bones of the leg, the use of standing height as the basis for describing sexual dimorphism has obvious problems.
    The skelic index (Fig. 10.1C) seems to suggest a general increase for *both* males and females, especially if the dip by the males of cohort 3 is ignored. As a measure of "leggedness," the skelic index reflects more directly the overall (and relative) long-bone growth in a population. That this should, therefore, increase in a population that is undergoing a general nutritional improvement due to modernization is not surprising.
    As Hall (1978) pointed out, the use of standing height alone, as is frequently done in studies of secular trend and sexual dimorphism, is

*As an incidental methodological recommendation, it is herewith proposed that the mean of these "subestimates" constitutes a useful indirect estimate of femur length.

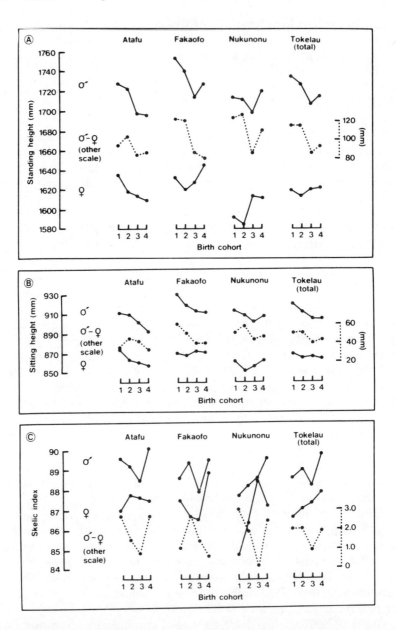

Figure 10.1 (A, B, and C). Mean values of standing height (A), sitting height (B), and skelic index (C) by sex and birth cohort, *within island*. Sexual dimorphism (in mm), shown as dotted lines, is given and related to its own (dotted line) scale.

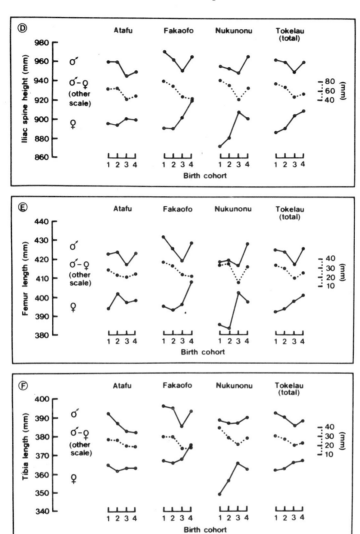

Figure 10.1 (D, E, and F). Mean values of iliac spine height (D), femur length (E), and tibia length (F) by sex and birth cohort, *within island*. Sexual dimorphism (in mm), shown as dotted lines, is given and related to its own (dotted line) scale.

not advisable, as any interpretations that involve nutritional or other (growth-affecting) environmental stress are likely to be misleading. Measurements should, therefore, be taken that will allow the estimation of the length of the leg long-bones, as well as the calculation of the skelic index.

CORRECTION FOR THE EFFECT OF AGE

Due to the cross-sectional nature of the data, standing height, sitting height, and skelic index were corrected for an estimated age effect by modifying an approach used by Himes and Mueller (1977). Adults aged between 25 and 35 were assumed to have attained maximum standing height. The linear regression coefficients predicting standing height from subischial height in this group were used to estimate the maximum attained standing height of older subjects in whom age had resulted in some degree of permanent height loss due to postural change and compression of the intervertebral discs. Obviously, this estimated maximum, while it will be less systematically biased (by age), will also be considerably less accurate than the *measured* (but biased) variable. Consequently, a mean annual effect due to aging was estimated (for males and females separately) by regressing on age the difference between the predicted and measured standing heights, for subjects aged 30 and over. A correction factor for both sexes of 0.9 mm/year was achieved by rounding off to one decimal place the values of the slopes of the regression lines. Both standing and sitting heights were then indirectly adjusted upwards by this amount for each year of the subject's age over 30. The skelic index was computed using the corrected variables.

Himes and Mueller point out (1977, p. 278) that "bowed legs or flat feet with aging are the other factors not detectable by using subischial length as a reference." While bowing of the legs could not be measured, that component of the age-related decrement which is due to foot posture was removed by subtracting the height of the medial malleolus from the subischial height before the latter was used both in the initial regressions of standing height on subischial height (in subjects aged 25 to 35) and in the subsequent equations estimating maximum attained height for older subjects.

SEXUAL DIMORPHISM AND SECULAR TREND IN TOKELAUANS

The patterns showing how the mean values of the six variables vary by birth cohort, and *within island*, are shown in Figure 10.1. The same values are regrouped in Figure 10.2 to show how these means vary by island, *within each of the four cohorts*. The consistency of the decrease in the size of all variables except sitting height shown by cohort 3 males is striking. The apparent secular trend to an increase in size of the long-bones in females, in the absence of a similar trend in

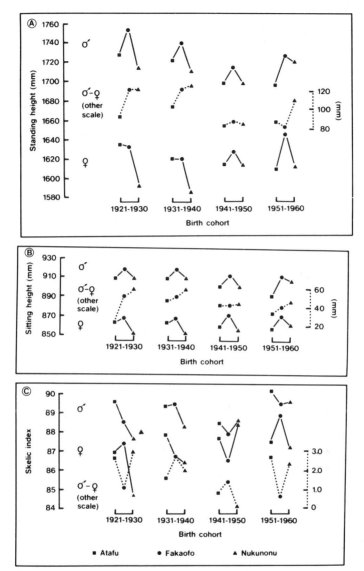

Figure 10.2 (**A, B,** and **C**). Mean values of standing height (**A**), sitting height (**B**), and skelic index (**C**) by sex and island, *within birth cohort*. Sexual dimorphism (in mm), shown as dotted lines, is given and related to its own (dotted line) scale.

males, is also of interest, particularly as the resulting trend to a decrease in sexual dimorphism resists explanation by conventional ideas regarding sexual dimorphism.

For the total sample the lowest degree of sexual dimorphism (right hand dotted figures in Figures 10.1 and 10.2) is determined by

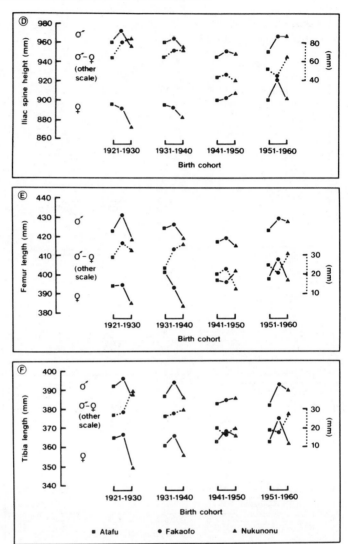

Figure 10.2 (D, E, and F). Mean values of iliac spine height (D), femur length (E), and tibia length (F) by sex and island, *within birth cohort*. Sexual dimorphism (in mm), shown as dotted lines, is given and related to its own (dotted line) scale.

the dip in male values of cohort 3 (1941-1950) together with the secular increase in female values. This can be observed in each of the (obviously highly correlated) variables, with the possible exception of sitting height, which for males do not increase in cohort 4 and for females tend to decrease rather than increase in the younger cohorts.

With respect to the Tokelau (total) pattern for most variables, the values for the male cohorts 1, 2, and 4 tend to fall in a straight line, a secular trend which is interrupted by the cohort 3 value. It seems reasonable to hypothesize that some event, affecting a significant proportion of this cohort, may have had an acute nutritional impact of limited duration, as the reduction in growth is not seen in the subsequent cohort. This does not, *a posteriori*, present much of a puzzle because, as was alluded to above, a nutritional catastrophe did occur in the Tokelaus in 1966 (i.e., when the 1941 to 1950 birth cohort, number 3, was aged 16 to 25). In January of that year a major hurricane did tremendous damage to the traditional Tokelau food-base, the coconut forests and breadfruit trees. The greatest shortages occurred in 1968 (Hooper and Huntsman 1973) when the cohort 3 males were *just prior to completing* their long-bone growth (i.e., aged 18 to 20 or so). Males in cohort 2 had completed all growth (aged 28 to 37) and most of those in cohort 4 (aged 8 to 17) were young enough to be able, with a measure of catch-up growth, to achieve their full height potential, constrained only by the overall nutritional situation. It is therefore suggested that only those males whose long-bones were *just* short of epiphyseal union were sufficiently affected by the nutritional shortages caused by the hurricane to reflect permanent (if subtle) evidence of a short period of subclinical malnutrition.

That females were for the most part unaffected, at least those in cohort 3, is readily explained. First, as pointed out by Wolański and Kasprzak (1976, p. 549), "both disadvantageous and advantageous stimuli induce change first in males; only a much stronger stimulus induces change in females." This is in keeping with the overall theory of a greater canalization (resistance to environmentally induced change) in females. Second, the fact that ossification tends to be completed in females about two or three years earlier than in males (Rodahl 1966) would suggest that *if* the food shortages had been sufficiently severe to affect female growth, this would be seen not in cohort 3 but in cohort 4. The latter cohort was aged 8 to 17 at the peak of the food shortages (1968) and most girls *just finishing* long-bone growth (i.e., those aged about 15 to 17) would have been in this group.

The question now is whether or not this hypothesis can be supported by reference to the actual record of events. Descriptions by Hooper and Huntsman (1973) indicate that they can. For instance in Nukunonu, the overall food shortages were reported as so severe that "by August 1968 the people were eating *takale* 'heart of palm' whose production kills the palms from which it is taken, and which is regarded by the people as a 'famine food' " (p. 392). Coupled with a subsequent increase in the ravages of the rhinoceros beetle, which attacks the coconut crop, the hurricane's impact was such that there were fears "the atoll might eventually be depopulated" (Hooper and Huntsman 1973, p. 392). During this period of food shortages, tight controls were imposed on access to food "with strict emphasis on the rights rather than the needs of particular individuals" (p. 405). It is therefore probable that many of the young (still growing) males, some of whom were nearing the completion of long-bone growth, experienced not only a reduced supply of nutrients, but at the same time were faced with an increased nutritional need, as these young males would have borne a significant share of the considerable increased work load (paddling, climbing, etc.) necessitated by the damage done by the hurricane. The consequent nutritional shortfall would account very well for the reduced mean size of the 1941 to 1950 cohort of males and the resulting reduction in size sexual dimorphism in that age group.

As already mentioned, the female pattern is quite a different one. Cohort 3 shows no decrease in mean size; on the contrary, it seems to reflect a continuation in most measures of a general size *increase*. Only in Nukunonu, where the hurricane "did the most damage . . . affecting the breadfruit so severely that the trees were not fruiting adequately even at the end of the following year" (Hooper and Huntsman 1973, p. 392), did females show a decline in size—and then not in those born between 1941 and 1950 (cohort 3) but in those of cohort 4.

Since long-bone growth is completed 2 to 3 years earlier in females than in males, the 18- to 27-year-olds of cohort 3 were probably already at their maximum height when the hurricane's impact on food supply was the greatest. However, the growth of Nukunonu females in cohort 4 does seem to have been detrimentally affected, as can be seen in Figure 10.1(**D, E,** and **F**). In this age group the degree of sexual dimorphism is consistently greater—influenced primarily by the increase in mean size shown by males. The increase in sexual dimorphism cannot, however, now be interpreted simply as an indication of improving nutritional status—but perhaps more as evidence of a delay in the female response (in terms of cohort mean size) to the food shortage on Nukunonu.

It is interesting to note that the greatest overall female increases in size are those experienced by the females on Nukunonu (Fig. 10.1). The older cohorts on this atoll also had the shortest mean stature and long-bone lengths compared with the other islands. It is not unreasonable to hypothesize that the farther a group's mean size is from its "potential" the greater its relative response to subsequent nutritional improvement. This is what seems to have happened with regard to Tokelau females. A secular trend to increased size, brought about by an overall nutritional improvement, was felt the most by the shortest females (i.e., those of Nukunonu). The observation that the smallest individuals, in terms of the variables under consideration, should, on average, see the greatest increases in size, has also been made by others (e.g., Frisancho, Cole, and Klayman 1977).

The smaller mean size of the two older Nukunonu cohorts (both male and female) is readily accounted for (in part at least) by the fact that Nukunonu's nutritional base, even prior to the hurricane, was inferior to that of Atafu and Fakaofo. Where the latter two islands grow crops of *pulaka* (a tuber that represents an important source of calories) "in artificial humus pits dug down to the fresh-water lens" (Hooper and Huntsman 1973, p. 367), Nukunonu has no such source of fresh water and hence no cultivation of *pulaka*. The fact that, unlike the other two atolls, "Nukunonu has never had a reliable well" (p. 367) may have further contributed to a general (if small) inferiority of nutritional status in times preceding the recently intensified (post-hurricane) importance of foods imported from New Zealand.

Considering the overall complexity of the relationship between long-bone growth in a population and environmental change, as is revealed in the Tokelau data, it becomes clear that both secular trend and sexual dimorphism must be interpreted cautiously *and together*. Markowitz (1955) points out that identifying a secular trend in stature during periods of acute environmental change (e.g., the World War II years in Europe) can depend very much on the year chosen as the basis for comparison. Thus "one finds absolute reductions during the later war years if 1941 is taken as a standard of comparison but absolute increases if 1938 is taken" (p. 261). Clearly, therefore, it is very important to consider whether or not the time period at issue involved significant nutritional changes—as the determination of a secular trend and the interpretation of any consequent variation in sexual dimorphism is not readily accomplished if other than chronic or long-term changes have affected the nutritional status of the population during that time.

DELAYED FEMALE RESPONSE TO NUTRITIONAL INADEQUACY

As pointed out earlier, a secular trend towards increasing stature in females in the *apparent* absence of a comparable increase in males has also been reported by Froelich (1970) and Greulich (1957, 1976). On the face of it this might be seen to be somewhat contrary to expectations, as the resulting decrease in sexual dimorphism (also observed in the Tokelauan data) is not consistent with the general picture of improving nutriture. However, the observation of a trend toward increased female stature in the absence of a similar trend for males may reflect not so much a generally greater biological efficiency of females (as is suggested by Greulich) but may indicate rather that a more rapid realization by males of a greater proportion of their growth potential may simply have *preceded* the observed female increases. Thus in the Tokelau data the males of cohort 1 may already reflect an increase in size achieved by earlier male cohorts and the observed increase in female size may reflect a considerable general delay in the female response to overall nutritional improvement. The observed decrease in sexual dimorphism can, therefore, *not* be interpreted without at the same time considering the possibility that it reflects a delay in the secular trend for females.

CONCLUSIONS

The model outlined above shows how subclinical malnutrition due to short-term food shortages may be detected in the achieved growth patterns of adult males and females. While the caveats of this type of cross-sectional study require strict attention, the careful avoidance of simplistic interpretations of sexual dimorphism for size (i.e., those without secular trend considerations and based solely on stature) should more than compensate for the lack of longitudinal data; in any case, unless one anthropometrist collected both sets of data in the latter situation, the validity of comparing measurements taken at two points in time is highly questionable. It is, furthermore, important to avoid the sole use of stature in such work, as this may obscure the nature and degree of sex differentials in the growth response to nutritional change.

The study of size sexual dimorphism and secular trend, especially with regard to leg long-bones, has thus been demonstrated to be of potential use in detecting such subclinical nutritional deficiencies as would make themselves felt in terms of only slightly reduced growth maxima.

BIBLIOGRAPHY

Acheson, R. M., and D. Hewitt. 1954. "Oxford Child Health Survey: Stature and Skeletal Maturation in the Preschool Child." *British Journal of Preventive and Social Medicine*, 8:59-65.

Frisancho, A. R., P. E. Cole, and J. E. Klayman. 1977. "Greater Contribution to Secular Trend among Offspring of Short Parents." *Human Biology*, 49:51-60.

Froelich, J. W.   1970.   "Migration and the Plasticity of Physique in the Japanese-Americans of Hawaii."   *American Journal of Physical Anthropology*, 32:429-442.

Greulich, W. W.   1957.   "A Comparison of the Physical Growth and Development of American-born and Native Japanese Children." *American Journal of Physical Anthropology*, 15(N.S.):489-515.

————.   1976.   "Some Secular Changes in the Growth of American-born and Native Japanese Children."   *American Journal of Physical Anthropology*, 45:553-568.

Greulich, W. W., C. S. Crismon, and M. L. Turner.   1953.   "The Physical Growth and Development of Children Who Survived the Atomic Bombing of Hiroshima or Nagasaki."   *Journal of Pediatrics*, 43:121-145.

Hall, R. L.   1978.   "Sexual Dimorphism for Size in Seven Nineteenth Century Northwest Coast Populations."   *Human Biology*, 50:159-171.

Himes, J. H., R. Martorell, J. P. Habicht, C. Yarbrough, R. M. Malina, and R. E. Klein.   1976.   "Sexual Dimorphism in Bone Growth as a Function of Body Size in Moderately Malnourished Guatemalan Preschool Age Children."   *American Journal of Physical Anthropology*, 45:331-336.

Himes, J. H., and W. H. Mueller.   1977.   "Aging and Secular Change in Adult Stature in Rural Colombia."   *American Journal of Physical Anthropology*, 46:275-279.

Hooper, A., and J. Huntsman.   1973.   "A Demographic History of the Tokelau Islands."   *Journal of the Polynesian Society*, 82:366-411.

Krogman, W. M., and R. M. Snodgrasse.   1947.   *A Manual of Anthropometry.* University of Chicago.   Mimeographed.

Markowitz, S. D.   1955.   "Retardation in Growth of Children in Europe and Asia during World War II."   *Human Biology*, 27:258-273.

Prior, I. A. M., A. Hooper, J. W. Huntsman, J. M. Stanhope, and C. E. Salmond.   1977.   "The Tokelau Island Migrant Study."   In *Population Structure and Human Variation*, edited by G. A. Harrison, pp. 165-186. Cambridge: Cambridge University Press.

Rodahl, K.   1966.   "Bone Development."   In *Human Development,* edited by F. Falkner, pp. 503-509.   Philadelphia: W. B. Saunders.

Stini, W. A.   1969.   "Nutritional Stress and Growth: Sex Difference in Adaptive Response."   *American Journal of Physical Anthropology*, 31:417-426.

————.   1972.   "Reduced Sexual Dimorphism in Upper Arm Muscle Circumference Associated with Protein Deficient Diet in a South American Population."   *American Journal of Physical Anthropology*, 36:341-352.

Tanner, J. M., J. Hiernaux, and S. Jarman.   1969.   "Growth and Physique Studies."   In *Human Biology: A Guide to Field Methods*, edited by J. S. Weiner and J. A. Lourie, pp. 1-42.   London: International Biological Programme.

Tobias, P. V.   1972.   "Growth and Stature in Southern African Populations." In *Human Biology of Environmental Change*, edited by D. J. M. Vorster, pp. 96-104.   London: International Biological Programme.

Wolański, N., and E. Kasprzak.   1976.   "Stature as a Measure of Effects of Environmental Change."   *Current Anthropology*, 17:548-552.

Three

Growth, Body Composition, and Proportionality

Eleven

Normal and Abnormal Sexual Dimorphic Patterns of Growth and Development

Leslie Sue Lieberman

The dominant activity of the human organism during the first two decades of life is growth and development (Malina 1975). Growth involves an increase in cell number (hyperplasia), an increase in cell size (hypertrophy), and an increase in cellular contents (accretion). Maturation implies cellular specialization. Humans, like most other mammals, exhibit sexual dimorphic differences in both growth and maturation. These sex differences are in response to genetic constraints, hormonal and environmental influences acting both pre- and postnatally.

The rate of the process is variable and depends on intrinsic or constitutional factors as well as on extrinsic or environmental factors: nutrients, temperature, and oxygen supply. Since the period of rapid cell division varies from one tissue to another, the period of maximum vulnerability varies. For example, the majority of brain cell divisions occur within 6 months after birth, whereas skeletal cells continue to divide for at least 15 to 20 years. Sexual dimorphic patterns of cell division are particularly evident at puberty. Testosterone and other androgens enhance the rate of linear growth and also stimulate osseous maturation. The presence of the Y-chromosome, however, may act to delay the onset of rapid bone growth during adolescence, and therefore contributes to a longer growth period in males.

In addition to the genes and hormones, other intrinsic factors affect growth: (1) mechanical forces of muscle use and strength influence the rate of growth and the size of bone; (2) muscle cell size

263

and number may be influenced by the nerve cells that innervate them; and (3) the vascular supply to a region can influence rate of growth.

The major era of maternal influence on growth is during the intrauterine period of life. The size of a full-term infant does not correlate well with the size of the father, however; it correlates better with the size of the mother. The practical application of this knowledge has been stressed by Mata (1978). His studies in Guatemalan rural villages demonstrate that smaller women have smaller babies. These infants have higher rates of morbidity and fatality from infectious disease, remain smaller, and do not perform as well as babies born of larger women. Malnutrition, as exemplified in this case, is the most common extrinsic cause of short stature and delayed maturation. Mata advised an intervention program to assure good nutrition for pregnant women and especially for their female offspring so that these infants would grow to be larger women. Clearly, height and weight are sensitive indicators of the health and well-being of an individual or, collectively, of a population. According to Tanner (as cited in Smith 1977) one of the best indications of how the people of a country are faring, and a potentially better one than the gross national product, is the size of its infants, children, and adults.

There are a number of ways to monitor growth. Assessment of stature is possibly of greater value than evaluation of weight. Linear growth rate is more consistent, provides a better indication of chronic disorders, and is a more veritable trait than weight growth. Statural growth depends on increase in cell number in the epiphyses of the skeleton. Bone age, based on the ossification rate of certain bones, provides another index of maturation.

Stature is a one-dimensional variable that increases about 3.5 times from birth to maturity, whereas weight is a three-dimensional variable that increases more than 20 times after birth (Smith 1977). Weight can be a better indicator than height of acute change; however, it is a combined measure of all tissues and is somewhat more difficult to interpret than stature.

The other standard measurement, head circumference, is a reflection of the size and the growth of the brain. In contradistinction to skeletal growth, the brain and its accessory structures, such as the eye, have achieved the majority of their growth in the first 2 years of life.

Measurements of growth can be plotted on a distance chart from which a percentile and standard deviation for age or for height may be determined. Repeated measurements may be plotted in terms of the rate of growth or velocity of growth in centimeters per year. Chronological age prior to birth is determined from age of conception,

2 weeks after the last menstrual period.   Many disorders that adversely affect linear growth in fetal life and in early infancy also impair brain growth; hence, it is important to detect these disorders at birth.   Monitoring of linear growth in early life may serve as a warning system for potential problems affecting later brain growth, physical growth, and behavior.

This chapter will examine both normal and abnormal age-related changes in growth and developmental patterns.   Emphasis will be placed on sexual dimorphic patterns and on sex differences in the prevalence of syndromes that have short or tall stature or delayed or accelerated maturation as components.   Both intrinsic (i.e., chromosomes, hormones) and extrinsic (i.e., nutrition, psychological stress) influences on growth and maturation will be examined. Methods for the assessment of growth will be briefly discussed in the next section.

METHODS OF STUDYING GROWTH AND DEVELOPMENT: RESEARCH DESIGN

Most growth studies are concerned either with observing in detail the growth of individuals or with setting up standards giving the normal variations in a given parameter, for example, stature.   Very few studies are directly concerned with dimorphic growth patterns of children in the same population.

Two research designs are commonly used in growth studies. These are the cross-sectional study and the longitudinal study.

Cross-Sectional Studies

Cross-sectional studies are those in which children are measured at each stage but no individual is measured more than once. Population standards and growth charts for clinical use are based primarily on cross-sectional data although they may be modified in light of information obtained through longitudinal studies.   Cross-sectional studies are particularly useful for estimating the population means and variances at successive ages.   Longitudinal studies are not as satisfactory for this purpose because the measurements at each age are not independent of each other.   A cross-sectional study, therefore, is the correct method of setting up population standards describing the mean and variation of height, weight, or some other parameter.

The main disadvantage to cross-sectional studies is that during periods of rapid growth there may be distortions of the curve because some children lag behind and others are advanced.   These distortions may be taken into account by statistical techniques of curve smoothing. An advantage of cross-sectional studies is that they are inexpensive to do and a large number of children may be measured in a single field study (Johnston 1980).

One option is a combined cross-sectional and longitudinal study. Different and often overlapping age cohorts of children are measured repeatedly and may be started at different times during the course of a study. In this way, there are overlaps and a better picture of the trajectory of development is achieved.

Longitudinal Studies

In studying growth patterns of an individual or group, the most effective technique is to collect repeated measures on the same individuals. These repeated measures constitute a longitudinal study. Measures taken at different ages for each subject can then be plotted forming distance curves. If a sample of individuals is measured once or many times, then the range of variation in the distance curves and achieved stature at any particular age can be estimated for a population. These distance curves may be compared between the sexes or among a number of different subgroups or populations. However, velocity curves plotting the rate of change of anthropometric traits must be based on repeated measures of the same individuals.

Longitudinal studies have important advantages and disadvantages. The main advantages are that they reveal accurately the growth patterns of individuals. Longitudinal studies enable the evaluation of changes in growth velocity and the patterning of a sequence of events such as the eruption of teeth and the development of secondary sexual characteristics. The main disadvantages for longitudinal studies are their duration, which may last up to 20 years for a complete growth study, and their costs. The second set of disadvantages involves sampling. It is impossible to carry out a longitudinal study on a sample sufficiently large to be truly representative of a population. The expense prohibits it and there is a great deal of subject attrition through time. However, a number of long-term studies have been done in the United States and other countries.

METHODS OF STUDYING GROWTH AND DEVELOPMENT: ANTHROPOMETRY

Somatic growth is measured by the technique of anthropometry. This methodology was originally developed by physical anthropologists but is now being utilized by individuals in a number of different disciplines including physicians and nutritionists. Anthropometric measurements are carefully done using standardized instruments and techniques (Cameron 1978).

The number of measurements that can be made of the body is almost limitless; the selection of measurements must be dictated by the purposes of the study. The human biologist, interested in relating physiological and ecological factors, may be interested in different measurements from those of the pediatrician who evaluates growth as a function of health. Some measurements will be common to virtually any study, such as stature and weight; others are unique to specific investigations, such as skinfold measurements.

One way of conceptualizing somatic growth is to cluster measurements. These clusters relate biologically similar aspects of growth, for example, stature and sitting height. Both measurements are along a linear axis of the body. In general, these reflect skeletal growth at the metaphyses. Body size, in contrast, may also be measured in terms of body breadth. In general, these measurements are made perpendicular to the long axis. The most common are biacromial breadth of the shoulder and bicrystal breadth of the hips. One set of size measurements that are somewhat different involve those of the head and face. Head circumference is one measurement widely used in the evaluation of health and nutritional status of infants and young children.

The basic measurement of body mass is weight. Weight and stature are the most widely taken pair of growth measurements. Both length (stature) and weight have an impressive amount of within sample variation for both sexes from birth through adolescence. Data in Table 11.1, summarizing variation at four age points, are based on longitudinal studies at the Denver Child Research Council (Hansman 1970).

TABLE 11.1

Coefficients of Variation of Body Length and Weight at Selected Ages Among Denver Children.

Length (%)			Weight (%)	
M	F	Age (yr)	M	F
4.5	3.5	Birth	15.3	13.7
3.0	3.8	5	9.1	10.7
3.3	4.6	10	13.7	17.5
4.0	3.6	15	15.2	14.4

Source: Hansman (1970) and Cameron (1978). Reprinted with permission from Plenum Publishing Corporation: Falkner, F. and J. M. Tanner (editors), 1978. *Human Growth, Vol. 2. Postnatal Growth*. New York: Plenum Press.

Body size and composition at birth reflect sexual dimorphic patterns of fetal development. The coefficients of variation for length are lower at birth for females than males but are higher thereafter. The coefficients of variation for weight are lower for females at birth and thereafter are higher than those for males.

Anthropometry is a technique for quantitatively expressing this variation in body form. Thus, it intimately involves the subject, instrument, and observer in an interactive situation that the observer is constantly attempting to standardize in order to measure the only important change, that of the growth of the subject (Cameron 1978). Both cross-sectional and longitudinal growth studies are the means by which individual growth patterns and differences in the tempo of growth can be measured.

Stature

Stature must be accurately measured, otherwise it is impossible to make reliable estimates of a child's rate of growth between successive measurements. Measurements are often carelessly taken in schools and in hospital clinics when they are not used to judge health or nutritional status or are not part of growth and development studies. Errors of 3 to 4 cm are not uncommon under these circumstances. The growth of even a healthy preadolescent child may only be about 6 cm per year. If measurements are made at intervals of 6 months, the child may have grown only about 3 cm. This amount of growth cannot be measured satisfactorily if the error of individual measurement exceeds 2 or 3 cm. For example, a positive error of 1.5 cm on the first occasion and a negative one of the same magnitude on the second one suggests that the child has not grown at all. Some error may be due to the measuring instruments. Either an anthropometer or a stadiometer, which is bolted to the wall, should be used. The horizontal bar of the stadiometer or the arm of the anthropometer should be checked to make sure that it is at right angles to the rod. Techniques for positioning the child and reading the measurements must be accurate and precise.

Weight

Weight is widely used as a measurement of growth. Weight fluctuates readily and reflects short-term alterations in nutrition, health status, or other environmentally or endogenously induced changes. It is a useful way to monitor general health and nutrition. A problem with measurement of weight, however, is that it does not distinguish body composition. A child who is light as compared with others of his or her age may be abnormally small; abnormally thin, lacking adipose stores; or malnourished, lacking protein or lean body mass. A child who is unusually heavy for his or her age might be too fat or might be a "big child." When weighing a youngster, age- and sex-adjusted standards should be used. The significance of a child's weight is judged better in relationship to stature.

Sitting Height

Another useful measure is the sitting height. Sitting height is measured when the subject is seated on a table or platform. It is a measurement from the buttocks to the vertex of the head. An anthropometer is usually used. This measurement allows a division of the stature into the trunk and head, and the leg lengths. Leg length can be estimated by subtracting the sitting height from the stature. Male and female growth velocity differences in leg length are evident in adolescence. A ratio of sitting height to standing height gives an indication of the contributions of the trunk and legs to total height. Males have relatively longer legs than females.

Circumferences

Head circumference is a useful indirect measurement of brain growth in infants and young children. Other frequently used girth measurements are upper arm, calf and chest circumferences.

Skinfold Measurements

Skinfold measurements are useful in calculating the amount of body fat. Regression equations have been developed to provide estimates of the fat and lean body mass. In many parts of the body, the skin and subcutaneous tissues are only loosely attached to the underlying structures, and, therefore, may be picked up between the thumb and forefinger as a fold. A number of different skinfold calipers are in use. In general, there is a specific pressure at the head of the calipers which is applied to the pinched, double thickness of skin and fat. A dial in millimeters indicates the thickness. The most widely used measures are the triceps skinfold and the subscapular skinfold.

During growth, the amount of subcutaneous fat deposited on the limbs is often different from that on the trunk. For this reason, it is advisable to take fat measurements on both limb and trunk sites. One disadvantage to skinfold measurements is that in very obese persons valid measurements are difficult to take.

Ratios of Measurements

Of great interest is the relationship between two parameters, for example, stature and weight. There are many methods that are used to express these relationships in both linear growth and in bulk. In the past, it was a common practice to divide one parameter by the other to make a ratio, for example, stature divided by sitting height. This procedure has a disadvantage because it discards information about the absolute values of the measurement. Unless the individual measurements are also reported, we do not know if a high ratio is due to tall sitting height or short stature. Another common way of relating two parameters is simply to plot one measurement against the other (i.e., weight for height). These plots often are expressed in age and sex specific centiles which can be used as standards against which to judge the growth of an individual child or to compare populations or subpopulations. Centiles which are frequently used include the third, fifth, twenty-fifth, fiftieth, seventy-fifth, ninetieth, ninety-seventh, and ninety-ninth centiles. Centiles are commonly used for birth weight (which may be the only information obtained about intrauterine growth), length, stature, stature velocity, weight, and weight velocity.

Growth Velocity

Distance curves are plots of the cumulative increments of growth over a portion of the lifetime of an individual or a population. These curves represent size attained at a particular age.

The distance curves do not give a description of the growth pattern, per se. In order to look at the speed of growth, that is, periods of greater or lesser growth velocity, a velocity curve is plotted. The terms "growth velocity" or "growth rate" refer to the increase in a given parameter (e.g., stature) in a specific period of time. Stature velocity is described in units of centimeters per year. The growth velocity curve is constructed by dividing the distance grown (that is, the difference between two successive measurements of stature or whatever dimension is being studied) by the time that has elapsed between the two measurements.

Distance curves reveal that males are taller than females from birth onward except during a brief period of preadolescence or early adolescence. Growth velocity curves indicate that the accelerated growth of puberty is approximately 2 years earlier for females than males and that a peak height velocity is reached approximately 2 years earlier for females. Growth deceleration for males may also be slower compared to females where there is a more rapid termination and a shorter period of accelerated growth.

The peak height velocity or the maximal velocity achieved during the adolescent spurt is an important landmark in the growth of all normal children. The age at which the child attains the peak height velocity as well as the actual value in centimeters per year can be derived from the velocity curve. This information is obtained only from repeated measures of the same individual. It cannot be obtained by measuring different individuals at each age. The growth velocity curve of an adolescent rises to maximum and then immediately begins to fall again. The maximum speed, Peak High Velocity (PHV), reached by different children varies greatly.

In the Harpenden Growth Study (Marshall 1977) girls averaged a peak height velocity of 9.0 cm/year while boys averaged a peak height velocity of 10.3 cm/year as estimated by drawing a curve of the individual measurements for each of the subjects. The standard deviation for females was 1.03 cm/year, whereas it was significantly greater for males at 1.54 cm/year. Girls' peak height velocity varied between 7 and 11 cm/year, which may indicate that they were much more canalized than the males, who ranged from 7.2 cm/yr to 13.4 cm/yr.

Marshall and Tanner (1969) observed a mean age at peak height velocity of 12.14 ± 0.14 years for British girls while boys reached a peak height velocity at 14.06 ± 0.14 years. Most girls reach their maximum growth rate between their 10th and 14th birthday; most boys reach their peak height velocity between their 12th and 16th birthday.

METHODS OF STUDYING GROWTH AND DEVELOPMENT: MEASURES OF MATURITY

The measurements of size, physique, and body composition are useful tools in evaluating growth and developmental changes. These measurements are usually reported in sex specific chronological age categories (Malina 1975). However, chronological age, particularly in abnormal growth, is only an estimate of developmental or maturational age. Therefore, in addition to anthropometrically derived measures of maturational age (i.e., height-age), biological age is frequently assessed by examination of other traits.

Dental Age

The eruption of teeth and the calcification of teeth follow a very regular pattern in normal development. Dental age is particularly useful during infancy and childhood but is not very useful during puberty because usually no new permanent teeth erupt between 12 and 18 years of age. Girls are 1 to 6 months ahead of boys in the eruption of the permanent dentition.

Bone Age

Bone age or skeletal age is perhaps the best method for assessing the developmental status of a child. Many disorders are expressed in terms of delayed or accelerated bone age in relationship to chronological age or height age. Osseous maturation is determined by comparing radiographs of the hand and wrist, or occasionally the knee, of a child to age and sex specific standards. The progressive calcification of the bones of the knee and of the 29 separate centers of bone growth in the hand and wrist complex are divided into a series of stages (Smith 1977). These stages are presented in atlases for comparison. Commonly used methods for estimating maturation include the Greulich-Pyle technique and the Tanner-Whitehouse (TW$_2$) technique (Roche 1978, 1980).

The tables developed by Bayley and Pinneau (1952) are most widely used for the prediction of adult stature for children from age 8 years (Marshall 1977; Roche 1980). The TW$_2$ method permits adult height estimates from age 4 years. The tables compare bone age to chronological age and give a percentage of the adult height attained by chronological age. Separate tables are used for delayed, average, or accelerated bone age.

Males age 4 to 13 and females aged 4 to 11 are predicted to within ±7 cm of their true adult height 95 percent of the time. This range falls for males to ±6 cm at 14 and ±1.6 cm at 17.5 years. Premenarcheal females 12 to 13 years have a range of ±4 to 5 cm while postmenarcheal females have a predictive range of ± 3–4 cm decreasing to ±1.5 cm at 15 years of age.

As anticipated, sex differences in bone age are most pronounced between the ages of 11.5 and 13.5 years. By age 17.5 years, the sex difference in skeletal age is only 3.9 months. This contrasts with a maximum sex difference of 35 months at 13 years of age.

Sexual Maturation

Sexual maturation is most frequently assessed using the Tanner system of five descriptive stages of development from preadolescent to adult for pubic hair, male genitalia, and breast development.

The development of these secondary sexual characteristics is associated with the adolescent growth spurt. Children without endocrine abnormalities will experience a growth spurt shortly after the beginning development of secondary sexual characteristics. Menarche occurs shortly after the peak height velocity. Most girls experience menarche when bone age is between 12.5 and 14.5 years (Marshall 1977). However, there is no strong predictive relationship between skeletal maturation and the development of secondary sexual characteristics. For example, bone age at which the breasts begin to develop in females is as variable as chronological age and a preadolescent child with an advanced bone age will not necessarily experience an early onset of puberty.

METHODS OF STUDYING GROWTH AND DEVELOPMENT: DIAGNOSIS OF GROWTH DISORDERS

There are several hundred different disorders in which growth deficiency is one feature; thus, it is important to develop a general approach to the evaluation and diagnosis of a patient with short or tall stature or delayed or advanced maturation. The diagnostic procedure should include both a detailed history of the family and the patient and a detailed physical evaluation including anthropometric measurements, radiographs, and, if applicable, assessment of sexual maturity as outlined above.

A family history is of great importance in determining if the delayed or accelerated growth is normal or abnormal for a particular individual. Knowing the stature of the parents and siblings as well as their pace of maturation is valuable information. For the mother the age of menarche is a standard that is usually remembered. Other questions that might have diagnostic value would include questions about attainment of stature relative to classmates or the age a male began to shave. Pregnancy histories are important. If the baby was small for gestational age or small for date, then a number of questions pertaining to the mother's socioeconomic status, and nutrition before and during pregnancy, ingestion of medication and alcohol, cigarette smoking behavior, and other relevant biological and behavioral variables should be noted in the maternal and pregnancy history.

Depending on the nature of the growth problem, specific instances of serious illness or gastrointestinal dysfunction as well as psychosocial adjustment should be noted. Longitudinal data on linear growth and weight should be obtained and evaluated to determine the age of onset of the growth problem.

During the physical evaluation, careful measurement of the stature and weight should be made. These should be plotted on a chart and compared to standards for the child's age and sex. For the younger child, head circumference may be useful measure. Height-age as well as weight-age should be determined and height for weight should be noted. Various methods, the most readily available of which are skinfold measurements, may be necessary to determine body composition in some disorders. In addition, hand/wrist x-rays may be of importance for determining osseous maturation. Tanner's standards or stages should be used to rate the development of secondary sexual characteristics in late childhood and adolescence. For example, in the male, the gonadotropin levels may be assessed by measurement of the growth of the testes. For the female, only the indirect effects of the gonadotropin-induced production of estrogen can be assessed by rating breast development and estrogenization of the vaginal mucosa.

There is no single laboratory test indicated for every patient with a growth disorder. Tests should be used specifically to confirm suspected diagnoses. Measurements of thyroid functions, gonado-tropin levels, pituitary hormones, adrenal hormones, and other products of endocrine activity may be made to aid in ruling out or confirming endocrinological disorders. The findings from the history and the examinations, sometimes supplemented by roentgenograms and laboratory tests, usually allow for the placement of the patient in a particular general diagnostic category. The largest categories are the normal variants of familial small stature and familial slow maturation.

The intrinsic and extrinsic factors that affect growth and maturation in children with and without growth disorders will be briefly examined in the next section.

FACTORS INFLUENCING GROWTH AND DEVELOPMENT

There are many factors that influence linear growth. These include genetic factors, nutrition, disease, seasonality, endocrine factors, and socioeconomic factors. From the perspective of sexual dimorphism, genetic factors, nutrition, endocrine factors, and secular trend show the most dramatic influences on growth differences between males and females.

Genetic Factors

Stature is one of the most heritable traits recognized in humans. The correlation coefficient for stature in monozygotic twins is 0.95 (Bulmer 1970). The average difference in height of like-sex monozygotic twins is 2.8 cm compared to a 12-cm difference for dizygotic twins of the same sex. Since many genes are involved in the determination of stature, the offspring of a normally tall parent and a short parent tend to be average in size, illustrating the principle of regression toward the mean with polygenic inheritance. There is usually a wide range of variability in the estimation of stature. The adult stature of children may be approximated by using the mid-parental height. Surprisingly, the size at birth does not correlate well either with mid-parental height (i.e., the mean height of the parents) or with the height of the same individual at maturity. Birth length correlates best with the size of the mother. Summarizing the data, Polani (1974) states that variation in birth size can be partitioned to include 18 percent ascribed to the genome of the fetus, 20 percent ascribed to the maternal genome, 32 percent ascribed to the maternal environmental factors, and the remaining 30 percent due to unknown factors.

The correlation of stature to parental height is evident by 2 years of age and does not change greatly from 2 to 9 years. During adolescent growth, the correlation with parental size becomes even stronger and is about 0.7 by age 18 years.

Correlations with the same-sex parents vary considerably from population to population. For example, in the wide range of material presented by Johnston (1978) the correlation of father and male child stature ranged from 0.11 to 0.35. Mean father-son height correlations for 9 European studies averaged 0.34. Mother and daughter height correlation in the same populations averaged 0.40. Parent-child correlations in 11 non-European populations were lower: 0.28 for father-son and 0.37 for mother-daughter. Weight correlations were also higher for mothers and daughters (Mueller 1976).

A number of authors have shown that there is wide genetic variability in the pace of growth and the osseous maturation. The pace of maturation, like size, appears to be under polygenic control. Therefore, the history of the pace of maturation of the parent may be quite important in interpreting the size and ultimate growth potential of a child and in ruling out other abnormalities associated with advanced or retarded growth and maturation.

At least some of the genes that affect pace of maturation and size are located in the X and Y chromosomes. Not only does the XX female mature at least 10 percent more rapidly than the XY male, but she is more rigorously channeled in her pace of growth. Garn and Rohmann (1962) found less variability in osseous maturation among girls than among boys and greater correlation between sisters in the sequence of osseous maturation than between brothers. The consequently greater size correlation among girls as compared to that found among boys further indicates an X linkage for some of the genes affecting growth. XYY males tend to be larger than XY males but they do not have higher levels of serum testosterone. Therefore, the attribute of larger size in XYY males is not due to increased testosterone in the presence of the extra chromosome (Baghdassarian, Bayard, and Borgaonkar et al. 1975).

Racial differences are largely a consequence of multiple gene differences. It is not surprising that there should be differences in size and in the pace of maturation among racial groups. Black infants tend to be a little smaller at birth and mature more rapidly than white infants. Relatively little difference in size between black and white children during childhood occurs, although black children tend to have less fat per kilogram of body weight and higher bone density than white children.

Disease

Bouts of illness can significantly affect growth in children. Decrements in growth and development also may be related to the synergism of infectious disease and malnutrition. Hewitt, Westropp, and Acheson (1955) analyzed annual height increments by illness severity, using five categories of illness in 650 children studied from 1 to 5 years of age in the Oxford Child Health Survey. They found a small but definite diminution of growth related to severity of illness. This reduction in growth was especially pronounced in males.

Endocrine Factors

Testosterone, the most important of the androgens, is the anabolic steroid produced in the adrenals of both males and females and in the testes of males. Testosterone has an important influence on increases in muscle cell number and size, increase in bone mass, accelerated epiphyseal maturation, and the appearance of secondary sexual characteristics. Androgens accelerate osseous maturation more rapidly than linear growth, and, hence, bring an early maturing male more rapidly to the stage of final height attainment. Thus, though testosterone and other androgens have profound effects on growth, they do not appear to be growth hormones in the sense that they increase the ultimate stature of the individual.

Estrogens accelerate the lateral growth of the pelvis and lead to increased hip width in females. Estrogens also accelerate the pace of osseous maturation without affecting linear growth as profoundly as testosterone. Thus, the female reaches final height attainment sooner than the male and has less of an adolescent growth spurt. Estrogens promote the accumulation of fat, enhancing some of the secondary sexual characteristics of females.

Pituitary growth hormone has a primary action on cell metabolism and affects the utilization of amino acids, glucose, and free fatty acids. Its predominant effect on linear growth is exerted through the stimulation of somatomedin production. Somatomedin enhances the rate of mitosis in cartilage cells at the epiphyseal plate, thereby affecting linear growth. This is accomplished without undue acceleration of osseous maturation; therefore, somatomedin may be considered to be a growth hormone.

Thyroid hormone is essential for normal energy metabolism to facilitate growth and maturation after birth. Excess thyroid hormone results in only mild acceleration of linear growth with moderate acceleration of osseous maturation and in increased metabolic rate. Thyroid deficiency results in reduced cell number; and if congenital, cell size is also reduced.

Insulin produced by the B-cells of the pancreas is vital in carbohydrate metabolism, and thus it is important in normal growth and development. Insulin and growth hormone work synergistically to promote protein synthesis. Insulin deficiency affects cell size but not cell number.

Parity

Castle (1941) found firstborns to be smaller than subsequent offspring by 0.34 cm in length and 0.18 kg in weight and 0.14 cm in head circumference. This may be due to relatively more uterine constraint on late fetal growth during the first pregnancy. The firstborn grows more rapidly during the first few postnatal months. This most likely represents catch-up growth compensating for the late fetal restraint on growth (Marshall 1977).

Seasonality

Seasonality in growth has been demonstrated for children (Bilewicz 1967). British children appear to grow faster from March through July than from September through February. Sex differences have not been noted. Marshall estimates that 30 percent of British children follow a seasonal pattern of growth (1977).

Nutrition

Stini (1972, 1975) has noted that male infants and children are more severely affected by malnutrition than females. Both weight and linear growth are affected. Stini has documented that in chronically malnourished populations, such as those in Colombia, males tend to show more marked decrements in both adipose tissue and protein stores as well as decreased stature and delayed osseous and sexual maturation compared to females in the same undernourished populations. The smaller body size of females may be an energetic advantage under conditions of nutritional stress.

Social Class or Socioeconomic Status

The lower the social class or socioeconomic status of the mother, the smaller the baby and child. Also, the lower the social class or socioeconomic status, the smaller the parents (Goldstein 1971). Therefore, the small size of the parents may be the major factor relating to both the size of the children and the low income status. Tanner (1962) noted that British children of the professional classes were one inch taller at 3 years of age and two inches taller at adolescence than children of laborers. Krogman (1972) reports that presidents at major universities average 2.5 cm taller than those at small colleges; railway presidents average 4 cm taller than railway station managers; bishops average 4.5 cm taller than rural ministers; and sales managers are taller than salesmen.

Secular Trend

During the past one to two hundred years there has been a profound change in the pace of maturation and in the extent of adult size of individuals in developed countries. Faster maturation has resulted in greater increments of growth, a larger size for age during childhood, and earlier advent of adolescence and of final height attainment. Secular changes in height are shown in Figures 11.1 and 11.2. Whereas a century ago the average male did not reach final height until 23 years of age, he now reaches it by 18 years. The average age of menarche in the female has dropped from approximately 17 years to approximately 13 years (Flint 1978). Thus, today maturation occurs about 25 percent faster than it did 100 years ago.

The accelerated maturation gives rise to profound sex differences in stature during childhood and adolescence. For example, the average 14-year-old boy of today is often at the same maturation level in size as the 18- to 19-year-old male of 100 years ago. But since the period of linear growth is shorter, the impact on final height attainment is only modest (Malina 1975). Some of the estimates of the increase in stature during the past century have been excessive because investigators compared the stature of former recruits who had not yet ceased growing to the stature of recent recruits of the same age who had reached their final height (Smith 1977).

Height Velocity in Boys

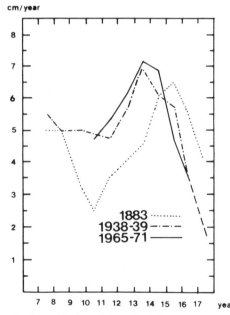

Figure 11.1.   Secular trend in height and adolescent growth spurt in boys. Redrawn from Falkner and Tanner (1978, p. 455). (Reprinted with permission from Plenum Publishing Corporation: Falkner, F. and J. M. Tanner [editors]. 1978. *Human Growth, Vol. 2. Postnatal Growth.* New York: Plenum Press.)

Height Velocity in Girls

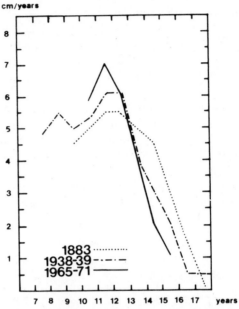

Figure 11.2.   Secular trend in height and adolescent growth spurt in girls. Redrawn from Falkner and Tanner (1978, p. 455). (Reprinted with permission from Plenum Publishing Corporation: Falkner, F. and J. M. Tanner [editors]. 1978. *Human Growth, Vol. 2. Postnatal Growth.* New York: Plenum Press.)

The cause or causes of these secular changes are not known. The most popular hypothesis is that it is a consequence of a decrease in growth-inhibiting factors—such as poor intrauterine, infant, and childhood nutrition, chronic childhood diseases—and improvements in sanitation and hygiene. In addition, genetic outbreeding creating hybrid vigor may be a factor, although studies among migrant groups (Hulse 1957) indicate that secular changes in height and weight and head circumference do occur without genetic admixture. There are now indications that the secular trend in stature and in decreased age of sexual maturation is leveling off among advantaged groups (Malina 1975).

Clearly, growth and development are influenced by a large number of other factors including hypoxia and altitude stress, temperature and climate, radiation, and psychological factors. Some of these factors will be examined in the section on abnormal growth patterns. Many of these factors work synergistically to enhance or retard growth. Interactions among these extrinsic factors coupled with complex genotype-environmental interactions have different effects on males and females. In general, females are better buffered against environmental insults and are able to more frequently maintain a normal trajectory of development and deviate less than males during the course of growth and development.

AGE-RELATED CHANGES AND SEXUAL DIMORPHIC PATTERNS IN NORMAL POSTNATAL GROWTH: INFANCY

The first year of life is characterized by extremely rapid growth (Tables 11.2 and 11.3). Differences in the mean birth weight between females (3.40 ± 0.57 kg) and males (3.50 ± 0.53 kg) reflect differences in prenatal growth patterns. More rapid weight gains occur in males after 34 weeks gestation (Smith 1977). The weight velocity is initially greater for males (8.93 ± 1.8 kg/yr) than for females (7.42 ± 1.91 kg/yr) but decreases more rapidly in males so that by 1 year of age the mean velocities for males and females are 3.33 ± 0.93 kg/year and 3.37 ± 0.99 kg/year, respectively. Birth weight doubling time reflects these velocity differences. Full-term German male infants doubled their birth weight in 4.5 months while female infants took 5.0 months (Brandt 1980). In California infant birth weight doubling time was even shorter, 3.6 months for males and 4.1 months for females (Neumann and Alpaugh 1976).

At birth males are larger than females, 50.0 ± 1.94 cm and 49.5 ± 1.94 cm, respectively. As in the case of weight, the length velocity is initially higher for males (47.0 cm/2 year) than females (41.0 cm/2 year) but falls more rapidly so that at 1 year of age the velocity for males is 13.40 cm/year and for females 14.70 cm/year.

This growth represents an increase in 60 to 65 percent in length and 250 to 300 percent in weight in the first year of life. In a Finnish longitudinal study (Kantero and Tiisala 1971a,b), males at 1 year of age had length increments exceeding females by 2.4 cm and weight increments exceeding females by 0.88 kg. Crown-rump length also shows a significant sex difference in the first year of life. Males had an increase in 45 percent over the birth value and females 42 percent (Hansman 1970).

The Denver Child Research Council's longitudinal study documents sex differences in the growth of horizontal dimensions (Hansman 1970). During the first year of life biiliac (hip) breadth and biacromial (shoulder) breadth averaged 55 percent of the birth value in males and 54 percent in females.

Head circumference is larger at birth for males (36.0 ± 1.97 cm) than for females (34.0 ± 1.60 cm). Males continue increases in head

TABLE 11.2

Sexual Dimorphic Patterns of Length, Height, Length Velocity, Height Velocity, Crown-Rump Length, Sitting Height, and Head Circumference Measurements from Birth to Nineteen Years.

Age	Length and Height F		M		Length Velocity F	Height Velocity F	Length Velocity M	Height Velocity M	Crown-Rump and Sitting Height F		M		Head Circumference F		M	
	Mean (cm)	S.D.	Mean (cm)	S.D.	Mean (cm/yr)	S.D.	Mean (cm/yr)	S.D.	Mean (cm)	S.D.	Mean (cm)	S.D.	Mean (cm)	S.D.	Mean (cm)	S.D.
Birth	49.5	1.94	50.0	1.94	41.00*	3.00	47.00	3.00					34.00	1.60	36.00	1.97
1 mo.									34.2	1.55	35.0	1.55				
3 mo.	59.0	2.16	60.7	2.16	32.00	2.63	36.00	2.63	38.0	1.42	39.0	1.42	39.60	1.52	40.20	1.70
6 mo.	65.5	2.34	68.2	2.34	22.50	2.34	24.00	2.34	42.2	1.57	43.1	1.67	42.60	1.44	43.65	1.60
9 mo.	70.2	2.52	72.7	2.52	16.45	2.15	16.25	2.15	44.7	1.67	45.5	1.67	44.62	1.44	45.60	1.60
12 mo.	74.2	2.69	76.3	2.69	14.70	1.98	13.40	1.98	46.5	1.71	47.4	1.71	45.45	1.41	46.65	1.60
1-1.5 yr.	80.5	3.01	82.1	3.01	11.20	1.75	10.50	1.75	49.4	1.83	50.2	1.83	46.90	1.38	48.10	1.49
2 yr.	85.6/84.6	3.3/3.3	86.9/85.9	3.30/3.30	9.15/9.30	1.43/1.64	8.90/9.00	1.48/1.64	51.8	1.95	52.7	1.95	47.90	1.37	49.03	1.49
3 yr.	93.0	3.83	94.2	3.83	7.90	1.34	7.88	1.34	55.2	2.25	56.0	2.25	49.33	1.25	50.37	1.41

Age																
4 yr.	100.4	4.30	101.6	4.30	7.03	1.15	7.00	1.12	58.5	2.34	59.2	2.33	50.20	1.28	51.12	1.36
5 yr.	108.3	4.74	108.3	4.74	6.48	1.09	6.48	1.03	61.4	2.50	62.0	2.38	50.80	1.28	51.60	1.33
6 yr.	114.6	5.17	114.6	5.14	6.09	0.95	6.09	0.91	64.4	2.70	64.7	2.40	51.20	1.28	51.88	1.33
7 yr.	120.5	5.46	120.5	5.46	5.82	0.87	5.79	0.87	66.9	2.90	67.2	2.45	51.50	1.28	52.12	1.33
8 yr.	125.0	5.73	126.2	5.75	5.55	0.80	5.55	0.77	69.1	3.08	69.5	2.55	51.70	1.28	52.29	1.33
9 yr.	130.5	5.86	131.6	6.00	5.47	0.78	5.35	0.76	71.3	3.22	71.7	2.70	51.90	1.28	52.43	1.36
10 yr.	136.0	5.94	136.9	6.20	5.47	0.83	5.16	0.70	73.4	3.36	73.8	2.90	52.15	1.30	52.70	1.49
11 yr.	141.7	5.96	142.0	6.37	6.50	1.01	5.01	0.68	76.3	3.50	75.7	3.13	52.65	1.33	53.10	1.54
12 yr.	149.5	5.98	146.9	6.48	8.33	1.10	4.98	0.79	79.6	3.70	77.6	3.39	53.20	1.33	53.60	1.54
13 yr.	156.8	6.00	152.2	6.55	5.50	1.05	6.55	1.03	82.3	3.88	80.1	3.72	53.62	1.28	54.10	1.54
14 yr.	160.6	6.00	160.6	6.59	2.36	0.84	9.45	1.20	84.6	3.40	83.2	4.18	53.97	1.20	54.59	1.54
15 yr.	161.9	6.00	168.7	6.61	0.60	0.52	5.86	1.13	86.2	3.18	86.5	4.52	54.18	1.14	54.85	1.49
16 yr.	162.2	6.00	172.7	6.63	0.20	0.52	2.65	0.91	87.0	3.10	89.6	4.12	54.27	1.14	55.00	1.46
17 yr.	162.2	6.00	174.3	6.65	0.00	0.50	1.00	0.50								
18 yr.	162.2	6.00	174.7	6.65	0.00	0.40	0.05	0.40								
19 yr.																

M = Male; F = Female; * = cm/2 yr.

Source: Adapted from Tanner (1973) and Smith (1977).

283

TABLE 11.3

Sexual Dimorphic Patterns of Weight, Weight Velocity, Triceps Skinfold, and Subscapular Measurements from Birth to Nineteen Years.

Age	Weight F		Weight M		Weight Velocity F		Weight Velocity M		Triceps Skinfold F		Triceps Skinfold M		Subscapular Skinfold F		Subscapular Skinfold M	
	Mean (kg)	S.D.	Mean (kg)	S.D.	Mean (kg/yr)	S.D.	Mean (kg/yr)	S.D.	Mean (mm)	S.D.	Mean (mm)	S.D.	Mean (mm)	S.D.	Mean (mm)	S.D.
Birth	3.40	0.57	3.50	0.53	7.42	1.91	8.93	1.80								
1 mo.					9.25	2.69	9.85	2.38	175.7	10.9	175.0	12.56	173.2	12.3	172.0	14.8
3 mo.	5.56	0.64	5.93	0.66	6.60	1.55	6.80	1.61	189.7	10.5	193.0	12.10	183.0	12.9	182.0	14.8
6 mo.	7.39	0.80	7.90	0.80	4.29	1.32	4.30	1.22	196.3	11.9	201.0	12.00	186.0	14.1	184.8	15.0
9 mo.	8.72	0.90	9.20	1.15	3.37	0.99	3.33	0.93	198.8	12.9	202.0	12.50	184.8	14.4	184.0	15.2
12 mo.	9.70	1.01	10.20	1.01	2.44	0.72	2.44	0.71	199.5	13.6	201.0	12.70	182.0	14.0	182.0	15.8
1.5 yr.	11.10	1.12	11.60	1.17	2.08	0.57	2.10	0.63	199.4	13.8	198.3	12.90	177.3	14.4	173.0	15.6
2 yr.	12.20	1.33	12.70	1.33	2.00	0.73	1.96	0.69	198.7	13.7	195.8	13.10	173.8	14.8	168.0	15.2
3 yr.	14.30	1.54	14.70	1.61	2.00	0.78	1.90	0.77	196.8	13.6	191.0	10.40	169.0	16.3	162.0	15.5
4 yr.	16.30	1.69	16.60	1.90	2.05	1.10	1.92	0.85	194.7	13.4	187.0	13.50	166.0	17.5	158.3	16.2
5 yr.	18.30	2.65	18.50	2.17					192.5	13.9	183.5	13.90	163.4	18.5	155.2	16.6

6 yr.	20.40	3.39	20.50	2.44	2.17	1.22	2.07	0.94	190.7	14.7	181.4	14.70	162.0	19.1	153.4	16.8
7 yr.	22.60	4.23	22.60	2.75	2.30	1.34	2.31	1.02	190.0	16.1	180.3	15.60	162.1	20.7	153.0	17.5
8 yr.	25.10	5.24	25.00	3.12	2.54	1.38	2.47	1.14	191.7	17.6	180.0	17.00	164.2	23.2	153.8	18.3
9 yr.	27.70	6.34	27.50	5.98	2.81	0.96	2.67	0.88	194.6	18.7	180.8	18.70	167.8	25.5	155.5	19.9
10 yr.	30.70	7.72	30.30	7.04	3.16	1.56	2.87	1.60	197.0	19.4	182.4	20.70	172.2	27.7	158.0	23.4
11 yr.	34.20	8.68	33.30	7.78	4.05	1.65	3.08	1.70	198.7	19.8	184.4	22.40	178.0	28.0	162.0	26.0
12 yr.	39.60	9.52	36.50	8.48	7.43	1.42	3.50	1.75	199.8	20.1	186.0	23.00	184.0	26.5	165.8	26.5
13 yr.	47.80	9.79	40.70	8.47	7.25	1.40	5.13	1.78	201.5	19.9	184.4	23.70	188.3	24.7	187.0	25.2
14 yr.	53.00	9.79	48.40	9.42	3.55	1.30	9.06	1.95	205.3	19.2	181.0	23.50	193.0	22.6	186.0	23.1
15 yr.	55.20	9.79	56.30	9.52	1.48	1.41	5.68	1.89	209.8	18.2	178.4	23.20	198.7	19.9	188.0	20.7
16 yr.	56.00	9.79	60.20	9.63	0.22	1.11	2.60	1.00	213.4	17.4	178.8	23.40	201.5	19.0	179.6	18.7
17 yr.	56.40	9.79	62.10	9.60					215.0	16.6	182.0	21.70	202.8	18.3	185.7	17.8
18 yr.	56.60	9.79	63.00	9.69					215.5	16.4	185.7	21.50	203.0	18.7	190.4	17.5
19 yr.									215.5	16.4	188.8	21.20	203.0	18.7	192.3	17.5

M = Male; F = Female.

Source: Adapted from Tanner (1973) and Smith (1977).

growth over females so that at 1 year of age head circumference values are 39 percent over birth values for males and 35 percent for females (Hansman 1970). In addition to these measurements, sex difference in the pace of osseous maturation is evident at 30 fetal weeks. The female average is 2 weeks beyond the male in bone age at the time of birth and is 8 weeks ahead by 1 year of age (Thompson, Bilewicz and Hytten 1968; Tanner, 1974; Smith, 1977).

Sexual dimorphic patterns also occur in body composition as measured by the triceps and subscapular skinfolds (Table 11.4). Females have smaller triceps skinfolds but larger subscapular skinfold measurements than males during the first years of life. At 1 year of age, sex differences in triceps skinfolds are greater for black and Indian infants than for whites (Johnston 1978; Johnston and Beller 1976). Huenemann's study (1974) of 6-month-olds found that although the triceps skinfold measurement was the same (8.0 mm) for both males and females the upper arm circumference was larger for males (15.4 cm) than for females (15.0).

In sum, the basic sexual dimorphic trend is the faster late fetal and early infancy growth rate of the male as compared to that of the female in length, weight, and head circumference. Sex differences persist in childhood but with a reduced velocity in growth rate until

TABLE 11.4
Skinfold Thickness in Newborn Infants.

		Triceps		Subscapular	
	Number	$\bar{x}$	*S.D.*	$\bar{x}$	*S.D.*
United States					
Whites[a]					
Males	32	4.0	1.1	3.8	1.2
Females	32	4.2	1.1	3.8	1.2
Blacks[a]					
Males	33	3.9	1.1	3.6	1.0
Females	34	4.3	1.1	4.0	1.1
Puerto Rican[a]					
Males	31	3.4	1.1	3.3	1.2
Females	34	3.9	1.3	3.5	1.3
England[b]					
Males	187	4.7	0.9	4.9	1.1
Females	144	4.7	1.0	5.2	1.2
Guatemala[c]					
Males	29	4.5	1.0	4.4	1.2
Females	16	4.7	0.9	4.3	0.8

Source: Adapted from [a]Johnston and Beller (1976); [b]Gambel (1965); [c]Malina et al. (1974).

the advent of adolescence. The early acceleration of male growth may be the consequence of testosterone, which is at levels of 250 mg/100 ml in the serum of the infant male in the first few postnatal months. Thereafter, the serum testosterone values are low in both sexes until adolescence (Forest 1974).

AGE-RELATED CHANGES AND SEXUAL DIMORPHIC PATTERNS IN NORMAL GROWTH: CHILDHOOD

The remaining preschool years (1 to 4 years) may be called the years of early childhood. From the standpoint of somatic growth, they are the years of developmental canalization. There is a slow and regular increase in most of the dimensions. Height velocities slow to 5 to 6 cm/year and weight velocities slow to 1.9 to 2.8 kg/year in pre-adolescent childhood. In years 1 through 4, growth in weight and length approach nearly a linear rate of increase as indicated by distance curves.

Percentage differences between length and weight at 1 year and height and weight at 4 years of age indicate that white females increase in length substantially more than white males although they weigh less. However, black males and females have approximately the same linear growth, but females weigh substantially less. Other cross-cultural work as presented in Table 11.5 indicates that in general children for this age group show sexual dimorphic trends in both length and weight. Females grow more rapidly in length but tend to weigh less than males. In spite of this basic pattern of change,

TABLE 11.5

Percentage Differences Between Length and Weight at One and Height and Weight at Four Years of Age from Various Studies.

	Length		Weight	
	Male	Female	Male	Female
Cross-sectional				
U.S.A. (white)	26.6	31.4	47.5	42.4
U.S.A. (black)	29.5	29.5	61.6	53.1
Indian	29.9	30.3	60.7	65.4
Mixed longitudinal				
U.S.A. (Denver)	29.2	31.2	54.4	61.3
U.K.	27.9	28.9	50.9	55.0
Guatemala	30.9	32.8	65.8	72.2

Source: Data compiled from Abraham et al. (1975); Indian Council of Medical Research (1972); Hansman (1970); Tanner et al. (1966a, b); and Yarbrough et al. (1975).

a considerable degree of independence exists in the growth of individuals from year to year. Increments of growth show low to moderate correlations within individuals between various age periods. The consistency of changes seems to be less pronounced in females than in males, with correlations of 0.37 for males and 0.16 for females for weight at birth and 5 years of age (Tanner et al. 1956). Coefficients of correlation for length for the same age groups were 0.42 for males and 0.34 for females (Tanner et al. 1956).

The relationship between increases in the dimensions of one part of the body in relation to the growth of the whole organism or other parts is called "allometry." In infants, the allometric growth is a steady change in various proportions of the body resulting in the legs becoming longer relative to the breadth and overall size of the head. These changes transform the "chunky" physique of the newborn into the more elongated physique of the child. This trend continues throughout the years of childhood.

Prior to the age of 5 years, proportional limb length is slightly greater for girls than for boys, although the average actual limb lengths may be the same because of slightly greater height for boys. The sitting height/height index is nearly the same for males and females until about 11 years of age when it becomes higher in females (Malina 1975).

Between the ages of 5 and 11 years, the proportion of limb length of the sexes is approximately the same. The average actual limb length is slightly greater for boys than for girls which gives the former a mechanical advantage in the performance by most physical skills. In addition, sex differences in the structure of the pelvis and the angle of the insertion of the head of the femur into the pelvis contribute to observed sex differences in running and jumping, particularly at adolescence. After 11 years of age, the proportional limb length becomes greater for boys than for girls. This factor together with the increment in height that occurs in boys in adolescence gives the adult male a very decided advantage over the female in the performance of leverage-related physical activities. Furthermore, the greater increase in shoulder width for boys after 11 years in comparison with the reduction in shoulder breadth for girls accentuates the sex differences in the arc of shoulder-arm action.

Triceps skinfold thickness in male and female children retains the sexual dimorphic pattern seen at birth. Males tend to have smaller skinfold dimensions and, therefore, less body fat than females. These comparisons are shown in Table 11.3. After 6 weeks of age, these sex differences become increased for the subscapular skinfold.

Overt changes in body proportion reflect proportional changes in body tissues with increasing years. Before 6 years of age, subcutaneous tissue measurements show a similar pattern for both sexes. Sex differences in mean gain of various body tissues during the circumpubertal period result in different proportions in bone, muscle, and fat for adolescent and adult males and females. The mean gain in subcutaneous fat in girls is generally higher and occurs over a longer duration than the average increase in boys. The mean gains in the breadth of bone and muscle in girls decline slightly from 6 to 9 years, after which there is a sharp increase through the 12th year with a gradual decline until the 15th year. On the other hand, the profile of mean tissue gains for boys indicates a fairly consistent gain from 6 to 11 years which marks the onset of a period of rapid gain extending through the 15th year followed by a year of less marked increase in bone and muscle.

In summary, early childhood is still a phase of rapid growth despite declining velocities. In middle childhood there is a constant gain in height and weight with relatively minor sex differences in growth and developmental patterns. Males, however, do retain their height and weight advantages until the chronologically earlier adolescent growth spurt of females.

AGE-RELATED CHANGES AND SEXUAL DIMORPHIC PATTERNS IN NORMAL GROWTH: ADOLESCENCE

Adolescence is the period of sex-hormone induced shifting growth. The amount of gonadotropin, especially luteinizing hormone, rises gradually over a period of years. This results in a slow increase in the levels of sex hormones which signal the start of adolescence. The acceleration in linear growth gradually increases with a peak growth velocity about 2 to 3 years after the advent of adolescence. Great variability is observed in the pace of maturation between males and females during adolescence. There are also great individual differences in the pace of growth and development among children of the same chronologic age.

The female matures more rapidly than the male throughout childhood and begins adolescence 2 years earlier at the average age of 11 to 12 years. Adrenal androgens are responsible for some of the growth changes. However, ovarian estrogen produces the most dramatic effects. The early signs are estrinization of the vaginal mucosa and the development of breasts, nipples, and areola. Pubic hair and subsequently axillary hair develop. The hips widen and body fat is maintained or enhanced. The peak height velocity occurs at the average age of 12.1 years; menarche occurs at approximately 13 years, after which there may be continued slow growth to the age of 17 years (Smith 1977).

Menarche, unlike some of these other events, is related to skeletal maturation. Approximately 85 percent of the females had bone ages between 13 and 14 years when they experienced their first menses (Marshall 1978).

Most females reached 95 percent of their mature height at ages close to 13 years and at the peak of the adolescent growth spurt. At this time bone age varies between 10 and 15 years. This implies that bone age is to some extent a measure of the percentage of the child's growth that has been completed; however, all girls do not attain the peak of the adolescent spurt when they have completed the same proportion of their total growth or skeletal maturation.

The male matures more slowly than the female and the rate of growth and maturation is less predictable. Thus, there is greater variability in the male in the age at which adolescence begins in its progression. The onset is heralded by gonadotropin-induced enlargement of the testes at about 9 to 12 years of age. Testosterone, a potent androgen, initiates skin changes such as acne, increased sweating response, and the development of pubic and facial hair. Linear growth accelerates reaching a peak average growth velocity of 10.3 cm at 14.1 years (Marshall and Tanner 1974). Shoulder breadth is increased and facial and bone structure is enlarged. The vocal cartilage extends and the voice deepens. The number and strength of muscle cells are almost doubled, which results in improved coordination and relative decrease in the amount of adipose tissue. Most linear growth has been achieved by the age of 18 years, with an average total of 1 cm in further growth taking place between 18 and 21 years. Cessation of linear growth occurs first in the distal parts (the hands and feet), then in the legs, the trunk, and the shoulder girdle. Skeletal ages are significantly less variable than chronological ages when males reach 95 percent of their final stature.

If the statures of a typical male and female are measured repeatedly through childhood and the measurements plotted by age, curves similar to those presented in Figure 11.3 are obtained. The female's curve begins to rise more steeply at about age 11 and the male's at about 13. This inflection represents the adolescent spurt at the average age for their sex.

Velocity curves measure the speed of growth in centimeters per year plotted against age. The absolute value of peak height velocity varies from child to child. Marshall and Tanner (1969, 1970) found a mean value of 10.3 cm/year with a standard deviation of 1.54 cm/year in 49 healthy males measured each month by a skilled observer. The corresponding velocity for 41 females in the same study was 9.0 cm/year with a standard deviation of 1.03 cm/year. When the

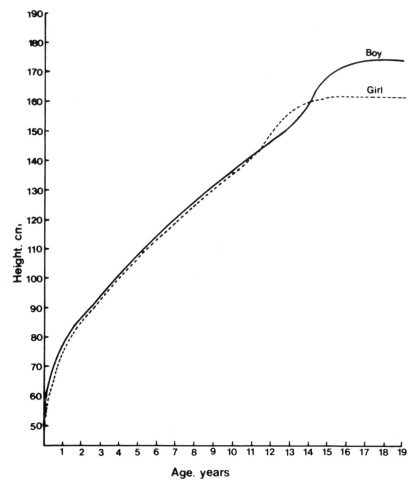

Figure 11.3. Height at different ages of a hypothetical boy and girl of the same birth length who grew at the mean rate and experienced the adolescent growth spurt at the mean age for their sex. Each finally reached the adult mean stature. Redrawn from Tanner et al. (1966).

velocity is calculated over a whole year centered on the peak height velocity, that is 6 months before and 6 months after the PHV, the average is 9.5 cm/year for males and 8.4 cm/year for females. The velocity of growth in both sexes just before the adolescent spurt begins is about 5 cm/year. During the year in which a male obtains his peak height velocity he usually gains between 7 and 12 cm in stature while a female gains between 6 and 11 cm. The maximum growth velocity is usually greater in children who reach their peak at an early age than those who do so later. Correlation between peak height velocity and age at which it occurs is 0.45 (Marshall 1978).

In females studied by Marshall and Tanner (1969) the mean age at peak height velocity was 12.14 ± 0.14 years with a standard deviation of 0.88 years. The corresponding age for males was 14.06 ± 0.13 years with a standard deviation of 0.92 years. These growth velocities differences are presented in Figure 11.4.

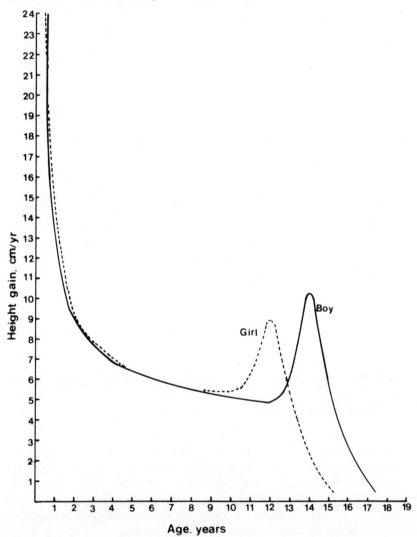

Figure 11.4. Growth velocity, in centimeters per year, at different ages. Redrawn from Tanner et al. (1966).

At puberty, the females tend to become taller than males. The sex differences factor which arises from the earlier adolescent spurt in females is of sufficient magnitude to make the short female taller than the short male but no taller than the average or tall male (Marshall 1978). The average female becomes taller than the average male, but only the tall female is taller than the 97th-percentile male. A calculation based on the data of Tanner et al. (1966a,b) shows that at 13.9 years, 7 percent of the females who reached PHV at the average age are taller than 13-year-old males who are at the 97th percentile and who also reach PHV at the average age for their sex. Males have, on the average, about 2 more years of preadolescent growth than females and are therefore some 10 cm taller when they begin their adolescent spurts than females who are of the corresponding age.

In practical terms, the difference is most important to the tall female and the small male because of the psychosocial implications of stature. The tall female may be taller than all her male peers and may become concerned that she could become an abnormally tall woman. Similarly, a small boy finds that he is at a disadvantage with larger peers and may be shorter than all of the girls for his age.

Growth during the adolescent spurt occurs in all skeletal dimensions. However, the increase in growth rate is not uniform throughout the skeleton. The spurt in stature, therefore, is initially due to a greater increase in the length of the legs than the trunk. Also, the spurt does not begin simultaneously in all parts of the body. For example, leg length reaches its peak growth velocity 6 months before the trunk (Marshall 1977). The foot attains its maximum size before any other region of the body with the possible exception of the head. In the anterior limbs, the arms appears to be of a similar gradient to that of the leg so that the forearm reaches its peak velocity about 6 months before the upper arm. The spurt in the trunk length is greater than that of the legs so peak height velocity is reached when the sum of the velocities of the two segments is maximal (Marshall 1977). The longer period of preadolescent growth in males is also largely responsible for the relatively longer leg length in males than in females. That is, men's legs are longer than women's in relation to the length of the trunk because the legs grow relatively faster than the trunk immediately before adolescence.

As a consequence of the earlier adolescence of females, their relatively shorter legs, and the prolonged growth of males, the sitting height/ height ratio (an index of the contribution of the trunk and legs to total height) becomes slightly higher in girls with the onset of the adolescent spurt and remains higher throughout the teenage years into adulthood. This ratio, of course, indicates relatively shorter legs in girls, or, alternately, relatively longer trunks. For equal stature, girls have shorter legs.

Sexual dimorphism in the shoulder and hip breadths appears because females have a larger adolescent spurt in hip width than males in relationship to statural increase. However, in absolute terms, the increase is no greater for females' hips than those of males (Figures 11.5 and 11.6). The girls' spurt in other dimensions is considerably less than that of the hips. Even before puberty, males have wider shoulders than females and this difference increases markedly at adolescence (Marshall 1978, Tanner 1962).

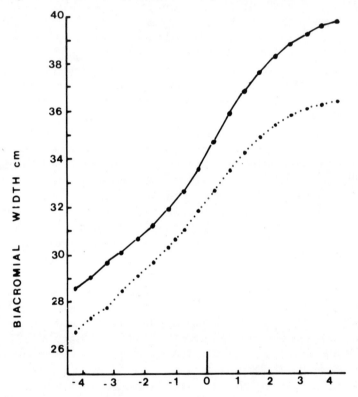

PEAK HEIGHT VELOCITY

Figure 11.5.   Growth in width of shoulders in girls and boys. In order to eliminate the difference in age at which the adolescent spurt occurs in the two sexes, the measurements have been plotted against a scale of years before and after peak height velocity. (Reprinted with permission from Plenum Publishing Corporation: Falkner, F. and J. M. Tanner [editors]. 1978. *Human Growth, Vol. 2. Postnatal Growth.*)

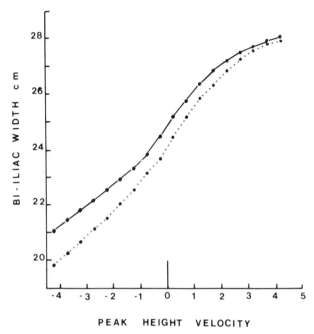

PEAK   HEIGHT   VELOCITY

Figure 11.6. Growth in width of hips in girls and boys. In order to eliminate the difference in age at which the adolescent spurt occurs in the two sexes, the measurements have been plotted against a scale of years before and after peak height velocity. (Reprinted with permission from Plenum Publishing Corporation: Falkner, F. and J. M. Tanner [editors]. 1978. *Human Growth, Vol. 2. Postnatal Growth.*)

As a consequence of these changes, in adulthood males are taller and heavier, have relatively longer legs, narrower hips and broader shoulders, and have less subcutaneous fat and more muscle and bone (i.e., greater lean body mass) than females. These sex differences in body form are primarily due to the effects of androgens acting upon the individual's preadolescent physique.

The cranium exhibits a pattern of postnatal growth different from the rest of the body. It approaches adult size quite early. However, certain changes do occur at adolescence. Females show more increases in soft tissue while males show more growth in the width of the cranial cavity (Hauspie 1980). The forward growth of the forehead at adolescence is due mainly to development of the brow ridges and frontal sinuses. This is more pronounced in males than in females. The middle and posterior cranial fossae do enlarge to some extent while the cranial base increases in length and is lowered.

The height of the cranium increases slowly in later childhood by about 2 to 3 mm between the ages of 5 and 7 in most children. Nevertheless, a clear adolescent spurt in this dimension has been observed in more than 50 percent of individuals studied longitudinally. The total height of the face increases rapidly during the first 2 or 3 years of life and then its growth slows down like that of the cranium. Yet, there is a definite spurt of growth at adolesence. This growth is greater in boys than in girls (Marshall 1977).

The growth of the whole naso-maxillary complex is directed in a forward and downward direction. Growth in height and length of the naso-maxillary complex is largely dependent upon alveolar growth in late childhood. Palatal width is finally fixed by the closure of the sagittal suture around the fifth year of age. Bizygomatic width increases up to the age of about 17 years.

Mandibular growth also continues to a late age, thereby showing sexual dimorphism in its final adult size. The greatest spurt is in the length and height of the mandible where 25 percent of the total growth of the ramus is completed between the ages of 12 and 20. As a result of this, the jaw becomes considerably longer in relationship to the front of the face and projects more prominently. These changes are much more marked in males than in females. The adolescent spurt does not, however, complete the growth of the chin, as further apposition of bone at the mandibular symphysis occurs usually between 15 and 23 years of age (Marshall 1977).

During adolescence, males show an absolute increase in muscle tissue and lean body mass and a small increase in fat. In contrast, females show an absolute increase in adipose tissue and/or decrease in the relative lean body mass compared to the fat mass. The sum of the triceps and subscapular skinfold measurements decreases in childhood. An increase in subcutaneous fat for females begins about 7 years of age and continues to about 17 years of age although skinfold measurements may continue to rise during adulthood. This growth in soft tissues corresponds to the weight velocity curves. Males show a more dramatic decrease until age 9 to 10 years, then an abrupt preadolescent increase followed by a slower increase and ending with lower skinfold measurements then females (Tanner and Whitehouse 1975).

Adulthood is the period of continued change. The epiphyses of leg bones become ossified and cease their linear growth by about 16 years in girls and 18 years in boys. There is about a 2 percent increase in length into the mid-20s. From 30 to 35 years, stature remains stable while adiposity increases. Thereafter, there is an insidious decrease in stature. The breadth of the bones in the face and the skull and the metacarpals may increase, however, even into the 60s and the ears may continue to lengthen into the 80s (Susanne 1980).

SEXUAL DIMORPHIC PATTERNS IN GROWTH DISORDERS

Those patients with aberrant growth patterns may be divided into predominantly two categories on the basis of (1) the age of onset of abnormal growth: pre- or postnatal; and (2) the cause: either primary, intrinsic to the skeletal cells, or secondary or extrinsic to these cells. Normal variants and abnormal variants of growth and development occurring prenatally and postnatally are listed in Tables 11.6, 11.7 and 11.8. In general, those factors contributing to the etiology of abnormal linear growth and/or weight gain do not affect the two sexes differentially.

Two etiological conditions produce sexually dimorphic differences in growth patterns. These are the chromosomal abnormalities and endocrinopathies.

To date, there are no effective modes of therapy to increase the stature of individuals with primary cellular growth deficiency disorders, if deficient growth has not been shown to be a consequence of a known endocrine disorder (Smith 1977). The precise reason or reasons for the growth deficiency in most conditions are unknown.

Secondary prenatal growth deficiencies are due to exogenous causes outside the skeletal system. These causes may be uterine crowding, as occurs with twins, or more commonly, maternal causes such as malnutrition, toxemia, hypertensive renal disease, cardiac disease, alcohol intake, or heavy cigarette smoking. Weight is affected relatively more than length. Very often, small birth weight infants will demonstrate catch-up growth within the first few weeks and months of life. Rapid catch-up growth within the first 3 to 6 postnatal months is a favorable sign for subsequent normal health and growth.

Postnatal onset growth deficiency involves primary growth deficiency related to chromosomal and genetic abnormalities and secondary postnatal onset growth deficiency related to a variety of

TABLE 11.6
Classification of Growth Deficiency: Normal Variants.

Features	Familial Short Stature	Familial Slow Maturation
Onset of growth deficiency	Postnatal	Postnatal (early childhood)
Rate of maturation	Normal	Slow
Family history	Short stature	Slow maturation
Final stature	Short	Normal limits
Therapy to increase eventual stature	None	None

Source: Adapted from Smith (1977, p. 64).

TABLE 11.7
Classification of Growth Deficiency: Abnormal Growth.

Features	Primary Skeletal Growth Deficiency	Secondary Growth Deficiency	
		Prenatal Onset	Postnatal Onset
Onset of growth deficiency	Usually prenatal	—	—
Rate of maturation	Variable, usually normal	Variable, slow to normal	Usually slow
Malproportion	Frequent	Variable	Unusual, except in rickets
Associated anomalies	Frequent	Variable	Unusual, except causative anomaly
General modes of etiology	Chromosomal abnormalities Mutant gene disorders, including osteochondro-dysplasias Syndromes of unknown etiology	Crowding (twins, etc.) Maternal: 1. Small mother 2. Low socioeconomic status 3. Malnutrition	1. Nutritional deficiency, neglect, poor absorption 2. Mental deficiency 3. Cardiac defect 4. Renal dysfunction 5. Respiratory insufficiency

	May or may not show post-natal catch-up growth	Specific treatment yields catch-up growth
	4. Hypertension	6. Growth hormone deficiency
	5. Toxemia	7. Thyroid hormone deficiency
	6. Renal disease	8. Still's disease
	7. Heart disease	9. Metabolic disorders
	8. Cigarette smoking	
	9. Heroin addiction	
	10. Ethanol intake	
	11. Hydantoin therapy	
	12. Warfarin therapy	
	13. Rubella	
	14. Cytomegalic inclusion disease	
	15. Toxoplasmosis	
	16. Syphilis	

Therapy to increase eventual stature	None to date		

Source: Adapted from Smith (1977, p. 64).

other factors outlined in Table 11.7. In general, these factors include malnutrition, deprivation syndromes, cardiac defects, respiratory insufficiency, renal dysfunction, and a host of endocrinological disorders. When the causes of the secondary postnatal onset growth deficiency have been recognized and corrected, there may be an amazing amount of catch-up growth. This dramatically emphasizes the fact that there is no primary growth disorder in the skeletal system. The extent of catch-up growth varies in accordance with the age of onset, the duration, the nature of the growth problem, and with the adequacy of therapy.

In the following sections, growth disorders will be examined with regard to time of onset and etiology. Emphasis will be placed on sexual dimorphic patterns in abnormal growth and development.

Growth Deficiency

The most common disorder of growth is short stature. Short stature may be due to: (1) normal (familial) shortness, (2) growth delay, (3) chromosomal abnormality, (4) intrauterine maldevelopment, (5) endocrine gland disorders, (6) cartilage and bone disorders, (7) nutritional disorders, (8) general diseases of the kidney, heart, etc., and (9) psychological causes.

Normal (familial) shortness.   A child is considered short if he or she is below the third percentile of appropriate standards. Based on parental heights the adult stature of the child may be estimated by a number of techniques (i.e., Bayley-Pinneau tables) (Roche 1980). Osseous maturation is equal to chronologic age in normal genetic shortness. There is no effective treatment for genetic short stature. Genetically short people secrete no less growth hormone than do tall people. Because of social norms, short stature in males will have more profound sociopsychological impact than for females. The physician should be aware of these dimorphic role differences that are influenced by stature.   Many physicians or counselors are wise enough to indicate that short stature can be an advantage.

Growth delay.   Growth delay is also seen frequently by physicians. Growth delay is not necessarily abnormal and may simply be a reflection of familial trends. Delays of up to 2 years in peak height velocity may be perfectly normal, but all children with delayed growth should be assessed through techniques used to estimate bone age. Both height age and bone age are less than chronological age in familial delayed maturation.

The child at birth is usually normal. The onset of slow growth is usually evident by 2 to 3 years of age. Smaller size is generally obvious by school age. The slow maturer is primarily slow in his or her rate of biological aging. Growth is prolonged and the advent of adolescence and final height attainment are late. This prolonged period of growth generally results in a final height that is within the normal range. Slow maturing girls tend to have a youthful body build, and slow maturing boys are often slender hipped and long legged. The psychologic impact of slow maturation tends to be greater in boys. The effect becomes increasingly greater as their peers begin to grow and they remain smaller.

Management of familial slow maturation may involve the administration of anabolic steroids if psychosocial adjustment and physical status necessitate therapy. In general, the purpose of hormonal administration is to accelerate growth and virilization so that the child will begin to adjust better to his peers.

Testosterone is effective in accelerating growth, particularly in boys. Unfortunately, it frequently accelerates bone age to a greater relative degree than height with the consequence of enhanced maturation but short adult stature. There are a number of drugs related to testosterone (i.e., oxandralone) whose action is less severe on bone age and sex characteristics than on the height spurt. These children have growth spurts that are dissimilar from those of children with a growth hormone deficiency, or chromosomal abnormality.

Chromosomal abnormalities. The two most common chromosome abnormalities producing short stature are Trisomy 21 or Down's syndrome and Turner's syndrome with the sex chromosome complement of a single X. Down's syndrome produces short stature in both sexes.

In Turner's syndrome, the child is phenotypically female. The child is a girl of short stature with some special physical peculiarity—such as puffy hands, webbing of the neck, broad chest, small nipples and characteristic facies, and low birth weight ($\overline{X}$ = 2.9 kg) (Polani 1974; Smith 1977). A Turner's syndrome child has a bone age that is delayed only slightly or not at all until the time of puberty. Because the child lacks functional ovaries, no pubertal development of the breasts takes place and there is no adolescent growth spurt. No treatment, including estrogen, is effective in markedly increasing height in Turner's syndrome though some male sex hormone-like preparations (oxandralone) and high doses of growth hormone have been moderately successful. The cause of short stature in Turner's syndrome females remains obscure. Growth hormone secretion is normal. The final height averages about 140 cm, though it depends upon the height of the parents since parental height correlations are maintained (Tanner 1978). Children with the mosaic Turner syndrome, that is, some cells carrying XO and others a full XX complement, also show the lack of sexual development and decreased stature. Males with sex chromosome abnormalities usually show excessive growth.

Intrauterine maldevelopment. Maldevelopment in utero may be due to a fault in the fertilized ovum, a fault in the placenta that brings less food and oxygen to the fetus, or to disease or starvation of the mother. Maldevelopment causes a restriction of growth and hence leads to small size at birth. The majority of small-for-date infants, particularly those born at term, develop within the normal height and weight centiles. Yet, they often do not fulfill their genetic potential and therefore appear somewhat small for their parents' heights. Their average centile is about 30th. Many of these children remain short, have diminished subcutaneous fat, and have a characteristic facial appearance. The face is often triangular with large eyes and a long lower jaw. The ears may be set low on the head and tend to stick out, the bridge of the nose is usually depressed, and the mouth turned down. Some of these children have marked asymmetry of the limbs or body with one arm or leg longer than the other or one side of the face or chest more developed. These conditions constitute a specific syndrome known as the Silver-Russell syndrome (Smith 1977). Mental developmental is usually normal.

Some of the children with relatively low birth weight and subsequent short stature have rare and more specific syndromes of maldevelopment, such as Prader-Willi syndrome. More recently, there has been an acknowledgment of an increase in the number of small children born with fetal alcohol syndrome as the result of maternal ingestion of alcohol.

In general, males are affected more severely than females by various factors, such as malnutrition, that are mediated through the mother. However, a study conducted by Davies (as reported in Smith 1977) indicates that females are more severely affected than males by heavy smoking (15 or more cigarettes per day) of mothers. Head circumference and length in particular are affected. Weight is not affected to the same extent. These comparisons are shown in Figure 11.7. The offspring of heavy smokers weighed 0.3 kg less and were 0.7 cm shorter at birth than those of nonsmoking women. The frequency of premature births is four times higher in women who smoke more than 30 cigarettes a day than in nonsmokers.

Endocrine gland disorders. A number of endocrinologic disorders affecting linear growth show sexually diferentiated patterns. The two chief endocrine disorders that cause short stature are growth hormone deficiency and thyroid deficiency. A third cause is disease of the adrenals or other glands leading to precocious puberty. In this case, the child grows rapidly and develops changes of puberty pathologically early. Growth stops very early and short stature results.

Growth hormone releasing factor is produced in the hypothalamus and stimulates the release of pituitary growth hormone by the anterior pituitary. There is an interdependency between the effects of pituitary growth hormone and somatomedin and the effects of thyroxin, insulin, and testosterone in terms of growth. Deficiencies in the hypothalamus-anterior-pituitary-somatomedin chain can give rise to a similar clinical phenotype most commonly thought of as hypopituitarism. Hypopituitarism a rare cause of growth deficiency estimated to have a frequency of 1: 30,000 individuals (Smith 1977). The most common cause is idiopathic hypopituitarism and it affects males in an excess of 2.5:1. Decreased hypothalamic function is probably the cause of deficient growth more commonly than is primary pituitary insufficiency.

About one-third of the cases of growth hormone deficiency are due to malformations of the central nervous system. The prevalence of craniopharyngioma or other tumors is higher in growth hormone deficient girls than boys (Marshall 1977). There is evidence of an inherited predisposition in some cases with about 3 to 5 percent of the index cases having brothers and sisters with the disorder. In a few families, one of the parents is affected (Marshall 1977).

Genetically determined instances of hypopituitarism have also been defined. These include an autosomal recessive anterior pituitary deficiency disorder and both an autosomal recessive and an autosomal dominant type of isolated growth hormone deficiency.

Children with hypopituitarism are simply small with normal skeletal proportions, facial appearance, and intelligence. They are usually fat although this condition diminishes with treatment. They also have delayed bone age. The diagnosis is confirmed by a lack of growth hormone production in response to a stimulation test. Deficiency in growth hormone may be complicated by deficiencies in other pituitary hormones. In most cases, growth hormone alone is involved, but commonly associated deficiencies occur in thyroid stimulating hormone, the gonadotrophins, and ACTH.

The treatment of growth hormone deficiency has been a major success of pediatrics since the first patient was given growth hormone by Rabin in 1958 in Boston (Tanner 1978). When treatment is started at a reasonably early age, at least before age 6, the results are usually excellent. Catch-up growth occurs on initial treatment and thereafter

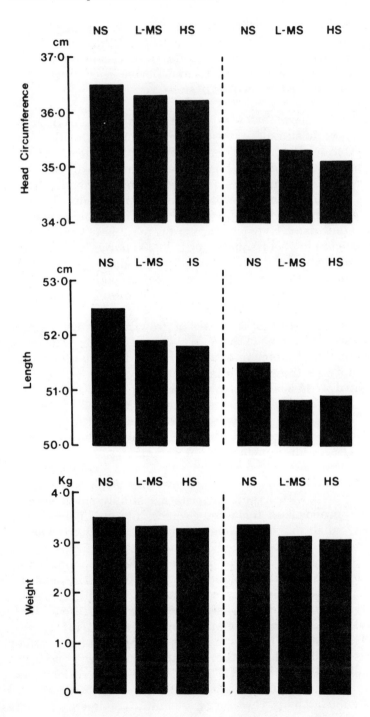

normal growth is maintained. Other hormone replacement therapy may also be needed.

Congenital hypothyroidism due to a partial or complete absence of the development of the thyroid gland occurs in about 1:7000 newborns and is more likely to occur in females—about 79 percent of the time. Less commonly, it is due to a genetically determined defect in the biosynthesis of thyroid hormones. A major concern in children with congential hypothyroidism is brain development. About 40 percent of the athyrotic hypothyroid babies treated with thyroid replacement therapy before 3 months of age eventually develop IQs above 90 (Smith 1977). The infant who is hypothyroid in utero does not usually manifest growth deficiencies until after birth. In fact, they tend to be larger than average at birth. This is the consequence of a longer than usual period of gestation.

Acquired hypothyroidism has an etiology which is rarely known. It is usually marked by a history of normal growth and development followed by a striking deceleration in linear growth even to the point of cessation of growth. Depending upon the degree of hypothyroidism there may be a lag in osseous and dental maturation. Again, thyroxin replacement will usually result in a normal developmental sequence for the child.

Insulin deficiency may lead to growth failure as the result of persistent catabolism. Overinsulinization leading to a chronic rebound state with excess cortisol can result in Cushingoid obesity and delayed maturation. Insulin deficiency may be accompanied by other hormone deficiencies such as thyroid deficiency, thereby compounding the growth disorders. In diabetic mothers, fetal growth is enhanced, producing large and fat babies (Smith 1977).

Sex steroid deficiency in androgen and estrogen production, except when they are part of a genetic syndrome, does not typically produce growth problems until adolescence. The lack of an adolescent growth spurt and a delay in sexual maturation are commonly associated with these deficiencies.

Cartilage and bone disorders. There are a large number of bone disorders that affect growth. They tend to be rare and usually are inherited. The most common is achondroplasia. Achondroplastic

Figure 11.7. Impact of maternal cigarette smoking on head circumference, length, and weight of boys (left of dashed line) and girls (right of dashed lines) in a study of 709 full-term infants. NS = nonsmokers; L = light to moderate smokers (under 15 cigarettes a day); and HS = heavy smokers (15 or more a day). (From Davies, D. P., Department of Child Health, Leicester Poly-Infirmary, Leicester, England [Smith 1977].)

dwarfs have short upper arms and thighs, normal length torso, large head, and characteristic face with depressed nasal bridge, small nose, and large forehead. They are of normal intelligence and health. Achondroplasia is inherited as an autosomal dominant allele although 80 to 85 percent of cases arise through mutation. Because of the nature of inheritance, the proportion of children afflicted is equally divided between males and females. There is no effective treatment at present.

A similar but less marked syndrome is hypochrondroplasia. In this condition also, only the limbs are short and the legs are responsible for the short stature. However, the face is normal. This disorder is also inherited as a dominant gene different from the achondroplasia gene.

Although most inherited bone and cartilage growth deficiencies are seen in both sexes, there are certain X-linked recessive syndromes, for example, spondyloepiphyseal dysplasia, that afflict more males than females. Children with this disorder show onset of growth deceleraton in mid-childhood.

In addition to the above syndromes, linear growth may be affected by a number of inborn errors of metabolism involving the deposition of minerals or the mobilization of protein and carbohydrate stores. One disease that shows sexual differences in prevalence is vitamin D-resistant rickets. This form of rickets is an X-linked recessive disorder that causes hypophosphatemic rickets with growth deficiency. Treatment is usually accomplished with high doses of Vitamin D of 50,000 or more units per day and phosphate. This disease affects males in significantly greater numbers than females.

In contrast to the above disorders, collagen-vascular diseases, such as lupus and rheumatoid arthritis, appear more frequently among females than males. These diseases are often accompanied by growth deficiency.

Nutritional disorders. The most frequent type of secondary or extrinsic growth deficiency disorder occurring postnatally is environmentally induced malnutrition. In many developing countries a larger proportion of malnutrition children are female; however, the most severely malnourished are male. As noted above, Stini (1972, 1975) has shown that females are better able to buffer the effects of malnutrition than males. Males exhibit a greater reduction in stature and lean body mass under conditions of nutritional stress.

Prolonged malabsorption of food stunts growth, as in the case of starvation. The most common disorder is coeliac disease. Coeliac disease is due to abnormal reaction of gut cells to glutens that are found primarily in wheat flour and flour-based foods. The treatment is a gluten-free diet.

Infants with diencephalic syndrome usually present with the problem of growth deficiency in terms of weight loss often to the point of emaciation. Most cases are due to a brain tumor in the diencephalon in the floor of the third ventrical. This particular syndrome occurs twice as often in boys as in girls. The onset of signs in 92 percent of the cases is during the first year of life, most often in the first 6 months. Poor weight gain with a loss of subcutaneous adipose tissue is a major feature that has not been explained on the basis of caloric deficiency. Despite the weight loss, linear growth is often at a normal, or even accelerated rate. Bone age is usually normal (Fishman and Peake 1970). Treatment may involve surgical removal of the tumor or radiotherapy. The course is variable and some patients survive many years.

General diseases of the kidney, heart, and other organs. A number of chronic general diseases cause short stature for reasons that are not clear. Those conditions of the heart and lungs that cause some degree of hypoxia to the tissues can lead to derangements in cellular metabolism resulting in delayed growth and maturation. However, heart lesions do not stunt growth. These diseases and teratologies do not show sex-specific prevalence patterns.

Psychological causes. Psychosocial stress may cause short stature in certain children. Such children may react by shutting off growth hormone secretion. Battered children or battered babies often show stunted growth. More frequently a child may have a psychogenic eating disorder; he or she may eat voraciously sometimes and not at all at others. Away from the deleterious home environment, these children exhibit amazing catch-up growth.

Anorexia nervosa is a disorder of eating that appears primarily as a psychiatric disorder and is most common in adolescent girls who have voluntarily limited their caloric intake. They become underweight to the point of being cachectic in appearance and weak. They alternate between hyperactivity and lethargy. Management is difficult and long-term efforts are required.

Growth Excess

The great majority of large children represent two variants of normal: (1) familial tall stature, and 2) familial rapid maturation. Those children with organic aberrations are relatively few and may be divided into two categories on the basis of the age of onset of rapid growth: prenatal or postnatal, and the cause: primary or intrinsic to the skeletal system, or secondary or extrinsic to the skeletal system.

The approach to the evaluation and the categorization of children with unusually tall stature is similar to that for growth deficiencies. Careful scrutiny for signs of sexual precocity may be especially important in the child with excess growth.

Normal (familial) tall stature. The normal variant of familial tall stature and familial rapid maturation represent the polygenically determined upper extremes of normal growth. Both variants give rise to large children for their chronlogical ages, but only familial tall stature generally results in tall adults. The major differences between these two categories are summarized in Table 11.8.

The category of familial tall stature includes those children who mature at a normal rate and reach adolescence and tall adult stature at the usual age. The family history generally reveals this to be a familial tendency. There are usually no associated problems other than the psychological problem of being unduly taller than one's peers. However, the psychosocial consequences can be quite serious and even devastating to the very tall adolescent girl.

In extreme cases the administration of sex hormones at a relatively early age will accelerate osseous maturation and bring about epiphyseal ossification before there has been an opportunity for full linear growth. In these children a predicted adult height should be determined from standards such as those listed in the Bayley-Pinneau tables. Unfortunately, parents often do not seek help for their children until they are close to the final height attainment. However, the ideal time to begin the early accelerated adolescence is between 9 and 13 years of age for females.

Advanced maturation. In the case of familial rapid maturation, the individual tends to be large as a child. The large child with a normal

TABLE 11.8
Large Size in Childhood: Normal Variants.

	Familial Tall Stature	Familial Rapid Maturation
Parental stature	Tall	Average
Onset of rapid growth	Infancy	Infancy
Facial appearance and bone age in childhood	Normal	Advanced
Onset of adolescence	Normal	Early
Final height attainment	Usual age	Early age
Adult stature	Tall	Average

Source: Smith (1977, p. 122).

pace of maturation will most likely become a tall adult. If, however, the child's bone age is advanced to the same degree as his or her height age, he or she will probably have a somewhat early adolescence and will achieve average adult stature, but at an early age. If the large child has osseous maturation accelerated beyond that expected for height age, he or she will most likely achieve final height attainment earlier than usual, but his or her adult height may be relatively short.

Rapid maturers tend to be relatively stocky in build. The more mature male often assumes leadership roles among his peers. His larger size and increased muscle strength also give him early advantages in athletics. The rapidly maturing female may not be as happy about her early maturation and large size and this may create some psychosocial problems for her during adolescence.

Chromosomal abnormalities. Males with Klinefelter's syndrome (XXY) and supermales (XYY) often show testicular agenesis or hypogonadism and consequent delayed maturation. These males are usually tall and have long legs. The birth weights of XXY infants ($\overline{X}$ = 3.15 kg) and XYY infants ($\overline{X}$ = 3.36 kg) are greater than those of infants with other chromosomal abnormalities (Polani 1974).

Schiebler and co-workers (1974) found the average XXY adult stature to be 180 cm (5'11") as compared to 174.1 cm for their normal adult brothers. The excess 6 cm in stature was accounted for by excess leg length. The relatively long legs and the diminished upper and lower segment ratio are present prior to adolescence in boys with XXY syndrome. Schiebler et al. (1974) have taken this as evidence of an allometric growth pattern due to a basic effect of the XXY genetic imbalance and not secondary to hypogonadism. Another possibility, however, is that a small amount of testosterone production in the preadolescent years plays a role in the growth of the legs and that the eunuchoid build at adolescence is the result of testosterone deficiency in childhood. Testosterone replacement therapy appropriate for age will prevent excessive stature and leg length (Smith 1977).

Intrauterine maldevelopment. Growth excess of prenatal onset includes "large for gestational age" babies and is sometimes referred to as "macrosomia." As with the prenatal onset growth deficiency disorders, there are often associated anomalies with or without disharmonic, malproportionate or asymmetric growth (Smith 1977). There are a number of rare primary prenatal onset growth disorders. More common, however, is the secondary prenatal onset growth excess related to maternal diabetes mellitus. These children, in particular, have a high birth weight and are large and fat but may have immature organ development.

Endocrine gland disorders. Many endocrinopathies lead to excessive growth and/or accelerated maturation. The condition of precocious gonadotropin-induced adolescence or precocious puberty is presumably due to an aberrant early stimulus from the hypothalamus causing an early onset of otherwise normal adolescence. This condition is most commonly idiopathic, although a variety of hypothalamic lesions including tumors may cause precocious puberty. Usually the serum or urinary levels of testosterone, estrogen, and gonadotropins are at normal levels in relation to sexual adolescent development. More females than males are affected. However, sexual precocity, particularly in males, is often familial.

With precocious puberty, linear growth is accelerated and there is rapid advancement of osseous maturation. The patient becomes a large, mature-looking child who is still immature in his or her psychosocial development. When the onset of precocious puberty is during the first few years, boys show a marked growth spurt then begin slowing down in growth by 6 years of age. Girls have less of a growth spurt and slowing of growth is evident by about 8 years. Final height is attained early and the adult stature, therefore, is relatively short (Smith 1977). Werder (1974) found a mean deficit in adult stature of 7.2 cm in females and 16.8 cm in males. Although the individuals were shorter in height, their relative statures still correlated with the height of their parents.

Psychologically, the problems are often greatest for sexually precocious females who are liable to begin menstruating before they are able to comprehend the situation. There is no fully satisfactory way to manage precocious puberty. Treatment with progesterone derivatives will usually suppress the estrogenic effects and limit both menstruation and continued breast enlargement in females. It does not appear to alter the pattern of growth. Other steroids also inhibit the effects of the gonadotropins but are not effective in suppressing accelerated growth.

Congenital adrenal hyperplasia is the most common endocrinopathy leading to accelerated growth. The basic defect is genetically determined. There is a limited production of hydrocortisone and excess ACTH production with concomitant adrenal hyperplasia. When excess of adrenal androgen exists from early fetal life, it invariably masculinizes the external genitalia in the female fetus. Postnatally there is an acceleration of growth with enlargement of muscle mass and of the phallus, giving rise to the "infant Hercules" designation. Osseous maturation is more accelerated than linear growth. Without therapeutic intervention, progressive virilization occurs in both sexes. Children reach final height attainment at an early chronologic age and hence, adult stature is relatively short.

Brook et al. (1974) found the mean adult stature in 15 untreated females to be 149 cm (4' 10" tall).

Treatment consists of hydrocortisone therapy. With treatment, there is usually an additional deceleration in the linear growth rate. The pace of osseous maturation is also slowed so that bone age more closely corresponds to chronologic age. In fact, the velocity of linear growth is a helpful indicator in management.

There are rare tumors of the testes in males and ovaries in females and the adrenals of either sex that lead to accelerated linear growth and increased or accelerated osseous maturation. Removal of the tumors results in deceleration of linear growth and in the pace of maturation. Androgenic tumors also lead to virilization of both males and females at an early age. The very rare estrogenic tumors may derive from the adrenal cortex or from the gonads. In females, secondary sexual characteristics and sexual maturation occur early. Broadening of the hips and an increase in adiposity may occur while linear growth and osseous maturation are accelerated. Removal of the tumors leads to deceleration in growth.

If sexual precocity has advanced the osseous maturation to an age at which adolescent changes occur, then previously suppressed gonadatropin-induced adolescence may appear when abnormal sources of androgens or estrogens are terminated. These normal secretions of hormones will tend to maintain accelerated growth and maturation and will induce final stature attainment at an early age.

Hypogonadism occurring in males allows for prolonged growth leading to increase in leg length versus trunk length before epiphyseal ossification takes place. As a consequence, males with inadequate testosterone production tend to be tall with long legs, the so-called eunuchoid build. One of the most common disorders is Klinefelter's syndrome, which has already been described.

Hyperthyroidism in both sexes results in a moderate acceleration in linear growth with a rather striking acceleration of osseous maturation during infancy. This marked acceleration in growth and osseous maturation may continue through childhood and adolescence.

Gigantism and acromegaly are rarely seen. These disorders are examples of the effects of long-term excess of human growth hormones. Clinical features relate to the age of onset. The very rare onset during childhood gives rise to gigantism with heights into the 7 to 9 feet range. Onset in late adolescence causes both gigantism and the more obvious features of acromegaly. Onset after epiphyseal fusion produces acromegaly. The excess growth in acromegaly is most striking in the large mandible, hands and feet, and in the increased thickness in bones of the calverium, the increased subcutaneous tissues, and coarse facies (Smith 1977).

Nutritional disorders. Excessive caloric intake will lead to advanced maturation and accelerated growth often accompanied by obesity. Many of these children show a familial pattern of obesity which is more common in females than in males (Smith 1977). Intervention for familial idiopathic obesity is usually unsuccessful. Obesity may be a feature of a number of endocrine disorders including hypopituitarism, Cushing's syndrome, hypothyroidism, hyperinsulinism, and hyperestrogenism.

Diseases of heart, lungs, kidneys, and other organs. Such diseases usually lead to delayed maturation and short stature rather than to accelerated growth.

Psychological factors. Psychological factors that are implicated in growth disorders also lead to growth deficits rather than augmentation.

SUMMARY

Sexual dimorphic patterns of growth are evident from the early prenatal weeks of life through adulthood. Sex differences are most evident during adolescence when females show an earlier accelerated growth velocity and earlier sexual maturation. The factors that influence growth—genes, hormones, nutrition, temperature, disease, and sociopsychological stress—often disrupt the trajectory of normal growth. The most common growth disorders of short stature and delayed maturation are due to intrinsic factors, such as chromosomal abnormalities or endocrine disorders, and the extrinsic factor of undernutrition. Relatively successful treatment programs are available to ameliorate most growth disorders. Early intervention is important, and the use of a standardized protocol for the detection of growth disorders is useful. Those syndromes that have growth abnormalities as a component have been stressed in this chapter. Many of these syndromes show sex differences in prevalence.

BIBLIOGRAPHY

Baghadassarian, A., F. Bayard, D. S. Borgaonkar, et al. 1975. "Testicular Function in XYY Men." *Johns Hopkins Medical Journal,* 136:15-24.
Bayley, N., and S. Pinneau. 1952. "Tables for Predicting Adult Height from Skeletal Age." *Journal of Pediatrics,* 40:423-441.
Bilewicz, W. Z. 1967. "A Note on Body Weight Measurements and Seasonal Variation." *Human Biology,* 39:241-250.

Brandt, I. 1980. "Postnatal Growth of Preterm and Full-Term Infants." In *Human Physical Growth and Maturation: Methodologies and Factors*, edited by F. E. Johnston, A. F. Roche, and C. Susanne, pp. 139-159. New York: Plenum Press.

Brook, C. G. D., M. Zachman, A. Prader, and G. Murset. 1974. "Experience with Long Term Therapy in Congenital Adrenal Hyperplasia." *Journal of Pediatrics*, 85:12-90.

Bulmer, M. G. 1970. *The Biology of Twinning in Man*. Oxford: Clarendon Press.

Cameron, N. 1978. "The Methods of Auxological Anthropometry." In *Human Growth, Vol. 2. Postnatal Growth*, edited by F. Falkner and J. M. Tanner, pp. 35-90. New York: Plenum Press.

Castle, W. E. 1941. "Size Inheritance." *American Naturalist*, 75:448-98.

Eveleth, P. B., and J. M. Tanner. 1976. *Worldwide Variation in Human Growth*. London: Cambridge University Press.

Falkner, F. and J. M. Tanner (editors). 1978. *Human Growth, Vol. 2. Postnatal Growth*. New York: Plenum Press.

Fishman, M. A., and G. T. Peake. 1970. "Paradoxical Growth in a Patient with Diencephalic Syndrome." *Pediatrics*, 45:973-982.

Flint, M. 1978. "Is There a Secular Trend in Age of Menopause?" *Maturitas*, 1:133-139.

Forest, M. G. 1974. "Plasma Androgens in Normal and Premature Newborns and Infants. Evidence for Maturation of the Gonadostat's Regulation." September. Buenos Aires: XIV International Congress of Pediatrics.

Gampel, B. 1965. "The Relation of Skinfold Thickness in the Neonate to Sex, Length of Gestation, Size at Birth, and Maternal Skinfold." *Human Biology*, 37:29-37.

Garn, S. M., and C. G. Rohmann. 1962. "X-Linked Inheritance of Developmental Timing in Man." *Nature*, 196:695-696.

————. 1966. "Interaction of Nutrition and Genetics in the Timing of Growth and Development." *Pediatric Clinics of North America*, 13:353-379.

Goldstein, H. 1971. "Factors Influencing Height of Seven Year Old Children—Results From the National Child Development Study." *Human Biology*, 43:92-111.

Hansman, C. 1970. "Anthropometry and Related Data." In *Human Growth and Development*, edited by R. W. McCammon. Springfield, Ill.: Charles C Thomas.

Hauspie, R. 1980. "Adolescent Growth." In *Human Physical Growth and Maturation: Methodologies and Factors*, edited by F. E. Johnson, A. F. Roche, and C. Susanne, pp. 161-175. New York: Plenum Press.

Hewitt, D., C. K. Westropp, and R. M. Acheson. 1955. "Oxford Child Health Survey, Effect of Childish Ailments on Skeletal Development," *British Journal of Preventive and Social Medicine*, 9:179-186.

Huenemann, R. L. 1974. "Environmental Factors Associated with Preschool Obesity. Obesity in Six-Month Old Children." *Journal of the American Dietetic Association*, 64:480-487.

Hulse, F. 1957. "Exogamie, et hétérosis." *Archive Suisse d'Anthropologie Genetique*, 22:103-125.

Indian Council of Medical Research. 1972. "Growth and Physical Development of Indian Infants and Children." New Delhi: Medical Enclave.

Johnston, F. E. 1978. "Somatic Growth of the Infant and Preschool Child." In *Human Growth, Vol. 2. Postnatal Growth*, edited by F. Falkner and J. M. Tanner, pp. 91-116. New York: Plenum Press.

_____. 1980. "Research Design and Sample Selection in Studies of Growth and Development." In *Human Physical Growth and Maturation: Methodologies and Factors*. NATO Advanced Study Institute Series, Vol. 3, edited by F. E. Johnston, A. F. Roche, and C. Susanne, pp. 5-19. New York: Plenum Press.

Johnston, F. E., and A. Beller. 1976. "Anthropometric Evaluation of the Body Composition of Black, White and Puerto Rican Newborns." *American Journal of Clinical Nutrition*, 29:61-65.

Kantero, R.-L., and R. Tiisala. 1971a. IV. "Height, Weight and Sitting Height Increments for Children From Birth to 10 Years." *Acta Paediatrica Scandinavica (Supplement)* 220:18-26.

_____. 1971b. V. "Growth of Head Circumference From Birth to 10 Years." *Acta Paediatrica Scandinavica (Supplement)* 220:27-32.

Krogman, W. M. 1972. *Child Growth*. Ann Arbor: University of Michigan Press.

Lindgren, G. 1978. "Growth of Schoolchildren with Early, Average, and Late Ages of Peak Height Velocity. *Annals of Human Biology*, 5:253-267.

Malina, R. M. 1975. *Growth and Development: The First Twenty Years in Man*. Minneapolis: Burgess Publishing Company.

Malina, R. M., J.-P. Habicht, C. Yarbrough, R. Martorell, and R. E. Klein. 1974. "Skinfold Thickness at Seven Sites in Rural Guatemalan Ladino Children Birth Through 7 Years of Age." *Human Biology*, 46:453-469.

Marshall, W. A. 1970. "Variations in the Pattern of Pubertal Changes in Boys." *Archives of Disease in Childhood*, 45:13-23.

_____. 1974. "Puberty." In *Scientific Foundations of Pediatrics*, edited by J. A. Davis and J. Dobbing. Philadelphia: W. B. Saunders.

_____. 1977. *Human Growth and Its Disorders*. New York: Academic Press.

_____. 1978. "Puberty." In *Human Growth, Vol. 2. Postnatal Growth*, edited by F. Falkner and J. M. Tanner, pp. 141-182. New York: Plenum Press.

Marshall, W. A., and J. M. Tanner. 1969. "Variations in the Pattern of Pubertal Changes in Girls." *Archives of Disease in Childhood*, 44:291-303.

Mata, L. J. 1978. *The Children of Santa Maria Cauqué: A Prospective Field Study of Health and Growth*. Cambridge, Mass.: MIT Press.

Mueller, W. H. 1976. "Parent-Child Correlations for Stature and Weight Among School Age Children: A Review of 24 Studies." *Human Biology*, 48:379-397.

Neumann, C. G., and M. Alpaugh. 1976. "Birthweight Doubling Time: A Fresh Look." *Pediatrics*, 57 (April):469-473.

Polani, P. E. 1974. "Size at Birth." Amsterdam: CIBA Foundation Symposium, ASP.

Prader, A. 1975. "Delayed Adolescence." *Clinics in Endocrinology and Metabolism*, 4:143-155.

Roche, A. F. 1978. "Bone Growth and Maturation." In *Human Growth, Vol.2. Postnatal Growth*, edited by F. Falkner and J. M. Tanner, pp. 317-356. New York: Plenum Press.

————. 1980. "The Measurement of Skeletal Maturation." In *Human Physical Growth and Maturation: Methodologies and Factors*, edited by F. E. Johnston, A. F. Roche, and C. Susanne, pp. 61-82. New York: Plenum Press.

Schiebler, D., C. G. D. Brook, H. P. Kird, M. Zachmann, and A. Prader. 1974. "Growth and Body Proportions in 54 Boys and Men With Klinefelter's Syndrome." *Helvetica Paediatrica Acta*, 29:325-333.

Smith, D. 1977. *Growth and Its Disorders: Basics and Standards, Approach and Classifications, Growth Deficiency Disorders, Growth Excess Disorders, Obesity.* Vol. 15, *Major Problems in Clinical Pediatrics*, edited by A. Schaffer. Philadelphia: W. B. Saunders.

Stini, William. 1972. "Reduced Sexual Dimorphism in Upper Arm Muscle Circumference Associated with Protein-Deficient Diet in a South American Population." *American Journal of Physical Anthropology*, 36:341-352.

————. 1975. "Adoptive Strategies of Human Populations Under Nutritional Stress." In *Bio-Social Interrelations in Population Adaptation*, edited by F. E. Johnston and E. S. Watts, pp. 19-41. The Hague: Mouton, World Anthropology Series.

Susanne, C. 1980. "Aging, Continuous Changes of Adulthood." In *Human Physical Growth and Maturation: Methodologies and Factors*, edited by F. E. Johnston, A. F. Roche, and C. Susanne, pp. 203-217. New York: Plenum Press.

Tanner, J. M. 1962. *Growth at Adolescence*, 2nd ed. Oxford: Blackwell.

————. 1973. "Physical Growth and Development." In *Textbook of Pediatrics*, edited by J. O. Forfar and G. C. Arneil. London: Churchill Livingstone.

————. 1974. "Variability in Growth and Maturity in Newborn Infants." In *Origins of Behavior: The Effect of the Infant on Its Care Giver*, edited by M. Lewis and L. Rosenblum. New York: John Wiley.

————. 1977. "Human Growth and Constitution (Part IV)." In *Human Biology: An Introduction to Human Evolution*, 2nd ed., edited by G. A. Harrison, J. S. Weiner, and N. A. Barnicot, pp. 301-385. New York: Oxford University Press.

————. 1978. *Fetus into Man.* Cambridge, Mass.: Harvard University Press.

Tanner, J. M., H. Goldstein, and R. H. Whitehouse. 1970. "Standards for Children's Height at Ages 2-9 Years Allowing for Height of Parents." *Archives of Disease in Childhood*, 45:755-762.

Tanner, J. M., M. J. R. Healy, R. D. Lockhart, J. D. MacKenzie, and R. H. Whitehouse. 1956. "Aberdeen Growth Study, I. The Prediction of Adult Body Measurements from Measurements Taken Each Year from Birth to 5 Years." *Archives of Disease in Childhood*, 31:272-281.

Tanner, J. M., and R. H. Whitehouse. 1975. "Revised Standards for Triceps and Subscapular Skinfolds in British Children." *Archives of Disease in Childhood*, 50:142-145.

Tanner, J. M., R. H. Whitehouse, and M. Takaishi. 1966a. "Standards from Birth to Maturity for Height, Weight, Height Velocity and Weight Velocity: British Children, 1965-I." *Archives of Disease in Childhood*, 41:454-471.

——. 1966b. "Standards From Birth to Maturity For Height, Weight, Height Velocity, and Weight Velocity: British Children, 1965-II." *Archives of Disease in Childhood*, 41:613-635.

Thompson, A. M., W. Z. Bilewicz, and F. E. Hytten. 1968. "The Assessment of Fetal Growth." *Journal of Obstetrics and Gynecology in the British Commonwealth*, 75:903-916.

Timiras, P. S. 1972. *Developmental Physiology and Aging*. New York: Macmillan.

van Wieringen, J. C. 1978. "Secular Growth Changes." In *Human Growth, Vol. 2. Postnatal Growth*, edited by F. Falkner and J. M. Tanner, pp. 445-474. New York: Plenum Press.

Werder, E. A. 1974. "Growth and Pubertal Development in Precocious Puberty." Presented to Centre International de l'Enfance. Paris. December.

Yarbrough, C., J.-P. Habicht, R. M. Malina, A. Lechtig, and R. E. Klein. 1975. "Length and Weight in Rural Guatemalan Ladino Children: Birth to Seven Years of Age." *American Journal of Physical Anthropology*, 42:439-449.

Twelve

Human Proportionality and Sexual Dimorphism

William D. Ross
Richard Ward

Dimorphism or the occurrence of two distinct forms of animals of the same species is often characterized by size and proportionality differences. The matter of size can be appreciated by use of simple measuring instruments and a weight balance. However, proportionality, or the size of a part relative to the whole, other part, or some external standard, requires an agreement on conventions for appraisal or quantification. The dilemma faced by investigators in adopting a convention is illustrated in the whimsical cartoon by John Dunn (Figure 12.1). Little Red Riding Hood's remark, "Grandmother, what large forearms you have!" is subject to misinterpretation. Even suppose she were able to use accepted anatomical landmarks to establish the true size of the forearm as the distance from the radiale to the stylion, the observation "large" must be qualified. "Large," relative to what?

The simplest procedure, with ample anthropological precedent, is to use a ratio. One might express relative size of the forearm with respect to stature, or to another body part. Conventionally, the brachioantibrachial index serves to quantify proportionality of the forearm.

$$\text{Brachioantibrachial Index} = 100 \times \left(\frac{\text{Forearm Length}}{\text{Upper Arm Length}} \right).$$

Normative standards such as those cited by Olivier (1960) may be used to make qualitative judgments about the relative length or

what large forearms you have, Grandmother

Figure 12.1.   What large forearms you have, Grandmother! (Cartoon by John Dunn. Audio Visual Department, Simon Fraser University.)

shortness of the forearm. In interpretation of ratios, however, the relative length may be a function of either the numerator or the denominator. For example, a judgment of there being a large forearm could be made if the upper arm were short in an absolute sense whereas the forearm might be normal for a particular sample. Therefore, ratios by themselves have little meaning unless studied in the context of the individual as a whole.

From a mathematical point of view, as discussed by Tanner (1964, p. 65) ratios "are neither as simple nor as informative as they seem." This is because they are an inextricable combination of the variance of the numerator and denominator. A correlation coefficient between ratios is a statistical enigma defying meaningful interpretation. Tanner recommends the use of a covariance analysis which describes how two measures vary with respect to one another. The approach is illustrated in his analysis of proportionality differences among Olympic athletes. For example, mean leg lengths were plotted against mean trunk length for each event on a bivariate grid, as illustrated in an abstracted version shown as Figure 12.2. The diagonal graph lines have the slope of the average within-event regression. If one assumes, as he did, that there is "parallelism between regressions for the different events," then by moving an individual bivariate plot parallel to the diagonal lines, a comparison with any point on another regression line may be made. Thus, a comparison of leg length can be made taking into account trunk length, because the tactic holds the differences in trunk length constant. In the example, the bivariate plot of the mean value for the 100/200 meter runners is moved diagonally to the right to bring it vertically in line with the position of the bivariate plot of the 400 meter runners. As a rough guide, Tanner recommends interpreting significance if the vertical differences are greater than one grid-width since the diagonal lines were drawn such that the vertical distance between

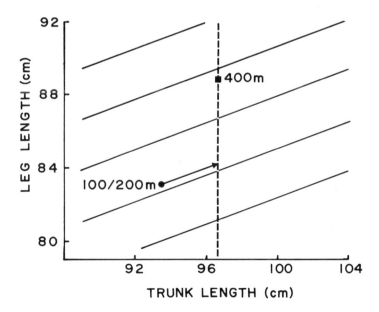

Figure 12.2. Mean leg and trunk lengths of 1960 Rome Olympic 100/200 meter and 400 meter runners, with diagonal within-event regression lines. Diagonal lines are spaced apart by a vertical distance equal to approximately two standard errors of the within-event regression for track athletes. (Abstracted from Tanner 1964, p. 66.)

them was approximately twice the standard error of the adjusted means for the track events. In the illustration, the 400 meter runners were shown to have proportionally longer legs than the 100/200 meter runners. This approach is particularly advantageous when regression lines can be determined for the total sample, and when the assumption of parallelism is tenable.

Another approach, where no such assumptions are required, is the use of a single reference model. This approach has a long tradition. Polykleitos in 750 B.C. arbitrarily constructed a canon, or model, showing ideal proportions, which he had produced by combining the most esthetically pleasing parts of 23 males. The resultant *Doryphorus*, or spearbearer, shown in Figure 12.3, has been used as a mimetic model by artists for centuries. Classically, the head height is one-eighth of the stature. This is illustrated in the outline drawing of the Doryphorus in Figure 12.3. The da Vinci Vitruvian

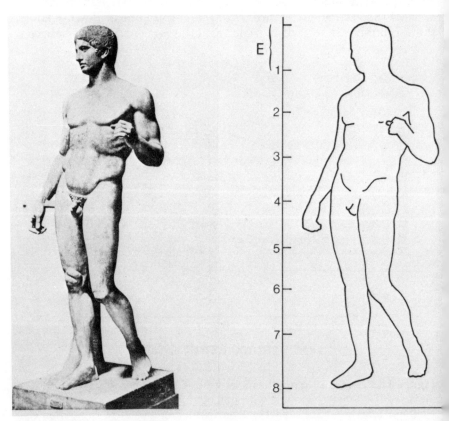

Figure 12.3. Doryphorus, or spearbearer, by Polykleitos 750 B.C. (**left**). Outline drawing (**right**) showing head height (E) to be one-eighth of stature.

man (Figure 12.4) is another example of a model representing the ideal proportions of man.   In Leonardo da Vinci's notebooks, as quoted by Goldwater and Treves (1947), the ideal proportions of the human figure were:

> From the chin to the starting of the hair is a tenth part of the figure. From the chin to the top of the head is an eighth part. And from the chin to the nostrils is a third part of the face. And the same from the nostrils to the eyebrows, and from the eyebrows to the starting of the hair. If you set your legs so far apart as to take a fourteenth part from your height, and you open and raise your arms until you touch the line of the crown of the head with your middle fingers, you must know that the centre of the circle formed by the extremities of the outstretched limbs will be the navel, and the space between the legs will form an equilateral triangle. The span of a man's outstretched arms is equal to his height. [P. 51]

It is somewhat anachronistic that canons for proportionality are scaled in many instances to that of a middle-aged, Caucasian male model. If one were to use a universal prototype it would probably be more female than male, under age 18, and racially indeterminate.

THE PHANTOM

The approach advocated by Ross and Wilson (1974) is to use a single, unisex reference human as a calculation device for quantifying proportional differences as illustrated in Figure 12.5. Arbitrarily they ascribed a standard stature of 170.18 cm (5 feet, 7 inches) to their model and defined over 100 measures (P) and their standard deviations (s) which have been slightly revised and augumented for this publication as shown in Tables 12.1 to 12.7.

It should be recognized that anthropometric technique is not invariable but reflects systematic differences as well as inter- and intraobserver error. The defined landmarks for the Phantom have been reported in a paper by Ross et al. (1978).   These specific techniques are similar to those reported by de Garay et al. (1974) and are currently advocated by the International Working Group on Kinanthropometry (IWGK)* as taught in their sponsored certification courses.

*Endorsed by the Research Committee of the International Council of Sport and Physical Education (N.G.O., A-level committee, UNESCO).

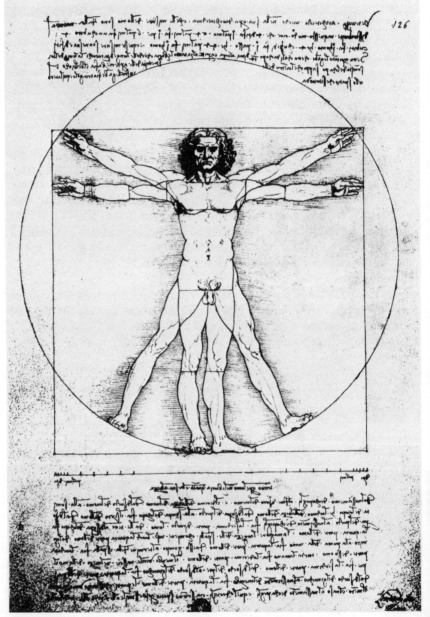

Figure 12.4.   Leonardo da Vinci's Vitruvian man.

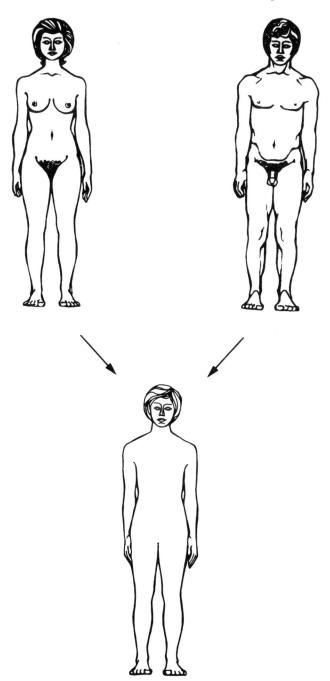

Figure 12.5.   Derivation of unisex Phantom from male and female data adjusted to standard stature. [Ross and Wilson 1974]

TABLE 12.1
Phantom Specifications.

	p	s
Stature (stretch) cm	170.18	6.29
Body mass, weight kg	64.58	8.60
Lean body mass kg	52.45	6.14
Fat mass kg	12.13	3.25
Percent fat	18.78	5.20
Density gm/cc	1.056	0.011
Bone mass kg	10.49	1.57
Muscle mass kg	25.55	2.99
Residual body mass kg	16.41	1.90
H in/$3\sqrt{W}$ lb	12.83	
H cm/$3\sqrt{W}$ kg	42.41	
$(3\sqrt{W}$ kg/H cm) X 10^3	23.58	
Somatotype*	5 - 4 - 2½	

*Heath and Carter (1976).

TABLE 12.2
Phantom Heights (Projected).

	p	s
Vertex (stretch stature)	170.18	6.29
Gnathion	148.81	5.65
Suprasternal	138.31	5.46
Infrasternal	119.50	4.96
Symphysion	87.05	4.35
Acromial	139.37	5.45
Radial	107.25	5.36
Stylion	82.68	4.13
Dactylion	63.83	3.38
Iliospinal*	94.11	4.71
Trochanteric*	86.40	4.32
Tibial (lateral or medial)*	44.82	2.56
Sphyrion (fibular)	7.10	0.85
Sphyrion (tibial)	8.01	0.96
Cervical	144.15	5.58
Gluteal arch*	88.33	4.41
Sitting height*	89.92	4.50
Span (dactylion-dactylion)	172.35	7.41

*These data revised from Ross and Wilson (1976).

TABLE 12.3
Phantom Lengths (Derived and Direct).

	p	s
Head height (vertex-gnathion)	27.27	1.02
Neck (gnathion-suprasternale)	9.48	1.71
Trunk (suprasternale-symphysion)	51.26	2.56
Back (cervicale-gluteal arch)	56.83	2.84
Upper extremity (acromiale-dactylion)	75.95	3.64
Upper extremity (acromiale-stylion)	57.10	2.74
Arm (acromiale-radiale)	32.53	1.77
Forearm (radiale-stylion)	24.57	1.37
Hand (stylion-dactylion)	18.85	0.85
Lower extremity length		
(stature-sitting height)*	81.06	4.05
Thigh 1 (stature-sitting height-tibiale)*	35.44	2.12
Thigh 2 (iliospinale-tibiale)*	49.29	2.96
Thigh 3 (trochanterion-tibiale)*	41.37	2.48
Tibia (tibiale mediale-t. sphyrion)*	36.81	2.10
Lower leg (tibiale laterale-f. sphyrion)*	37.72	2.15
Foot length (standing,		
akropodion-pternion)	25.50	1.16
Foot length (flat unweighted,		
akropodion-pternion)*	24.81	1.15

*These data revised from Ross and Wilson (1976).

It should be appreciated, however, that the Phantom model does not require absolute adherence to those techniques if comparisons are made to a control where the anthropometric technique is consistent. For example, the IWGK definition of the landmark for the acromiale for the Phantom is consistent with that of the 1898 Geneva Convention reproduced by Stewart (1952, p. 205) as being the "superior and external border of the acromion process" as contrasted to the definition of the International Biological Program handbook as being "the inferior edge of the most external border of the acromion process" (Weiner and Lourie 1969, p. 8). In comparison to the Phantom, the IWGK procedure would yield greater values than the IBP procedure. However, the comparison of differences between experimental versus control subjects would yield similar results provided each were measured by the same procedure regardless of which one it was. For this reason, the Phantom is technique independent for within-sample analyses or wherever the anthropometric technique is common for all subjects. This provides a particular advantage in secular trend studies or in longitudinal growth analyses.

TABLE 12.4
Phantom Girths.

	p	*s*
Head	56.00	1.44
Neck	34.91	1.73
Shoulders	104.86	6.23
Chest (mesosternale, end tidal)	87.86	5.18
Abdominal 1 (waist)	71.91	4.45
Abdominal 2 (umbilical)	79.06	6.95
Abdominal AV (mean 1 and 2)	75.48	5.74
Hips	94.67	5.58
Thigh (1 cm distal, gluteal line)	55.82	4.23
Knee	36.04	2.17
Calf (standing)	35.25	2.30
Ankel	21.71	1.33
Arm (fully flexed and tensed)	29.41	2.37
Arm (relaxed, mid-acromiale-radiale)	26.89	2.33
Forearm (relaxed)	25.13	1.41
Wrist 1 (distal styloids)	16.35	0.72
Wrist 2 (proximal styloids)	16.38	0.72
Arm girth relaxed (-π x triceps skinfold cm)*	22.05	1.91
Chest girth (-π x subscapular skinfold cm)*	82.46	4.86
Thigh girth (-π x front thigh skinfold cm)*	47.34	3.59
Calf girth (-π x medial calf skinfold cm)*	30.22	1.97

*Fat-corrected girths for fractionation of both mass procedure.

TABLE 12.5
Phantom Breadths.

	p	*s*
Biacromial	38.04	1.92
Bideltoid	43.50	2.40
Transverse chest (mesosternale)	27.92	1.74
Biiliocristal	28.84	1.75
Bitrochanteric	32.66	1.80
Chest depth (AP, mesosternale)	17.50	1.38
Biepicondylar humerus	6.48	0.35
Wrist (max. stylion-ulnare)	5.21	0.28
Hand (distal II-V metacarpals)	8.28	0.50
Biepicondylar femur	9.52	0.48
Transverse tibia	9.12	0.47
Bimalleolare	6.68	0.36
Transverse foot (standing)	9.61	0.60
Transverse foot (resting flat, unweighted)	8.96	0.56
Foot (standing, distal I-V metatarsals)	10.34	0.65

TABLE 12.6
Phantom Skinfolds (Harpenden Caliper).

	p	s
Triceps	15.4	4.47
Subscapular (diagonal)	17.2	5.07
Subscapular (vertical)	17.5	5.17
Chest	11.8	3.27
Biceps	8.0	2.00
Suprailiac	15.4	4.47
Abdominal	25.4	7.78
Iliac crest	22.4	6.80
Front thigh	27.0	8.33
Rear thigh	31.1	9.69
Medial calf	16.0	4.67

TABLE 12.7
Phantom Head and Face Measures.

	p	s
Classic head height (vertex-gnathion)	27.27	1.02
Head length (glabella-occiput)	19.15	0.68
Head breadth (transverse parietal)	15.08	0.58
Head height (vertex-tragion)	13.31	0.75
Bizygomatic breadth	13.66	0.57
Bigonial breadth	10.59	0.58
Morphological face height (nasion-gnathion)	11.94	0.69
Nose length (nasion-subnasale)	5.21	0.48

General Formula

The general formula for use of the Phantom geometrically scales all measures to the Phantom stature (170.18 cm), obtains the difference from the given Phantom values (p), and expresses this in terms of the standard deviation distances (s) as follows:

$$Z = \frac{1}{S}\left[V\left(\frac{170.18}{h}\right)^d - P \right]$$

where

Z is a proportionality value or z-value;
V is the size of any given variable;
170.18 is the Phantom stature constant;

h is the subject's obtained stature;

d is a dimensional exponent. When scaled geometrically, $d =$ 1 for all lengths, breadths, girths, and skinfold distances; $d = 2$ for all areas, and $d = 3$ for all weights and volumes;

P is the given Phantom value for variable V;

S is the Phantom standard deviation value for variable based on a hypothetical universal human population.

A z-value of 0.00 indicates that the subject for variable v is proportionally the same as the Phantom. A z-value greater than 0.00 means that the subject is proportionally greater than the Phantom for variable v, whereas a z-value of less than 0.00 shows that the subject is proportionally smaller than the Phantom for that item. The value of the Phantom is not as a normative model but primarily as a calculation device for comparing individuals and groups. It does not obviate the need for normative data; to the contrary, it encourages such compilation.

Sample mean and standard deviation z-values should be calculated from individually obtained z-values. However, when those are not available they may be derived with some loss of precision from mean raw score values. The implicit assumption made when calculating z-values from reported means is that there is a perfect correlation between stature and the size of the variable in question in the particular sample. This usually is not the case; however, the differences are seldom great enough to invalidate the use of this technique of calculating mean z-values from anthropometric means of a sample.

To illustrate this point, a comparison was made of the z-values for the 100/200 m and 400 m runners from Tanner's study shown previously. Tanner had reported individual data on height and leg length, as well as in the form of group means. We were, therefore, able to calculate mean z-values in both ways. The preferred procedure of calculating individual z-values and then producing a mean z-value was compared with the alternate procedure of calculating a mean z-value from mean data as shown in Table 12.8. For this particular comparison the mean of z-values calculated from the individual values was the same as that calculated from mean scores. However, this latter procedure is not preferred for two reasons. First, it is not as precise, and second, and more importantly, it does not provide for calculation of variances and standard deviations that are essential for descriptive and inferential statistical purposes. The results of the t-test for a significant difference between mean z-values for the two groups indicated that the 400 m runners had significantly proportionally longer legs than the 100/200 m runners ($t = 2.19$, $\alpha = 0.05$, $d.f. = 21$).

TABLE 12.8

Mean Leg Length z-Scores of Olympic 100/200 Meter and 400 Meter Runners, Calculated from Individual Data, and Also from Mean Reported Data.*

		Individual Data		Mean Data
	(n)	$(\overline{X})$	$(S.D.)$	$(\overline{X})$
100/200 m	12	−0.25	0.44	−0.25
400 m	11	0.11	0.32	0.12

*From data reported by Tanner (1964).

The conclusion agreed with that of the covariate analysis described previously when an inspectional test of significance was made by regarding a graphic distance greater than two standard errors of the mean as significant, i.e., $2(\sigma/\sqrt{n}\,)$.

SEXUAL DIFFERENTIATION

Human variability is affected by a plethora of genetic and environmental influences. Jost (1972) established that sexual differentiation is a sequential and ordered process: genetic sex, established at conception, determines gonadal sex, which, in turn, regulates phenotypic sexual development. During embryonic development, the gonads inherently tend to become ovaries, and a female phenotype develops during the fetal stage. However, in the presence of the Y-linked gene product H-Y antigen, the gonads form testes, which, during fetal development, secrete the hormones necessary to produce the male phenotype (Ohno 1976). As discussed in a later section, studies of sex chronosomal aneuploidy help show specific effects.

PROPORTIONAL SEXUAL DIMORPHISM

In order to quantify gross structural differences between male and female phenotypes, the Phantom strategem may be used. The difference between z-values for male and female data may be conceived as a measure of sexual dimorphism. In muscular girths, for example, positive differences would indicate that the male would be proportionally larger in girths, whereas negative differences such as encountered in skinfold thicknesses would indicate the female would be proportionally larger. No difference in z-values between male and female data would indicate no proportional sexual dimorphism, whereas a large positive or negative value would indicate that a high degree of proportional sexual dimorphism existed.

PERINATAL PROPORTIONAL GROWTH PHENOMENA

Absolute differences in height and weight for infant males and females have been reported in the literature. A summary by Tanner (1978) indicates that boys tend, on the average, to be slightly larger at birth than girls, however the difference is small and remains so until the girls accelerate in height and weight during their adolescent growth spurt.

Girls, however, mature faster than boys and this is evident even in the perinatal period. At birth, girls are approximately 4 to 6 weeks further along their predetermined course to maturity and even when only halfway through the fetal period the female skeleton has been shown to be some 3 weeks more advanced than that of the male. Girls are more mature in some other organ systems at birth as well, and Tanner proposes that this may be a reason why more girls than boys survive at birth. The assumption made is that a greater degree of maturity at birth increases the chances of survival of the individual.

Height and weight are classically used as indicators of health and well-being, either as two individual variables or combined as a ratio or ponderal index. Many studies have been carried out, with large samples of infants, to produce normative growth charts for both intrauterine and postnatal growth.

It has been shown that there are relationships between infant mortality, infant weight at birth, and length of gestation. Unfortunately, the consideration of weight and length of gestation alone is insufficient. Height (or more appropriately, the length) of an infant is also a critical factor, since an infant weight of 3.5 kg would have very different meaning depending on whether the child was 47 cm long or 51 cm long. Investigators have realized this and have used various height-weight ratios to study the two values simultaneously. The dimensional rationale and assumptions of similarity systems for comparison of variables have been specified and discussed in historical context by Ross et al. (1980a). In growth analyses, the geometrical similarity system is used almost exclusively. In this system, if shape and composition are constant, an increase in any linear measure is accompanied by the square of the increase for any area and the cube of the increase for volumes and masses. If height and weight preserve the 3:1 theoretical exponential or dimensional relationship, the variables can be combined in a ratio assuming geometrical similarity.

There are a number of these combinations. The most popular is weight divided by the cube of the height, the so-called "ponderal index." Mathematically, its reciprocal, used to determine the ectomorphic component in somatotyping, has the same meaning as a scaling device since a linearity scale is simply the inverse of a ponderosity scale. As described by Ross et al. (1980a), a convenient alternative for these height-weight ratios is to use proportional body weight obtained by multiplying obtained body weight by the cube of the ratio of 170.18 and obtained height, i.e., $w(170.18/h)^3$. The proportional body weight can also be expressed as a Phantom z-value by using 64.58 and 8.60 constants for the p and s values for body weight in the Phantom formula. This in no way alters the mathematical interpretation. Body weight is scaled to a geometrical similarity system and should be interpreted accordingly.

As for all z-values, positive or negative values quantify proportionality differences greater or lesser than the Phantom which has a value of 0.00. In growth analyses, if a z-value is constant from time to time, we know that growth in height and weight is geometrically similar. Declining z-values for proportional body weight with time indicate a trend toward linearity. That is, height is increasing faster than body weight for a geometrically similar system (i.e., one where shape and composition are constant and the variables are changing according to geometrical rules). Increasing proportional body weight values in a growth series indicate that the body weight is increasing faster than height for a geometrical system, the individual growing more ponderous with time.

PERINATAL PROPORTIONALITY PATTERNS

Upon the application of the Phantom stratagem to longitudinal data of Mexican boys and girls, as reported by Faulhaber (1976), it was noticed that proportional weight (Figure 12.6) and several other proportional variables—such as sitting height, biacromial breadth, and calf girth—showed a proportionality deflection, or peak in z-value, at about age 2 months. Subsequent scrutiny of the world literature by our colleague, G. Lau-Pau (1980) showed that the finding of this proportionality deflection was not an artifact of the Mexican data but was a bona fide phenomenon of infant growth. It should be pointed out that z-values for weight were calculated from mean crown-heel lengths and weights reported in the literature, a tactic that we have previously explained as being usually adequate, yet needing care in interpretation. In addition it was stated that the stratagem is technique independent provided the measurements are consistent for compared groups of individuals. For this reason it is possible to use the Phantom height value in the calculation of proportional weight z-value even though the height of the infant is, in fact, recumbent length. In some studies, conversion to standing stature (at around 2.5 years of age) will be marked by a slight

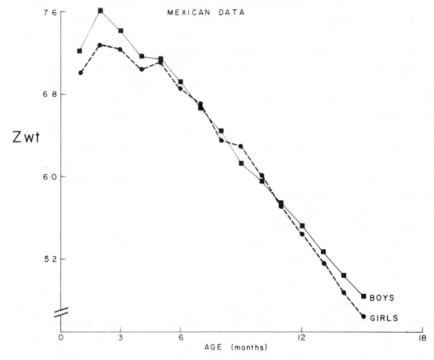

Figure 12.6. Proportional body mass (Zwt) in Mexican boys and girls from reported mean values of height and weight from a longitudinal study. [Faulhaber 1976]

deflection in the curves since recumbent length has a slightly greater value than standing stature.

A proportionality deflection was obtained in 25 out of the 28 reports where usable data were found. Of these positive studies, 6 were cross-sectional and the remaining were longitudinal. Two of the three studies that did not show a deflection were cross-sectional and were started on 2- and 3-month-old infants; therefore the peak might have been missed.

In compiling calculated z-values for proportional body weight with adjusted means according to the numbers of subjects in each sample, a composite picture of the phenomenon was constructed as shown in Figure 12.6. All data have been aligned according to the gestational age at birth, rather than the time from birth, as the growth process begins at conception. Both cross-sectional and longitudinal data have been used in the production of this graph. The cadaver data of Scammon and Calkins (1929) on fetuses have been used to give an indication of proportional weight in early fetal life, along with the proposed intrauterine growth norms for several populations proposed by various investigators (Boersma and Mbise 1979, Ghosh et al. 1971). The graph is only intended as an indication of the overall change in proportional weight that occurs. It is not intended as a normative chart since it was composed from reported data on subjects of both sexes and various nationalities and socioeconomic levels. The composite curve must, therefore, be viewed as an approximation of the actual situation of the developing infant. A cogent research need is for such curves to be developed from available data bases where extraneous factors can be more adequately controlled.

In absolute rather than proportional values, Tanner (1978) reports peak intrauterine length velocity occurring around the 20th week, followed by peak intrauterine weight velocity about the 32nd week. As shown in Figure 12.7, the proportional body weight graph which reflects both variables decreases steadily from the 15th to 28th gestational week due to the length velocity dominance, then rises sharply as weight velocity exerts its influence.

The vertical dotted line represents the 40th week of gestation, the normal full-term period. An initial peak in proportional weight is seen at term; however, during the first few days of infant life there is a drop in proportional weight. This may be partly due to a loss of body weight in the infant, which is well documented in the literature. This weight loss in the normal infant is usually in the region of 5 to 7 percent of body weight. It is presumed that this is mainly a fluid loss along with fecal matter. The proportional weight then increases to a second peak at around 3 months from term. The infant then begins a steady decrease in proportional weight. From this curve it can be seen that there are definite proportional weight changes occurring in the infant. However the question remains as to the true relevance of this phenomenon. In order to look at the developmental differences in full birth weight and true premature (less than 37 weeks gestation) infants, means of proportional weight for each group were calculated from data from studies that had classified infants according to these categories. From these two curves, shown in Figure 12.8, it can be seen that in the full birth weight infants the initial decrease in proportional weight is very marked. An interesting feature of the curves is that the true premature infants increase in proportional weight to reach a similar peak at the same time after conception as the full birth weight infants. The premature infant curve does not show the proportional weight decrease immediately after birth. This does not preclude the existence of the proportional weight loss in the premature infant. The means for the premature infants are composed of infants with varying gestational ages of less than 37 weeks at birth:

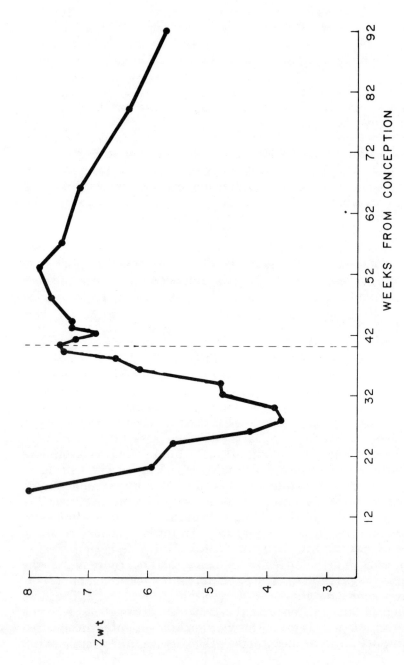

Figure 12.7. Postulated proportional body weight (Zwt) from reported height and weight data from multiple sources in the literature, aligned according to gestational age at birth.

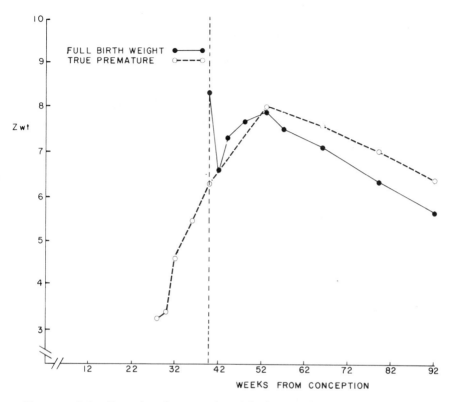

Figure 12.8. Postulated proportional body weight (Zwt) for full birth weight and true premature infants from reported height and weight data from multiple sources in the literature, aligned according to gestational age at birth.

The proportional weight decrease, therefore, may be occurring to some extent but it is smoothed out when the average curve is produced.

A simple explanation could be that length accelerations account for the proportional weight deflection. However, the data belie this conclusion since the proportionality deflection should be common to all anthropometric variables. In the Mexico data it was encountered in some variables, such as sitting height and calf girth, but not in others, such as head girth. There was no evidence whatsoever of a proportionality deflection in head girth, in any of the samples.

The facts of differential growth of the head are awesome. Typically the child is four head heights (vertex-menton) long, whereas the adult is eight head heights tall. If we apply geometrical scaling, the adult head is twice the size of the infant head, and eight times the volume or weight. In terms of the Phantom, infant head girths are proportionally remote from adult samples having a head girth z-value of 42.0 at birth. Growth is marked by a consistent decline until 0.00 z or thereabouts, characteristic of the adult dimensions.

One of the questions that needs to be answered is whether infants with excessively low or even excessively high proportional birth weights are the infants who will be at particular risk to death and disease, and therefore would require close attention. Body weight and gestational age are presently used as indicators of risk. However, would proportional weight and gestational age provide more sensitive indicators of risk?

PROPORTIONAL SEXUAL DIMORPHISM IN INFANTS

It has been stated that boys tend to be longer and heavier than girls at birth. The question we now ask is whether the boys and girls, in fact, achieve similar proportional weights or whether there is some intrinsic difference in the weight to height relationship between the sexes. At present we do not ourselves possess good longitudinal measurements on infants from birth. What we do have are reported means of height and weight in various longitudinal and cross-sectional studies. Figures 12.9a and 12.9b show a graphical representation of z-values for weight calculated from three studies where boys and girls were compared. These studies include a sample from Finland (Saarinen and Siimes 1979), one from Zurich (Falkner et al. 1958), and two samples from California—one black, one white (Wingerd et al. 1971). Comparisons between studies are confounded by technique differences and also by differences in physique due to race and socioeconomic status. However, there appears to be some degree of sexual differentiation in proportional weight in each study. Present in each curve is the proportionality peak that we have previously discussed. The girls seem to show a comparable trend in proportionality to the boys except that they tend to be proportionally lighter at certain stages. The differences, however, appear minimal, except at the 2 to 3 month proportionality deflection where the boys have consistently greater proportional body weight values. Body weight gives an indication of total body growth. It appears, however, that the proportionality deflection is not a total body growth phenomenon, but is a differential growth phenomenon of various tissues of the body. For instance, Figures 12.10 and 12.11 show z-values for sitting height and head girth, respectively, for the first 8 months of life in the Mexico data. Sitting height reflects the same deflection that proportional weight exhibited, yet head girth does not.

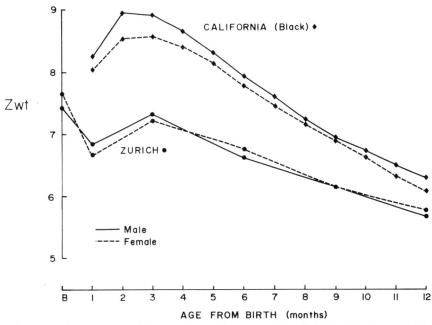

Figure 12.9a. Sexual dimorphism in proportional infant body weight (Zwt), calculated from reported mean data from California (Wingerd et al. 1971) and Zurich (Falkner et al. 1958).

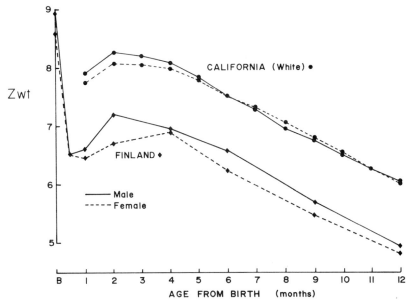

Figure 12.9b. Sexual dimorphism in proportional body weight (Zwt), calculated from reported data from California (Wingerd et al. 1971) and Finland (Saarinen and Siimes 1979).

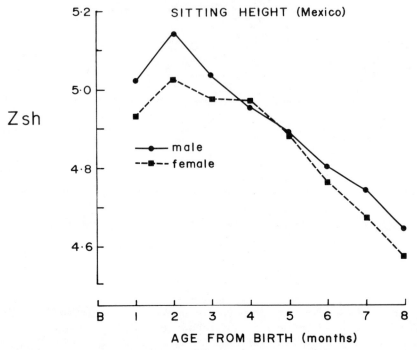

Figure 12.10. Proportional sitting height (Zsh) from Mexican male and female data reported by Faulhaber (1976).

Apart from the absence or presence of a proportionality deflection, an interesting trend is apparent. The females' z-values are generally lower at each age, in both variables. It has been stated previously that at birth females are ahead of males in skeletal maturity. Both sitting height and head girth are skeletal measures, both show a trend for decreasing z-values with maturity. Therefore the question we pose is: Do lower mean z-values for sitting height and head girth infer a greater degree of skeletal maturity in the females? Unfortunately we do not have the evidence to answer this question, we can only speculate. The whole question of infant proportional sexual dimorphism in body weight and other measures invites further study.

PROPORTIONAL GROWTH FROM INFANCY TO ADOLESCENCE

The adolescent growth spurt is a well-established biological fact. During puberty there are rapid changes in size, shape, and composi-

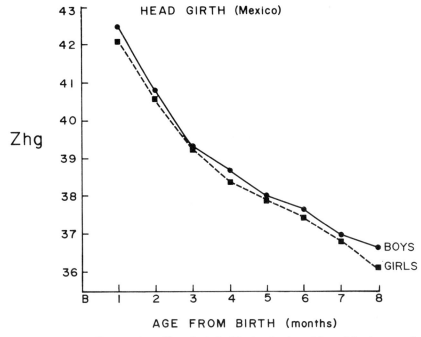

Figure 12.11. Proportional head girth (Zhg) calculated from Mexican male and female data reported by Faulhaber (1976).

tion. These changes tend to follow similar patterns in boys and girls, but it is the magnitude and timing of the changes that cause the vast phenotypic differences in males and females in adulthood. Girls are only marginally shorter than boys before puberty, whereas afterward, the male is substantially taller, being on average 12 to 13 cm greater in height. Concomitant with this change in height are changes in body proportions that distinguish the characteristic profiles between the sexes. Boys develop wider shoulders and greater overall musculature. Girls develop the wider hips characteristic of their gender. Use of the Phantom stratagem will enable quantification of these and other proportionality differences.

The developmental pattern from the peak proportional weight values at 2 to 3 months of life is toward linearity. This move to linearity in both boys and girls continues until adolescence, where sexual dimorphism becomes pronounced. Typical cross-sectional data have been reported by Eiben (1978). In the Kormend Growth Study, one of the most ambitious secular trend investigations undertaken, he measured samples of West Hungarian children and youth in 1958, 1968, and 1978. Although the data have yet to be fully resolved, comparison of the data in 1958 and 1968 showed that the latter sample was taller and heavier than the former. However, the secular trend was greater in height than weight because the 1968 youngsters showed smaller proportional weight values at each age than the 1958 sample.

The proportional weight values obtained in 1968 are shown in Figure 12.12. The continuation of the developmental pattern toward linearity from peak values in early infancy persists from the age of 3 to 9, with no apparent difference between boy and girls. It is only in the circumpubertal period that any sex differential becomes evident. This is dramatically illustrated by the fact that whereas after puberty the male exhibits only a slight rise in proportional weight which plateaus, the female shows a striking increase, ostensibly due to the deposition of secondary sexual fat. Although the male encounters a large increase in muscle bulk, as we shall discuss later, this is counteracted by the simultaneous large increase in height. After

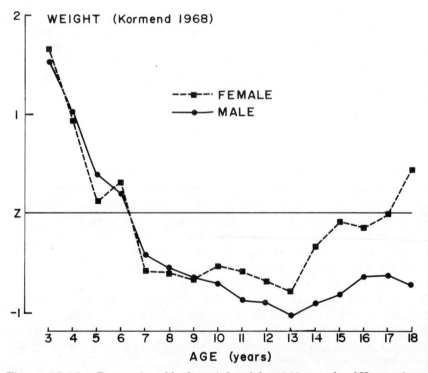

Figure 12.12. Proportional body weight of the 1968 sample of Hungarian males and females from the Kormend Growth Study after Eiben (1978).

puberty the female has attained a more rounded and ponderous form in comparison to that of the male.

Tanner (1978, p. 69) summarizes the changes in proportions associated with the adolescent growth spurt by stating that there is a fairly regular order in which the dimensions of the body parts accelerate. Leg length reaches a peak 6 to 9 months ahead of trunk length, and shoulder and chest breadths are the last to reach their peaks. Males have proportionally longer leg lengths due to a typically later onset of puberty that allows a longer growing period. The proportional increase in lower limb length is illustrated in Figure 12.13 from cross-sectional data on Spinale height from the Coquitlam Growth Study (COGRO) in which 451 females and 484 males between the ages of 6 and 16 were measured in a comprehensive anthropometric protocol, described by Ross et al. (1980b). Spinale height (or the height of the inferior border of the anterior superior iliac spine from the floor in an erect subject) is essentially a measure of total leg length, although it may be affected to some extent by pelvic changes during puberty. The data showed that this value increases up to around puberty, after which time it decreases slightly due to the

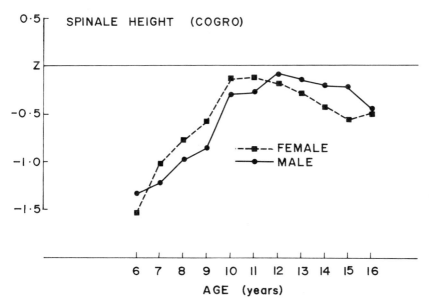

Figure 12.13. Proportional spinale height from Canadian males and females from the Coquitlam Growth Study (COGRO) reported by Ross et al. (1980b).

continued spurt in growth of the trunk. Girls were shown to have proportionally longer legs than boys up to puberty. However as their spurt in trunk length occurred the boys then began to experience their peak in growth of leg length to achieve a proportional leg length greater than that of the girls. This trend is also indicated in the sitting height data collected in the COGRO Study as well as in the leg length data of the Kormend Study presented by Eiben (1978). This difference in proportional leg length has been attributed to the difference in onset of puberty between the sexes. We have also found this phenomenon in postpubescent boys, with the later maturing boy having proportionally longer legs than the early maturing boy. Growth in arm length shows a similar trend to that of the leg. The data on the upper extremity (acromiale-dactylion) as reported by Eiben (1978) has been replotted as shown in Figure 12.14. Little significant difference in proportional arm length between the sexes is seen until approximately 8 years of age. Subsequently, boys tend to have proportionally longer arms than the girls. Again this is a feature of the longer growing time available to boys before puberty.

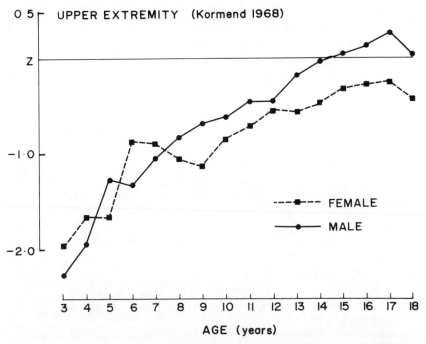

Figure 12.14. Proportional upper extremity length of the 1968 sample of Hungarian males and females from Kormend Growth Study after Eiben (1978).

In addition to reporting z-values plotted with age as the independent variable, it is often useful to show interrelations of proportionality scores as a profile for any given age. Such charts have been used to summarize the proportionality differences found between the sexes at three different ages in the COGRO Study. Figure 12.15 shows the proportionality profiles for children aged 7, 12, and 15 years. The variables chosen for inclusion in the charts represent the growth in dimension of the bony measurements of the children. Any number of variables may be included on a chart and it is up to the investigators' discretion to select variables that are representative. Variables we have chosen as being representative of the proportional changes in bony measurements are sitting height, tibiale height (lower leg length), forearm length, wrist girth, ankle girth, biacromial (shoulder) breadth, and biiliocristal (hip) breadth. At 7 years of age the major differences between the sexes are in ankle and wrist girths, with biacromial and biiliocristal breadths showing a small degree of the dimorphism more typical of postadolescence. At 12 years of age the overall pattern moves closer to that of the Phantom as the children attain proportions more similar to adulthood. Again the greatest dimorphism is in proportional wrist girth. The biiliocristal breadth in girls becomes almost identical to the boys due to the spurt in height of the girls that has not yet been accompanied by the flaring of the hips. At 15 years of age the typical shoulder-hip dimorphism is apparent. The girls are proportionally narrower in biacromial breadth, and proportionally wider in biiliocristal breadth. The girls are also proportionally smaller in upper limb dimensions and proportionally shorter in lower leg length.

A well-known feature of the morphological changes at puberty is the large increase in muscle bulk of the boys under the action of testosterone. This phenomenon is apparent in Figure 12.16 which describes the z-values for fat-corrected relaxed arm girth in the COGRO sample. When considering any fleshy girth, the measurement includes components of bone, muscle, and subcutaneous fat. If we wish to look at muscular hypertrophy then it is necessary to take into account the amount of subcutaneous fat present. This may be achieved by reducing the girth measurement by a factor proportional to the amount of subcutaneous fat present. The technique that we use for this adjustment is to take a skinfold measurement at the level of the girth, and then to use it in the following equation:

Fat-Corrected Girth = Girth $- (\pi \times$ Skinfold$/10)$.

In the case of the relaxed arm girth we have used the triceps skinfold as being representative of the fat around the arm at the level

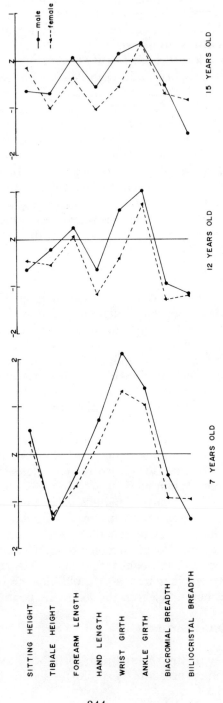

Figure 12.15. Proportionality profiles for Canadian males and females aged 7, ,12, and 15 years, from the Coquitlam Growth Study (COGRO) reported by Ross et al. (1980b).

344

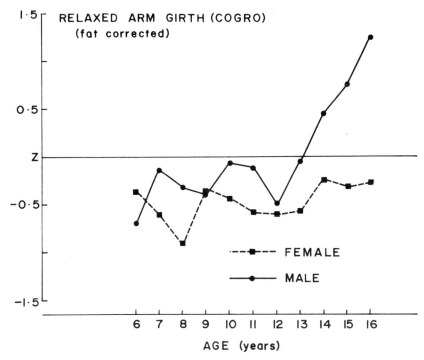

Figure 12.16. Proportional relaxed arm girth corrected by triceps skinfold from males and females from the Coquitlam Growth Study (COGRO) reported by Ross et al. (1980b).

that the girth is taken. Therefore, in Figure 12.16 the z-values represent changes in muscle and bone and not those in the thickness of the subcutaneous fat. The fat-corrected arm girth z-values show little consistent pattern up to 12 years of age. However, after 12 years of age there was a striking proportional increase in muscle in the boys, whereas in the girls it rises only marginally and then reaches a plateau. This same trend was also reflected in forearm girth, calf girth, and thigh girth in the COGRO data. This differential muscle increase is also manifest in such performance variables as maximal aerobic power (Bailey et al. 1978).

Biacromial and biiliocristal breadths (essentially measures of shoulder and hip widths, respectively) have been examined previously. It was shown that there is an increase in proportional shoulder width in males and an increase in proportional hip width in females. Both of these variables have z-values that are scaled to the same Phantom height. An advantage of the Phantom stratagem is that any variable may be scaled to any other variable (not necessarily height). The shoulder-hip dimorphism has long been used as a measure of bodily androgyny, and Tanner (1978, p. 66) proposed the discriminant function (3 × Biacromial Diameter − 1 × Biiliac Diameter) as a measure of androgyny that is less biased by sheer body size than a simple ratio of shoulder/hip widths would be. A measure of shoulder-hip dimorphism may be produced by calculating z-values for biiliocristal breadth, but using biacromial breadth of the subject instead of subject height in the Phantom formula. Figure 12.17 shows the result of this maneuver on the COGRO sample. Clear proportionality differences between the sexes are shown after the age of 11. After this age, the girls have proportionally larger hips relative to shoulder widths than the boys. A higher z-value indicates wider hips proportionally. From this example it can be seen that an almost infinite number of relationships between variables may be investigated in the form of z-values. It is, however, the task of the investigator to decide which relationships have validity to and meaning for the problem under consideration.

SOMATOTYPE SEXUAL DIMORPHISM

Since Sheldon, Stevens, and Tucker (1940) coined the word "somatotype," and developed the appropriate methodology, it has become common practice in human biology to describe the morphological characteristics of a sample using the concept of a three-component rating system. In recent years, a revised and

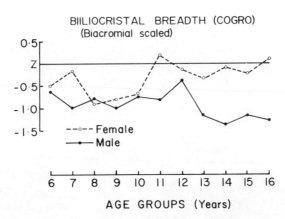

Figure 12.17. Proportional biiliocristal breadth scaled to biacromial breadth rather than height for females and males from the Coquitlam Growth Study (COGRO) reported by Ross et al. (1980b).

elaborated method, first proposed by Heath and Carter (1967), has supplanted the original photoscopic system and other variants. The new method expresses the present morphological conformation with its underlying composition as a three-component rating (endomorphy, mesomorphy, and ectomorphy). Endomorphy is a rating of relative fatness; mesomorphy is a rating of relative musculoskeletal development; ectomorphy is a rating of relative linearity. The method is described in detail by Carter (1975, 1980).

A somatochart is a convenient way for visually representing the dispersion of sample somatotypes. Tri-dimensional scaling of the somatotype and parametric analyses have been developed for testing significance of true representation of the somatotype as a "somatopoint" on X, Y, Z coordinate axes. However, the phenomenon of sexual dimorphism in somatotype distributions can be appreciated from simple displays on the somatochart.

Although somewhat leaner and perhaps fitter than other general population samples, the distribution of somatotypes shown in Figures 12.18 and 12.19 illustrates typical dispersion. The female sample,

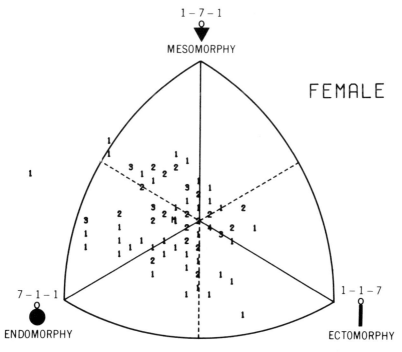

Figure 12.18. Heath-Carter Somatotype distribution for Canadian female university sample selected from three British Columbia, Canada, universities ($N = 94$).

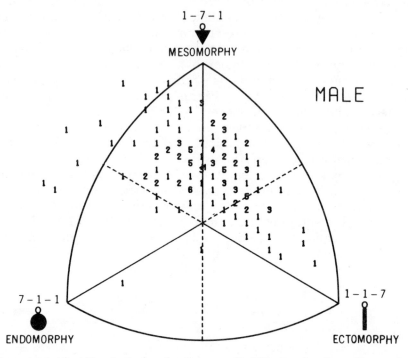

Figure 12.19.   Heath-Carter Somatotype distribution for Canadian male university sample selected from three British Columbia, Canada, universities (*N* = 153).

while located more to the south-western, endomorphic pole of the somatochart than the male sample, is not totally discontinuous from the male dispersion. The male sample while displaced to the north-eastern, ectomesomorphic sector, overlaps with the more mesomorphic of the female subjects.

In all samples where environmental conditions are similar for both sexes, the mean male somatotype is consistently more ecto-mesomorphic than that of the females. This is apparent in Figure 12.20 which shows mean somatoplots for various ethnic groups. The sexual dimorphism is represented by a vector: the circle representing the female mean and the point of the arrow representing the male mean for that particular ethnic group. The data are those reported by Carter and augmented by our own Canadian reference sample. The most mesomorphic of the samples was the Manus (M) from the territory of Papua-New Guinea, reported by Heath and Carter (1971). The females were more mesomorphic than most of the male samples, yet, the Manus males were still substantially more so. In select

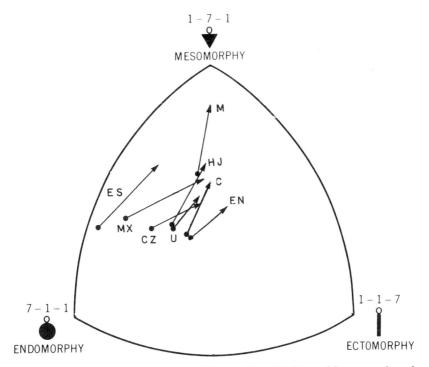

Figure 12.20. Somatotype sexual dimorphism illustrated by mean female and male vectors for ES (Eskimo), MX (Mexico), CZ (CSSR), U (U.S.A.), M (Manus), HJ (Hawaiian Japanese), C (Canada), EN (England). Carter (1980) was the source for other than Canada data.

athletic samples, the male-female vectors, shown in Figure 12.21, illustrate the same somatotypic dimorphic tendency.

Thus, while male and female distributions of somatotypes are not dichotomous but provide overlap, the general tendency is for males to be more ectomesomorphic than females provided selective factors are common to both sexes. However, there are many females who are more ectomesomorphic than males, particularly if the females are athletes and the males are not under similar selection and training restraints.

ADULT PROPORTIONALITY

One investigator asked Dr. Lindsay Carter, "What does the somatotype tell us that lengths, breadths, girths, and skinfold thicknesses on a subject will not tell us?" His answer, "The subject is a 2-5-3." The

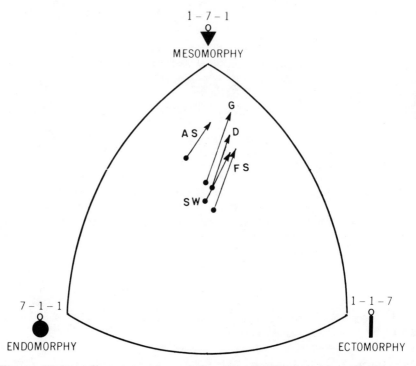

Figure 12.21.   Somatotype sexual dimorphism illustrated by mean female and male vectors for AS (Canadian alpine skiers); 1976 Olympic athletes SW (swimmers), G (gymnasts), D (divers); and FS (Canadian figure skaters). Data from Carter (1980) and Ross et al. (1977).

value of the somatotype is that it compresses a lot of information into a reliable form that can be easily comprehended. However, within a sample of subjects with 2-5-3 somatotypes, there are size and proportionality differences that may have biological or functional importance. The Phantom stratagem does not obviate the need for somatotyping, since somatotyping provides the simplest, most economical description of the human form. The Phantom stratagem provides for more detailed description and analyses.

The male and female samples shown in Table 12.9 were selected as prototypes of nonathletically select university students who, if anything, had a bias towards an active life-style, having been selected from a general education exercise management class, a non-major teacher education class in elementary school physical education, and a campus residence from three British Columbia universities.

TABLE 12.9
Canadian Tri-University Sample (CANREF). Mean and Standard
Deviations for Age, Height, and Weight of Males and Females.

	Male		Female	
	$(\overline{X})$	(S.D.)	$(\overline{X})$	(S.D.)
Age (dec. years)	21.53	3.96	20.63	2.60
Height (cm)	178.5	7.1	165.7	6.1
Weight (kg)	72.4	8.6	57.5	6.4

*For males, $N = 152$; for females, $N = 94$.

Twenty-two of the 39 obtained and derived anthropometric variables were transformed to z-values as summarized in Table 12.10. In order to view proportionality dimorphism between female and male z-values, differences were obtained and displayed by showing displacement of female from male means as shown in Figure 12.22. For example, the mean value for fat-corrected relaxed arm girth for the females was -0.57 z and for the males was $+1.92$ z, the female value would, therefore, be displaced from the males by a difference of -2.49 z. Twice the standard error about the zero adjusted mean male z-values is represented by the stippled shadow, whereas the deviation about the displaced female z-values is represented by plus and minus two standard error horizontal bars.

The proportionality profile shown as Figure 12.22 shows females to be similar to males in proportional body weight. However, the makeup of the proportional weight shows a high degree of sexual dimorphism in the proportionally smaller muscle girths, bone breadths, larger biiliocristal breadth, and smaller in each of the five skinfolds which are represented as a mean value. There is also a tendency for females to have proportionally shorter distal parts of the extremities: forearm, tibial height, and foot length. The proportional hand length and other derived lengths do not appear to have a high degree of sexual dimorphism.

Interestingly, the lower extremity or weight-bearing structures appear to have less proportional sexual dimorphism than the upper extremities. That is, compared to the males, within the female sample the females appeared to have proportionally larger femur than humerus breadth, and proportionally larger thigh and calf girths than arm girth. The circumstantial evidence is that stress induced by weight bearing caused structural development that is similar in males and females, whereas there may not be the same common stress pattern in the upper extremities. There is evidence that persistent stress in tennis, for example, can cause muscular and bone

TABLE 12.10
Mean z-Values and Their Standard Errors for Male[a] and Female[b] Canadian Tri-University Sample (CANREF).

Variable	Male (x)	Male (s$_x$)	Female (x)	Female (s$_x$)	Mean Difference[c]
Weight	−0.21	0.06	−0.27	0.07	−0.06
Total arm	−0.15	0.05	−0.50	0.05	−0.35
Upper arm (acromiale-dactylion)	−0.23	0.06	−0.35	0.06	−0.12
Arm (acromiale-radiale)	−0.30	0.07	−0.90	0.08	−0.60
Hand (stylion-dactylion)	0.34	0.10	0.02	0.14	−0.32
Leg (stature-sit ht.)	−0.10	0.05	−0.43	0.05	−0.33
Spinale ht.	−0.01	0.04	−0.16	0.07	−0.15
Tibiale ht.	0.07	0.05	−0.39	0.05	−0.46
Foot length	−0.22	0.06	−0.87	0.08	−0.65
Biepicondylar humerus width	1.04	0.07	−0.16	0.09	−1.20
Biepicondylar femur width	−0.21	0.07	−0.74	0.09	−0.53
Arm girth relaxed (f.c.)[d]	1.92	0.09	−0.57	0.11	−2.49
Chest girth (f.c.)[d]	1.10	0.08	0.10	0.10	−1.00
Thigh girth (f.c.)[d]	0.61	0.09	0.32	0.09	−0.29
Calf girth (f.c.)[d]	1.38	0.08	0.29	0.13	−1.09
A.P. chest	0.85	0.09	−0.03	0.11	−0.88
Transverse chest	−0.71	0.07	−1.61	0.08	−0.90
Biacromial breadth	0.05	0.08	−0.82	0.08	−0.87
Biiliocristal breadth	−1.24	0.07	−0.36	0.10	+0.88
Sitting height	−0.09	0.05	0.21	0.05	+0.30

[a]$N = 152$.
[b]$N = 94$.
[c]Female z-values minus male z-values are shown as the mean difference.
[d]f.c. = fat-corrected.

hypertrophy (Copley, 1978). How much this is an effective factor in narrowing the bone and muscle proportionality dimorphism is an interesting question with insufficient experimental data for its resolution.

FRACTIONATION OF BODY MASS

If, as discussed by Drinkwater and Ross (1980), we assume that fat, bone, muscle, and residual body masses deviate from Phantom values as the mean of indicator variables, we can fractionate body mass

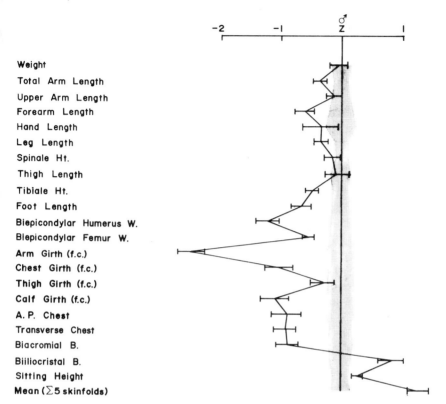

Figure 12.22. Proportional sexual dimorphism showing female z-value differences from male z-values scaled as 0.00, female bars are $+$ and $-$ 2 standard errors of z-values.

accordingly. For example, if the mean of the skinfolds is -1.0 z we should expect the fat mass to deviate from the Phantom values shown in Table 12.1 in the same way, i.e., $12.13 - 3.25$, to yield 8.88 kg fat mass. This would then have to be rescaled to the subject's actual size by dividing by $(170.18/h)^3$.

In using skinfolds to estimate fat, bone breadths for bone, skinfold-corrected girths for muscle, and torso measures for residual masses, it is possible to fractionate total body mass according to the above principle by the following general formula:

$$M = \frac{\bar{z} \times s + p}{\left(\dfrac{170.18}{h}\right)^d}$$

where:

M   is any mass such as fat mass, skeletal mass, muscle mass, or residual mass;

z is the obtained mean Phantom z-value for the subset associated with a given mass;

p is the Phantom value for the mass;

s is the standard deviation of the Phantom value for the mass;

h is the obtained height for the subject;

3   is the dimensional exponent (in this procedure d is equal to 3 since a geometric similarity system is assumed, and in this system the cube of a linear measure is proportional to a volume or a mass of constant density); and

170.18 is the Phantom height constant.

As summarized in Table 12.11, the total of the fractionated fat, bone, muscle, and residual masses accounted for total body mass in the male sample with a predicted total body mass, both rounded off to 72.3 kg. The predicted total in the female samples of 56.8 kg was only 0.7 kg less than the obtained value.

The males were leaner, having about 7.3 percent less fat and 0.9 percent less residual mass than the females. They were more

TABLE 12.11

Fractionation of Body Mass for Male and Female Canadian Tri-University Sample.

	Fat		Bone		Muscle		Residual	
	(M)	**(F)**	**(M)**	**(F)**	**(M)**	**(F)**	**(M)**	**(F)**
z	−1.61	−0.28	0.05	−0.64	1.25	0.04	−0.26	−0.70
S.E.	0.06	0.10	0.06	0.08	0.07	0.09	0.05	0.06
kg	7.94	10.40	12.18	8.75	33.80	23.68	18.36	13.93
S.D.	2.77	2.99	1.58	1.20	4.07	2.70	2.03	1.50
%	10.90	18.20	16.87	15.39	46.79	41.83	25.45	24.58

	Males	**Females**
N	152	94
Predicted weight (kg)	72.29	56.78
Obtained weight (kg)	72.35	57.48
Percentage difference	0.03	−1.16

musculoskeletally robust, having about 5.0 percent more muscle and 1.5 percent more skeletal mass.

In preliminary analysis of the fractionated body masses of the athletes studied in the Montreal Olympic Games (MOGAP) we note there are only two classifications for estimated fat. The females ranged from about 9 to 12 percent, whereas the males were generally below 8 percent. There was no clear sexual dimorphism in bone, muscle, and residual masses since the selective and training factors appeared to override the normal sexual differentiation in structure. Female runners had about 2 percent less proportional muscle mass than male runners but were 4 percent more muscular than our normal male reference sample. The specific effects of training are confounded by selection factors and hence it is impossible to ascribe causal relationships.

SEXUAL DIMORPHISM AND GENETIC ABERRATION

The specific effect of the presence or absence of sex chromosomes may be studied indirectly by the use of the Phantom stratagem, as demonstrated by Miller et al. (1980). Using data reported by Milne, Lauder, and Price (1974) and Eiben, Sandor, and Lazlo (1974) they found z-value differences between four sex chromosomal aneuploidy samples and their normal male and female controls; these are identified in Table 12.12. If there was a specific effect related to the number of Y chromosomes and the number of X chromosomes, we should expect a systematic proportionality pattern characterizing each of the aneuploidy-control differences. This was manifest in the profiles, as shown in Figure 12.23. If we conceive of the aneuploidy order of 47,XYY; 47,XXY; 47,XXX; and 45,X as a dimorphism continuum, it appears the specific effect associated with the presence or absence of Y and X chromosomes systematically alters normal patterns. Presumably this would cause an additive difference when aneuploidy groups 47,XYY and 47,XXY are compared to normal

TABLE 12.12
Chromosomal Aneuploidy Group Comparisons.

Aneuploidy Group	N	Control Group	N
47,XYY	29	46,XY	102
47,XXY	50	46,XY	188
47,XXX	26	46,XX	124
45,X	16	46,XX	164

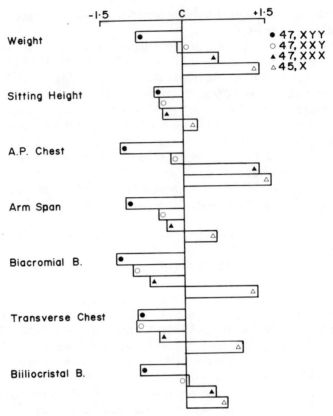

Figure 12.23.   Sex chromosomal aneuploidy versus control (C) differences showing systematic departures according to presence of Y and X chromosomes after Miller et al. (1980).

46,XX females, or 47,XXX or 45,X subjects are compared to normal 46,XY males. From consideration of Figure 12.23 it can be seen that there is an increase in ponderosity as we move from 47,XYY to 45,X. This same trend is reflected not only in proportional body weight but in each of the variables. Thus there would appear to be a specific effect on proportionality attributable to the presence or absence of X and Y chromosomes.

When the sex chromosomes themselves are intact as in Down's syndrome (trisomy 21), one would expect normal sexual dimorphism in proportionality z-values. This is patently the situation as illustrated in the z-values (Figure 12.24) for sitting height that were calculated from data by Rarick and Seefeldt (1974). Despite the distortion in proportional sitting height caused by the genetic aberration present in the Down's syndrome subjects, there is still

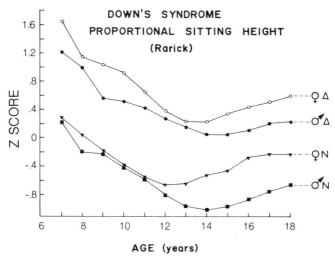

Figure 12.24. Proportional sitting height of male and female Down's syndrome and normal control subjects showing syndrome differences but within-sample male-female similarity calculated from data by Rarick and Seefeldt (1974).

present the same sexual dimorphism that is seen in the normal control sample.

SUMMARY

Recognizing the inherent mathematical limitations of the correlation of ratios and the difficulty of applying covariance analyses beyond a given sample, an alternate stratagem for proportionality assessment was discussed. This involved the use of a unisex reference human, or Phantom, that geometrically scaled all variables to a common stature and expressed differences in z-values from specified Phantom measures (p) and their standard deviations based on an arbitrary human population (s).

The general formula for application of the Phantom stratagem with a complete and recently revised list of p and s values was presented enabling the reader to calculate z-values and make comparison between male and female samples using a simple hand calculator.

Although boys tend to be slightly taller and heavier at birth than girls, girls mature faster than boys. In terms of proportional body weight, trivial differences were noted between boys and girls in early infancy. Both sexes, however, appear to have a proportional weight deflection or spurt at around 2 months of age. This has been shown in proportionality values other than proportional weight, such as sitting height and calf girth. Full explanation of the phenomenon awaits a well-controlled longitudinal study with monthly or even biweekly measurements.

During the adolescent growth spurt there are dramatic changes in proportionality characteristics. Proportional body weight values continue to decline from infancy to early childhood. Girls show increased proportional weight values from initiation of the growth spurt which precedes that of the boys. The boys' growth spurt increase does not keep pace with the girls' and they end up being somewhat more linear at age 18.

Proportionality values for other variables as well as weight revealed a changing pattern in bone measurements at ages 7, 12, and 15. Boys were seen to be proportionally larger in forearm length, hand length, wrist girth, and biacromial breadth at all ages. The shoulder-hip dimorphism was illustrated by the use of a z-value for biiliocristal breadth with biacromial breadth as the scaling factor. The tremendous increase in proportional muscularity was shown by the z-values for fat-corrected relaxed arm girth which increased sharply in boys around puberty. The girls, however, showed no significant rise.

In viewing an adult sample recruited from three universities, a typical somatotype display showed males to be displaced in a northeasterly direction of the somatochart (i.e., they were more ectomesomorphic or lean-muscular) than the females. Vectors between mean somatoplots for various ethnic and athletic samples showed the displacement to be a general sexual dimorphic characteristic whenever the sample selection was similar for males and females.

The reference samples of Canadian males and females were compared by proportionality profiles that showed the greatest sexual dimorphism to be in proportional skinfolds, which were greater in females, and fat-corrected muscle girths, which were smaller in females.

A further application of the Phantom stratagem for the anthropometric fractionation of body mass showed that the Canadian reference samples had the greatest male-female differences in muscle and fat masses.

The specific effect of the sex chromosomes associated with sexual dimorphism in proportionality was explored comparing sex chromosomal aneuploidy groups with appropriate norms. Marked differences with decreasing linearity were noted in aneuploidy-control differences for 47,XYY, 47,XXY, 47,XXX, and 45,X syndromes. Where the sex chromosomes were intact, as illustrated by data in Down's syndrome, normal male-female proportionality differences were maintained, even though the syndrome groups were markedly different from the normal controls. These and other aspects of sexual dimorphism and proportional growth phenomena await further elucidation. The Phantom stratagem appears to be a simple procedure and useful in dealing with longitudinal and cross-sectional data to sort out genetic and environmental influences that give rise to sexual dimorphism.

BIBLIOGRAPHY

Bailey, D. A., W. D. Ross, R. L. Mirwald, and C. Weese. 1978. "Size Dissociation of Maximal Aerobic Power during Growth in Boys." *Medicine Sport*, 11:140-151 (Basel: Karger).

Boersma, E. R., and R. L. Mbise. 1979. "Intrauterine Growth of Live-born Tanzanian Infants." *Tropical and Geographical Medicine*, 31:7-19.

Carter, J. E. L. 1975. *The Heath-Carter Somatotype Method.* San Diego: San Diego State University.

———. 1980. "The Contributions of Somatotyping to Kinanthropometry." In *Kinanthropometry II. International Series on Sport Sciences* Vol. 9, edited by M. Ostyn, G. Beunen, and J. Simons, pp. 409-422. Baltimore: University Park Press.

Copley, B. B. 1978. "The Effect of Intensive Tennis Playing on Certain Morphological Parameters. *Journal of Anatomy*, 126(3):666.

Drinkwater, D. T., and W. D. Ross. 1980. "Anthropometric Fractionation of Body Mass." In *Kinanthropometry II. International Series on Sport Sciences* Vol. 9, edited by M. Ostyn, G. Beunen, and J. Simons, pp. 178-189. Baltimore: University Park Press.

Eiben, O. G. 1978. "Changes in Body Measurements and Proportion of Children, Based on Kormend Growth Study." In *Auxology: Human Growth in Health and Disorder. Proceedings of the Serono Symposia*, Vol. 13, edited by L. Gedda and P. Parisi, pp. 187-198. London: Academic Press.

Eiben, O. G., G. Sandor, and J. Lazlo. 1974. "Turner-Syndromasok Testalkata." *Anthropologiai Kozlemenyek* (Budapest), 18:41-48.

Falkner, F., M. P. Pernot-Roy, H. Habich, J. Senecal, and G. Masse. 1958. "Some International Comparisons of Physical Growth in the Two First Years of Life." *Courrier of the International Children's Centre*, VIII(1):1-11.

Faulhaber, J. 1976. "Algunos Cambios Morfologicos Durante el Crecimiento." Unpublished paper. Available from Instituto Nacional de Anthropologia e Historia. Mexican Cordova 43-45 Y, Mexico.

de Garay, A. L., L. Levine, and J. E. Lindsay Carter (eds.). 1974. *Genetic and Anthropological Studies of Olympic Athletes.* New York: Academic Press.

Ghosh, S., S. K. Bhargava, S. Madhavan, A. D. Taskar, V. Bhargava, and S. K. Nigam. 1971. "Intrauterine Growth of North Indian Babies." *Pediatrics*, 47(5):826.

Goldwater, R., and M. Treves (eds.). 1947. *Artists on Art*. London: Kegan Paul, p. 51.

Heath, B. H., and J. E. L. Carter. 1967. "A Modified Somatotype Method." *American Journal of Physical Anthropology*, 27:57-74.

_____. 1971. "Growth and Somatotype Patterns of Manus Children, Territory of Papua and New Guinea: Application of a Modified Somatotype Method to the Study of Growth Patterns." *American Journal of Physical Anthropology*, 35:49-67.

Jost, A. 1972. "A New Look at the Mechanisms Controlling Sex Differentiation in Mammals." *Johns Hopkins Medical Journal*, 130:38-53.

Lau-Pau, G. 1980. "Perinatal Patterns of Proportional Growth." B. Sc. unpublished honors thesis. Simon Fraser University, Burnaby, B.C., Canada.

Miller, R., W. D. Ross, A. Rapp, and M. Roede. 1980. "Sex Chromosome Aneuploidy and Anthropometry: A New Proportionality Assessment Using the Phantom Stratagem." *American Journal of Medical Genetics*, 5:125-135.

Milne, J. S., I. J. Lauder, and W. H. Price. 1974. "Anthropometry in Sex Chromosome Abnormality." *Clinical Genetics*, 5:96-106.

Ohno, S. 1976. "Major Regulatory Genes for Mammalian Sexual Development." *Cell*, 7:315-321.

Olivier, G. 1960. *Pratique Anthropologique*. Paris: Vigot Frères.

Rarick, G. L., and V. D. Seefeldt. 1974. "Observations from Longitudinal Data on Growth in Stature and Sitting Height of Children with Down's Syndrome." *Journal of Mental Deficiency Research*, 9:24.

Ross, W. D., and N. C. Wilson. 1974. "A Strategem for Proportional Growth Assessment." In *Children and Exercise, VIth International Symposium on Pediatric Work Physiology*, den Haan, 1973, edited by J. Borms and M. Hebbelinck, pp. 169-182. *Acta Pediatrica Belgica* Supplement 28.

Ross, W. D., S. R. Brown, J. W. Yu, and R. A. Faulkner. 1977. "Somatotype of Canadian Figure Skaters." *Journal of Sports Medicine and Physical Fitness*, 17(2):195-205.

Ross, W. D., S. R. Brown, M. Hebbelinck, and R. A. Faulkner. 1978. "Kinanthropometry Terminology and Landmarks." In *Physical Fitness Assessment Principles, Practices and Application*, edited by R. J. Shephard and H. La Vallee, pp. 44-50. Springfield, Ill.: Charles C Thomas.

Ross, W. D., D. T. Drinkwater, D.A. Bailey, G. R. Marshall, and R. M. Leaky. 1980a. "Kinanthropometry: Traditions and New Perspectives." In *Kinanthropometry II*, edited by M. Ostyn, G. Beunen, J. Simons, pp. 3-27. Baltimore, Md.: University Park Press.

Ross, W. D., D. T. Drinkwater, N. Whittingham, and R. A. Faulkner. 1980b. "Anthropometric Prototypes Age 6 to 18 Years." In *Pediatric Work Physiology IX*, edited by K. Berg and B. O. Eriksson, pp. 3-12. Baltimore, Md.: University Park Press.

Saarinen, U. M., and M. A. Siimes. 1979. "Role of Prolonged Breast Feeding in Infant Growth." *Acta Paediatrica Scandinavica*, 68:245-250.

Scammon, R. E., and L. A. Calkins. 1929. *The Development and Growth of the External Dimensions of the Human Body in the Fetal Period.* Minneapolis: University of Minnesota Press.

Sheldon, W. H., S. S. Stevens, and W. B. Tucker. 1940. *The Varieties of Human Physique.* New York: Harper Bros.

Stewart, T. D. 1952. *Hrdlička's Practical Anthropometry*, 4th ed. Philadelphia: Wistar Institute, p. 205.

Tanner, J. M. 1978. *Foetus into Man: Physical Growth from Conception to Maturity.* Cambridge, Mass: Harvard University Press.

_____., with the assistance of R. H. Whitehouse and S. Jarman. 1964. *The Physique of the Olympic Athlete. A Study of 137 Track and Field Athletes at the XVIIth Olympic Games, Rome 1960.* London: George Allen Unwin.

Weiner, J. S., and J. A. Lourie. 1969. *Human Biology: A Guide to Field Methods.* IBP Handbook No. 9. Oxford: Blackwell Scientific Publications, p. 8.

Wingerd, J., E. J. Schoen, and I. L. Solomon. 1971. "Growth Standards in the First Two Years of Life Based on Measurements of White and Black Children in a Prepaid Health Care Program." *Pediatrics*, 47:818-825.

Thirteen

Absolute and Relative Sex Differences in Body Composition*

Quantitative sex differences in soft tissue composition are marked by their variability. Sexual dimorphism can change by an order of magnitude from one anatomical region to the next. This quality, which contrasts with the patent dimorphism of stature or weight, stems from the complex and mutable structure of soft tissue. Of these tissues, fat has a role in morphological variation that makes it central to any consideration of sexual dimorphism in living populations. Accordingly, adipose tissue and its relation to other soft tissues form the focus of this chapter.

Adipose tissue comprises approximately 15 percent of body weight in the young adult male and about 27 percent in his female counterpart. By comparison, muscle tissue represents an average 52 percent and 40 percent of body weight in men and women, respectively (Andersen 1963; Keys and Brozek 1953; Malina 1969, 1978). These means belie the greater variability of fat tissue. It may range from a few kilograms in the trained male athlete to well over 100 kg in the obese of either sex.

In turn, fat tissue is not purely fat. It contains about 62 percent ether-soluble extracts including phospholipids, glycolipids, sterols,

*The author wishes to express his appreciation to Dr. Stanley M. Garn for generous access to the University of Michigan Tecumseh Project data, and to Drs. Garn, Victor Katch, A. Roberto Frisancho, Frank Falkner, and C. Loring Brace for thoughtful criticism regarding many of the ideas contained in this chapter.

and glycerides; about 24 percent cellular solids; and roughly 14 percent extracellular fluids (Moore et al. 1963; Siri 1956). The composition of the glycerides has been found to vary somewhat by sex, age, and race (Insull and Bartsch 1967), while the other components are reasonably stable.

Another way of considering fat is through its relation to body water. Total body water (TBW) can be partitioned into intracellular water (ICW), which constitutes about 35 percent of adult body weight, and extracellular water (ECW), which makes up about 25 percent of body weight (Friis-Hansen 1971; Siri 1956). Because ICW, and by extension, TBW, are invested primarily in lean tissues, they make useful indirect measures of body composition. The fraction of water in lean tissue has been assumed to be a slightly less than 73 percent, and the water in fat tissue has been found to vary from 10 to 30 percent depending on age, health, and hydration (Keys and Brozek 1953).

The relation between total body water and fatness has theoretical and methological implications for the study of sex differences in body composition. In the basic two-component model (Morales et al. 1945), the proportion of total body water in lean tissue is assumed constant and independent of the fat tissue. The relationship can be expressed as follows: $TBW = \alpha(1 - A) + \beta A$, where A is the proportion of fat tissues and α and β are the constant water fractions of lean and fat, respectively. Extracellular water also is assumed constant (cf. Siri 1956).

Using this expression, it can be demonstrated that in a completely fat-free body, TBW will approach 73 percent, while in a very obese body this figure may be halved. Arithmetically, lean tissue is the predominant source of TBW. However, the potential range of variation of fatness makes it the effective determinant of variability in total body water. As a case in point, adult women are nearly twice as fat as men. This difference in adiposity gives women some 3 percent more TBW directly from fat and some 11 percent less TBW indirectly lost through the reduction in percent lean.

From the two-component model have come such estimators of body composition as lean body mass (LBM), fat-free weight (FFW), fat weight (FW) and lean body weight (LBW) (cf. Behnke, Feen, and Welham 1942; Behnke 1959; Brozek 1963; Garn 1957; Pace and Rathbun 1945; von Dobeln 1959). The theoretical conundrums inherent to the two-component model are well known (Brozek and Grande 1955; Brozek et al. 1963; Keys and Brozek 1953; Siri 1956; Wedgewood 1963; but see Kodama 1971 or Sheng and Huggins 1979 for dissenting views). Strictly speaking, the lean body mass appears neither as invariant nor as independent of fatness as the two-component model requires. The error introduced by these problems is small when the model is used with individuals of near average fatness but increases for the very lean or very fat. Moreover, the biological meaning of such concepts as lean body mass is sometimes abstruse. However, despite these caveats, measures such as LBM or FW provide useful comparisons between sex and age groups, and they are demonstrably more informative than whole body parameters such as weight or density (cf. Brozek 1961). In the discussion that follows, indirect measures of body composition (such as those just noted) are used in conjunction with direct measures such as radiographic fat breadths or skinfold thicknesses in order to evaluate adequately soft tissue body composition.

Finally, it should be noted that sexual dimorphism is of two types, absolute and proportionate. The first is that calculated from absolute differences between men and women. The second, also termed "relative sexual dimorphism," is calculated independently of size. Such measurements, often expressed as ratios, are common throughout the natural sciences, but have been less favored by investigators of human sex differences. In this chapter, both absolute and relative measures of sexual dimorphism are used in order to enhance biological meaning.

SOFT TISSUE SEXUAL DIMORPHISM DURING CHILDHOOD

Sexual dimorphism in the body composition of children and adolescents reflects the complex dynamics of growth. The various growth criteria—accumulated tissue, incremental change, velocity ratios, and so forth—can yield quite disparate estimates of soft tissue sexual dimorphism (Roede and van't Hof 1978; Tanner 1951, 1962). Further complications are introduced by simple mathematical relationships. For instance, breadth in an expanding annular tissue such as limb fat can be constant, yet tissue area and volume increase. In addition, the allometric relationships of growing tissues are complex and poorly understood.

For all of this, some aspects of sex differences in body composition are straightforward. Most strikingly, from birth to death females are systematically fatter than males.

A clear relation has not been established between soft tissue sex differences and gestational age or birth weight (Dauncey, Gandy, and Gairdner 1977; Friis-Hansen 1963, 1971). Chemical analyses of stillborn infants under 2400 gm indicated no significant differences in body composition (Hunt and Giles 1956), but several other investigations have found sex differences in term (Dauncey, Gandy, and

Gairdner 1977; Owen, Jensen, and Fomon 1962; Owen et al. 1966; Yssing and Friis-Hansen 1965) and premature (Friis-Hansen 1963; Gampel 1965) infants. Representative data indicate a sex difference of about 4 percent in intracellular water, 2 percent in total body water, and 0.4 percent in density at birth (Table 13.1). This sex difference in body composition also is apparent in subcutaneous fatness. In a study of 79 male and 67 female newborns, Garn (1958) found only slight sex differences in absolute thoracic fat breadth, but a significantly greater ratio of fat breadth to body weight in girls (0.93) than in boys (0.83). Greater absolute skinfold thickness in female neonates was reported by Parizkova (1963), and Gampel (1965) found female newborns to have significantly greater subcutaneous fat per unit body weight at all gestational ages. Gampel also found no sex difference in skinfold compressibility changes with gestational age.

During the first month of life, sex differences in body composition may increase slightly (Owen et al. 1966) but thereafter diminish to under 2 percent in TBW by 1 year. Some caution in interpreting these data is called for because of the high variance in dehydration during the first months of life. However, it appears that girls have slightly smaller decrements of total body water loss from 1 through 9 months. Moreover, between the fourth and ninth month the initial sex difference in ICW becomes trivial (Owen, Jensen, and Fomon 1962). These data may indicate slight sex differences in either lean growth velocity or extracellular water loss. No completely satisfactory explanation has been advanced.

Subcutaneous fatness is more straightforwardly dimorphic during the first year. Girl infants have greater fat thicknesses at all sites (Garn 1956; Garn, Greaney, and Young 1956; Maresh 1962, 1966; Owen et al. 1966; Reynolds 1944; Stuart and Sobel 1946). Overall, sex differences in subcutaneous fatness during this period are on the order of 4 to 6 percent or 10 to 12 percent relative to body weight (Table 13.2).

TABLE 13.1
Newborn Sex Differences in Body Composition.

	Boys	Girls	Difference (%)
Body weight (gm)	3330	3321	0.3
TBW (%)	76.6	74.3	2.3
ECW (%)	39.6	39.3	0.3
ICW (%)	36.0	31.8	4.0
Body density	1.026	1.022	0.4

Source: Adapted from Yssing and Friis-Hansen 1965.

TABLE 13.2
Summed Subcutaneous Fat and Skin Thicknesses.

Age	Boys		Girls	
(months)	Mean (mm)	*S.D.*	Mean (mm)	*S.D.*
2	52.8	12.0	56.4	9.1
4	72.4	14.0	75.9	11.6
6	83.2	15.7	87.2	15.0
12	82.0	19.8	83.2	15.2

Source: Adapted from Owen et al. 1966, p. 251. Reprinted with permission from W. B. Saunders, Inc.: Owen, G. M., L. J. Filer, M. Maresh, and S. J. Fomon. 1966. "Sex-related Differences in Body Composition in Infancy." In *Human Development*, F. Falker, ed. Philadelphia: Saunders.

GROWTH OF FAT AND LEAN TISSUE

After the first year, sex differences in fatness increase slowly until prior to puberty. In terms of body water, males gain more TBW and ICW per unit weight or height (Cheek, Mellits, and Elliott 1966; Friis-Hansen 1957; Mellits and Cheek 1970; Moore et al. 1963). This trend is shown in Table 13.3. It can be seen that the slope of TBW as a function of weight and of height is systematically greater in boys. The equations are linear for both weight and height, but a break in slope occurs in the relationship between TBW and height at about 6 years for girls and 10 years for boys (Cheek et al. 1966). It is unclear whether these breaks represent developmental benchmarks or the upswing of sigmoid growth curves. In either case, the general relationship reflects differential acquisition of fat and lean.

The timings of sex differences in the growth of fat and of lean are not congruent. Early in childhood, sexual dimorphism in soft tissue is predominately due to fat growth. Both sexes show decrements in growth of fat from about the ninth month to the seventh year. However, girls lose somewhat less fat, leading to a relatively greater amount of fat tissue throughout childhood. This phenomenon is illustrated in Figure 13.1 for triceps and subscapular skinfolds. It is apparent that the sex differences in decrements varies according to anatomical site and age, but the basic form of the curve holds for these and for other fat locations.

Lean body mass growth over the same period is positive, although there is a slow loss of velocity from the first year through the seventh in females and the first year through the ninth in males (cf. Stuart and Sobel 1946; Tanner 1962). Sex differences in incremental growth are slight. Thus the changes in body water during the period described above are explained best by differential rates of fat loss.

TABLE 13.3
Growth of Total Body Water.

Boys
 TBW = 1.065 + 0.603 (Wt.)
 TBW = −6.77 + 0.170 (Ht.) when Ht. ≤ 132.7 cm
 TBW = −66.75 + 0.623 (Ht.) when Ht. ≥ 132.7 cm

Girls
 TBW = 1.87 + 0.493 (Wt.)
 TBW = −3.806 + 0.127 (Ht.) when Ht. ≤ 110.8 cm
 TBW = −27.85 + 0.344 (Ht.) when Ht. ≥ 110.8 cm

Source: Adapted from Mellits and Cheek 1970. Reprinted with permission from ©The Society for Research in Child Development, Inc., at the University of Chicago Press: Mellits, E. D., and D. B. Cheek. 1970. "The assessment of body water and fatness from infancy to adulthood." In: *Physical Growth and Body Composition: Papers from the Kyoto Symposium on Anthropological Aspects of Human Growth*, J. Brozek, ed. *Monographs of the Society for Research in Children's Development*, 35(7): 12-27.

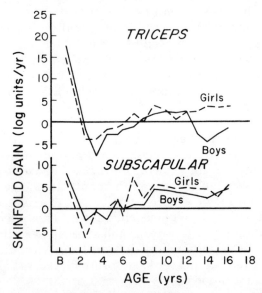

Figure 13.1. Growth of subcutaneous fat in boys and girls is shown for two skinfold sites. Each sex loses fat thickness from infancy to middle childhood. However, girls' decrements are smaller, resulting in greater total fatness. (Adapted from Tanner 1962, p. 23. Reprinted with permission from Blackwell Scientific Publications, Ltd.: Tanner, J. M. 1962. *Growth at Adolescence*, 2nd ed. Oxford: Blackwell.)

As early as the sixth year, growth of lean tissue also becomes a factor in compositional dimorphism. This is evident first in measures of actively metabolizing cell mass, such as potassium (Burmeister 1965), body water (Cheek et al. 1966), or creatinine excretion (Malina 1969). Sex differences in the growth of skeletal muscle appear somewhat later (Tanner 1962).

Table 13.4 indicates these initial sex differences in terms of total body potassium between the ages of 6 and 18. The earliest detectable sex difference of 0.01 gm potassium per kilogram body weight increases some 50 times by the end of adolescence. Other data estimating the growth of lean are in general agreement with these (Andersen 1963; Andersen and Langham 1959; Flynn et al. 1975; Pierson, Lin, and Phillips 1974).

This contrast in growth of lean is complemented by another in growth of fat. After the sixth year, velocity of adipose tissue growth is positive, but girls add more fat per unit weight or unit height than boys (Mellits and Cheek 1970; Reynolds 1944, 1946; Stuart, Hill, and Shaw 1940; Tanner 1962).

Table 13.5 presents these relationships in terms of equations for calculation of lean body mass or fat mass. It can be seen that boys gain an average of about 2.1 percent in LBM for every centimeter of height, while girls gain about 1.8 percent. By comparison, boys gain approximately 2.5 percent and girls 2.7 percent in FW for each centimeter of height. Thus sex differences in growth of soft tissue are influenced by total body size independently of age. The significance of this fact is elaborated later in the chapter.

TABLE 13.4
Sex Differences in Total Potassium.

Age (yrs.)	Males (gm/kg)	Females (gm/kg)	Difference (gm/kg)
6-7	2.01	2.00	0.01
7-8	2.08	1.97	0.11
8-9	2.04	1.94	0.10
9-10	2.14	1.92	0.22
10-11	2.12	1.91	0.21
11-12	2.10	1.85	0.25
12-13	2.10	1.87	0.23
13-14	2.06	1.82	0.24
14-15	2.18	1.79	0.39
15-16	2.23	1.74	0.49
16-17	2.26	1.71	0.55
17-18	2.28	1.75	0.53

Source: Adapted from Burmeister 1965.

TABLE 13.5
Growth of Lean Body and Fat Mass.

Males

$$LBW = 1.44e^{0.0212 \text{ Ht.}}$$
$$FW = 12.116 - 0.215 \text{ Ht.} + 0.00114 \text{ (Ht.)}^2$$

Females

$$LBW = 2.06e^{0.0184 \text{ Ht.}}$$
$$FW = 27.514 - 0.538 \text{ (Ht.)} + 0.00279 \text{ (Ht.)}^2$$

Source: Forbes 1972; Mellits and Cheek 1970. Reprinted with permission from © The Society for Research in Child Development at the University of Chicago Press: Mellits, E. D., and D. B. Cheek. 1970. "The Assessment of Body Water and Fatness from Infancy to Adulthood." *Monographs of the Society for Research in Children's Development*, 35(7): 12-27, and with permission from Williams and Wilkins Co.: Forbes, G. B. 1972. "Relation of Lean Body Mass to Height in Children and Adolescents." *Pediatric Research*, 6:32-37.

The net effect of differential velocities of fat and lean growth is illustrated in Figure 13.2. In terms of accumulated fat and fat-free mass, boys have a greater fat-free weight and smaller fat weight than girls at all ages shown. The absolute sex difference in fatness is roughly constant until menarche, while the absolute sex difference in lean is winnowed for the 2 years in which girls' growth velocity exceeds boys'.

SUBCUTANEOUS TISSUE

Sexual dimorphism in subcutaneous fatness inreases slowly from early childhood through the tenth year (Figure 13.3). Median female skinfold or radiographic breadth averages 25 percent greater during childhood (cf. National Center for Health Statistics 1972; Tanner and Whitehouse 1975), and at some anatomical sites girls in the 10th percentile of fatness are absolutely fatter than boys in the 50th percentile (Stuart and Sobel 1946; Stuart et al. 1962).

The nature of this variability in the magnitude of sex differences from one anatomical region to another is unresolved. In the large cross-sectional sample illustrated in Figure 13.3, fatness was most dimorphic in the lower trunk. However, other data have shown greater sexual dimorphism during childhood in the upper body. In one well-known longitudinal study (Reynolds 1944), boys averaged

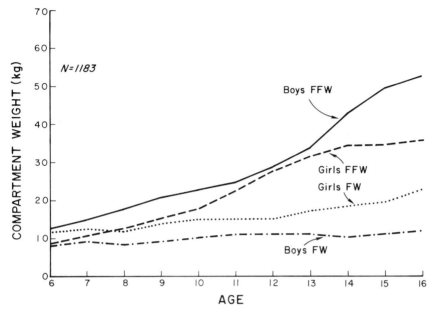

Figure 13.2. Fat and fat-free weights of children, calculated using height-corrected regressions of weight on summed skinfolds (cf. Brozek 1963). These sex differences increase very slowly until late childhood, at which time fat dimorphism is slightly reduced and lean dimorphism is sharply reduced. (Calculated using unpublished data from the University of Michigan Tecumseh Project courtesy of S. M. Garn.)

12.6 percent less calf fat breadth than girls, which can be compared to 25.7 percent less brachial fat breadth (Baker, Hunt, and Sen 1958) and 18.4 percent less thoracic fat breadth (Bailey 1977) than girls.

If size is taken into account by expressing fat breadth as a fraction of total limb breadth, sexual dimorphism in calf fat is increased very slightly to 13.3 percent, but sex differences in brachial fat are decreased to 20.9 percent. It should be noted here that the variance surrounding these differences is sufficiently high that gender assignment based on children's subcutaneous fatness has been termed little better than guesswork (Tanner 1962).

Ratios are biologically meaningful when numerator and denominator show covariance. As one might expect, associations between either fat or muscle and limb diameter have been found to be highly significant (Reynolds 1944, 1949; Malina and Johnston 1967), with correlation coefficients on the order of 0.7 to 0.9. However, between-tissue correlations generally are far lower and are significant ($r = 0.3$ to 0.4) only for fat and bone (Baker, Hunt, and Sen 1958; Malina and

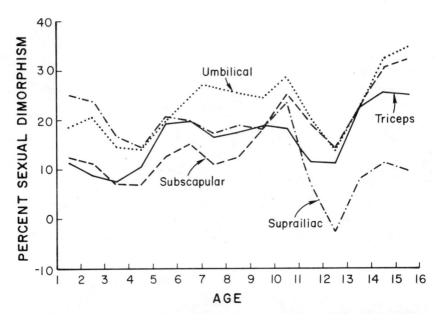

Figure 13.3. Childhood and adolescent sexual dimorphism in four skinfolds. Lower trunk fatness is most dimorphic in this sample of subjects. Puberty is marked by a temporary decline in sex differences in subcutaneous fat thickness. (Unpublished data from the University of Michigan Tecumseh Project courtesy of S. M. Garn.)

Johnston 1967; Reynolds 1949; but see Maresh 1966 or Tanner 1965 for different estimates). No major sex differences are apparent in these intercorrelations, but same-tissue correlations between anatomical regions are higher in males, from 0.6 to 0.8, than in girls, from 0.3 to 0.5 (Garn 1955; Malina and Johnston 1967). These findings thus indicate higher variability of single tissue distribution over the female body, but no real sex differences in the interrelationship of different tissues at a given location.

A related problem concerns the correspondence between subcutaneous and internal fat. Reported correlations between selected skinfolds and total body density range from -0.4 to -0.9 (cf. Parizkova 1961; Forbes and Amirhakimi 1970). Inferential evidence suggests that from childhood onward females store proportionately more fat internally (Forbes and Amirhakimi 1970; Pascale et al. 1956). This follows from the observation that changes in female subcutaneous fat thickness are associated with a smaller change in body density than similar changes in males. However, other interpretations are possible (Forbes 1962; Forbes and Amirhakimi 1970). Anatomical studies of animals (Pitts and Bullard 1968) offer little additional insight regarding sex differences in fat distribution.

ADOLESCENCE

Maturational timing is the initial determinant of changes in soft tissue sex differences during adolescence. Minimum velocity of fat growth coincides with peak height velocity, which is at about 12 years in girls and 13.5 years in boys (National Center for Health Statistics 1974; Tanner 1974; Tanner and Whitehouse 1976). Growth of the lean body mass is nearly the inverse of this, with peak velocity roughly coincident with peak height velocity.

The effect of this differential timing is summarized in Figure 13.4. The ratio of lean body mass to height is slightly dimorphic from middle childhood (see Table 13.5) but the sex difference is not notable until after male peak height velocity in the fourteenth year. By comparison, sex differences in the ratio of fat mass to total mass (e.g., percent fat) are apparent from female peak height velocity in the thirteenth year. As noted previously, these ratios demonstrate that boys gain more lean than girls during their height accelerations.

The reduction in fat sexual dimorphism shown in Figures 13.3 and 13.4 during the twelfth and thirteenth years can be attributed to a stasis in female fat deposition occurring in conjunction with a prepubertal fat growth acceleration in the male. However, not all investigations have found such a specific decline in fat sexual dimorphism (cf. Burmeister and Bingert 1967; Maresh 1966; Rauh and Shumsky 1968). Moreover, the reduction in sexual dimorphism appears to be more pronounced in trunk than in limb subcutaneous fat. This is due to the continued decrements of limb fat growth in males for some years after peak height velocity (Garn and Haskell 1959; Tanner 1962), while female limb fat growth is checked only temporarily during peak height velocity. The result is maintenance of sexual dimorphism in limb fat throughout puberty.

SIZE CHANGE AND SEXUAL DIMORPHISM

The influence of body size on soft tissue sexual dimorphism in children was noted earlier. However, the precise nature of the interaction is poorly understood. One approach to the problem has been to partition size into vertical and horizontal frame components

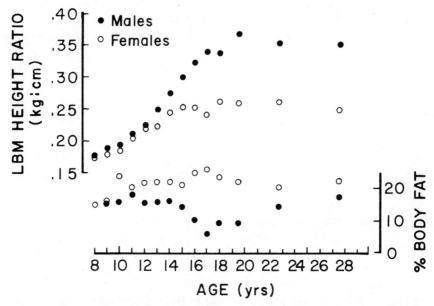

Figure 13.4. Proportional lean and fat mass, determined using K^{40}, from late childhood through the third decade. Slight sex differences during childhood become pronounced following puberty, with the increase in fat sexual dimorphism preceding that in lean. These trends can be compared to the more obvious childhood dimorphism in absolute mass of fat and lean shown in Figure 13.2. (Adapted from Forbes and Hursh 1963, p. 261. Reprinted with permission from the New York Academy of Sciences: Forbes, G. B. and J. Hursh. 1963. "Age and sex trends in lean body mass calculated from K^{40} measurements: With a note on the theoretical basis for the procedure." *Annals of the New York Academy of Sciences*, 110:225-263.)

and measure the effects of each on compositional sex differences using matched pair analysis within age groups (Bailey 1977). Figure 13.5 illustrates the results. Boys and girls of similar height differed by 5.2 kg in fat weight and 4.8 kilograms in fat-free weight. These data can be compared to the unmatched children in Figure 13.2, who averaged 4.6 kg difference in fat weight and 5.3 kg in fat-free weight. Children of similar stature are thus somewhat more dimorphic in fat and somewhat less dimorphic in lean.

A smaller number of children were of similar bony chest breadth. They differed by about 7 kg in fat weight, but were within 0.25 kg of the same fat-free weight. Thus children of similar breadth are still more dimorphic in fat and essentially nondimorphic in lean tissue.

Boys and girls of similar height or breadth come from opposite ends of their respective size distributions. The finding that small boys

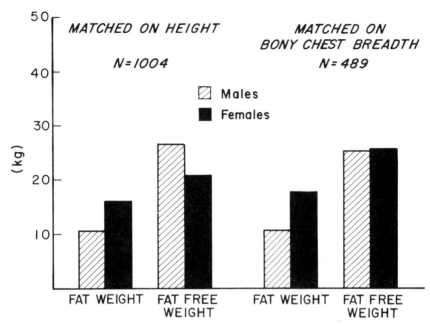

Figure 13.5. The influence of sex differences in frame size on compositional sexual dimorphism in children aged 6-11. Boys and girls of equal height are more dimorphic in fat weight and less dimorphic in fat-free weight. Boys and girls of equal bony chest breadth are yet more dimorphic in fatness but non-dimorphic in fat-free weight. (Calculated using unpublished data from the University of Michigan Tecumseh Project courtesy of S. M. Garn.)

and large girls differ substantially less in lean tissues and considerably more in fat tissue agrees with Forbes' observation that the tall of either sex are disproportionately lean (1972, 1974); one may add that the short of either sex appear to be disproportionately fat. The curvilinear nature of the relationship is indicated in Table 13.5. It is more problematic to explain the greater change in sexual dimorphism evoked by matching for frame breadth. This suggests sex differences in the association between soft tissue and skeletal conformation, but further study is needed to provide a secure answer. It is clear enough, however, that stature is not the only aspect of size that influences soft tissue sexual dimorphism in children.

ADULT SOFT TISSUE DIMORPHISM

The central trend in adult body composition is fat deposition. Over six decades, women's fatness increases from about 26 percent of the body weight to over 44 percent, averaging about 36 percent, or some 23 kg of tissue. Men are less fat by a third, averaging 22 to 24 percent or about 14 kg of tissue. However, relative to their initial fatness, men actually gain more fat—going from 12 percent to over 30 percent—than do women. In absolute terms, women's 0.2 kg of fat increase per year is twice that of men (cf. Brozek et al. 1963; Katch and Weltman 1975; Pierson, Lin, and Phillips 1974; Norris, Lundy, and Shock 1963; Young et al. 1963). The sex differences in body fatness are greatest in the sixth decade of life (National Center for Health Statistics 1970; Ten-State Nutrition Survey 1972; Young et al. 1963).

By contrast, the more stable lean body mass is greatest in males during the third decade and in females during adolescence (Forbes 1976). Males average 62 to 65 kg and females 42 to 48 kg of lean between 20 to 70 years of age (cf. Behnke 1963; Behnke and Wilmore 1974; Forbes 1976; Norris, Lundy, and Shock 1963). Longitudinal data indicate that the greater lean mass of the male is lost more rapidly after the third decade, approximating 2 to 3 kg per decade compared to a female loss of about 1.5 kg per decade (cf. Forbes 1976; Pierson et al. 1974; Shukla et al. 1973). The causes of this sex difference are unclear.

Similar trends are observable in body water compartments. Relative to body weight, men average 13 to 14 percent more total body water than women and 7 to 8 percent more intracellular water (Allen, Andersen, and Langham 1963; Moore et al. 1963). Both sexes lose TBW with age. Expressed as a percentage of total body weight, the loss of TBW is curvilinear (Table 13.6). The rate of loss in either sex is largely a function of ICW water loss, which, in turn, reflects alterations in body composition. It is not completely clear whether the proportion of lean to fat changes or the ratio remains constant but lean becomes less hydrated as it is infiltrated by connective tissue (Allen et al. 1960; Edelman et al. 1952a,b). In either case, by 60 years of age the sex difference in liters of TBW is half what it was at 20 years.

TABLE 13.6
Changes in Adult Total Body Water with Age.

Age	Male % TBW	Female % TBW	Difference % TBW
18-22	61.5	52.2	9.3
22-30	58.5	51.1	7.4
30-40	56.1	51.1	5.0
40-50	55.6	49.0	6.6
50-60	54.4	47.8	6.6
60-80	54.1	46.2	7.9

Source: Adapted from Allen, Andersen, and Langham 1960.

The relation of body water to weight provides a further example of how scale affects calculated sexual dimorphism. If absolute body water is related to age and weight with parabolic equations, the resultant plot is linear. Figure 13.6 shows the influence of sex differences in weight on TBW and ICW. Men and women of equal weight differ in TBW by approximately 6.5 liters and in ICW by about 4 liters, compared to the average differences of roughly 13.5 liters and 8 liters, respectively. These TBW differences in men and women of equal weight represent sex differences in compositional proportions.

ADULT SUBCUTANEOUS FATNESS

Sex differences in external fat are marked throughout adulthood (cf. National Center for Health Statistics 1970; Ten-State Nutrition Survey 1972). As shown in Figure 13.7, women's skinfolds average some 19 percent thicker than men's over six decades and the triceps is fully 40 percent larger in females. It is evident that the sex difference in triceps fatness established during adolescence is nearly doubled, whereas sex differences in trunk fatness remain near adolescent levels. In general, adult limb fatness is more highly dimorphic than adult trunk fatness (Edwards 1951; Garn 1957; Garn and Saalberg 1953; Reynolds and Asakawa 1950; Tanner 1965).

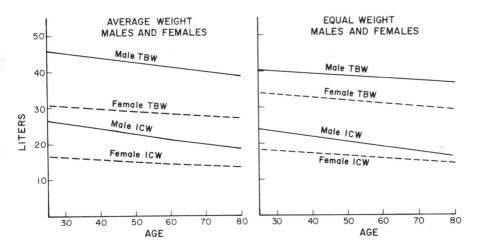

Figure 13.6. The effect of sex differences in body mass on sexual dimorphism in total body water (TBW) and intracellular water (ICW). Rate of loss of body water with age is similar in the two groups, but sexual dimorphism in TBW and ICW is more than halved by weight equalization. (Calculated from data in Moore et al. 1963.)

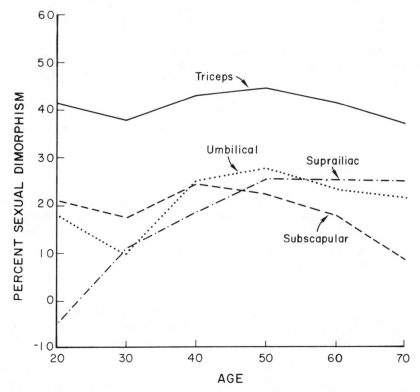

Figure 13.7. Adult sex differences in subcutaneous fatness increase through the fifth decade. In adults limb fatness is more dimorphic than trunk fatness. (Calculated using unpublished data from the University of Michigan Tecumseh Project, courtesy of S. M. Garn.)

There is a great deal of variability in the strength of sex differences in subcutaneous fatness. Table 13.7 indicates average young adult male and female values and percent sexual dimorphism, calculated as $100(M/F-1)$, for 17 skinfolds (Bailey 1980). Sexual dimorphism ranges from 4.0 percent greater suprailiac thickness in males to 60.6 percent greater lateral midthigh thickness in females. In general, the lower limb is most dimorphic, followed by the upper limb. Trunk dimorphism is moderate to slight.

Comparison of these data to those in Figure 13.8 reveals considerable differences in the sexual dimorphism of the umbilical and subscapular skinfolds. This underscores the population specificity of subcutaneous fat distribution, which further complicates investigation of sex differences. There is some indication that a basic contrast of trunk with limb fatness is population independent (cf. Badora 1975;

TABLE 13.7
Male and Female Skinfold Thickness and Sexual Dimorphism.

Skinfold	Males X̄(mm)	S.D.	Females X̄(mm)	S.D.	Percent Sexual Dimorphism*
Mandibular	7.0	2.2	7.5	1.9	−5.8
Lateral neck	5.4	1.2	5.6	1.2	−4.4
Acromion	7.1	1.7	8.3	2.4	−13.9
Biceps	4.3	1.3	6.7	2.6	−34.7
Triceps	9.0	3.7	14.9	4.6	−39.9
Anterior forearm	4.4	1.1	6.9	3.0	−36.7
Lateral forearm	5.5	1.6	8.0	3.0	−30.3
Subscapular	11.9	4.4	12.2	3.7	−2.1
Axillary	9.4	3.5	10.4	3.5	−10.1
Umbilical	15.7	8.0	16.3	6.2	−3.7
Suprailiac	17.4	8.0	16.7	6.4	4.0
Dorsal iliac	11.3	5.9	15.2	5.8	−25.6
Anterior upper thigh	10.2	4.0	16.2	6.1	−37.2
Anterior mid-thigh	12.0	4.7	23.9	6.9	−49.7
Lateral mid-thigh	8.7	3.6	22.1	7.8	−60.6
Lateral max. calf	8.7	2.8	13.8	4.4	−36.8
Med. max. calf	8.0	2.8	15.7	5.3	−49.2

*Calculated as $100(M/F - 1)$. Using this formula, larger male means will be positive and larger female means negative.
Source: Author's data.

Bailey 1980; Garn 1955; Mueller and Reid 1979), although the particulars of distribution are population-specific.

ADULT SIZE AND SEX DIFFERENCES IN BODY COMPOSITION

The comparative stability of the lean body mass in the adult allows more precise investigation of how size affects sexual dimorphism in soft tissue. Techniques described earlier are inappropriate for adults because of the lessened overlap in size parameters. However, analysis of covariance permits mathematical equalization of independent size variables and subsequent calculation of adjusted dependent variable means (Draper and Smith 1966). This use of the algorithm is elaborated in Bailey and Katch (1981).

As shown in Table 13.8 for 4057 adults over four decades, adjustment of sex differences in frame size substantially alters calculated sexual dimorphism of fatness. Uncorrected values follow

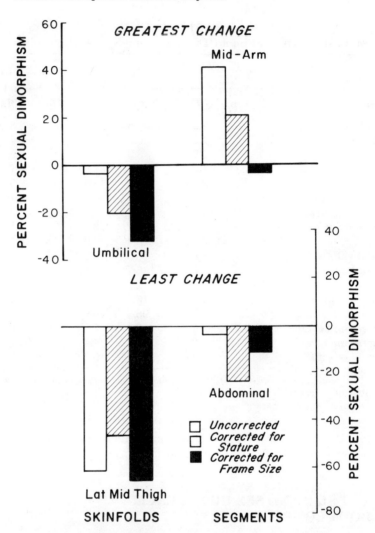

Figure 13.8.   The influence of size on sex differences in subcutaneous fat and body segment volume of young adult subjects. The greatest effect of total frame size equalization is on umbilical fatness and mid-arm volume. Size correction has the least effect on lateral mid-thigh fat and abdominal volume. No relationship is apparent between initial sexual dimorphism and propensity for change. (Author's data.)

those indicated in Figure 13.6. A general increase in sexual dimorphism is evident with age, particularly for the suprailiac and umbilical skinfolds. When height is statistically equalized, sex differences in fatness are altered slightly in the younger but not in the older subjects. However, sex differences are altered considerably

TABLE 13.8
Effects of Size on Subcutaneous Fatness.

	Percent Sexual Dimorphism*		
	Uncorrected	Corrected for Stature	Corrected for Stature and BCB
18-25			
Triceps	−34.6	−36.8	−55.3
Subscapular	−12.9	−13.2	−40.7
Suprailiac	16.2	10.9	−27.7
Umbilical	−6.2	−11.6	−44.5
25-35			
Triceps	−34.8	−36.0	−49.9
Subscapular	−9.2	−6.3	−30.0
Suprailiac	22.2	21.4	−13.4
Umbilical	−0.1	−2.6	−26.9
35-45			
Triceps	−37.3	−39.6	−55.7
Subscapular	−9.5	−9.5	−34.5
Suprailiac	3.8	5.6	−27.3
Umbilical	−8.5	−8.6	−34.8
45-55			
Triceps	−43.2	−44.8	−61.6
Subscapular	−19.5	−19.7	−41.6
Suprailiac	−18.7	−19.2	−41.7
Umbilical	−23.1	−23.9	−44.3

*Calculated as $100(M/F - 1)$. Using this formula, greater male means will be positive, greater female means will be negative.
Source: Unpublished data, University of Michigan Tecumseh Project, courtesy of S. M. Garn.

when both height and bony chest breadth (BCB) are adjusted. At all ages females of similar size to males are markedly fatter. The smallest sex difference after correction for size is 13.4 percent and the largest is 61.6 percent. These data indicate that, proportionately, females are a great deal fatter than calculation of average sex differences would lead us to believe (cf. Reynolds and Asakawa 1950).

The model can be extended to assay greater variability in subcutaneous fatness and in body size. Table 13.9 shows relative sexual dimorphism for 17 skinfolds corrected for height and for frame size, in this case height and eight frame diameters including biacromial, biiliac, bitrochanteric, chest, wrist, elbow, knee, and ankle.

Correction for stature increases the relative sex differences in skinfold thickness from 0.1 percent for the acromion skinfold to 18.9

TABLE 13.9
Absolute and Relative Sex Differences in Skinfold Thickness.

Skinfold	Percent Sexual Dimorphism*		
	Uncorrected	Corrected for Height	Corrected for Frame Size
Mandibular	−5.8	−12.7	−19.3
Lateral neck	−4.4	−11.3	−18.5
Acromion	−13.9	−14.0	−22.0
Biceps	−34.7	−49.7	−59.5
Triceps	−39.9	−46.1	−53.4
Anterior forearm	−36.7	−45.8	−52.9
Lateral forearm	−30.3	−41.3	−50.0
Subscapular	−2.1	−11.3	−24.4
Axillary	−10.1	−20.5	−27.6
Umbilical	−3.7	−20.2	−32.1
Suprailiac	4.0	−14.9	−22.3
Dorsal iliac	−25.6	−37.0	−48.1
Anterior upper thigh	−37.2	−49.5	−58.7
Anterior mid-thigh	−49.7	−53.2	−67.5
Lateral mid-thigh	−60.6	−55.2	−64.7
Lateral max. calf	−36.8	−39.6	−42.7
Medial max. calf	−49.2	−54.8	−60.6

*Calculated as $100(M/F - 1)$. Using this formula, larger male means will be positive and larger female means will be negative.
Source: Author's data.

percent for the suprailiac skinfold. Full frame size correction increases average skinfold thickness 8.6 percent over statural correction alone and 16.9 percent over the uncorrected state.

It is apparent from the range of response to size adjustment that some regions of the body are more sensitive to scale than others. In general, sex differences in lower trunk and anterior upper leg fatness are most increased by size equalization, while sex differences in calf and upper torso fatness are least affected. Magnitude of change caused by size adjustment is not associated with initial sexual dimorphism. This variability in response to size correction suggests that subcutaneous fat sites are subject to varying degrees of genetic regulation. This may explain so-called "sex specific" distributions of fat that appear to correspond roughly with those skinfolds least affected by size.

VOLUME AND BODY SIZE

The end product of variation in internal structure is variation in external size and shape. It is of some interest to examine the limited information available concerning sex differences in volume.

Sexual dimorphism in adult total body volume, measured hydrostatically, is on the order of 20 percent (Freedson et al. 1979; Katch and Weltman 1975). College-age men average 69 liters volume and college-age women average 56 liters. Middle-aged subjects have been found to be larger and slightly more dimorphic, with average male volumes of 78 liters and female volumes of 59 liters. This is a sex difference of about 25 percent. Whether this increase in sexual dimorphism reflects sex specific increases in fatness and bulk or cross-sectional sampling is not clear.

Segmental volumes vary substantially in the degree of sexual dimorphism (Table 13.10). Volumetric sex differences.range from under 17 percent for the head and neck to over 60 percent for the upper limb. The 33 percent difference in sexual dimorphism between upper and lower limbs is noteworthy.

The volumes of body segments, like other dimensions of soft tissue, are influenced by total body size. This effect is particularly evident if small segments are delimited. The linked segment approach of Dempster (Dempster and Gaughan 1967) has been utilized to calculate segmental volumes from anthropometric measurements (Katch, Weltman, and Gold 1974; Katch and Weltman 1975; Sady et al. 1978). Table 13.11 presents data on the effects of size on 16 segmental volumes using analysis of covariance techniques

TABLE 13.10
Body Segment Volumes of Men and Women (Water Displacement).

Segment	Males $\overline{X}$(ml)	Females $\overline{X}$(ml)	Percent Sexual Dimorphism
Left upper limb	3937	2424	62.4
Right upper limb	4066	2483	63.8
Left hand	479	305	56.6
Right hand	497	295	68.5
Left lower limb	10976	8519	28.8
Right lower limb	10818	8296	30.4
Left foot	1205	879	37.0
Right foot	1221	883	38.5
Head and neck	5325	4554	16.9
Buttocks	10635	8540	24.5

Source: Adapted from Katch and Weltman 1975.

TABLE 13.11
Absolute and Relative Sex Differences in Segment Volume (Geometric).

Segment	Percent Sexual Dimorphism*		
	Uncorrected	Corrected for Height	Corrected for Frame Size
Chest	23.3	4.4	−0.4
Abdominal	−3.9	−23.7	−11.6
Pelvic	27.9	−1.1	−9.3
Gluteal	−6.6	−21.0	−40.2
Mid-thigh	7.2	−7.2	−22.8
Lower thigh	18.9	5.5	5.6
Upper knee	24.2	8.9	2.1
Lower knee	17.2	−6.7	−26.2
Upper calf	12.2	−13.6	−18.4
Lower calf	23.9	7.7	−0.5
Upper arm	24.6	16.1	1.8
Mid-arm	40.9	20.7	−3.9
Lower arm	48.7	32.8	16.8
Upper forearm	52.5	37.2	15.3
Mid-forearm	54.7	42.7	22.4
Lower forearm	67.4	44.0	25.2

*Calculated as $100(M/F - 1)$. Using this formula, larger male means will be positive and larger female means will be negative.
Source: Author's data.

described earlier. The uncorrected volumes of the forearm are most dimorphic and the volumes of the middle trunk the least dimorphic. Following equalization of stature, 5 segments were relatively larger in women and 10 segments were from 4.4 to 44 percent larger in men. The degree of change—a measure of sensitivity to scale—ranged from 8.5 percent in the upper arm to 29.0 percent in the pelvis. Full frame size correction created a somewhat different pattern of dimorphism. A majority of segments were larger in females, reaching 40.2 percent for the gluteal segment. The lower forearm remained the most positively dimorphic (male larger) segment.

The effect of equalizing frame size includes an increase in relative female fatness, thereby increasing female volume. However, the variability in sexual dimorphism from one anatomical region to another is not explained adequately by this shift in relative fatness (Bailey and Katch 1981).

The overall effects of body size on fatness and on segmental volume are summarized in Figure 13.8.

CONCLUSIONS

Sex differences in soft tissue composition have been shown to vary according to age and anatomical site. Some trends are evident. Sex differences in fatness increase slowly from birth to puberty, become more pronounced from then into middle age, and stabilize thereafter. Generally speaking, these differences are strongest in the extremities. Insofar as can be determined, internal fat reserves are less variable, leading to smaller sex differences in total body fat.

Two types of sexual dimorphism have been defined. Absolute sexual dimorphism is most representative of average populational differences. Relative or proportionate sexual dimorphism, independent of size or mass, can provide additional information concerning the interrelationship of tissues or compartments, and may provide the most relevant data regarding genetic and environmental components of sexual dimorphism.

Finally, the variability of sexual dimorphism has been underscored. This variability challenges the investigator to produce models and analyses sufficiently sophisticated to describe the complexity of soft tissue body composition.

BIBLIOGRAPHY

Allen, T. H., E. C. Andersen, and W. H. Langham. 1960. "Total Body Potassium and Gross Composition in Relation to Age." *Journal of Gerontology*, 15:348-357.

Andersen, E. C. 1963. "The Three Component Body Composition Analysis Based on Potassium and Water Determinations." *Annals of the New York Academy of Sciences*, 110:189-210.

Andersen, E. C., and W. H. Langham. 1959. "Average Potassium Concentration of the Human Body as a Function of Age." *Science*, 130:713-714.

Badora, G. 1975. "The Distribution of Subcutaneous Fat Tissue in Young Women and Men." *Studies in Physical Anthropology, Polish Academy of Sciences No. 1*:91-107.

Bailey, S. M. 1977. "Sex Differences in Body Composition for Children of Similar Size (abstract)." *American Journal of Physical Anthropology*, 47:116.

————. 1980. Patterns of Variation in Human Sexual Dimorphism. Ph.D. Dissertation, University of Michigan. Univ. Microfilms: Ann Arbor.

Bailey, S. M., and V. L. Katch. 1981. "The Effects of Body Size on Sexual Dimorphism in Fatness, Volume and Muscularity." *Human Biology*, 53:337-349.

Baker, P. T., E. E. Hunt, and T. Sen. 1958. "The Growth and Inter-relationships of Skinfolds and Brachial Tissues in Man." *American Journal of Physical Anthropology*, 16:39-58.

Behnke, A. R. 1959. "The Estimation of Lean Body Weight from Skeletal Measurements." *Human Biology*, 31:295-315.

_____. 1963. "Anthropometric Evaluation of Body Composition Throughout Life." *Annals of the New York Academy of Sciences*, 110:450-464.

Behnke, A. R., B. G. Feen, and W. C. Welham. 1942. "The Specific Gravity of Healthy Men." *Journal of the American Medical Association*, 118:495-498.

Behnke, A. R., and J. J. Wilmore. 1974. *The Evaluation and Regulation of Body Build and Composition*. Englewood Cliffs, N.J.: Prentice-Hall.

Brozek, J. 1961. "Body Composition." *Science*, 134:920-930.

_____. 1963. "Quantitative Description of Body Composition: Anthropology's 'Fourth Dimension'." *Current Anthropology*, 4:3-39.

Brozek, J., and F. Grande. 1955. "Body Composition in Man: Correlation Analysis versus Physiological Approach." *Human Biology*, 27:22.

Brozek, J., F. Grande, J. Andersen, and A. Keys. 1963. "Densitometric Analysis of Body Composition: Revision of Some Quantitative Assumptions." *Annals of the New York Academy of Sciences*, 110:113-140.

Brozek, J., J. K. Kihlberg, H. L. Taylor, and A. Keys. 1963. "Skinfold Distributions in Middle-Aged American Men: A Contribution to Norms of Leanness-Fatness." *Annals of the New York Academy of Sciences*, 110:492-502.

Burmeister, W. 1965. "Body Cell Mass as the Basis of Allometric Growth Functions." *Annals of Pediatrics*, 204:65-72.

Burmeister, W., and A. Bingert. 1967. "Die Quantitaven Veränderungen der Menschlichen Zellmasse Zwischen dem 8 und 90 Lebensjahr." *Klinical Wochenschrift*, 45:409.

Cheek, D. B., E. D. Mellits, and D. Elliott. 1966. "Body Water, Height and Weight during Growth in Normal Children." *American Journal of Diseases of Childhood*, 112:312-317.

Dauncey, M. J., G. Gandy, and D. Gairdner. 1977. "Assessment of Total Body Fat in Infancy from Skinfold Thickness Measurements." *Archives of Disease in Childhood*, 52:223-227.

Dempster, W. T., and G. Gaughan. 1967. "Properties of Body Segments Based on Size and Weight." *American Journal of Anatomy*, 120:33-54.

von Dobeln, W. 1959. "Anthropometric Determination of Fat-free Body Weight." *Acta Medica Scandinavica* (*Supplement*) 126.

Draper, N. .R., and H. Smith. 1966. *Applied Regression Analysis*. New York: Wiley & Sons.

Edelman, I. S., J. M. Olney, A. J. James, C. Brooks, and F. Moore. 1952a. "Body Composition: Studies in the Human Being by the Dilution Principle." *Science* 115:447.

Edelman, I. S., H. B. Haley, P. R. Schloerb, D. B. Sheldon, B. J. Friis-Hansen, G. Stoll, and F. Moore. 1952b. "Further Observations on Total Body Water: Normal Values Throughout the Life Span." *Surgery, Gynecology, and Obstetrics*, 95:1.

Edwards, D. A. W. 1951. "Differences in the Distribution of Subcutaneous Fat with Sex and Maturity." *Clinical Science*, 10:305-315.

Flynn, M. A., J. Clark, J. Reid, and G. Chase. 1975. "A Longitudinal Study of Total Body Potassium in Normal Children." *Pediatric Research*, 9:834-836.

Forbes, G. B. 1972. "Relation of Lean Body Mass to Height in Children and Adolescents." *Pediatric Research*, 6:32-37.

––––––. 1974. "Stature and Lean Body Mass." *American Journal of Clinical Nutrition*, 27:595-598.

––––––. 1976. "The Adult Decline in Lean Body Mass." *Human Biology*, 48:161-173.

Forbes, G. B., and G. H. Amirhakimi. 1970. "Skinfold Thickness and Body Fat in Children." *Human Biology*, 42:401-418.

Forbes, G. B., and J. Hursh. 1963. "Age and Sex Trends in Lean Body Mass Calculated from K^{40} Measurements: With a Note on the Theoretical Basis for the Procedure." *Annals of the New York Academy of Sciences*, 110:255-263.

Freedson, P., S. Sady, V. Katch, and H. Reynolds. 1979. "Total Body Volume in Females: Validation of a Theoretical Model." *Human Biology*, 51:499-506.

Friis-Hansen, B. 1957. "Changes in Body Water Compartments During Growth." *Acta Paediatrica Scandinavica*, 46:207-208.

––––––. 1963. "The Body Density of Newborn Infants." *Acta Paediatrica Scandinavica*, 52:513-521.

––––––. 1971. Body Composition during Growth." *Pediatrics*, 47:264-274.

Gampel, B. 1965. "The Relation of Skinfold Thickness in the Neonate to Sex, Length of Gestation, Size at Birth and Maternal Skinfold." *Human Biology*, 37:29-37.

Garn, S. M. 1955. "Relative Fat Patterning: An Individual Characteristic." *Human Biology*, 27:75-89.

––––––. 1956. "Fat Thickness and Growth Progress during Infancy." *Human Biology*, 28:232.

––––––. 1957. "Fat Weight and Fat Placement in the Female." *Science*, 125:1091-1092.

––––––. 1958. "Fat, Body Size and Growth in the Newborn." *Human Biology*, 30:265-280.

Garn, S. M., and J. A. Haskell. 1959. "Fat Changes during Adolescence." *Science*, 129:1615-1616.

Garn, S. M., and J. Saalberg. 1953. "Sex and Age Differences in the Composition of the Adult Leg." *Human Biology*, 27:39-49.

Garn, S. M., G. R. Greaney, and R. W. Young. 1956. "Fat Thickness and Growth Progress during Infancy." *Human Biology*, 28:232-250.

Hunt, E. E., Jr., and E. Giles. 1956. "Allometric Growth of Body Composition in Man and Other Mammals." *Human Biology*, 28:253.

Insull, W., Jr., and G. E. Bartsch. 1967. "Fatty Acid Composition of Human Adipose Tissue Related to Age, Sex and Race." *American Journal of Clinical Nutrition*, 20:13-23.

Katch, V., and A. Weltman. 1975. "Predictability of Body Segment Volume in Living Subjects." *Human Biology*, 47:203-218.

Katch, V., A. Weltman, and E. Gold. 1974. "Validity of Anthropometric Measurements and the Segment-Zone Method for Estimating Segmental and Total Body Volume." *Medicine and Science in Sports*, 6:271-276.

Keys, A., and J. Brozek. 1953. "Body Fat in Adult Man." *Physiological Reviews*, 32:245-325.

Kodama, A. M. 1971. "In Vivo and in Vitro Determination of Body Fat and Body Water in the Hamster." *Journal of Applied Physiology*, 31:318-322.

Malina, R. M. 1969. "Quantification of Fat, Muscle and Bone in Man." *Clinical Orthopedic Related Research*, 65:9.

_____. 1978. "Growth of Muscle Tissue and Muscle Mass." In *Human Growth* Vol. 2, edited by F. Falkner and J. M. Tanner, pp. 273-274. New York: Plenum.

Malina, R. M., and F. Johnston. 1967. "Relations Between Bone, Muscle, and Fat Widths in the Upper Arms and Calves of Boys and Girls Studied Cross-Sectionally at Ages 6-16 Years." *Human Biology*, 39:211-223.

Maresh, M. M. 1962. "Bone, Muscle and Fat Measurements." *Pediatrics*, 28:971-984.

_____. 1966. "Changes in Tissue Widths during Growth." *American Journal of Diseases of Childhood*, 111:142-155.

Mellits, E. D., and D. B. Cheek. 1970. "The Assessment of Body Water and Fatness from Infancy to Adulthood." *Monographs of the Society for Research in Children's Development*, 35(7):12-27.

Moore, F. D., K. H. Olesen, J. D. McMurray, H. V. Parker, M. Ball, and C. M. Boyden. 1963. *The Body Cell Mass and Its Supporting Environment.* Philadelphia: W. B. Saunders.

Morales, M. F., E. N. Rathbun, R. E. Smith, and N. Pace. 1945. "Studies on Body Composition: Theoretical Considerations Regarding the Major Body Tissue Components, with Suggestions for Applications to Man." *Journal of Biological Chemistry*, 158:677-684.

Mueller, W. H., and R. Reid. 1979. "A Multivariate Analysis of Fatness and Relative Fat Patterning. *American Journal of Physical Anthropology*, 50:199-208.

National Center for Health Statistics. 1970. "Skinfolds, Body Girths, Biacromial Diameters and Selected Anthropometric Indices of Adults in the United States 1960-1962." Washington, D.C.: DHEW, Series 11 (No. 35).

_____. 1972. "Skinfold Thickness of Children in the United States 6 to 11 Years." Washington, D.C.: DHEW, Series 11, No. 120.

_____. 1974. "Skinfold Thickness of Youths in the United States 12-17 Years." Vital and Health Statistics Series 11, No. 132.

Norris, A. H., T. Lundy, and N. W. Shock. 1963. "Trends in Selected Indices of Body Composition in Men Between the Ages 30 and 80 Years." *Annals of the New York Academy of Sciences*, 110:623-639.

Owen, G. M., R. L. Jensen, and S. Fomon. 1962. "Sex-Related Difference in Total Body Water and Exchangeable Chloride during Infancy." *Journal of Pediatrics*, 60:858-868.

Owen, G. M., L. J. Filer, M. Maresh, and S. J. Fomon. 1966. "Sex-related Differences in Body Composition in Infancy." In *Human Development*, edited by F. Falkner, pp. 246-253. Philadelphia: W. B. Saunders.

Pace, N., and E. N. Rathbun. 1945. "Studies on Body Composition: The Body Water and Chemically Combined Nitrogen Content in Relation to Fat Content." *Journal of Biological Chemistry*, 158:685-692.

Parizkova, J. 1961. "Age Trends in Normal and Obese Children." *Journal of Applied Physiology*, 16:173-174.

————. 1963. "Impact of Age, Diet and Exercise on Man's Body Composition." *Annals of the New York Academy of Sciences*, 110:861.

Pascale, J. R., M. Grossman, H. Sloane, and P. Frankel. 1956. "Correlations Between Thickness of Skinfolds and Body Density in 88 Soldiers." *Human Biology*, 28:165.

Pierson, N. R., D. H. Y. Lin, and R. A. Phillips. 1974. "Total Body Potassium in Health: Effects of Age, Sex, Height and Fat." *American Journal of Physiology*, 226:206-212.

Pitts, G., and T. Bullard. 1968. "Some Interspecific Aspects of Body Composition in Mammals." In *Body Composition in Animals and Man*. National Academy of Sciences Pub. No. 1598, Washington, D.C.

Rauh, J. L. and D. A. Shumsky. 1968. "Lean and Non-Lean Body Mass Estimates in Urban School Children." In *Human Growth*, edited by D. B. Cheek. Philadelphia: Lea & Febiger.

Reynolds, E. L. 1944. "Differential Tissue Growth in the Leg during Childhood." *Child Development*, 15:181-205.

————. 1946. "Sexual Maturation and the Growth of Fat, Muscle and Bone in Girls." *Child Development*, 17:121-144.

————. 1949. "The Fat-Bone Index as a Sex-Differentiating Character in Man." *Human Biology*, 21:199-204.

Reynolds, E. L., and T. Asakawa. 1950. "A Comparison of Certain Aspects of Body Structure and Body Shape in 200 Adults." *American Journal of Physical Anthropology*, 8:343-366.

Roede, M. J., and M. A. van'T Hof. 1978. "Errors Associated with the Estimation of Intersection of Male and Female Growth Curves." *Human Biology*, 50:411-423.

Sady, S., P. Freedson, V. L. Katch, and H. M. Reynolds. 1978. "Anthropometric Model of Total Body Volume for Males of Different Sizes." *Human Biology*, 50:529-540.

Sheng, H. P., and R. A. Huggins. 1979. "A Review of Body Composition Studies with Emphasis on Total Body Water and Fat." *American Journal of Clinical Nutrition*, 32:630-647.

Shukla, K. K., K. J. Ellis, C. S. Dombrowski, and S. H. Cohen. 1973. "Physiological Variation of Total-Body Potassium in Man." *American Journal of Physiology*, 224:271-274.

Siri, W. 1956. "The Gross Composition of the Human Body." *Advances in Biological and Medical Physics*, 4:239-280.

Stuart, H. C., and E. H. Sobel. 1946. "The Thickness of the Skin and Subcutaneous Fat Tissue by Age and Sex in Childhood." *Journal of Pediatrics*, 28:637-647.

Stuart, H. C., P. Hill, and C. Shaw. 1940. "The Growth of Bone, Muscle and Overlying Tissues as Revealed by Studies of Roentgenograms of the Leg Area." Monographs of the Society for Research in Child Development 5(3).

Stuart, H. C., R. B. Reed, I. Valadian, and J. Cornoni. 1962. "Growth of Fat Tissue." *Bibliographica Paediatrica*, 79:71-89.

Tanner, J. M. 1951. "Notes on Reporting of Growth Data." *Human Biology*, 23:93-159.

_____. 1962. *Growth at Adolescence*, 2nd ed. Oxford: Blackwell.

_____. 1965. "Radiographic Studies of Body Composition in Children and Adults." In *Human Body Composition*, edited by J. Brozek, pp. 211-236. Oxford: Pergamon Press.

_____. 1974. "Sequence and Tempo in the Somatic Changes in Puberty." In *Control of the Onset of Puberty*, edited by M. Grumbach, G. Grave, and F. Mayer. New York: John Wiley & Sons.

Tanner, J. M., and R. H. Whitehouse. 1975. "Revised Standards for Triceps and Subscapular Skinfolds in British Children." *Archives of Disease in Childhood*, 50:142.

_____. 1976. "Clinical Longitudinal Standards for Height, Weight, Height Velocity and Weight Velocity and the Stages of Puberty." *Archives of Disease in Childhood*, 51:170-179.

Ten-State Nutrition Survey of 1968-1970. 1972. Washington, D.C.: Department of Health, Education, and Welfare, Document HO, HSM 72-8130.

Wedgewood, R. J. 1963. "Inconstancy of the Lean Body Mass." *Annals of the New York Academy of Sciences*, 110:141-152.

Young, C. M., J. Blodin, R. Tensuan, and J. H. Fryer. 1963. "Body Composition Studies of 'Older Women,' Thirty to Seventy Years of Age." *Annals of the New York Academy of Sciences*, 10:589-606.

Yssing, M., and B. Friis-Hansen. 1965. "Body Composition of Newborn Infants." *Acta Paediatrica Scandinavica (Supplement)* 159:117-118.

Fourteen

Sexual Dimorphism and Nutrient Reserves

William A. Stini

The topic of nutrient reserves is one that can be addressed at several levels. Mammals, being a class of organisms sharing the trait of relatively high metabolic activity, have been endowed with the capacity to accumulate nutrient reserves throughout the life cycle. The means by which crucial demands are met change as demands change. Several, but not all, important functional relationships between individual and species survival and the maintenance of endogenous reserves will serve to illustrate the evolutionary role of such reserves in our own species' history.

SEXUAL REPRODUCTION AND NUTRIENT RESERVES

There is considerable asymmetry in the size of the gametes contributed by mammalian parents in the process of zygote formation. The mammalian spermatozoon is little more than a vehicle for the transport of a haploid chromosome set. Its function is to deliver the genetic information needed to complement that already present in the mature ovum. Sperm mobility requires an energy supply mainly to permit sustained undulations of the flagellum that help to propel the spermatozoon to the site of fertilization in the fallopian tube. Most, if not all, of the energy supporting this activity is obtained from carbohydrates (fructose) and citric acid contained in seminal fluid. In effect, the spermatozoon is supplied with its nutrient requirements by being bathed in an energy-rich medium. The spermatozoon is thereby permitted to perform its sole function, fertilization of the ovum, with a simple anatomical structure unburdened with elaborate systems for the storage and delivery of nutrients. In view of its short life (2 to 4 days after ejaculation) and limited range of activities, the spermatozoon is adapted effectively to its functional role through the minimization of its mass. Part of the maturation process undergone by the spermatozoon involves the loss of cytoplasmic fluid in the chromatin-bearing head region. The mature spermatozoon, then, is identifiable by its high chromatin density. Its small size (0.05 mm) and mass reflect the high specificity of its role. Numbers are important, however, with an estimated 300 million spermatozoa being transferred during a single copulation.

It appears that a sperm count lower than 50 million/ml of seminal fluid is indicative of infertility in the human male. There is some uncertainty about the reason for such large numbers of spermatozoa being necessary in order for fertilization to occur, but it is thought that the enzymatic activity of many spermatozoa is necessary to permit one of them to penetrate the zona pellucida of the ovum.

Production of large numbers of spermatozoa guarantees many recombinatory events involving the parental chromosome set. The original epithelial cell's diploid chromosome set of 22 autosomal pairs can yield up to 2^{22} haploid combinations, each of which may be accompanied by either an X or Y chromosome. The system thus works continually to produce variation through recombination of genetic traits carried by the parent. Additional variation can arise as a result of crossing over and, in view of the enormous number of cell divisions involved, occasional copying errors. When the amount of variation this system makes possible is added to that occurring in the female parent, the capacity to maintain variability in the species is seen to be nearly inexhaustible. The evolutionary success of sexual reproduction is thought to derive largely from its effectiveness in that respect. The predominance of sexual reproduction among higher organisms is generally regarded as the outcome of that success.

Maintenance of variability is presumably as important in female gametogenesis as in the male. However, the means by which it is accomplished differ significantly. Whereas the process of spermiogenesis has, in its later stages, the reduction of cytoplasmic mass to the level seen in the mature spermatozoon, mechanisms of oogenesis ensure that cytoplasmic mass remains high. As a result of these mechanisms, the zygote begins the process of cleavage with substantial nutrient reserves. How these nutrient reserves are preserved, while at the same time the advantages of chromosomal recombination are retained, is a matter of considerable interest.

In many respects, oogenesis and spermatogenesis parallel each other. Where they differ is in the number of offspring ultimately produced through division of the parent oogonia or spermatogonia; the maturation process involves two divisions yielding four haploid spermatids that will become spermatozoa. The process undergone by the maturing oogonia involves two successive divisions each yielding a polar body. The polar body produced with each division contains a haploid chromosome set just as does the maturing ovum, but its cytoplasmic content is much smaller. Since the first polar body produced may, itself, divide, the usual outcome of oogenesis is one mature ovum and three polar bodies. The ovum has retained most of the cytoplasm and is usually the cell that will be fertilized. Because of the preservation of cytoplasm inherent in the system, the ovum at the time of fertilization is one of the largest of human cells. It is capable of undergoing a number of divisions initiating the differentiation process while drawing mainly on endogenous nutrient resources. Implantation in the uterine wall and access to maternally supplied nutrients does not occur for at least 10 days after fertilization. The role of nutrient reserves retained by the ovum is, therefore, a crucial one in the process of human reproduction.

From an evolutionary perspective, important aspects of the aforementioned characteristics of human reproduction include the following: (1) the benefits of ensuring continued production of variation are of sufficient value to warrant substantial gametic wastage in the form of surplus spermatozoa and polar bodies, and (2) the emphasis on quantity in gametic production by males differs fundamentally from the emphasis on quality inherent in the monthly production of a single mature ovum in the female. Thus, at the gametic level, humans exhibit the interplay of two major evolutionary tactics: In the male, variability is assured by the production of large numbers of gametes; in the female, a small number of gametes is provided with substantial nutrient reserves to begin the process of growth, differentiation, and development. The genotypes endowed with generous reserves are in a more favorable circumstance for survival. Whereas success in producing a new individual is awarded to an infinitesimally small proportion of male gametes, the proportion of potentially successful female gametes is much higher.

Because of these intrinsic factors, the level of parental investment in the survival of a specific gamete differs substantially between mammalian males and females. But in fact, the difference goes much further than gametic characteristics alone would indicate. This is because the role of the male in the reproductive process can, and often is, limited to the fertilization of the egg borne by a female. The biological relationship of the male parent and offspring can end there without necessarily jeopardizing the offspring's chances of survival. In a number of species, no contribution to the welfare of the offspring is made by the male parent beyond the act of insemination. Even in humans, the potential for such limited contribution exists, and, on occasion, is realized. The modest investment in the reproductive process characterizing the male as compared to the female translates into a fundamentally different form of selective pressure. For the male, genetic survival derives from successful competition for the opportunity to fertilize the eggs borne by females. This activity is episodic, sometimes being limited to a short period of days or weeks during the year in a number of species. In no species, with the possible exception of humans, is the net energy investment of the male equivalent to that of the female. While both sexes participate in the process of fertilization, the costs of gestation and lactation are carried exclusively by the female. While food procurement and food sharing may involve both sexes, the nurture of the young is a function of the mother to a far greater extent than of the father.

The assymmetry of the distribution of the burden of nurturing the young through the crucial early stages of life is reflected in physiological and morphological differences that, in their aggregate, we recognize as sexual dimorphism. In some mammals, sexual dimorphism is far more pronounced than in others. Even among primate species, there is wide variation in the degree of sexual dimorphism exhibited. The size difference between male and female baboons, for instance, is substantially greater than that seen in gibbons. Human sexual size dimorphism falls somewhere in between that of gibbons and that of baboons.

A survey of human populations around the world (Stini 1972a) identified a range of male/female ratios for stature of from 104/100 to 110/100 (Table 14.1). These differences, even at the top of the range, are really quite modest. But the truly significant aspects of sexual dimorphism go far beyond differences in stature. As a matter of fact, greater stature in males might, if viewed simplistically, obscure the more important fact that females are endowed with greater nutrient reserves that are dictated by their role in the reproductive process. Since some of the most significant aspects of sexual dimorphism reside predominantly in soft tissue, they are often not fully discernible through analysis of osteological remains. Substantial increments in lean body mass, as occur during hypertrophy of skeletal muscle, can usually be identified through examination of the bones, but variations in adiposity, the primary site of caloric reserves, are less easily detected. For this and for other reasons that will emerge in subsequent discussion, the analysis of osteological remains may not

TABLE 14.1
Male Stature as a Percent of Female Stature: Highest and Lowest
Values Recorded in Europe and Africa.

High Values		Low Values	
Europe		Europe	
Macedonians	109.0	Germans (N. Algau)	106.7
Swedes	109.0	Germans (S. Algau)	106.4
Yugoslavs	108.5	Norwegians	106.2
Bulgarians	108.4	Ukrainians	106.2
Portugese	108.2	Genevans	106.1
Welsh	108.2	German Swiss	106.0
Gypsies	108.0	Poles	105.8
Czechs	107.8	Highland Bernois	105.7
Estonians	107.7		
Africa		Africa	
Lera	108.8	Bassari	106.1
Venda	108.8	Bisago	105.5
Baka-Bayaka	107.6	Gondar	106.2*
		Mbuti	105.1
		Mangisa	104.7
		Lari	104.6

*Dellapotas (1969).
Source: From Stini (1972a).

provide conclusive evidence of the effect of nutritional stress or
disease on the expression of sexually dimorphic characters. Osteological remains do, however, yield considerable direct and indirect traces
of nutritional and disease status and often are the best evidence
available for drawing inferences concerning the state of health of
extinct populations.

MATERNAL RESERVES AND REPRODUCTIVE SUCCESS

Natural selection operates through the mechanism of differential
reproductive success. No matter how successful the individual is in
terms of resource control, intrapersonal dominance, or even longevity,
lack of progeny spells genetic death. Even though the concept of
inclusive fitness has led to some modification of the strict-selectionist
interpretation of evolutionary theory, it must be conceded that any
population with a large proportion of sterile females will find itself at
a competitive disadvantage with respect to populations of generally
high fertility. This is especially true where mortalities are high and
the life span is short. The most direct means of altering a population's

gene pool is through prevention of reproduction by specific genotypes. We might expect, therefore, that traits closely associated with reproductive success have been under strong selective pressure throughout the species's history and continue to be so. In view of sex differences in parental investment and role in the human reproductive process, biological differences of substantial scope and magnitude are predictable.

In humans, female secondary sexual characteristics are, in large part, a direct reflection of the childbearing and lactation functions. It is necessary to recognize that, in terms of its deleterious impact on reproductive success, a stillborn infant is more costly than an early spontaneous abortion. Even more costly is infant mortality, since it means an even lengthier withdrawal of the mother from the pool of actively reproducing females. We must recognize then, that in addition to physiological and morphological adaptations to the childbearing function, mechanisms for the support of the infant for an extended postpartum period must also exist. A breakdown in any of the adaptive mechanisms in the sequence from fertilization through gestation, parturition, and lactation would compromise the genetic future of the mother. The male parent, who may have been successful in fertilizing other females, has a smaller stake in the survival of any specific fetus. Thus, the force of natural selection is exerted preferentially on the female. Differences between the sexes attributable to the support and nurture of the fetus and infant by the female are reinforced and emphasized through the intimacy of their effect on genetic survival.

The genetic future of male genotypes is affected by these female adaptations since males who are successful in mating with females capable of producing viable offspring will leave more progeny. Consequently, traits that enhance male success in attracting such females will gain a selective advantage. Anatomical and physiological characteristics that enhance success of certain males in maximizing their contribution to the gene pool of future generations will increase in frequency over time. From the foregoing discussion, it should be apparent that the pathways of adaptation in this crucial area differ fundamentally between the sexes of our species. During much of the history of the species, evolutionary change in sex-related traits in females has either paralleled or diverged from that of males. Only in the very recent past has the opportunity for convergence arisen, and the possible effect of recent relaxation in selective pressures related to sex roles remains to be seen.

SELECTIVE FORCES OF SPECIAL SIGNIFICANCE
IN HUMAN EVOLUTION

Contemporary humans are the products of an evolutionary sequence that can be traced back to an apelike ancestor. Earlier phases of human evolutionary history, that is, those preceding the Late Pliocene/Early Pleistocene epochs, remain the object of much speculation. From the bulk of the evidence currently available, it seems highly probable that all of the contemporary higher primates are derived from a prosimian-like form of Early Tertiary origin. Paleontological evidence for the ancestral forms making up the inferred sequence is exceedingly meager. Students of human evolution have, therefore, been compelled to attempt hypothetical reconstruction of the anatomical and physiological characteristics of these ancestors. In order to use the evidence available from studies of contemporary primates, it has generally been assumed that a prosimian-like primate ancestor would resemble contemporary prosimians in many ways. This assumption can most certainly be challenged, of course, but reconstructions of the habitats of these Early Tertiary forms lend support to claims that they at least had access to a wide range of nutrient resources resembling those exploited by contemporary forms. The paleontological and paleo-ecological evidence that is available is consistent with the assumption that Early Tertiary primate ancestors consumed a heterogeneous diet that included insects, fruits, and other vegetable products. If this was indeed the case, the foundations for human dietary versatility were laid early in the history of the primates. The corollary of this conclusion is that the heavy reliance on vegetable diets currently prevalent among primates is a relatively recent specialization. The increasingly common observations by primate ethologists of animal protein consumption by primates raises the possibility that most if not all contemporary primates are potential omnivores.

One contemporary primate species, *Homo sapiens*, is unquestionably omnivorous. While lacking the capacity to digest cellulose, contemporary humans are endowed with an array of organs and enzymes capable of extracting energy, amino acids, minerals, and vitamins from an extraordinary variety of food sources. Although a number of living primates appear to be specialized to some degree in their dietary repertoire, humans have maintained and perhaps enlarged the range of foods that can be exploited. As reference to the recommended daily allowances (Table 14.2) for humans shows, heterogeneity has become an important factor in human dietary requirements, and the human taste for culinary variety is rooted in

TABLE 14.2
Human Nutritional Requirements and Their Major Dietary Sources.

Nutrient Requirement	Dietary Sources	Where Obtained
Energy	Carbohydrates, proteins, and fats	Plant and animal products
Amino acids and nitrogen	Proteins	Plant and animal tissues
Essential fatty acids	Fats	Vegetable oils, nuts, animal fat
Fat-soluble vitamins	Vitamin A—preformed or as caratenoids	Green and yellow vegetables, animal liver, egg and dairy products
	Vitamin D—cholecalciferol	Fatty fish, eggs, liver, butter
	Vitamin E—tocopherols, tocotrienols	Vegetable oils, some in plant and animal tissues
	Vitamin C—almost exclusively of plant origin	Citrus fruits, raw vegetables, some in animal liver
	Thiamin—plant and animal sources	Yeast, legumes, meat, fish, poultry, eggs and dairy products, fruits, vegetables, and cereals
	Riboflavin—animal and plant sources	Yeast, meat, fish, poultry, eggs, dairy products, legumes, fruits, vegetables, cereals

Water-soluble vitamins (Vitamin C, thiamin, riboflavin, niacin, vitamin B-6, folacin, vitamin B-12)	Niacin—animal and plant sources	Meat, fish, poultry, eggs, dairy products, fruits and vegetables, cereals
	Vitamin B-6 (Pyridoxine), animal, and plant sources	Muscle meats, liver, vegetables, whole-grain cereals, egg yolk
	Folacin—animal and plant sources	Wheat germ, liver, kidney, yeast, mushrooms, fruits, vegetables
	Vitamin B-12—foods of animal origin	Liver, kidney, milk, meat
Minerals	Calcium—animal and vegetable sources	Milk and dairy products, meat, fish, poultry, eggs, cereals and legumes, fruits, vegetables
	Phosphorus—foods rich in protein	Meat, fish, poultry, eggs, cereals
	Magnesium—vegetable and animal sources	Vegetables, legumes, seafood, nuts, cereals, dairy products
	Iron—animal and vegetable sources	Liver, meat, fish, poultry, eggs, cereals, fruits, vegetables
	Zinc—animal and vegetable sources	Seafood, meat, eggs, cereals, legumes, nuts, vegetables, dairy products
	Iodine—water, seafoods, animal and some vegetable products	Seafood, dairy products, eggs, milk, some in vegetables and grains

the biological need to satisfy a wide range of nutrient demands. Some nutrients are essential on a recurrent basis in large quantities whereas others need to be present in only minute amounts to satisfy metabolic needs. Thus, while the need for energy is constant and results in total degradation of the carbohydrates from which it is normally derived, the need for certain trace minerals can be satisfied by daily intakes expressed in milligrams with only trace quantities being present at any one time. Certain minerals and vitamins are not metabolized but are lost in the process of cell turnover. Vitamins catalize specific biochemical reactions of physiological importance and thus do not, strictly speaking, enter into those reactions; they therefore could, theoretically, remain in the body indefinitely. In practice, however, there is always some loss to excretion and, therefore, a need for replacement. Similarly, metals may enter into the formation of organometallic compounds of considerable longevity. Even when such compounds are broken down, their metallic components are promptly reclaimed to be incorporated in newly synthesized compounds, sometimes of the same category. The exchange of iron atoms between hemoglobin molecules incorporated in the stroma of red blood cells, hemoglobin attached to haptoglobin molecules, and those attached to transferrin are examples of a physiological system adapted to minimize the loss of a critical element although the cells incorporating it have a limited life span (120 days for the average human red blood cell).

The result of the recycling systems associated with metabolism of most nutrients is their parsimonious consumption. As the consequences of depletion can often be life-threatening, most nutrients are also accumulated in reserves capable of being drawn upon when dietary intake falls below the level of consumption or loss. There is, in general, a correlation between the size of the reserve and the demand for a given nutrient. In the present context, calorie and protein reserves will be a primary concern. This is, in part, because a great deal is known about them and, in part, because they are an important component of tissues exhibiting significant sexual dimorphism in humans. While an extensive treatment of vitamin and mineral reserves would be of interest in a consideration of sexual dimorphism and reproductive success, especially with respect to the B vitamins and iron, they will be dealt with only peripherally here.

CYCLES OF FEAST AND FAMINE AND HUMAN STARVATION

Human dietary versatility is accompanied by the need for a variety of nutrients. Among the more stringent requirements to be met is that involving complementarity of essential amino acid intake. The clinical condition known as kwashiorkor, or PCM (protein-calorie malnutrition), arises, wholly or in part, from either insufficient amino acid intake or from a deficiency of one or more of the essential amino acids. Although the remainder of the essential amino acids may be available in abundance, the one in short supply becomes limiting. Over the years, it has been shown that the clinical implications of amino acid deficiency or imbalance can be serious or even fatal. Since complete reliance on a totally vegetarian diet creates high risk of such deficiency, it is probable that human ancestors consumed at least some animal protein on a regular basis. This is not to say that it is impossible to satisfy all essential amino acid requirements through consumption of an all-vegetable diet. However, complementarity of essential amino acid absorption requires that all nine of them be ingested within a few hours of each other. Seasonal factors and geographical determinants of plant distribution make it exceedingly unlikely that foraging vegetarians would have evolved retaining the essential amino acid requirements of contemporary humans.

Animal domestication is a recent event in human evolutionary history. Before the Neolithic period, it is probable that animal protein was obtained through hunting, fishing, and gathering birds' eggs, invertebrates, and young animals. It is highly unlikely that "hungry seasons" did not occur from time to time. Survival of the species, in consideration of known requirements for amino acids, could only be possible if some means of carrying the individual through periods of protein deficiency existed. The consequences of a protein-deficient diet would be especially destructive for gestating or lactating females. If the 9 months of gestation are added to 6 to 9 months of lactation, the result is a total period of 15 to 18 months of enhanced protein demand. Women living in areas where "hungry seasons" are annual occurrences would thus be certain to experience nutritional stress every time pregnancy occurred. While every human population probably did not experience annual hungry seasons, those practicing subsistence agriculture would be likely to have experienced periodically such times of insufficient or unbalanced amino acid intake.

Perturbations in the reproductive process are of special significance among the mechanisms of natural selection. Physiological adaptations that permit the preservation of conceptuses through the vulnerable early stages of growth and development have a high probability of becoming part of the genetic endowment of the population.

In view of the foregoing discussion, it would be anticipated that the traits having the highest selective value are those coming into play at the time when parental investment was greatest. Thus, adaptations that increase the survivorship of term infants would be of greater selective significance than those in force during gestation. The human infant's period of dependency becomes a factor of considerable significance in this phase of maternal adaptation. The human infant is virtually helpless at birth and its rate of neurological maturation and musculoskeletal development are such that upright walking does not occur until about a year after birth. The capacity for independent, unassisted feeding is also late to appear. Human babies are uniquely dependent among all the mammals. As a consequence, the demand upon maternal support systems is steady, intense, and of long duration.

Breastfeeding of the human infant is capable of supplying all of its nutrient requirements for the first 6 months postpartum. The composition of human milk is unique among the mammals, but is similar to that of other higher primates. Table 14.3 lists the major constituents of mature human milk. In Table 14.4, comparisons with the milk of some other mammals is made along with the amount of time each species requires to double birth weight. As can be seen in Table 14.4, the more rapidly growing newborns are those supplied

TABLE 14.3
Mature Human Versus Cow's Milk.

Composition	Human Milk	Cow's Milk
Water/100 ml	87.1	87.3
Energy kcal/100 ml	75	69
Total solids, gm/100 ml	12.9	12.7
Protein	1.1	3.3
Fat	4.5	3.7
Lactose	6.8	4.8
Ash	0.21	0.72
Proteins % of total protein		
Casein	40	82
Whey proteins	60	18
Ash, major components/liter		
Calcium (mg)	340	1250
Phosphorus (mg)	140	960
Vitamins/liter		
Vitamin A (IV)	1898	1025
Thiamin	160	440
Riboflavin	360	1750
Niacin	1470	940
Vitamin C (mg)	43	11

Source: Fomon, S. V. (1967).

TABLE 14.4
Comparison of Milk Protein Content and Time Required To Double Birth Weight in Several Mammalian Species.

Species	Days Required to Double Birth Weight	Percent Protein Content in Milk
Man	180	1.6
Horse	60	2.0
Cow	47	3.5
Goat	19	4.3
Pig	18	5.9
Sheep	10	6.5
Dog	8	7.1
Rabbit	6	10.4

with a milk of high protein content. Human milk is noteworthy for its relatively low protein concentration. At the same time, it is well endowed with lactose and lipids. The high energy requirements of the infant's rapidly growing brain and its rapid myelinization are supported by these important nutrients.

During times of nutritional deprivation, maternal reserves are crucial to the maintenance of the quality and quantity of milk available to the infant. Energy, amino acids, minerals, vitamins, and electrolytes must also be supplied in sufficient quantities to supply both growth and metabolic requirements of the infant. Energy can be stored in the form of glycogen in muscles and liver and in fat. Glycogen reserves are depleted rapidly during starvation, fat being the primary energy reserve when dietary intake does not supply total metabolic requirements. Table 14.5 compares the metabolic requirements of the human female in the nonpregnant, pregnant, and lactating states. The metabolic costs of pregnancy increase throughout gestation and become greatest during lactation. It can be readily seen that a woman whose nutritional intake has been at or below minimum requirements will be forced into a state of depletion while lactating. Moreover, although protein makes up a relatively small proportion of milk, it is a critical component. This is especially true during the first 5 to 10 days postpartum when colostrum is being produced. The protein content of colostrum is nearly three times that of mature human milk (Table 14.6).

Both colostrum and mature milk have an important role in the establishment of the infant's immune response. For this reason, the protein components, although only a small part of the total mass, are an exceedingly important fraction of human milk. The maternal physiological and anatomical adaptations involved in its mainte-

TABLE 14.5

Energy and Protein Requirements of Human Females, Median Height and Weight.

Age	Weight (kg)	Height (cm)	Energy Needs (kcal)	Range	Protein (gm)
11-14	46	157	2200	1500-3000	46
15-18	55	163	2100	1200-3000	46
19-22	55	163	2100	1700-2500	44
23-50	55	163	2000	1600-2400	44
51-75	55	163	1800	1400-2200	44
Pregnant			+300		+30
Lactating			+500		+20

Source: Food and Nutrition Board, *Recommended Dietary Allowances*, 9th ed. Committee on Dietary Allowances, Food and Nutrition Board, National Academy of Sciences, Washington, D.C., 1980.

nance are therefore of high selective significance and, since limited to the female, act as a focus for divergent adaptive strategies of males and females.

THE ROLE OF BREASTFEEDING IN INFANT SURVIVAL

The breastfed infant is given an important advantage in the attainment of resistance to measles and a number of other diseases. There are several reasons for this, among them the continued activity of the maternal immune system in conferring immunity to the infant. There are several distinct aspects to this conferred immunity. Among them are:

1. Passive immunity functioning topically on tissues of the upper respiratory and gastrointestinal tract.
2. Cellular immunity in the form of lymphocytes capable of phagocytosis and other forms of interaction with pathogenic organisms.

Some elements of the maternal contribution to disease resistance in the human newborn are of special concern. The justification for regarding the first 9 months of the human life span as an "extero-uterine fetal" phase of the life cycle (Jelliffe and Jelliffe 1978) will be seen as the data are presented.

Certain diseases of childhood are of special concern. Among them are measles and mumps. Measles, for instance, may produce mortality rates as high as 20 percent, as seen in parts of Africa, Latin

TABLE 14.6
Comparison of Colostrum, Mature Human Milk, and Cow's Milk.

Composition	Human Colostrum	Mature Milk (Human)	Cow's Milk
Energy (kcal/100 ml)	60	75	66
Protein (gm/100 ml)	3.2	1.1	3.5
Casein (%)	44	40	82
Whey (%)	56	60	18
Lactose (gm/100 ml)	5.7	6.8	4.9
Fat (gm/100 ml)	2.5	4.5	3.7

America, and India (Ifekwunigwe et al. 1980). In North America and in most European countries mortality rates on the order of 0.2 percent are currently being observed. Nutrition and pathogen clearly interact to influence the virulence of disease organisms producing these disparate mortality statistics.   Another frequently encountered pathogen for the newborn is *Escherichia coli*. First exposure to this ubiquitous and potentially dangerous bacterium often occurs during parturition. Immunity to *E. coli* is specifically transmitted via milk and colostrum lymphocytes;   such lymphocytes are not normally present in the blood of adult humans.

For some time, the role of the cellular component in human milk remained unknown. Moreover, it appeared highly unlikely that cells could survive passage through the stomach and small intestine and remain viable. The low pH of the stomach was believed to present a formidable barrier to successful establishment of maternal cellular factors in the gastrointestinal tract of the neonate. Studies currently under way at a number of universities have identified a number of mechanisms by which such survival is made possible (for instance, see Head 1977). The ingestion of breast milk has been shown to produce a transient rise in the pH of the stomach contents. A pH of 6.0 (compared to the normal 3.5) is maintained sufficiently long to permit constituents of milk to enter the small intestine before the higher acid state is reestablished. It is during this interval that cellular immune components are thought to make their way into the neonate's intestinal tract.

Perhaps most intriguing is the manner in which the specificity of the immune response is maintained. Here again the maternal and neonatal systems interact with an intimacy approximating that of gestation.   The close proximity of the mother and infant during breastfeeding ensures their simultaneous exposure to pathogens. Maternal behavior such as kissing and nuzzling (and in many mammalian species, frequent vigorous licking) allows the pathogen the infant harbors to enter the mother's respiratory and gastro-intestinal tracts. It has been shown that the lymphatic circulation of the gastrointestinal tract also supplies the mammaries. Thus, the immune components entering the breast milk are those synthesized specifically in response to the antigenicity of the pathogens present. The fetal-maternal system of immunity persists in this form as long as breastfeeding continues. The effectiveness and efficiency of the mechanism is impressive. A reference to Table 14.7 gives some idea of the forms of pathogenic organisms most commonly generating immune responses that have been detected in breast milk.

The lymphocytes transferred are, in some cases, capable of secreting antibodies, particularly those of the IgA category. These cells are also of the non-complement fixing variety generally associated with those indigenous to the gut. As a group, such cells are also more acid resistant than other cell types so that their chances of passing through the stomach unharmed are further enhanced.

Another important aspect of the biochemistry of breastmilk is its capacity to transmit folate to the infant (Table 14.8). As a consequence of the abundant folate levels in both serum and erythrocyte fractions (Tamura, Yoshimura, and Arakawa 1980), the breastfed infant is not constrained in the important process of DNA synthesis essential for establishment of cellular immunity along with other forms of cellular proliferation. It has been shown that inadequate folate levels are associated with reduced numbers of leucocytes and a reduced capacity to synthesize antibodies.

TABLE 14.7
Comparison of Blood and Milk Lymphocytes' Reactivity to Stimuli.

Cell Stimulant	Blood Lymphocyte	Milk Lymphocyte
Phytohemagglutinin Concanavalin A	+	+ −
Allogeneic cells	+	+
Mumps	+	+
Measles	+	+
Tuberculin	+	+
Candida albicans	+	−
Tetanus toxoid	+	−
Streptokinase	+	−
Escherichia coli	−	+

Source: Adapted from Head (1977).

TABLE 14.8
Folate Levels in Mothers and Breast-Fed Infants.

	Plasma	RBC (ηg/ml)	Milk
Mothers	5.9 ± 3.5 (N = 39)	232.7 ± 83.6 (N = 39)	141.4 ± 47.9 (N = 39)
Infants	29.0 ± 13.6 (N = 25)	491.1 ± 185.5 (N = 25)	

Source: Tamura T., Yoshumura, Y., and Arakawa T., "Human milk folate and folate status in lactating mothers and their infants." *Am. J. Clin. Nutr.* 33:193-197, 1980.

VARIATIONS IN MILK COMPOSITION

Early work on the composition of human milk concentrated on the major constituents; fat, protein, lactose, and total ash were usually the only routine determinations made. It was not for several years that the analysis of major and minor minerals, of specific amino acids, and of individual fatty acids could be reported accurately. As the amount of available data increased, it became necessary to condense this information into an easily accessible form; the NAS publication by Macy, Kelly, and Sloan (1953) served that purpose for work completed at that time. This publication made it obvious, however, that there was a large discrepancy in the published values for each of the major constituents. This variation resulted, in part, from a lack of standardization in milk collection procedures. It is now known that composition values for human milk are applicable only under the specific conditions of that one study.

The composition of human milk is known to undergo significant changes in the transition from colostrum (or "early milk") to mature milk. Most authors define colostrum as the milk produced during the first 5 days postpartum. Some define an additional "transition" period, from Day 5 to Day 10. Many authors, however, continue to label all samples simply as "milk," with no specification as to "mature," "colostrum," or "transitional."

Human colostrum contains an average of 2.3 to 3.2 gm protein per 100 ml, while mature milk averages 1.1 gm/100 ml. Fat level increases from 2.95 gm/100 ml colostrum to 3.52 gm/100 ml in the transition period, and finally reaches an average level of 4.54 gm/100 ml in the fully mature stage. Lactose levels increase slightly during the transition from colostrum to mature milk, from 5.7 gm/100 ml to an average of 6.8 gm/100 ml. Total ash declines rapidly from an initial value of 308 mg/100 ml colostrum to an average of 267 mg/100 ml transitional milk to a final level of 202 mg/100 ml mature milk.

In addition to the changes that occur during the transition from colostrum to mature milk, the constituents of milk continue to vary as lactation progresses from one month to another. Some of these changes are significant, others vary only slightly. Protein declines as the duration of lactation progresses, although the absolute concentration and the rate of decline vary from one subject to another. The total nitrogen content in breast milk decreases rapidly during the first 20 days, decreasing slowly thereafter. Nonprotein nitrogen remains fairly constant throughout lactation. The α-lactalbumin and lactoferrin, which are hormonally controlled, decrease during lactation.

The total amino acid composition of milk is almost identical among women of different ethnic origin and changes little in concentration throughout lactation. Fat levels, known to have the highest variability of any constituent of human milk, have not been shown to increase or decrease significantly with the duration of lactation, nor has lactose been shown to vary in a consistent pattern. It has been demonstrated by Hanafy, Seddick, and Habib (1972) that the daily yield of milk from healthy mothers increases slightly as lactation proceeds from Month 1 to Month 12. Hefnawi et al. (1972) found milk yield to increase significantly from the second month postpartum to a maximum at the seventh month, followed by a gradual decline up to the twelfth month of lactation. The lack of agreement might stem from the use of subjects who were not of the same age, parity, race, health status, or interdelivery stages. In addition, the authors did not measure milk yield in the same manner; one study employed a mechanical pump and measured the amount of milk obtained, while the other set of data was determined by weighing the infant before and after a test feed.

Not only does the consumption of human milk vary from one month to another, but considerable variation occurs within a single feeding. In addition, a diurnal variation can be defined within a single day. It has been shown that fat levels rise consistently during a single feeding, although the magnitude of the increase can vary from 6 to 79 percent and the pattern of the rise (linear, curvilinear, or irregular) can differ as well. According to Hytten (1954a-c), lactose concentration varies inversely to fat, dropping from a maximum level at the start of a feeding to a minimum at the completion of the feeding. Macy, Kelly, and Sloan (1953) did not confirm this relationship. Some authors find no significant differences in lactose concentrations at the early and later part of a feeding, and others find only a slight change. Protein levels are thought to increase during the course of a feeding, but the degree of change is not as great as for fat. Only a few studies have tried to define the diurnal variation in the composition of human milk. Total yield was found to be greatest at 6 A.M., after which the yield per feeding declined to variable degrees. Fat content rises from 5 A.M. to 10 A.M., where it peaks, then declines gradually. Lactose shows no consistent change throughout the day, nor does protein seem to vary systematically.

In addition to the effect of time on the composition of human milk, several other factors are known to influence both the quality and quantity of milk secreted. Dietary intake, whether expressed in terms of overall adequacy or defined for specific nutrients, can alter the composition of human milk. Women who are chronically under-nourished have been shown to produce milk that is not significantly lower in quality than milk from well-nourished women. Not all reports, however, are in agreement with these findings. Hanafy, Seddick, and Habib (1972) found that milk from chronically mal-nourished women was lower in protein, lactose, and fat; in addition, the total yield per day was significantly lower. Karmarkar and Ramakrishan (1960) investigated the relation between dietary intake of protein, fat, carbohydrate, and selected minerals and the milk levels of these same nutrients using a composite of a single day's intake. They found a general increase in the level of milk protein as dietary protein increased; this trend was valid, however, only up to a certain point, after which milk protein remained constant despite further increases in dietary protein. As dietary fat increased, so did the level of milk fat, again only up to a certain point. Dietary carbohydrate was not significantly correlated with the lactose content of human milk, nor was a relationship shown for calcium, phosphorus, or iron. Bourges, Martinez, and Chavez (1977) reported that dietary supplementation with a high protein, milk-based beverage resulted in a higher daily output of milk (650 ml versus 550 ml in nonsupplemented women). There was, however, a general dilution effect, so that the actual concentration of most nutrients actually declined.

Several recent studies have focused specifically upon the role of dietary intake in determining the fatty acid content of human milk. Milk fat can originate from three sources: *de novo* synthesis within the mammary gland itself, transfer of depot fat via the bloodstream, or transport of dietary fat via circulating lipoproteins and chylomi-crons. In general, it has been found that on a low carbohydrate diet, the fatty acid intake of a lactating woman tends to be reflected in the fatty acid pattern of the milk. If the diet is high in saturated fats, the milk will contain a high level of stearic acid and a relatively low level of linoleic. On the contrary, if the diet is high in polyunsaturated fatty acids, the milk also will contain a greater proportion of linoleic. This type of effect can be significant as early as 2 days after the specific dietary regime is initiated. As dietary carbohydrate increases, however, the effect of dietary fat on milk fat becomes less significant. If both the fat content and total calories are low, the milk fatty acid pattern is similar to that of depot fat, indicating the source of the milk fat. However, considering all other factors that are involved, diet lipids influence trans fatty acids and polyunsaturated/saturated ratios of the fatty acids in human milk. Although increases or decreases in dietary cholesterol will affect plasma cholesterol levels, these effects do not carry over to the cholesterol concentration of human milk. The typical American diet, over the past 10 to 20 years, has gradually shifted from the use of mostly saturated fats to a greater reliance on polyunsaturated fatty acids; linoleic acid, in particular, has shown a two- to threefold increase in dietary consumption. This has resulted in a significant difference in the fatty acid composition of milk from women sampled in the 1970s compared to human milk analyzed in the 1940 to 1960 period. Milk tested within the last few years showed a higher percent of long chain fatty acids and twice as much linoleic acid as milk sampled 20 years ago. It is interesting to note that the total milk fat output and the total milk volume does not change significantly as these various dietary manipulations of fat, carbohydrate, and total calories occur.

SEX DIFFERENCES IN HUMAN BODY COMPOSITION

It is instructive to note that humans are among the fattest of mammals (Pitts and Bullard 1968). A very lean human may have 10 percent of total body weight made up of fat. It is not uncommon for the proportion of fat to run as high as 35 percent in contemporary industrialized countries. Among many mammalian species, fat serves largely as insulation. This is especially true among marine species for which immersion in cold water creates the potential for chilling to a dangerously low temperature. Whales maintain a fat proportion of about 35 percent, an amount giving them sufficient insulation to range from polar to tropical waters during the course of an annual migration. In the anatomy of sea mammals, subcutaneous fat deposits act as an insulating blanket surrounding the body's core and creating a relatively inert barrier. This barrier is positioned so that it moderates the steep thermal gradient between the body core and the surrounding sea water.

While a generous layer of subcutaneous fat serves admirably as a barrier reducing the loss of metabolic heat in a cold environment, under heat stress it can become a distinct disadvantage. Most of the evidence available supports the argument that human evolution occurred in the Old World tropics. Heat stress was more often encountered than cold stress during most of human history. Penetration of the temperate and frigid zones came only after technological innovations emerged to supplement physiological adjustments for coping with problems of thermoregulation. All human populations are well equipped to dissipate metabolic heat. Convection, conduction, radiation, and evaporation all come into play in this process. Sweating is an especially effective heat dissipating mechanism, and humans sweat far more than any other animal. The ability to sweat has permitted humans to engage in strenuous activity throughout the day in hot climates and must be counted among the traits indicating a tropical origin for the species.

There is an apparent paradox in the simultaneous possession of a high proportion of fat, much of it in subcutaneous deposits, and a highly evolved mechanism for heat dissipation through sweating. There is, of course, substantial variation in the amount of subcutaneous fat present within and between human populations. But the fact remains that, on the average, Arctic populations are no more generously endowed than tropical ones. This could not be the case if the function of subcutaneous fat were primarily one of insulation. Other mammalian species do exhibit a gradient of fat percentages with fat percentage positively correlated with distance from the equator (Table 14.9). If the probability of severe cold exposure is relatively low, possession of a percentage of body fat similar to that seen in cold-adapted marine mammals is better explained as evidence of a substantial reserve of nutrients. Even where fat deposits appear most closely associated with adaptation to cold climates, as in the thermogenesis of brown fat, the process is an energy-consuming one as opposed to the passive role attributable to insulation (Aherne and Hull 1966; Himms-Hagen 1969; Leduc and Rivest 1969; LeBlanc and Villamaire 1970; LeBlanc 1975).

TABLE 14.9
Comparison of Fat Percentage of Total Weight in Mammals Found in Differeing Climates.

Fat (%)	Alaska	Virginia	Brazil
1-10	9	14	4
11-20	4	4	2
> 20	1	0	0

Source: Pitts and Bullard (1968).

Sweating has a cost in nutrients as well, but does not generate a caloric expenditure comparable to that associated with thermogenesis. It is correct to say that human thermogenesis is, on the whole, far more dependent upon fat for energy than for insulation and that both subcutaneous and depot fat are best viewed as energy reserves.

If we accept the role of fat in humans as being mostly the site of energy reserves we must conclude that our species is extremely well-endowed with such reserves when compared to most other mammals. Of special interest is the difference in the amount of these reserves seen in human females compared to males. Reference to Table 14.10 will show the degree to which human males and females differ in this respect throughout life. The difference in energy reserves that female fat deposits represent is, in large part, attributable to the high energy costs of the female role in the reproductive process. It is true, however, that a crucial factor in the maintenance of the newborn and in the establishment of its immune response is the availability of amino acids in sufficient quantity and balance to support the synthesis of antibodies and lymphocytes. Human males, on the average, have substantially greater lean body mass than human females. Thus, the circulating pool of amino acids being exchanged between skeletal muscle and plasma is smaller in females. Amino acids are not, in the strict sense, stored. Instead, surplus circulating amino acids will be converted to carbohydrate throughout gluconeogenesis and either catabolized or stored following glycogenesis. Since humans are incapable of synthesizing nine of the amino acids necessary for protein synthesis, no amount of energy reserve will compensate for insufficient or unbalanced protein intake. This is a factor that would seem to place the poorly nourished and lactating female in an

TABLE 14.10
Relationship of Adipose Tissue to Body Weight in Adult Humans.

Age	Ratio of Adipose Tissue Mass : Body Mass	
(years)	Male	Female
25	0.14	0.26
40	0.22	0.32
55	0.25	0.38

Source: Edward Masoro. "Other physiologic changes with age." In *Epidemiology of Aging*, Adrian Ostfeld and Don V. Gibson (eds.). DHEW Publication No. (NIH) 77-711, 1975.

extremely vulnerable state. Clearly, the fact that both past and present human populations survived and reproduced during extended periods of inadequate protein intake is a strong indication that effective adaptive mechanisms have been evolved. Some clues regarding their nature can be obtained from observations of the etiology of human starvation.

Young and Scrimshaw (1971) followed the process of weight reduction during starvation to identify changes in body composition. The observations they cite show that starving humans do not survive by simply metabolizing fat. In the early stages of starvation, glycogenolysis occurs in the liver. The glucose so released supplies energy needs for only a few hours. Gluconeogenesis associated with the breakdown of serum amino acids is a more important endogenous resource. Among the amino acids, the nonessential alanine is the most important source of energy through gluconeogenesis, but essential amino acids being cycled out of muscle may also be so converted. When the amino acid complement of skeletal muscle is reduced in this manner, there is an inevitable loss of certain minerals. The effect of this loss on electrolyte balance is such that fluid loss follows. This is the reason for the rapid decline in body weight during the first 5 days of fasting.

Consumption of body fat becomes the primary source of energy in the next phase of starvation. Each gram of fat yields 9 kilocalories (kcal) of energy. The total resting requirement of the adult male is between 1600 and 1800 kcal/day. About 200 gm of fat can therefore supply the energy requirements of a resting adult male for a day. Females have lower requirements due both to body size and to their lower metabolic rate.

When body fat is consumed to supply metabolic needs, it is generally believed that adipocytes release their lipid complement without significant change in cell number. Thus, cycles of weight loss followed by weight gain can be repeated many times during a lifetime without replacement of the cells themselves. It is not known whether depletion of amino acids from skeletal muscle is similar in its lack of impact on cell number. Observations of the impact of early protein-calorie malnutrition on the amount of muscle present in the arm give evidence that males are more affected than females. Under conditions of chronic inadequacy of protein intake, male arm muscle circumference is reduced to a far greater extent than female. The result of this difference is a reduction in size dimorphism for lean body mass. Table 14.11 provides a comparison of the sexual dimorphism in arm muscle circumference seen in a well-fed (U.S.A.) population and one exposed to chronically low protein intake (Colombia). While the reduction in soft tissue so produced may not be easily detectable in

TABLE 14.11

Mean Upper Arm Muscle Area of Adults of Both Sexes: U.S.A. and Colombian Values.

	Colombia		U.S.A.		Colombia as Percentage of U.S.A.	
	Arm Muscle Area (mm^2)	Body Wt. (kg)	Arm Muscle Area (mm^2)	Body Wt. (kg)	Muscle Area	Body Wt.
Male	4267	60	6464	70	66	85
Female	3450	51	4272	58	81	88
Female as % of Male	81	85	66	83		

Source: from William A. Stini. "Adaptive strategies of human populations under nutritional stress." In *Biosocial Interrelations in Population Adaptation*, E. Watts, F. E. Johnston, and G. W. Lasker (eds.). The Hague: Mouton, 1975, p. 28.

osteological remains, careful attention to muscle attachments, particularly in the vicinity of the weight-bearing joints, may yield heretofore overlooked evidence of nutritional inadequacies of prehistoric populations.

There is undoubtedly a limit to the amount by which muscle mass can be reduced while retaining sufficient strength and endurance to perform essential work. It is not a simple matter to calculate precisely how much muscle must be present to avoid impairment of functional capacity.   Parizkova and Merhaustova (1970) observed that in comparisons of well-fed Czech and less well-fed, and therefore smaller, Tunisian children, the Tunisians exhibited superior functional capacity in a variety of activities. Certainly mere size is no guarantee of superior work capacity outside of a limited number of activities where a large body is a special advantage, as in the lifting of heavy weights. In the absence of such a concrete advantage, a larger body may be decidedly disadvantageous especially where nutritional resources are scarce.   This is because inertia alone dictates an increased energy cost for each increment of mass to be moved. Moreover the higher the activity level, the greater the incremental cost (Tables 14.12 and 14.13). Lean body mass increments also increase amino acid requirements. Thus, larger, more muscular individuals are more vulnerable to the stress of undernutrition and/or protein deprivation than are smaller, lighter ones. Early exposure to nutritional deprivation can reduce body size substantially.   The mechanisms of muscle mass reduction are discussed elsewhere (Stini 1975; Aubert, Suquet, and Lemonnier 1980). From an evolutionary standpoint, there are more constraints on reductions in exchangeable amino acid pool in females than in males. Males can alter activity patterns to accommodate changes in body composition. Most human activity is carried out at work levels far below maximal. Thus, there is

TABLE 14.12

Comparison of Caloric Requirements of a 70-kg U.S. Male with Those of a 60-kg Colombian Male at Similar Activity Levels.

	U.S.A.	Colombia
Mean body weight (kg)	70	60
Caloric costs (kcal)		
Resting (8 hours)	570	480
Very light activity (6 hours)	630	540
Light labor (8 hours)	1624	1392
Moderate labor (2 hours)	602	516
Total	3426	2918

Source: Stini (1975, p. 22).

TABLE 14.13

Energy Expenditures (kcal/min) of Mature Reference Man and Woman at Various Activity Levels.

Activity Category	Time (hr)	Man, 70 kg		Woman, 58 kg	
		Rate (kcal/min)	Total (kcal)	Rate (kcal/min)	Total (kcal)
Sleeping	8	1.0-1.2	540	0.9-1.1	440
Very light	12	2.5	1300	2.0	900
Light	3	2.5-4.9	600	2.0-3.9	450
Moderate	1	5.0-7.4	300	4.0-5.9	240
Heavy	0	7.5-12.0		6.0-10.0	
Total	24		2740		2030

Source: Food and Nutrition Board (1980, p. 24).

latitude for size reductions that may be translated into reductions in nutrient requirements for males.

The exigencies of reproduction for females, involving gestation and lactation, allow less flexibility. Severe reductions in energy or amino acids available during pregnancy or breastfeeding would be destructive to a crucial process in the maintenance of population number. While males may be labile in their growth performance, females are more tightly canalized. The sexes respond to different selective pressures under nutritional stress with the result being enhancement of sexual dimorphism for body size during times of abundance and its reduction when deprivation is of long duration.

SUMMARY AND CONCLUSIONS

In terms of the parental investment in the production of human offspring, the female's contribution is far greater than the male's. In important ways, the role of the male has the property of guaranteeing substantial variability. While female gametogenesis is also a source of variability, the process is one in which enhancement of survivorship of the zygote is an important element. As might be anticipated under conditions where maternal investment is great, there are numerous physiological adjustments available to protect and support the conceptus. Even after birth, the human newborn remains highly dependent upon the maternal organism for nutrients, warmth, support, and the initiation of immunities.

The heavy demands made on the maternal organism during gestation and lactation may make it impossible to balance nutrient intake and metabolic requirements. Especially during famines or shortages of specific nutrient resources, the human female requires nutrient reserves in order to sustain the metabolic needs of herself and her offspring. The existence of sexual dimorphism in human body composition is, in large part, attributable to these requirements.

Males are larger and more muscular than females in all human populations; however, the growth and development of males is more susceptible to environmental alteration than that of females. Females have a higher proportion of fat, and in view of the emphasis on energy-consuming processes in climatic adaptations, these deposits are almost certainly energy reserves and not a thermoregulatory device.

Nutrient reserves are clearly of high adaptive significance in mammalian species where homeostasis is maintained at the expense of a high energy input. Lactation is also a mammalian characteristic of direct significance to the reproductive process. The support of lactation creates a demand for reserves in females without parallel in males. The divergent pathways of the selection process created by the different reserve requirements of males and females is at the root of many important aspects of human sexual dimorphism.

BIBLIOGRAPHY

Aherne, W., and D. Hull. 1966. "Brown Adipose Tissue and Heat Production in the Newborn Infant. *Journal of Pathology and Bacteriology*, 91:223-234.

Aubert, R., J.-P. Suquet, and B. Lemonnier. 1980. "Long-Term Morphological and Metabolic Effects of Early Under- and Over-Nutrition in Mice." *Journal of Nutrition*, 110:649-661.

Bourges, H., C. Martinez, and A. Chavez. 1977. "Effect of Dietary Supplements on Nutrient Content of Milk from Mothers in a Rural Mexican Town." Paper read before Western Hemisphere Nutrition Congress V, Quebec, Canada.

Dellaportas, G. J. 1969. "Growth of School Children in Gondar Area, Ethiopia." *Human Biology*, 41:218-222.

Fomon, S. V. 1967. *Infant Nutrition*. Philadelphia: Saunders.

Food and Nutrition Board. 1980. *Recommended Dietary Allowances*, 9th ed. Washington, D.C.: National Academy of Sciences.

Hanafy, M., Y. Seddick, and Y. Habib. 1972. "Maternal Nutrition and Lactation Performance." *Journal of Tropical Pediatrics, Environmental and Child Health*, 18:187.

Head, J. R. 1977. "Immunology of Lactation." *Seminars in Perinatology*, 1:195-210.

Hefnawi, F., M. Badraoui, N. Younis, and F. Hassib. 1972. "Lactation Patterns in Egyptian Women. Milk Yield During the First Year of Lactation." *Journal of Biosocial Science*, 4:397-401.

Hiernaux, J. 1968. "Variabilité du dimorphisme sexuel de la stature en Afrique Subsaharienne et en Europe." *Sonderdruck aus Anthropologie und Human genetik*. Stuttgart: Gustav Fischer Verlag.

Himms-Hagen, J. 1969. "The Role of Brown Adipose Tissue in the Calorigenic Effect of Adrenaline and Noradrenaline in Cold-Acclimatized Rats." *Journal of Physiology* (London), 205:393-403.

Hull, D. 1974. "The Function and Development of Adipose Tissue." In *Scientific Foundation of Paediatrics*, edited by J. A. Daves and J. Dobbing, pp. 440-455. Philadelphia: W. B. Saunders.

Hytten, F. 1954a. "Clinical and Chemical Studies in Human Lactation. II. Variation in Major Constituents During a Feeding." *British Medical Journal*, I:176.

———. 1954b. "Clinical and Chemical Studies in Human Lactation III. Diurnal Variation in Major Constituents of Milk." *British Medical Journal*, I:179.

———. 1954c. "Clinical and Chemical Studies in Human Lactation V. Individual Differences in Composition of Milk." *British Medical Journal*, I:253.

Ifekwunigwe, A. E., N. Grasset, R. Glass, and S. Foster. 1980. "Immune Response to Measles and Smallpox Vaccinations in Malnourished Children." *American Journal of Clinical Nutrition*, 33:621-624.

Jelliffe, D. B., and E. F. P. Jelliffe. 1978. "The Volume and Composition of Human Milk in Poorly Nourished Communities." *American Journal of Clinical Nutrition*, 31:492.

Karmarkar, M., and C. Ramakrishan. 1960. "Studies on Human Lactation: Relation Between the Dietary Intake of Lactating Women and the Chemical Composition of Milk with Regard to Principal and Certain Inorganic Constituents." *Acta Paediatrica Belgica*, 49:599.

LeBlanc, J. 1975. *Man in the Cold*. Springfield, Ill.: Charles C Thomas.

LeBlanc, J., and A. Villemaire. 1970. "Thyroxine and Noradrenaline or Adrenaline Sensitivity, Cold Resistance, and Brown Fat." *American Journal of Physiology*, 218:1742-1745.

Leduc, J., and P. Rivest. 1969. "Effets de l'ablation de la graisse brune interscapulaire sur l'acclimatation au froid chez la rat." *Revue Canadienne de Biologie*, 28:49-66.

Macy, I., H. Kelly, and R. Sloan. 1953. "The Composition of Milks." National Research Council Publication No. 254. Washington, D.C.: National Academy of Sciences.

Masoro, E. 1977. "Other Physiologic Changes with Age." In *Epidemiology of Aging*, edited by A. M. Ostfeld. Washington, D.C.: DHEW Publication No. NIH77-711.

Morgan, B. L. G., and D. V. Naismith. 1980. "Value of Dietary Protein for Hyperplastic Growth at Restricted Energy Intakes." *Journal of Nutrition*, 110:618-626.

Parizkova, J., and J. Merhaustova. 1970. "The Comparison of Somatic Development, Body Composition and Functional Characteristics in Tunisian and Czech Boys of 11 and 12 Years." *Human Biology*, 42:391-400.

Pitts, G. C., and T. R. Bullard. 1968. "Some Interspecific Aspects of Body Composition in Mammals." In *Body Composition in Animals and Man*, pp. 45-70. Washington, D.C.: National Academy of Science Publication No. 1598.

Stini, W. A. 1972a. "Malnutrition, Body Size and Proportion." *Ecology of Food and Nutrition*, 1/1:125-132.

_____ . 1972b. "Reduced Sexual Dimorphism in Upper Arm Muscle Circumference Associated with Protein-Deficient Diet in a South American Population." *American Journal of Physical Anthropology*, 363:341-352.

_____ . 1975. "Adaptive Strategies of Human Populations Under Nutritional Stress." In *Biosocial Interrelations in Population Adaptation*, edited by E. Watts, F. E. Johnston, and G. L. Lasker, pp. 19-41. The Hague: Mouton.

Tamura, T., Y. Yoshimura, and T. Arakawa. 1980. "Human Milk Folate and Folate Status in Lactating Mothers and Their Infants." *American Journal of Clinical Nutrition*, 33:193-197.

Young, V. R., and N. S. Scrimshaw. 1971. "The Physiology of Starvation." *Scientific American*, 225:14-25.

Index

421